DevOps for Databases

A practical guide to applying DevOps best practices to
data-persistent technologies

David Jambor

BIRMINGHAM—MUMBAI

DevOps for Databases

Copyright © 2023 Packt Publishing

Group Product Manager: Preet Ahuja

Publishing Product Manager: Arindam Majumder

Book Project Manager: Ashwin Kharwa

Senior Editor: Athikho Sapuni Rishana

Technical Editor: Rajat Sharma

Copy Editor: Safis Editing

Proofreader: Safis Editing

Indexer: Pratik Shirodkar

Production Designer: Prashant Ghare

DevRel Marketing Coordinator: Rohan Dobhal

First published: November 2023

Production reference: 1301123

Published by Packt Publishing Ltd.

Grosvenor House

11 St Paul's Square

Birmingham

B3 1RB, UK.

ISBN 978-1-83763-730-0

www.packtpub.com

This book is lovingly dedicated to my family, friends, and colleagues, whose unwavering support and wisdom have been the bedrock of this journey. You have transformed my aspirations into reality. To my family, for your endless encouragement; to my friends, for your invaluable companionship; and to my colleagues, for your inspiring camaraderie – this accomplishment is as much yours as it is mine. Thank you for shaping my life and inspiring every page of this book. Without you, this would not have been possible.

Contributors

About the author

David Jambor is a seasoned technology expert with a 16-year career in building, designing, and managing large-scale, mission-critical systems. He has spent a decade honing his expertise in DevOps and data-persisting technologies, and he is widely regarded as an authority in the field. Currently serving as the head of DevOps, data, and analytics at Amazon Web Services in the UK, David brings with him a wealth of experience from previous roles at top-tier companies, such as Vodafone, Sky, Oracle, Symantec, Lufthansa, and IBM.

In addition to his professional achievements, David is a prominent figure in the DevOps community, frequently presenting technical and strategy-focused talks at various international events. He is also a respected judge and advisor for multiple DevOps awards, and he provides valuable support to technology vendors.

About the reviewer

Sandor Szabo has worked for over 16 years in different fields of IT, mainly focusing on supporting and maintaining large-scale systems worldwide. Several high-profile companies such as Lufthansa Systems, AT&T, Sky UK, and Huawei broadened his view on technologies and principles relating to highly available applications and databases, cloud technologies, DevOps, CI/CD, automation, business continuity, and project, team, and product ownership.

He received a BSc in engineering information technology from John Von Neumann Faculty of Informatics at the University of Obuda in Hungary. He is currently employed by Nokia full-time, where he is one of the product owners and security leads of Nokia Continuous Delivery software.

I'd like to thank my family, who understood that the effort and time invested in this project were important to me. I also would like to thank the author of this book, who shared his knowledge and valuable insights, and Packt Publishing, who made it possible for me to participate in such an interesting project! I also learned a lot from this book, and I hope you enjoy the content, just like I did while reviewing it!

Table of Contents

3

DBAs in the World of DevOps   49

Part 2: Persisting Data in the Cloud

4

Cloud Migration and Modern Data(base) Evolution   65

7

AI, ML, and Big Data   177

Part 3: The Right Tool for the Job

8

Zero-Touch Operations   201

Part 4: Build and Operate

11

13

Operators and Self-Healing Data Persistent Systems   307

14

Bringing Them Together   333

Part 5: The Future of Data

15

Specializing in Data   361

16

The Exciting New World of Data — 373

Preface

In today's rapidly evolving world of DevOps, traditional silos are a thing of the past. No longer are there strictly database admins; instead, SRE or DevOps engineers are experts at databases. This blurring of the lines has led to increased responsibilities, and in high-performing DevOps teams, it means being responsible for everything end to end.

This book is your ultimate guide to mastering DevOps for databases. Beginning with real-world examples of DevOps implementation and its significance in modern data-persisting technologies, the book progresses into different types of database technologies, highlighting their strengths, weaknesses, and commonalities. You'll learn through practical examples about design, implementation, testing, and operations. You will then learn about common design patterns, combining them with tooling, technology, and strategy for different types of data-persisting technology. Moreover, it will guide you through creating end-to-end complex implementation, deployment, and cloud infrastructure strategies defined as code.

By the end of this book, you will be equipped with the knowledge and tools to design, build, and operate complex systems efficiently. Whether you're a seasoned DevOps professional or a newcomer, this book is a must-have resource to achieve success in the ever-changing world of DevOps.

Who this book is for

This book is primarily targeted at SREs, DevOps engineers, and system engineers who are interested in large-scale systems, with a heavy focus on data-persisting technologies. This book will also help database administrators who are looking to step up into the DevOps world.

What this book covers

Chapter 1, *Implementing DevOps in Real Life*, embarks on an exploratory journey into the rich history and fundamental principles of DevOps. We'll uncover the compelling reasons behind its inception, evaluate its transformative impact on the tech industry, and delve into the substantial value it adds to organizational workflows. Moreover, this chapter serves as a practical guide, outlining common goals, objectives, and implementation patterns in DevOps. These insights are designed to offer you, the reader, a clear roadmap, potentially saving you considerable time and effort as you apply these concepts in real-world scenarios.

Chapter 2, Large-Scale Data Persistent Systems, focuses on the cutting-edge practices and prevailing trends in modern infrastructure design, particularly as they relate to large-scale data persistence systems. We will dissect the substantial impacts these practices have on data-persisting technologies and the unique challenges they present. Additionally, this chapter bridges the gap between these evolving technologies and DevOps, highlighting how DevOps methodologies can be the key to meeting increased demands and higher expectations, even with leaner team structures. This discussion aims to provide a comprehensive understanding of how integrated DevOps strategies can effectively address and streamline these complex data persistence challenges.

Chapter 3, DBAs in the World of DevOps, introduces a pivotal shift in the role of **Database Administrators** (**DBAs**) within the dynamic world of DevOps. We will explore the concept of the "DevOps DBA" – a professional who transcends the traditional boundaries of DBA roles to embrace a broader scope as a DevOps/**Site Reliability Engineering** (**SRE**) specialist with a focus on databases. Through practical examples and real-life anecdotes, we will delve into the best practices for a DevOps DBA, examining the expanded expectations and responsibilities that come with this evolved role. You will gain insights into the transition process for a DBA stepping into this multifaceted position, understanding how these practices are applied in real-world scenarios and the benefits they yield. This chapter emphasizes the importance of implementation practices, underscoring the critical role of collaboration among developer teams, testers, and operations personnel in forging a successful DevOps model.

Chapter 4, Data(base) Evolution, offers a panoramic view of the evolution of databases, charting the path through significant technological milestones, such as the advent of the first non-relational databases. Our exploration places a strong emphasis on understanding the reasons behind the emergence of each new technology, dissecting the customer demands they were developed to meet and their enduring relevance in today's fast-paced tech landscape. We will also briefly explore the rise of analytical systems and their synergistic pairing with cutting-edge **Machine Learning** (**ML**) and AI technologies. This chapter aims to provide a comprehensive overview of database evolution, offering insights into how these developments have shaped and continue to influence the field of data management.

Chapter 5, Relational Databases, presents a detailed exploration of select, pivotal relational databases. We will delve into the intricate design patterns that define these databases, alongside an in-depth analysis of their configuration details. A critical focus of this chapter is on understanding the performance characteristics and resiliency properties of these systems. By providing a comprehensive look at these key aspects, the chapter aims to equip you with a thorough understanding of relational databases, essential for effective database management and optimization in various technological environments.

Chapter 6, Non-Relational Databases, offers an in-depth analysis of select, crucial non-relational databases. We dive into their unique design patterns, unraveling the nuances of their configuration details. A significant portion of the chapter is dedicated to examining the performance characteristics and resilience features of these databases. This comprehensive overview is designed to provide you with a deep understanding of non-relational databases, highlighting their distinct advantages and applications. This knowledge is vital to effectively utilize and optimize these databases in various technological landscapes, particularly where traditional relational databases may not be the best fit.

Chapter 7, Big Data, AI, and ML, provides a comprehensive overview of various data persisting technologies that are at the forefront of today's tech landscape, including analytical systems, big data lakes, and the integration of AI and ML. We will delve into the design patterns of these technologies, scrutinize their configuration details, and evaluate their performance and resiliency characteristics. A special emphasis will be placed on understanding the intended outcomes and fundamental reasons behind the adoption of these technologies. Additionally, we will explore common utilization examples, such as how AI drawing capabilities leverage a combination of data lakes, visual stores, AI services, and algorithms. This chapter aims to provide a holistic view of these advanced technologies, highlighting their roles and impacts in the modern digital world.

Chapter 8, Zero-Touch Operations, serves as a comprehensive guide to mastering requirement-gathering techniques, a crucial step in identifying the right technologies and configurations for your needs. We will walk you through methods to gather meaningful insights from various stakeholders – including business, technical, and customer perspectives – to compile a robust dataset before initiating any project. This knowledge, combined with the DevOps principles and technological insights covered in earlier chapters, will equip you with the necessary framework to make informed strategic and technology decisions.

A key focus of this chapter is on defining "what good looks like" in different scenarios, offering clear patterns for various combinations of strategies and technologies. We also delve into the concept of Zero-Touch operations, a cornerstone of modern operational best practices. The chapter explains the critical need for this strict policy, which prohibits manual intervention in operational life cycle events, and how its implementation can significantly enhance operational efficiency, reduce **Mean Time to Repair** (**MTTR**), and boost system availability. We will also discuss the unique challenges and nuances of applying Zero Touch principles to data-persisting technologies, providing a detailed roadmap for successful implementation.

Chapter 9, Design and Implementation, delves into the practical aspects of database design and implementation, highlighting the integral role of the DevOps DBA. We will present a range of common design patterns, now enriched with an integrated approach that combines tooling, technology, and strategy, tailored for various types of data persisting technology.

The chapter is structured to provide a comprehensive understanding of implementing different database systems. We will explore two relational database implementations, each employing distinct tooling and strategic approaches. Similarly, two non-relational database systems will be examined, again with unique combinations of tools and strategies. Additionally, we will delve into the implementation of an analytical system that integrates AI and ML technologies.

By offering these diverse examples, the chapter aims to equip you with a broad spectrum of knowledge and practical insights. This will enable DevOps DBAs and technology professionals to effectively navigate through the complexities of database design and implementation, from initial concept to production.

Chapter 10, Tooling for Database Automation, is dedicated to exploring the array of tools commonly utilized by DevOps and SRE teams in the realm of database management. We will delve into the concept and importance of data automation, defined as the process of programmatically updating data on open data portals, as opposed to manual updates. This approach is crucial for the sustainability and efficiency of any open data program.

We will examine a variety of tools that are instrumental in facilitating this automation, discussing their functionalities, applications, and how they integrate into broader database management and maintenance processes. The chapter aims to provide a thorough understanding of how these tools can optimize database operations, ensuring data is consistently up to date, accurate, and accessible. This insight will be invaluable for professionals seeking to enhance their database management strategies through effective automation.

Chapter 11, End-to-End Ownership Model, focuses on the shift from traditional infrastructure and operational strategies, which often involved segmented team functions, to a more integrated approach that aligns with the core DevOps objective of end-to-end team ownership. We will explore the implications of this strategy and provide real-life examples of where such holistic approaches are currently being successfully implemented in the industry.

A key aspect of this shift is the increasing emphasis on empowering development teams. This has led to a transformation of legacy team structures, moving away from role-specific functions to enabling development teams with the capabilities needed to manage the entire journey from start to finish. This chapter will delve into the unique challenges that arise, particularly in the context of databases and related technologies, and offer insights into how these challenges can be effectively addressed.

Through this discussion, we aim to provide a clear understanding of the end-to-end ownership model, illustrating how teams can successfully transition to this model, thereby enhancing efficiency, collaboration, and overall project success in the realm of DevOps.

Chapter 12, Immutable and Idempotent Logic, examines the modern strategic approaches of using immutable objects and idempotent orchestrations in managing and operating infrastructure resources, specifically how these concepts apply to database technologies. The inherent challenge here is that data, by its nature, is mutable, and the servers or services associated with databases often don't align seamlessly with strategies based on immutability.

We will explore strategies to adopt the core principles of immutability and idempotence in the realm of databases. The focus will be on how to leverage these concepts to enhance the resiliency and availability of database systems, without compromising the integrity and safety of the data. This chapter aims to bridge the gap between these modern operational strategies and the practical realities of database management, offering insights into creating more robust, efficient, and reliable database systems.

Chapter 13, Operators and Self-Healing, delves into the advanced realm of automation for DevOps DBAs, building on the themes of automation discussed in previous chapters and especially focusing on Kubernetes Operators for database technologies. We will examine real-world examples, such as the Couchbase Operator, to understand how these operators facilitate self-healing mechanisms in database systems and the circumstances under which they may fall short of expectations.

The chapter will also take you through the concept of fully managed database solutions, comparing and contrasting them with operator-based systems. This comparative analysis will shed light on the strengths and limitations of each approach, helping you to make informed decisions about which strategy best suits your specific needs and environments. The goal is to equip DevOps DBA professionals with the knowledge and tools necessary to navigate the evolving landscape of database automation, ensuring robust, efficient, and self-sufficient database operations.

Chapter 14, Bring Them Together, serves as a culmination of all the concepts and strategies discussed throughout the book. We will undertake an engaging exercise that traces the life cycle of a theoretical project, from its inception to its operation in a production environment. This exercise will encompass every stage of project development, beginning with requirement gathering and progressing through design, implementation, and deployment, all the way to operation and maintenance.

Throughout this journey, we will apply the diverse technologies and methodologies covered in previous chapters, integrating them to demonstrate how they can work in concert. This hands-on approach will not only reinforce the lessons learned but also provide practical insights into how these technologies and strategies can be synergistically utilized in real-world scenarios. The aim is to offer a holistic view of project management in a DevOps context, showcasing how various elements – from database management to automation and operational strategies – come together to create a cohesive and efficient workflow.

Chapter 15, Specializing in Data – the Author's Personal Experience and Evolution into DevOps and Database DevOps, is where I offer a personal narrative of my professional journey over the past 15+ years, evolving alongside the rapidly changing tech industry. This account is more than just a chronicle of professional experiences; it's a story of the highs and lows, the challenges faced, and the triumphs achieved.

I will share insights into how I specialized in the realms of data, DevOps, and database DevOps, providing a behind-the-scenes look at the shifts and trends I witnessed and adapted to. This chapter aims to offer a unique perspective, shedding light on the reasons why this journey has been, and continues to be, incredibly exciting and fulfilling.

Through anecdotes and reflections, the goal is to inspire and inform you, illustrating the dynamic and ever-evolving nature of a career in technology, particularly in areas as crucial and transformative as DevOps and database management. This personal account is intended to not only chronicle a professional journey but also to convey the passion and enthusiasm that have fueled my career in this exciting field.

Chapter 16, The Exciting World of Data – What The Future Might Look Like for a DevOps DBA, ventures into speculative territory, envisioning the future of data management and the evolving role of the DevOps DBA. Drawing upon current trends and industry developments, we will look forward and attempt to predict the upcoming challenges and opportunities that await in this dynamic field.

This chapter will explore potential technological advancements, industry shifts, and emerging methodologies that could reshape the landscape of DevOps and database administration. We'll discuss how these changes might impact the day-to-day responsibilities of a DevOps DBA and the skill sets that will become increasingly valuable.

Our goal is to provide a thoughtful and informed glimpse into what the future may hold, offering insights that can help professionals in this field prepare for and adapt to the changes ahead. By anticipating the direction in which the industry is headed, this chapter seeks to inspire DevOps DBAs to remain at the forefront of innovation and continue to drive their careers in exciting and meaningful directions.

To get the most out of this book

To maximize the benefits of this book on DevOps for databases, you should ideally possess the following:

- A foundational understanding of cloud technologies and environments, as the book delves into cloud infrastructure strategies and their integration with database technologies
- Familiarity with automation tools such as Ansible and Terraform, which are crucial for implementing the "as code" strategies for infrastructure deployment and database orchestration discussed in the book
- Basic knowledge of database systems, both relational and non-relational, as the book covers a range of database technologies through a DevOps lens
- An appreciation of DevOps principles and practices, as the book is tailored for those looking to apply these methodologies specifically to data-persisting technologies and large-scale systems

This background will enable you to fully engage with the advanced concepts and practical applications presented in the book.

Conventions used

There are a number of text conventions used throughout this book.

`Code in text`: Indicates code words in text, database table names, folder names, filenames, file extensions, pathnames, dummy URLs, user input, and Twitter handles. Here is an example: "Here's a YAML file (`deployment-and-service.yaml`) for Kubernetes."

A block of code is set as follows:

```
import redis
# create a Redis client
client = redis.Redis(host='my-redis-host', port=6379)
# cache a value
client.set('my-key', 'my-value')
```

```
# retrieve a cached value
value = client.get('my-key')
```

When we wish to draw your attention to a particular part of a code block, the relevant lines or items are set in bold:

```
import redis
# create a Redis client
client = redis.Redis(host='my-redis-host', port=6379)
```

Any command-line input or output is written as follows:

```
ansible-playbook -i inventory/hosts playbooks/postgres.yml
```

Bold: Indicates a new term, an important word, or words that you see on screen. For instance, words in menus or dialog boxes appear in **bold**. Here is an example: "To create a new dashboard in Datadog, go to the **Dashboards** page and click **New Dashboard**."

> Tips or important notes
> Appear like this.

Get in touch

Feedback from our readers is always welcome.

General feedback: If you have questions about any aspect of this book, email us at customercare@packtpub.com and mention the book title in the subject of your message.

Errata: Although we have taken every care to ensure the accuracy of our content, mistakes do happen. If you have found a mistake in this book, we would be grateful if you would report this to us. Please visit www.packtpub.com/support/errata and fill in the form.

Piracy: If you come across any illegal copies of our works in any form on the internet, we would be grateful if you would provide us with the location address or website name. Please contact us at copyright@packtpub.com with a link to the material.

If you are interested in becoming an author: If there is a topic that you have expertise in and you are interested in either writing or contributing to a book, please visit authors.packtpub.com.

Share Your Thoughts

Once you've read *DevOps for Databases*, we'd love to hear your thoughts! Scan the QR code below to go straight to the Amazon review page for this book and share your feedback.

https://packt.link/r/183763730X

Your review is important to us and the tech community and will help us make sure we're delivering excellent quality content.

Download a free PDF copy of this book

Thanks for purchasing this book!

Do you like to read on the go but are unable to carry your print books everywhere? Is your eBook purchase not compatible with the device of your choice?

Don't worry, now with every Packt book you get a DRM-free PDF version of that book at no cost.

Read anywhere, any place, on any device. Search, copy, and paste code from your favorite technical books directly into your application.

The perks don't stop there, you can get exclusive access to discounts, newsletters, and great free content in your inbox daily

Follow these simple steps to get the benefits:

1. Scan the QR code or visit the link below

https://packt.link/free-ebook/978-1-83763-730-0

2. Submit your proof of purchase
3. That's it! We'll send your free PDF and other benefits to your email directly

Part 1:
Database DevOps

Welcome to our insightful exploration of DevOps in the realm of data management and database technologies. This book is a journey through various facets of DevOps, blending theory with practical applications, and covering topics from the fundamentals of DevOps to advanced discussions on databases, big data, AI, and ML. Each chapter builds upon the last, offering a cohesive narrative for both new entrants and seasoned professionals in the field.

If you are new to the DevOps world, this part of the book will introduce you to the exciting world of DevOps. If you are an experienced database professional who has not yet had a chance to experience DevOps practices at scale, you are in for a great and surprising journey with this part. DevOps plays a core role in modern software development and operational best practices, unifying the building and running of systems with an emphasis on automation and monitoring at all stages. DevOps plays a key role in modern systems design and operation with a heavy focus on end-to-end ownership and autonomous operation. You will be introduced to DevOps fundamentals and best practices.

This part comprises the following chapters:

- *Chapter 1, Implementing DevOps in Real Life*
- *Chapter 2, Large-Scale Data Persistent Systems*
- *Chapter 3, DBAs in the World of DevOps*

1

Data at Scale with DevOps

Welcome to the first chapter! In this book, you will learn the fundamentals of DevOps, its impact on the industry, and how to apply it to modern data persistence technologies.

When I first encountered the term **DevOps** years ago, I initially saw it as a way to grant development teams unrestricted access to production environments. This made me nervous, especially because there seemed to be a lack of clear accountability at that time, making the move toward DevOps appear risky.

At the time (around 2010), the roles of developers and operations were divided by a very strict line. Developers could gain read-only privileges, but that's about it. What I did not see back then was that this was the first step in blurring the lines between development and operation teams. We already had many siloed teams pointing fingers at one another. This made the work slow, segmented, and frustrating. I was worried this would just increase complexity and cause an even greater challenge. Luckily, today's world of DevOps is very different, and we can all improve it together even further!

There are no more dividing lines between the development and operations teams – they are one team with a common objective. This improves quality, speed, and agility! This also means that traditional roles such as database admin are changing as well. We now have **site reliability engineers** (**SREs**) or DevOps engineers who are experts at using databases and able to perform operational and development tasks alike. Blurring the line means you increase the responsibilities, and in a high-performing DevOps team, this means you are responsible for everything from end to end. Modern tooling and orchestration frameworks can help you do way more than ever before, but it's a very different landscape than it was many years ago.

This book will introduce you to this amazing new world, walk you through the journey that leads us to this ever-changing world of DevOps today, and give some indications as to where we might go next.

By the end of this book, you will be able to not only demonstrate your theoretical knowledge but also design, build, and operate complex systems with a heavy focus on data persistence technologies.

DevOps and data persistence technologies have a love-hate relationship, which makes this topic even more interesting.

In this chapter, we will take a deep dive into the following topics:

- The modern data landscape

- Why speed matters

- Data management strategies

- The early days of DevOps

- SRE versus DevOps

- Engineering principles

- Objectives – SLOs/SLIs

The modern data landscape

Have you ever wondered how much data we generate every single day? Or the effort required to store and access your data on demand? What about the infrastructure or the services required to make all of this happen? Not to mention the engineering effort put in to make all of this happen. If you have, you are in the right place. These questions inspired me to dive deep into the realms of DevOps and SRE and inspired the creation of this book.

Technology impacts almost every aspect of our lives. We are more connected than ever, with access to more information and services than we even realize. It's not just our computers, phones, or tablets that are connected to the internet, but our cars, cameras, watches, televisions, speakers, and more. The more digital native we become, the bigger our digital footprint grows.

A digital footprint, also known as a digital shadow, is a collection of data that represents an individual's interactions and activities across digital platforms and the internet. This data can be categorized as either **passive**, where it's generated without direct interaction – such as browsing history – or **active**, resulting from deliberate online actions such as social media posts or emails. Your digital footprint serves as an online record of your digital presence, and it can have lasting implications for your privacy and reputation.

As of 2022, researchers estimate that out of 8 billion people (the world's population as of 2022), approximately 5 billion utilize the internet daily. Compared to the 2 billion that was measured in 2012, this is a 250% increase over 10 years. This is an incredible increase. See the following figure for reference:

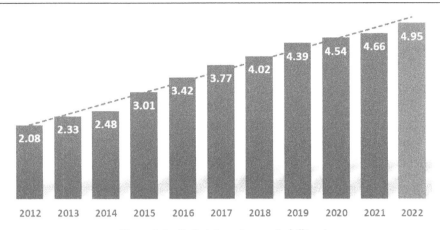

Figure 1.1 – Daily internet users (in billions)

Each person who has a digital presence generates digital footprints in two ways.

The first is actively. When you browse a website, upload a picture, send an email, or make a video call, you generate data that will be utilized and stored for some time. The other, less obvious way is passive data generation. If you, like me, utilize digital services with push notifications on or have GPS enabled on your phone with a timeline, for example, you are generating data every minute of the day – even if you do not use these services actively. Prime examples can be any **Internet of Things (IoT)** devices, something such as an internet-enabled security camera – even if you are not actively using it, it's still generating data and constantly uploading it to your service provider for safekeeping. IoT devices are the secondary source of data generators right after us active internet surfers. Researchers estimate that approximately 13 billion IoT devices are being connected and in daily use as of 2022, with the expectation that this figure will become close to 30 billion by the end of 2030. See the following figure for reference:

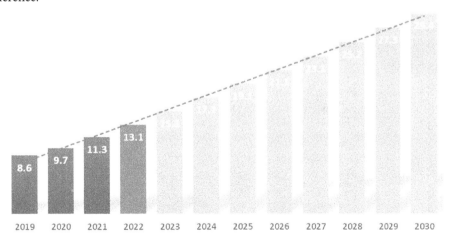

Figure 1.2 – Connected IoT devices (in the billions)

Combining the 5 billion active internet users with the 13 billion connected IoT devices, it is easy to guess that our combined digital footprint must be ginormous. Yet trying to guess the exact number is much harder than you might think. Give it a try.

As of 2023, it is estimated that we generate approximately 3.5 exabytes of data every single day. This is about 1 exabyte more than what was estimated in 2021. To help visualize how much data we are talking about, let me try to put this into perspective. Let's say you have a notebook (or one of the latest phones) with 1 TB of storage capacity. If you were to use this 1 TB storage to store all this information, it would be full in less than 0.025 seconds. An alternative way to think about it is that we can fill 3,670,016 devices with 1 TB storage within 24 hours.

How do we generate data today?

Well, for starters, we collectively send approximately 333.2 billion emails per day. This means that more than 3.5 million emails are sent per second. We also make over 0.5 billion hours of video calls, stream more than 200 million hours of media content, and share more than 5 billion videos and photos every single day.

So, yes, that's a lot of us armed with many devices (on average, one active internet user had about 2.6 IoT devices in 2022) generating an unbelievable amount of data every single day. But the challenge does not stop at the amount of data alone. The speed and reliability of interacting with it are just as important as, if not more important than, the storage itself. Have you ever searched for one of your photos to show someone, but it was slow and took forever to find, so you gave up? We have all been there, but can you remember just how much time after doing this that you decided to abandon your search?

As technology advances, we gain quicker access to information and multitask more efficiently, which may be contributing to a gradual decline in our attention spans. Research shows that in 2000, the average attention span was 12 seconds. Since then, significant technological milestones have occurred: the advent of the iPhone, YouTube, various generations of mobile networks, Wikipedia, and Spotify, to name a few. Internet speed has also soared, moving from an average of 127 kilobits per second in 2000 to 4.4 Mbps by 2010, and hitting an average of 50.8 Mbps by 2020 – with some areas experiencing speeds well over 200 Mbps today.

As the digital landscape accelerates, so do our expectations, resulting in further erosion of our attention spans. By 2015, that 12-second average had fallen to just 8.25 seconds and dropped slightly below 8 seconds by 2022.

Why speed matters

If you consider your attention span the full amount of time you would consider spending to complete a simple task, such as showing photos or videos to a friend, this means searching for it is just a small percentage of your total time. Let's say you are using a type of cloud service to search for your photo or video. What would you consider to be an acceptable amount of time between you hitting *search* and receiving your content?

I still remember the time when "buffering" was a given thing, but if you see something similar today, you would find it unacceptable. According to multiple studies, the ideal load time for "average content," such as photos or videos, is somewhere between 1 and 2 seconds. 53% of mobile site visits are abandoned if pages take longer than three seconds to load. A further two-second delay in load time results in abandonment rates of up to 87%.

This shows us that storing our data is not enough – making it accessible reliably and with blazing speed is not only nice to have but an absolute necessity in today's world.

Data management strategies

There are many strategies out there, and we will need to use most of them to meet and hopefully exceed our customers' expectations. Reading this book, you will learn about some of the key data management strategies at length. For now, however, I would like to bring six of these techniques to your attention. We will take a much closer look at each of these in the upcoming chapters:

- **Bring your data closer**: The closer the data is to users, the faster they can access it. Yes, it may sound obvious, but users can be anywhere in the world, and they might even be traveling while trying to access their data. For them, these details do not matter, but the expectation will remain the same.

  There are many different ways to keep data physically close. One of the most successful strategies is called **edge computing**, which is a distributed computing paradigm that brings computation and data storage closer to the sources of data. This is expected to improve response times and save bandwidth. Edge computing is an architecture rather than a specific technology (and a topology), and is a location-sensitive form of distributed computing.

The other very obvious strategy is to utilize the closest data center possible when utilizing a cloud provider. AWS, for example, spans 96 Availability Zones within 30 geographic Regions around the world as of 2022. Google Cloud offers a very similar 106 zones and 35 regions as of 2023.

Leveraging the nearest physical location can greatly decrease your latency and therefore your customer experience.

- **Reduce the length of your data journey**: Again, this is a very obvious one. Try to avoid any unnecessary steps to create the shortest journey between the end user and their data. Usually, the shortest will be the fastest (obviously it's not that simple, but as a best practice, it can be applied). The greater the number of actions you do to retrieve the required information, the greater computational power you utilize, which directly increases the cost associated with the operation. It also linearly increases the complexity and most of the time increases latency and cost as well.

- **Choose the right database solutions**: There are many database solutions out there that you can categorize based on type, such as relational to non-relational (or NoSQL), the distribution being centralized or distributed, and so on. Each category has a high number of sub-categories and each can offer a unique set of solutions to your particular use case. It's really hard to find the right tool for the job, considering that requirements are always changing. We will dive deeper into each type of system and their pros and cons a bit later in this book.

- **Apply clever analytics**: Analytical systems, if applied correctly, can be a real game changer in terms of optimization, speed, and security. Analytics tools are there to help develop insights and understand trends and can be the basis of many business and operational decisions. Analytical services are well placed to provide the best performance and cost for each analytics job. They also automate many of the manual and time-consuming tasks involved in running analytics, all with high performance, so that customers can quickly gain insights.

- **Leverage machine learning (ML) and artificial intelligence (AI) to try to predict the future**: ML and AI are critical for a modern data strategy to help businesses and customers predict what will happen *in the future* and build intelligence into their systems and applications. With the right security and governance control combined with AI and ML capabilities, you can make automated actions regarding where data is physically located, who has access to it, and what can be done with it at every step of the data journey. This will enable you to stick with the highest standards and greatest performance when it comes to data management.

- **Scale on demand**: The aforementioned strategies are underpinned by the method you choose to operate your systems. This is where DevOps (and SRE) plays a crucial part and can be the deciding factor between success and failure. All major cloud providers provide you with literally hundreds of platform choices for virtually every workload (AWS offered 475 instance types at the end of 2022). Most major businesses have a very "curvy" utilization trend, which is why they find the on-demand offering of the cloud very attractive from a financial point of view.

You should only pay for resources when you need them and pay nothing when you don't. This is one of the big benefits of using cloud services. However, this model only works in practice if the correct design and operational practices and the right automation and compatible tooling are utilized.

A real-life example

A leading telecommunications company was set to unveil their most anticipated device of the year at precisely 2 P.M., a detail well publicized to all customers. As noon approached, their online store saw typical levels of traffic. By 1 P.M., it was slightly above average. However, a surge of customers flooded the site just 10 minutes before the launch, aiming to be among the first to secure the new phone. By the time the clock struck 2 P.M., the website had shattered previous records for unique visitors. In the 20 minutes from 1:50 P.M. to 2:10 P.M., the visitor count skyrocketed, increasing twelvefold.

This influx triggered an automated scaling event that expanded the company's infrastructure from its baseline (designated as 1x) to an unprecedented 32x. Remarkably, this massive scaling was needed only for the initial half-hour. After that, it scaled down to 12x by 2:30 P.M., further reduced to 4x by 3 P.M., and returned to its baseline of 1x by 10 P.M.

This seamless adaptability was made possible through a strategic blend of declarative orchestration frameworks, **infrastructure as code** (**IaC**) methodologies, and fully automated CI/CD pipelines. To summarize, the challenge is big. To be able to operate reliably yet cost-effectively, with consistent speed and security, all the while automatically scaling these services up and down on demand without human interaction in a matter of minutes, you need a set of best practices on how to design, build, test, and operate these systems. This sounds like DevOps.

The early days of DevOps

I first came across DevOps around 2014 or so, just after the first annual *State of DevOps* report was published. At the time, the idea sounded great, but I had no idea how it worked. It felt like – at least to me – it was still in its infancy or I was not knowledgeable and experienced enough to see the big picture just yet. Probably the latter. Anyway, a lot has happened since then, and the industry picked up the pace. Agile, CI/CD, DevSecOps, GitOps, and other approaches emerged on the back of the original idea, which was to bring software developers and operations together.

DevOps emerged as a response to longstanding frictions between **developers** (**Devs**) and **operations** (**Ops**) within the IT industry. The term *obvious* seems apt here because, for anyone involved in IT during that period, the tension was palpable and constant. Devs traditionally focused solely on creating or fixing features, handing them off to Ops for deployment and ongoing management. Conversely, Ops prioritized maintaining a stable production environment, often without the expertise to fully comprehend the code they were implementing.

This set up an inherent conflict: introducing new elements into a production environment is risky, so operational stability usually involves minimizing changes. This gave rise to a "Devs versus Ops" culture, a divide that DevOps sought to bridge. However, achieving this required both sides to evolve and adapt.

In the past, traditional operational roles such as system administrators, network engineers, and monitoring teams largely relied on manual processes. I can recall my initial stint at IBM, where the pinnacle of automation was a Bash script. Much of the work in those days – such as setting up physical infrastructure, configuring routing and firewalls, or manually handling failovers – was done by hand.

While SysAdmin and networking roles remain essential, even in the cloud era, the trend is clearly toward automation. This shift enhances system reliability as automated configurations are both traceable and reproducible. If systems fail, they can be swiftly and accurately rebuilt.

Though foundational knowledge of network and systems engineering is irreplaceable, the push toward automation necessitates software skills – a proficiency often lacking among traditional operational engineers. What began with simple Bash scripts has evolved to include more complex programming languages such as Perl and Python, and specialized automation languages such as Puppet, Ansible, and Terraform.

In terms of the development side, the development team worked with very long development life cycles. They performed risky and infrequent "big-bang" releases that almost every time caused massive headaches for the Ops teams and posed a reliability/stability risk to the business. Slowly but steadily, Dev teams moved to a more frequent, gradual approach that tolerated failures better. Today, we call this Agile development.

If you look at it from this point of view, you can say that a set of common practices designed to reduce friction between Dev and Ops teams is the basis of DevOps. However, simple common practices could not solve the Dev versus Ops mentality that the industry possessed at the time. Shared responsibility between Devs and Ops was necessary to drive this movement to success. Automation that enables the promotion of new features into production rapidly and safely in a repeatable manner could only be achieved if the two teams worked together, shared a common objective, and were accountable (and responsible) for the outcome together. This is where SRE came into the picture.

SRE versus DevOps

SRE originated at Google. In the words of Ben Treynor (VP of engineering at Google), "*SRE is what happens when you ask a software engineer to design an operations function.*"

If you want to put it simply (again, I am quoting Google here), "*Class SRE implements DevOps.*"

SRE is the (software) engineering discipline that aims to bridge the gap between Devs and Ops by treating all aspects of operations (infrastructure, monitoring, testing, and so on) as software, therefore implementing DevOps in its ultimate form. This is fully automated, with zero manual interaction, treating every single change to any of its components (again referring to any changes to infrastructure, monitoring, testing, and so on) as a release. Every change is done via a pipeline, in a version-controlled and tested manner. If a release fails, or a production issue is observed and traced back to a change, you can simply roll back your changes to the previously known, healthy state.

The fact that it is treated as any other software release allows the Dev teams to take on more responsibility and take part in Ops, almost fully blurring the line between the Dev and Ops functions. Ultimately, this creates a *You build it, you run it* culture – which makes "end-to-end" ownership possible.

So, are SRE and DevOps the same thing? No, they are not. SRE is an engineering function that can also be described as a specific implementation of DevOps that focuses specifically on building and running reliable systems, whereas DevOps is a set of practices that is more broadly focused on bringing the traditional Dev and Ops functions closer together.

Regardless of which way you go, you want to ensure that you set an objective, engineering principles, and a tooling strategy that can help you make consistent decisions as you embark on your journey as a DevOps/SRE professional.

Engineering principles

I offer the following engineering principles to start with:

- Zero-touch automation for everything (if it's manual – and you have to do it multiple times a month – it should be automated)
- Project-agnostic solutions (defined in the configuration to avoid re-development for new projects, any tool/module should be reusable)
- IaC (infrastructure should be immutable where possible and defined as code; provisioning tools should be reusable)
- **Continuous delivery** (**CD**) with **continuous integration** (**CI**) (common approaches and environments across your delivery cycle; any service should be deployable immediately)
- Reliability and security validated at every release (penetration testing, chaos testing, and more should be added to the CI/CD pipeline; always identify the point of flavors at your earliest)
- Be data-driven (real-time data should be utilized to make decisions)

To fully realize your engineering goals and adhere to your principles without compromise, you should make "immutable IaC" a priority objective.

To enable this, I would recommend the following IaC principles:

- Systems can be easily reproduced
- Systems are immutable
- Systems are disposable
- Systems are consistent
- Processes are repeatable
- Code/config are version-controlled

Once you have defined your goals, it's time for you to choose the right tools for the job. To do that, you must ensure these tools are allowed to utilize the following:

- **Declarative orchestration framework(s)**:
  - The declarative orchestration approach uses structural models that describe the desired application structure and state. These are interpreted by a deployment engine to enforce this state.

- It enables us to define the end state and interact in a declarative manner, thus making managing the application less resource-intensive (faster speed to market and cheaper costs).

The following is an example Terraform file (main.tf):

```
provider "aws" {
  region = "us-west-2"
}


# Create an S3 bucket
resource "aws_s3_bucket" "my_bucket" {
  bucket = "my-unique-bucket-name"
  acl    = "private"
}


# Create an EC2 instance
resource "aws_instance" "my_instance" {
  ami            = "ami-0c55b159cbfafe1f0" # This is an example
Amazon Linux 2 AMI ID; use the appropriate AMI ID for your needs
  instance_type = "t2.micro"

  tags = {
    Name = "MyInstance"
  }
}
```

- **Declarative resource definition**:

  - In a declarative style, you simply say what resources you would like, and any properties they should have so that you can create and deploy an entire infrastructure declaratively. For example, you can deploy not only agents (or sidecars) but also the network infrastructure, storage systems, and any other resources you may need.

  - This enables us to define what our infrastructure resources should look like and force the orchestrator to create it (focus on the how while leveraging declarative orchestration).

The following is an example that uses Kubernetes, which is a popular container orchestration platform that exemplifies the concept of declarative resource definition. In this example, we'll define a Deployment for a simple web server and a Service to expose it.

Here's a YAML file (deployment-and-service.yaml) for Kubernetes:

```
# Deployment definition to create a web server pod
apiVersion: apps/v1
kind: Deployment
metadata:
  name: my-web-server
```

```
spec:
  replicas: 2
  selector:
    matchLabels:
      app: web-server
  template:
    metadata:
      labels:
        app: web-server
    spec:
      containers:
      - name: nginx
        image: nginx:1.17
        ports:
        - containerPort: 80

---
# Service definition to expose the web server
apiVersion: v1
kind: Service
metadata:
  name: my-web-service
spec:
  selector:
    app: web-server
  ports:
    - protocol: TCP
      port: 80
```

- **Idempotency**:

  - This allows you to create and deploy an entire infrastructure declaratively. For example, you can deploy not only agents (or sidecars) but also the network infrastructure, storage systems, and any other resources you may need. Idempotency is the property that an operation may be applied multiple times with the result not differing from the first application. Restated, this means multiple identical requests should have the same effect as a single request.

  - Idempotency enables the same request to be sent multiple times but the result given is always the same (same as declared, never different).

- **No secrets and environment config in code**:

  - The main cloud providers all have a secure way to manage secrets. These solutions provide a good way to store secrets or environment config values for the application you host on their services.

- Everything should be self-served and manageable in a standardized manner and therefore secrets and configs must be declarative and well defined to work with the aforementioned requirements.

- **Convention over configuration**:

  - Also known as environment tag-based convention over configuration, convention over configuration is a simple concept that is primarily used in programming. It means that the environment in which you work (systems, libraries, languages, and so on) assumes many logical situations by default, so if you adapt to them rather than creating your own rules each time, programming becomes an easier and more productive task.

  - This means that developers have to make fewer decisions when they're developing and there are always logical default options. These logical default options have been created out of convention, not configuration.

- **Automation scripts packaged into an image**:

  - This enables immutability and encourages sharing. No longer is a script located on a server and then has to be copied to others – instead, it can be shipped just like the rest of our code, enabling scripts to be available in a registry rather than dependent on others.

Thanks to the amazing progress in this field in the past 10+ years, customer expectations are sky-high when it comes to modern solutions. As we established earlier, if content does not load in under two seconds, it is considered to be slow. If you have to wait longer than 3 to 5 seconds, you are likely to abandon it. This is very similar to availability and customer happiness. When we talk about customer happiness (which evolved from customer experience), a concept you cannot measure and therefore cannot be data-driven, setting the right goals/objectives can be crucial to how you design your solutions.

Objectives – SLOs/SLIs

Service-level objectives (**SLOs**), which is a concept that's referenced many times in Google's SRE handbook, can be a great help to set your direction from the start. Choosing the right objective, however, can be trickier than you might think.

My personal experience aligns with Google's recommendation, which suggests that an SLO – which sets the target for the reliability of a service's customers – should be under 100%.

This is due to multiple reasons. Achieving 100% is not just very hard and extremely expensive, but almost impossible given that almost all services have soft/hard dependencies on other services. If just one of your dependencies offers less than 100% availability, your SLO cannot be met. Also, even with every precaution you can make, and every redundancy in place, there is a non-zero probability that something (or many things) will fail, resulting in less than 100% availability. More importantly, even if you could achieve 100% reliability of your services, the customers would very likely not experience that. The path your customers must take (the systems they have to use) to access your services is likely to have less than 100% SLO.

Most commercial internet providers, for example, offer 99% availability. This also means that as you go higher and higher, let's say from 99% to 99.9% or IBM's extreme five nines (99.999%), the cost of achieving and maintaining this availability will be significantly more expensive the more "nines" you add, but your customers will experience less and less of your efforts, which makes the objective questionable.

Above the selected SLO threshold, almost all users should be "happy," and below this threshold, users are likely to be unhappy, raise concerns, or just stop using the service.

Once you've agreed that you should look for an SLO less than 100%, but likely somewhere above or around 99%, how do you define the right baseline?

This is where **service-level indicators (SLIs)**, **service-level agreements (SLAs)**, and error budgets come into play. I will not detail all of these here, but if you are interested, please refer to Google's SRE book (`https://sre.google/books/`) for more details on the subject.

Let's say you picked an SLO of 99.9% – which is, based on my personal experience, the most common go-to for businesses these days. You now have to consider your core operational metrics. **DevOps Research and Assessment (DORA)** suggests four key metrics that indicate the performance of a DevOps team, ranking them from "low" to "elite," where "elite" teams are more likely to meet or even exceed their goals and delight their customers compared to "low" ranking teams.

These four metrics are as follows:

- **Lead time for change**, a metric that quantifies the duration from code commit to production deployment, is in my view one of the most crucial indicators. It serves as a measure of your team's agility and responsiveness. How swiftly can you resolve a bug? Think about it this way:

  - **Low-performing**: 1 month to 6 months of lead time

  - **Medium-performing**: 1 week to 1 month of lead time

  - **High-performing**: 1 day to 1 week of lead time

  - **Elite-performing**: Less than 1 day of lead time

- **Deployment frequency**, which measures the successful release count to production. The key word here is *successful*, as a Dev team that constantly pushes broken code through the pipeline is not great:

  - **Low-performing**: 1 month to 6 months between deployments

  - **Medium-performing**: 1 week to 1 month between deployments

  - **High-performing**: 1 day to 1 week between deployments

  - **Elite-performing**: Multiple deployments per day/less than 1 day between deployments

- **Change failure rate**, which measures the percentage of deployments that result in a failure in production that requires a bug fix or rollback. The goal is to release as frequently as possible, but what is the point if your team is constantly rolling back those changes, or causing an incident by releasing a bad update? By tracking it, you can see how often your team is fixing something that could have been avoided:

- **Low-performing**: 45% to 60% CFR

- **Medium-performing**: 15% to 45% CFR

- **High-performing**: 0% to 15% CFR

- **Elite-performing**: 0% to 15% CFR

- **Mean time to restore** (**MTTR**) measures how long it takes an organization to recover from a failure. This is measured from the initial moment of an outage until the incident team has recovered all services and operations. Another key and related metric is **mean time to acknowledge** (**MTTA**), which measures the time it takes to be aware of and confirm an issue in production:

  - **Low-performing**: 1 week to 1 month of downtime

  - **Medium- and high-performing**: Less than 24 hours of downtime

  - **Elite-performing**: Less than 1 hour of downtime

In conclusion, SLOs are crucial in setting reliability targets for a service, with a recommendation for these to be under 100% to account for dependencies and potential service failures. Utilizing tools such as SLIs, SLAs, and error budgets is essential in defining the appropriate SLO baseline, usually around or above 99%. We have also highlighted the importance of core operational metrics, as suggested by DORA, in assessing the performance of a DevOps team. These metrics, including lead time for change, deployment frequency, change failure rate, and MTTR, provide tangible criteria to measure and improve a team's efficiency and effectiveness in service delivery and incident response.

Summary

DevOps presents challenges; introduce data and those challenges intensify. This book aims to explore that intricate landscape.

Consider this: immutable objects and IaC with declarative orchestration frameworks often yield secure, dependable, and repeatable results. But what happens when you must manage entities that resist immutability? Think about databases or message queues that house data that can't be replicated easily. These technologies are integral to production but demand unique attention.

Picture this: a Formula 1 car swaps out an entire tire assembly in mere seconds during a pit stop. Similarly, with immutable objects such as load balancers, a quick destroy-and-recreate action often solves issues. It's convenient and rapid, but try applying this quick-swap approach to databases and you risk data corruption. You must exercise caution when dealing with mutable, data-persistent technologies.

Fast forward to recent years, and you'll find attempts to facilitate database automation via **custom resource definitions** (**CRDs**) or operators. However, such methods have proven costly and complex, shifting the trend toward managed services. Yet, for many, outsourcing data operations isn't the ideal solution, given the priority of data security.

Navigating DevOps and SRE best practices reveals the looming complexities in managing data-centric technologies. Despite the valuable automation tools at our disposal, maintaining the highest DevOps standards while capitalizing on this automation is anything but straightforward. We'll delve into these challenges and potential solutions in the chapters to come.

2

Large-Scale
Data-Persistent Systems

In our contemporary digital landscape, data stands as the cornerstone for organizations in diverse sectors. The facility to efficiently store, retrieve, and manage this data is vital for making educated choices, refining business workflows, and establishing a market advantage. This introduces the importance of data persistence technologies.

Data persistence is the quality of sustaining data beyond the operational life of a particular software or hardware system. It safeguards data so that it stays both available and retrievable, even after events such as system reboots or power failures. Technologies that enable data persistence ensure reliable storage and access to invaluable data over extended periods.

Originally, the goal of data persistence was met through filesystems that housed data on disk drives. However, as data has expanded both in volume and intricacy, more innovative and capable methods of data persistence have come to the fore. Organizations now have a plethora of choices, each with its unique merits and ideal use cases.

One dominant form of data persistence is the relational database. These databases categorize data into schema-defined tables, enabling easy query execution, indexing, and data integrity enforcement. Relational databases primarily use **Structured Query Language** (**SQL**) for data manipulation, making them a sturdy choice for structured data storage.

Another significant category encompasses NoSQL databases. These databases are crafted to manage unstructured or semi-structured data that changes swiftly. With their flexible schema design, horizontal scaling, and **high availability** (**HA**), NoSQL databases are particularly apt for big data scenarios, real-time applications, and distributed computing environments.

More recently, in-memory databases and key-value stores have come into vogue. In-memory databases keep data in the main memory of a system, which allows for rapid data access and transactions. These are particularly beneficial for applications demanding real-time analytics and low-latency operations.

Key-value stores, conversely, store data in uncomplicated key-value relationships, providing swift and scalable storage solutions. They are often used for caching mechanisms, session handling, and saving user settings.

Besides databases, the realm of data persistence also includes various types of filesystems, object storage solutions, cloud-based storage options, and distributed filesystems. Each of these comes with specific features and capacities tailored to address different data storage needs.

In summary, data persistence technologies serve as key pillars in modern strategies for data management and storage. They allow organizations to securely store, access, and manage data, thus assuring its long-term availability and reliability. Whether dealing with structured data in relational databases, unstructured data in NoSQL databases, or data residing in memory or in cloud storage, choosing the appropriate data persistence technology is crucial for any organization aspiring to fully leverage its data assets.

In this chapter, we'll explore the historical progression of these technologies, as well as their shared and unique characteristics. We hope you find the journey enlightening!

The following are the main topics in this chapter:

- A brief history of data
- Database evolution
- Data warehouses
- Data lakes

A brief history of data

The evolution of computers and databases has been a fascinating journey that has transformed the world we live in. From the first mechanical calculators to modern-day supercomputers, computers have come a long way in terms of their processing power, storage capacity, and speed. Similarly, databases have evolved from simple filesystems to highly sophisticated systems capable of managing massive amounts of data. This essay examines the history of computer and database evolution and their relationships.

The early days of computing

The history of computing dates back to the early 1800s, when the first mechanical calculators were built to aid in mathematical computations. Charles Babbage, an English mathematician, is credited with designing the first programmable mechanical computer, the Analytical Engine, in the 1830s. However, the machine was never built due to lack of funding.

In the late 1800s, Herman Hollerith, an American inventor, developed a machine that could read punched cards and tabulate statistical data. This machine was used to process US census data, reducing the time taken to tabulate the data from several years to a few months. This marked the beginning of the use of computers in data processing.

The first electronic computers were developed in the 1940s, during World War II. The need for faster calculations to aid in the war effort led to the development of the first electronic computers. The first electronic computer, the **Electronic Numerical Integrator and Computer** (**ENIAC**), was developed by John Mauchly and J. Presper Eckert in 1945. The machine was massive, occupying an entire room, and had limited processing power. It was used to calculate ballistic trajectories for the US military.

The development of electronic computers continued in the 1950s, with the introduction of the first commercially available computer, the **Universal Automatic Computer** (**UNIVAC**). This machine was developed by Mauchly and Eckert and was used for scientific and business applications.

The 1960s and 1970s saw the development of mainframe computers, which were large, powerful computers used by large organizations for data processing. These machines were expensive and required specialized skills to operate. However, they were reliable and could handle massive amounts of data.

The 1980s saw the introduction of personal computers, which were small, affordable computers designed for individual use. The first personal computer, the IBM PC, was introduced in 1981. These machines were popular among individuals and small businesses due to their affordability and ease of use. The introduction of **graphical user interfaces** (**GUIs**) in the 1980s also made personal computers more accessible to non-technical users.

The 1990s saw the rise of the internet and the development of the World Wide Web. This led to the development of new applications and technologies, such as web browsers and e-commerce. The proliferation of personal computers and the internet also led to the development of client-server architectures, where applications were split between the client (the user's computer) and the server (the remote computer).

The rise of relational databases

In the early days of computing, data was stored in flat files, which made it difficult to manage and retrieve data. In the 1960s, IBM developed the first relational database, which allowed data to be stored in tables with relationships between them. This made it easier to manage and retrieve data.

The development of relational databases led to the creation of SQL, a standard language for managing relational databases. SQL allows users to query and manipulate data using a simple syntax, making it easier for non-technical users to access data.

The 1970s saw the development of the first commercial relational database, Oracle, which was developed by Larry Ellison, Bob Miner, and Ed Oates. Oracle quickly became the dominant relational database on the market, and it is still widely used today.

The 1980s saw the development of **object-oriented** (**OO**) databases, which allowed data to be stored in objects with properties and methods. This made it easier to manage complex data structures, such as those used in software applications.

The 1990s saw the rise of distributed databases, which allowed data to be stored and managed across multiple servers. This made it easier to manage large amounts of data and provided better scalability and reliability.

In the 2000s, NoSQL databases were developed, which used non-relational data models. These databases were designed to handle large amounts of unstructured data, such as social media data and sensor data. NoSQL databases provide better scalability and performance than relational databases for certain types of applications.

Computers and databases are closely related, as databases are used to store and manage data that is processed by computers. The development of faster and more powerful computers has led to the development of more sophisticated databases that can handle larger amounts of data and provide better performance.

The evolution of database technologies has also influenced the development of computer applications. For example, the rise of OO databases in the 1980s led to the development of **OO programming** (**OOP**) languages, such as Java and C++. These languages allowed developers to build applications that could interact with OO databases more easily.

Similarly, the rise of distributed databases in the 1990s led to the development of distributed computing technologies, such as Hadoop and MapReduce. These technologies allow large amounts of data to be processed across multiple servers, making it possible to handle massive amounts of data.

In recent years, the use of cloud computing has become increasingly popular, providing on-demand access to computing resources and databases. Cloud databases, such as **Amazon Web Services** (**AWS**) and Microsoft Azure, provide scalable and flexible solutions for storing and managing data.

Conclusion

The evolution of computers and databases has transformed the world we live in, making it possible to store, manage, and process massive amounts of data. From the first mechanical calculators to modern-day supercomputers, computers have come a long way in terms of their processing power, storage capacity, and speed. Similarly, databases have evolved from simple filesystems to highly sophisticated systems capable of managing massive amounts of data.

The relationship between computers and databases is a close one, with the development of one influencing the development of the other. The evolution of database technologies has influenced the development of computer applications, and the development of faster and more powerful computers has led to the development of more sophisticated databases.

As we move forward, the use of **artificial intelligence** (**AI**) and **machine learning** (**ML**) is set to drive further innovation in the field of computing and databases. These technologies will enable us to process and analyze data in ways that were previously not possible, leading to new insights and discoveries.

Database evolution

In this section, we will briefly discuss how databases have evolved over time.

Hierarchical database models

Hierarchical databases are a type of **database management system** (**DBMS**) that follows a hierarchical structure for organizing data. This structure is similar to a tree, with the root node at the top and child nodes branching out from it. Each child node can have multiple child nodes of its own, and so on, creating a hierarchical structure of data.

In this model, data is organized into records, which are stored in a hierarchy of parent-child relationships. Each record is linked to one or more child records, forming a tree-like structure. The parent record is called the **owner** record, and the child records are called **member** records. The owner record can have one or more member records, but each member record can only have one owner record.

One of the key features of hierarchical databases is the use of pointers or links to connect records. These links define parent-child relationships between records and allow for efficient retrieval of data. The use of pointers is also what makes hierarchical databases fast and efficient, as they can quickly navigate through the database to find the desired records.

Hierarchical databases were first introduced in the 1960s as a way to organize large amounts of data in mainframe computers. IBM's **Information Management System** (**IMS**) is one of the most well-known hierarchical databases, and it is still used today in many large enterprises.

Advantages of hierarchical databases

One of the main advantages of hierarchical databases is their speed and efficiency. Because data is organized in a tree-like structure and linked using pointers, hierarchical databases can quickly retrieve data by following these links. This makes them ideal for applications that require fast access to large amounts of data, such as banking and finance systems.

Another advantage of hierarchical databases is their simplicity. The hierarchical structure is easy to understand and implement, making it a popular choice for small-to-medium-sized applications. This simplicity also makes it easier to maintain and update the database, as changes can be made quickly and efficiently.

Disadvantages of hierarchical databases

One major disadvantage of hierarchical databases is their inflexibility. Because data is organized in a strict hierarchy, it can be difficult to add or modify data without disrupting the structure of the database. This can make it challenging to adapt to changing business needs or to integrate with other systems.

Another disadvantage of hierarchical databases is their lack of support for complex relationships between data. For example, if you wanted to represent a many-to-many relationship between two sets of data, it would be difficult to do so using a hierarchical structure. This can limit the types of applications that can be built using hierarchical databases, especially those that require more complex data relationships.

Furthermore, hierarchical databases can also suffer from data redundancy issues. Since each record can only have one owner record, duplicate data may need to be stored in multiple locations in the database. This can cause data inconsistencies and increase the storage requirements of the database.

Hierarchical databases are also limited in terms of their scalability. As the size of the database grows, the hierarchical structure can become more complex and difficult to manage. This can lead to performance issues and make it challenging to scale the database to meet the needs of larger applications.

Despite these limitations, hierarchical databases continue to be used in many industries today. They are particularly well suited for applications that require fast and efficient retrieval of data, such as banking and finance systems. They can also be useful for smaller applications where simplicity is a priority and the data relationships are relatively straightforward.

Examples of hierarchical databases

As mentioned earlier, IBM's IMS is one of the most well-known hierarchical databases. IMS was originally developed in the 1960s for IBM's mainframe computers and is still widely used today in large enterprises. IMS is used in a variety of industries, including banking, insurance, and telecommunications, and is known for its speed and reliability.

Another example of a hierarchical database is the Windows Registry, which is used to store system settings and configuration data on Windows operating systems. The registry is organized in a hierarchical structure, with keys representing the parent-child relationships between data. This makes it easy to navigate and retrieve system settings quickly.

In conclusion, hierarchical databases are a type of DBMS that organizes data in a tree-like structure with parent-child relationships. They are known for their speed and efficiency, as well as their simplicity and ease of maintenance. However, they can be inflexible and limited in terms of their ability to represent complex data relationships. Despite these limitations, hierarchical databases continue to be used in many industries today, particularly in applications that require fast and efficient retrieval of data.

Here's an example structure of a hierarchical database model represented in JSON:

```json
{
    "FamilyTree": {
      "Grandparent": {
        "Name": "Alice",
        "Children": [
          {
            "Name": "Bob",
            "Children": [
              {
                "Name": "Charlie"
              }
            ]
          },
          {
            "Name": "Diana",
            "Children": [
              {
                "Name": "Eva"
              }
            ]
          }
        ]
      }
    }
}
```

This JSON file illustrates a tree-like structure, which is characteristic of hierarchical databases. Here, `Alice` is the grandparent and has two children, `Bob` and `Diana`, each with their own children (`Charlie` and `Eva`, respectively).

This hierarchical database model is useful for representing organizational structures, family trees, or any other data that has a tree-like structure. However, it can be limiting if the data needs to be queried in more complex ways, such as retrieving all employees who have a certain job title regardless of their position in the hierarchy. In those cases, a different database model, such as a relational database, may be more appropriate.

Network database model

The network database model is a type of DBMS that is designed to store and query data in a hierarchical structure. It was first introduced in the late 1960s as an improvement over the earlier hierarchical database model, and it was widely used throughout the 1970s and 1980s.

The network database model is based on the concept of a network, where data is organized into a series of interconnected nodes or records. These records are linked together through a series of relationships, which form a network of interconnected data.

In the network database model, each record or node in the network is called an entity, and each relationship between entities is called a set. A set can be thought of as a pointer or link that connects one entity to another. Sets can also have attributes, which are properties that describe the relationship between entities.

One of the key features of the network database model is the ability to represent complex relationships between entities. For example, an entity in the network can have multiple parents or children, and relationships can be defined between entities that are not directly connected.

To illustrate this, consider a simple example of a network database for a library. The database might have entities for books, authors, publishers, and borrowers. Each book entity might have sets that link it to an author, a publisher, and one or more borrower entities. Each borrower entity might have a set that links it to one or more book entities.

The network database model can be implemented using a variety of different data structures, including linked lists, trees, and graphs. These data structures are used to represent the relationships between entities and to facilitate efficient queries of the data.

One of the primary advantages of the network database model is its flexibility. Because it allows for complex relationships between entities, it can be used to model a wide variety of data structures and relationships.

However, the network database model also has some limitations. One of the main challenges with this model is that it can be difficult to maintain consistency and integrity when there are multiple relationships between entities. For example, if a book entity is linked to multiple borrower entities, it can be difficult to ensure that the borrower records are updated correctly when the book is checked out or returned.

Another limitation of the network database model is that it can be less intuitive than other database models, such as the relational database model. Because the network model relies heavily on sets and relationships, it can be more difficult to understand and work with than a table-based model.

Despite these limitations, the network database model still has some important use cases and advantages. One of the primary advantages of the network database model is its ability to handle complex data structures and relationships. This makes it particularly well suited for applications that require hierarchical or recursive data structures, such as product structures, **bills of materials (BOMs)**, and organization charts.

Another advantage of the network database model is its ability to handle large volumes of data. Because the data is organized hierarchically, it can be efficiently accessed and queried even when dealing with large datasets.

In addition, the network database model can be more performant than other database models in certain situations. For example, when dealing with complex relationships between entities, the network model can be faster than the relational model, which requires multiple joins to retrieve the same data.

Another advantage of the network database model is its ability to support multiple access paths to the data. Because the data is organized hierarchically, it can be accessed through multiple paths, allowing for greater flexibility in querying and reporting.

Despite these advantages, the network database model has largely been superseded by the relational database model, which has become the dominant database model in use today. This is largely due to the fact that the relational model is more intuitive and easier to use than the network model, particularly for non-technical users.

In addition, the relational model offers better support for data integrity and consistency, making it a better choice for applications where data accuracy and reliability are critical.

That being said, the network database model still has some important use cases, particularly in niche applications where its strengths in handling hierarchical and recursive data structures are particularly valuable.

In terms of implementation, the network database model can be implemented using a variety of different data structures, including linked lists, trees, and graphs. These data structures are used to represent the relationships between entities and to facilitate efficient queries of the data.

In summary, the network database model is a hierarchical DBMS that allows for complex relationships between entities. While it has some limitations compared to other database models, it remains a valuable tool for applications that require hierarchical or recursive data structures, such as product structures, BOMs, and organization charts.

Here is an example of a network database structure in JSON format:

```
{
  "Courses": [
    {
      "CourseID": "Math101",
      "Students": ["Alice", "Bob"]
    },
    {
      "CourseID": "History202",
      "Students": ["Bob", "Charlie"]
    }
  ],
  "Students": [
    {
      "Name": "Alice",
```

```
      "Courses": ["Math101"]
    },
    {
      "Name": "Bob",
      "Courses": ["Math101", "History202"]
    },
    {
      "Name": "Charlie",
      "Courses": ["History202"]
    }
  ]
}
```

In this example, the `Courses` array contains courses and their enrolled students. The `Students` array contains students and the courses they are enrolled in. Notice how `Bob` is a child node for both `Math101` and `History202`, demonstrating the multiple parent-child relationships that are typical in a network database model.

This JSON structure represents a simple example of a network database model, where data is organized hierarchically into a series of interconnected nodes or records.

Relational databases

The relational database model is a widely used method for organizing and managing data in computer systems. It was first introduced by Edgar F. Codd in 1970 and has since become the foundation for many modern DBMSs. In this technical deep dive, we will explore the key concepts and components that make up the relational database model.

Concepts of the relational database model

The relational database model is based on several key concepts, including entities, attributes, relationships, and constraints:

- **Entities**: An entity is a real-world object or concept that can be identified and described. In a relational database, an entity is typically represented as a table or relation. Each row in the table represents an instance of the entity, and each column represents an attribute or property of the entity. For example, in a database for a retail store, the entities might include customers, products, and orders.

- **Attributes**: An attribute is a characteristic or property of an entity. In a relational database, attributes correspond to columns in a table or relation. For example, a customer entity might have attributes such as name, address, and phone number.

- **Relationships**: Relationships define how entities are related to each other. In a relational database, relationships are typically represented by foreign keys, which are columns in one table that refer to the primary key of another table. For example, in a database for a retail store, the `orders` table might have a foreign key column that refers to the `customer` table's primary key, indicating which customer placed the order.

- **Constraints**: Constraints are rules that limit the values that can be stored in a database. There are several types of constraints in a relational database, including primary keys, foreign keys, unique constraints, and check constraints. These constraints help ensure data integrity and consistency. For example, a primary key constraint ensures that each row in a table is unique, while a foreign key constraint ensures that the values in a column refer to valid primary key values in another table.

Components of the relational database model

The relational database model is made up of several key components, including tables, columns, rows, and keys:

- **Tables**: In the relational database model, data is organized into tables or relations. Each table represents an entity, and each row in the table represents an instance of the entity. For example, a customer table might contain rows for each individual customer.

- **Columns**: Columns in a table represent attributes or properties of the entity represented by the table. Each column has a name and a data type, which specifies the type of data that can be stored in the column. Common data types include integers, strings, dates, and Booleans. Columns also have a set of constraints that can be applied to restrict values that can be stored in the column.

- **Rows**: Rows in a table represent individual instances of the entity represented by the table. Each row contains values for each of the table's columns, representing the specific values for each attribute of the entity. For example, a row in a customer table might contain values for the customer's name, address, and phone number.

- **Keys**: Keys are used to uniquely identify rows in a table and establish relationships between tables. There are several types of keys in the relational database model, including primary keys, foreign keys, and composite keys.

- **Primary keys**: A primary key is a column or set of columns in a table that uniquely identifies each row in the table. This key is used to enforce data integrity and ensure that each row in the table is unique. For example, a customer table might use the customer ID as its primary key.

- **Foreign keys**: A foreign key is a column or set of columns in a table that refers to the primary key of another table. This key is used to establish relationships between tables and enforce referential integrity. For example, an orders table might have a foreign key column that refers to the primary key of the customer table.

- **Composite keys**: A composite key is a key that consists of multiple columns in a table. This key is used when no single column can uniquely identify a row in the table. For example, a table that stores customer orders might use a composite key consisting of the order ID and the customer ID.

Advantages of the relational database model

The relational database model offers several advantages over other data storage methods, including the following:

- **Data consistency and integrity**: The use of constraints and keys helps ensure that data is consistent and accurate across tables

- **Scalability**: The relational database model can scale to handle large amounts of data and complex relationships between entities

- **Flexibility**: The use of tables and relationships allows data to be organized and accessed in a flexible and efficient manner

- **Data security**: The use of access controls and permissions helps ensure that sensitive data is protected from unauthorized access

Limitations of the relational database model

While the relational database model offers many advantages, it also has some limitations, including the following:

- **Performance**: The use of joins and relationships can sometimes result in slower query performance, particularly for large datasets

- **Complexity**: The relational database model can be complex to design and manage, particularly for large or complex databases

- **Lack of flexibility**: The rigid structure of the relational database model can make it difficult to make changes to the data schema or add new functionality to the database

- **Data duplication**: In some cases, the relational database model can result in data duplication across tables, which can lead to inconsistencies and inefficiencies

- **Limited support for unstructured data**: The relational database model is designed primarily for structured data, and may not be well suited for storing and querying unstructured data such as images or text documents

Alternatives to the relational database model

While the relational database model is widely used and well established, there are several alternative data storage methods that address some of its limitations, including the following:

- **NoSQL databases**: NoSQL databases use a more flexible data model that is not based on tables and relationships. This can offer improved scalability and performance for certain types of data.

- **Graph databases**: Graph databases are designed specifically for storing and querying relationships between entities. They can be particularly useful for analyzing complex networks or social graphs.

- **OO databases**: OO databases store data as objects, which can offer improved support for complex data structures and relationships.

In conclusion, the relational database model is a widely used and well-established method for organizing and managing data in computer systems. It is based on the concepts of entities, attributes, relationships, and constraints, and is made up of tables, columns, rows, and keys. While the relational database model offers many advantages, it also has some limitations, including performance, complexity, and lack of flexibility. Several alternative data storage methods address some of these limitations, including NoSQL databases, graph databases, and OO databases.

Example

Relational databases are typically represented in a tabular format, whereas JSON is a hierarchical data format. However, it is possible to represent relational data in JSON format by using nested objects and arrays.

Here's an example of a simple relational database represented in JSON:

```
```
{
  "customers": [
    {
      "id": 1,
      "name": "John",
      "email": "john@example.com"
    },
    {
      "id": 2,
      "name": "Jane",
      "email": "jane@example.com"
    }
  ],
  "orders": [
    {
      "id": 1,
```
```

```
        "customer_id": 1,
        "order_date": "2022-03-15",
        "total_amount": 100.00
      },
      {
        "id": 2,
        "customer_id": 2,
        "order_date": "2022-03-16",
        "total_amount": 200.00
      }
    ]
  }
```

In this example, we have two tables: `customers` and `orders`. The `customers` table has three columns: `id`, `name`, and `email`, and the `orders` table has four columns: `id`, `customer_id`, `order_date`, and `total_amount`. The `customer_id` column in the `orders` table is a foreign key that references the `id` column in the `customers` table.

Using this JSON representation, we can easily retrieve all orders associated with a particular customer by searching for the customer's ID in the `customer_id` column of the `orders` table.

Here's the same example in a tabular format:

```
Customers table:

| id | name  | email            |
| 1  | John  | john@example.com |
| 2  | Jane  | jane@example.com |
Orders table:

| id | customer_id | order_date | total_amount |
| 1  | 1           | 2022-03-15 | 100.00       |
| 2  | 2           | 2022-03-16 | 200.00       |
```

In the tabular format, each table is represented as a set of rows and columns. The `customers` table has three columns: `id`, `name`, and `email`, and two rows representing two customers. The `orders` table has four columns: `id`, `customer_id`, `order_date`, and `total_amount`, and two rows representing two orders. The `customer_id` column in the `orders` table serves as a foreign key that references the `id` column in the `customers` table, linking the two tables together.

OO databases

The OO database model is a type of DBMS that uses an OOP language to create, store, and retrieve data. It is based on the principles of OOP, which means it treats data as objects. In this model, data is represented as objects that have attributes and methods, just as in OOP.

In the OO database model, data is stored in an OO database, which is a collection of objects that are organized into classes. A class is a blueprint for creating objects that have the same attributes and methods. Objects are instances of a class, and each object has its own unique set of values for its attributes.

One of the main advantages of the OO database model is that it allows for complex data structures to be created and stored in the database. This is because objects can be nested inside other objects, allowing for more complex relationships between data.

Another advantage of the OO database model is that it is highly flexible. Because data is stored as objects, it is easy to add new attributes and methods to objects as needed. This makes it easy to modify the database schema as requirements change, without having to make significant changes to the underlying database structure.

One of the challenges of the OO database model is that it can be difficult to map it onto a traditional **relational DBMS** (**RDBMS**). This is because the OO model uses a different structure and different operations than a traditional RDBMS. Some OO databases have attempted to bridge this gap by providing a relational view of the OO data, but this can come at the cost of some of the flexibility and performance advantages of the OO model.

To address this challenge, some OO databases have been developed that are specifically designed to support the OO model. These databases typically provide a range of features that are not available in traditional RDBMSs, such as support for complex data structures, support for inheritance and polymorphism, and support for object versioning and transactions.

One of the key features of the OO database model is support for inheritance and polymorphism. Inheritance allows objects to inherit attributes and methods from their parent classes, making it easy to create new objects that are similar to existing ones. Polymorphism allows objects to be treated as instances of their parent classes, which can simplify code and make it more flexible.

Another important feature of the OO database model is support for transactions. Transactions allow multiple operations to be grouped together into a single unit of work, which ensures that either all of the operations are completed successfully or none of them are completed at all. This helps to ensure the integrity of the data in the database and can be particularly important in applications where data consistency is critical.

OO databases can store a wide variety of data types, including text, images, audio, and video. This makes them well suited for applications that deal with multimedia data, such as video editing software or digital asset management systems.

One potential disadvantage of the OO database model is that it can be less efficient than a traditional RDBMS when it comes to queries that involve complex joins or aggregations. This is because the OO model is optimized for accessing individual objects, rather than for performing complex queries across multiple objects.

To address this challenge, some OO databases have included support for SQL, which allows developers to perform complex queries using a familiar syntax. However, this can come at the cost of some of the flexibility and performance advantages of the OO model.

Another potential disadvantage of the OO database model is that it can be more difficult to learn and use than a traditional RDBMS. This is because it requires developers to learn a new programming paradigm and to become familiar with the specific features and syntax of the OO database system they are using.

Overall, the OO database model is a powerful and flexible approach to database management that is well suited for applications that deal with complex data structures and multimedia data. While it can be more challenging to learn and use than a traditional RDBMS, it offers significant advantages in terms of flexibility, performance, and data integrity. As such, it is an important option for developers and organizations that need to manage complex data in a flexible and efficient way.

Example

JSON is often used to represent OO data structures in web applications. Here is an example of an OO data structure represented in JSON:

```
```
{
  "person": {
    "name": "John Smith",
    "age": 35,
    "address": {
      "street": "123 Main St",
      "city": "Anytown",
      "state": "CA",
      "zip": "12345"
    },
    "phoneNumbers": [
      {
        "type": "home",
        "number": "555-555-1234"
      },
      {
        "type": "work",
        "number": "555-555-5678"
      }
```
```

```
        ]
    }
}

```

In this example, there is a top-level object called `person` that represents a person with a name, age, address, and phone numbers. The name and age are represented as simple attributes of the `person` object. The address is represented as a nested object with its own set of attributes, including the street, city, state, and zip code.

The phone numbers are represented as an array of objects, where each object represents a phone number with a type (for example, `home` or `work`) and a number.

NoSQL database paradigms

NoSQL databases are a class of non-relational databases that are designed to handle large volumes of unstructured or semi-structured data. Unlike traditional relational databases, which store data in tables with strict schema definitions, NoSQL databases allow for more flexible and dynamic data models.

They are often used in big data and web applications, where scalability and performance are critical. They can handle high volumes of data and support distributed architectures, making them ideal for applications that require HA and **fault tolerance** (**FT**).

NoSQL databases have paradigms because they are designed to handle different types of data and workloads than traditional relational databases. These paradigms are essentially different models for organizing and storing data, and they offer different trade-offs in terms of scalability, performance, consistency, and ease of use.

For example, document-oriented databases such as MongoDB and Couchbase store data as flexible, JSON-like documents that can be easily nested and denormalized. This makes them well suited for storing complex, unstructured data, such as social media posts or product catalogs, and for supporting agile development workflows.

Key-value stores such as **REmote DIctionary Server** (**Redis**) and Riak, on the other hand, store data as simple, unstructured key-value pairs that can be quickly accessed and updated. This makes them ideal for high-speed data caching and session management, as well as for supporting real-time applications such as chat and gaming.

Column-family stores such as Apache Cassandra and HBase store data as columns rather than rows, which allows them to support very large datasets and high write throughput. This makes them well suited for big data analytics and other applications that require massive scalability.

Each of these paradigms offers different benefits and trade-offs, and choosing the right one depends on the specific requirements of the application.

Let's dive deeper into them.

Document-oriented databases

Document-oriented databases are designed to store data in a document format, such as JSON, BSON, or XML. Each document can have a different structure, which makes them flexible and easy to scale horizontally. Document databases are often used for web applications, **content management systems** (**CMSs**), and e-commerce sites.

Examples: MongoDB, Couchbase, Amazon DocumentDB, Azure Cosmos DB.

The pros are as follows:

- **Flexible schema**: Document-oriented databases allow for flexible and dynamic schema design, which makes it easier to handle unstructured or semi-structured data

- **High performance**: Document databases can provide high performance and low latency because they can store all related data in a single document, which reduces the need for joins and other complex queries

- **Horizontal scalability**: Document-oriented databases can easily scale horizontally by adding more nodes to the cluster, which makes them well suited for high-traffic applications

The cons are as follows:

- **Limited transaction support**: Some document-oriented databases do not support ACID transactions, which can make it challenging to maintain data consistency in high-concurrency environments

- **Data duplication**: Because each document can have a different structure, there can be data duplication across documents, which can increase storage requirements

- **Limited query flexibility**: Document-oriented databases are optimized for querying within a single document, which can make it challenging to perform complex queries across multiple documents

> **Fun fact**
>
> One example of a document-oriented database is MongoDB. In MongoDB, data is stored in documents, which are JSON-like data structures that can have nested fields and arrays. Each document can have a unique identifier, called an **ObjectId**, which is automatically generated by MongoDB.
>
> For example, suppose you are building a blog application, and you want to store blog posts in a database. In MongoDB, you could represent each blog post as a document, like this:
>
> ```
> ```
> ```
> {
>   "_id": ObjectId("6151a3a3bce2f46f5d2b2e8a"),
>   "title": "My First Blog Post",
>   "body": "Lorem ipsum dolor sit amet, consectetur adipiscing
> elit...",
>   "author": "John Doe",
>   "tags": ["mongodb", "database", "blogging"],
>   "created_at": ISODate("2022-10-01T12:30:00Z"),
>   "updated_at": ISODate("2022-10-02T15:45:00Z")
> }
> ```
> ```
> ```
>
> In this example, each blog post is represented as a document with a unique `_id` field, a `title` field, a `body` field, an `author` field, a `tags` field (which is an array of strings), and `created_at` and `updated_at` fields (which are `ISODate` objects representing when the post was created and last updated, respectively).
>
> You can then use MongoDB's query language to retrieve or manipulate these documents based on their fields and values.

Key-value databases

Key-value databases store data as a collection of key-value pairs, where each key is unique and maps to a value. Key-value databases are simple and fast, making them suitable for caching and session management. They are often used for real-time applications and distributed systems.

Examples: Redis, Riak, Amazon DynamoDB, Azure Cache for Redis.

The pros are as follows:

- **High performance**: Key-value databases are designed for high-performance and low-latency access to data, making them ideal for real-time applications

- **Scalability**: Key-value databases can easily scale horizontally by adding more nodes to the cluster, which makes them well suited for high-traffic applications

- **Low overhead**: Key-value databases have minimal overhead and can be used for caching and session management without adding significant overhead to the application

The cons are as follows:

- **Limited query support**: Key-value databases are optimized for key-value lookups and do not support complex queries or aggregations

- **Limited data modeling**: Key-value databases do not support relationships between data, which can make it challenging to model complex data structures

- **Limited support for secondary indexes**: Some key-value databases do not support secondary indexes, which can make it challenging to perform efficient queries on non-primary keys

---

Fun fact

One example of a key-value database is Redis. In Redis, data is stored as key-value pairs, where keys are unique identifiers that map to values. Redis supports various data types for values, such as strings, hashes, lists, sets, and sorted sets.

For example, suppose you are building an e-commerce application, and you want to store shopping cart information for each user. In Redis, you could represent each user's shopping cart as a key-value pair, where the key is the user's ID and the value is a hash containing the items in the cart and their quantities, like this:

```
```
> HSET cart:1234 item:apple 2
(integer) 1
> HSET cart:1234 item:banana 1
(integer) 1
> HSET cart:1234 item:orange 3
(integer) 1
```
```

In this example, the `cart:1234` key maps to a hash with three fields: `item:apple`, `item:banana`, and `item:orange`. The values of these fields represent the quantities of the corresponding items in the user's shopping cart.

You can then use Redis commands to retrieve or manipulate these key-value pairs based on their keys and values. For example, you can use the `HGETALL` command to retrieve all the fields and values of a hash, or the `HINCRBY` command to increment the quantity of a specific item in a hash.

Column-family databases

Column-family databases are designed to store data in column families, which are groups of columns that are stored together. Each column family can have a different schema, allowing for flexible and efficient data storage. Column-family databases are often used for large-scale data processing and analytics.

Examples: Apache Cassandra, Apache HBase, Amazon Keyspaces, Azure Cosmos DB.

The pros are as follows:

- **Scalability**: Column-family databases can easily scale horizontally by adding more nodes to the cluster, making them well suited for large-scale distributed systems.

- **High performance**: Column-family databases can provide high performance and low latency because they store related data in a single-column family, which reduces the need for joins and other complex queries

- **Flexible schema**: Column-family databases allow for flexible and dynamic schema design, which makes it easier to handle unstructured or semi-structured data

The cons are as follows:

- **Limited transaction support**: Some column-family databases do not support ACID transactions, which can make it challenging to maintain data consistency in high-concurrency environments

- **Complex data modeling**: Column-family databases require careful consideration of the data model, which can make them challenging to use for applications with complex relationships between data points

- **Limited query support**: Column-family databases are optimized for querying within a single-column family, which can make it challenging to perform complex queries across multiple-column families

Fun fact

One example of a column-oriented database is Apache Cassandra. In a column-oriented database, data is stored in columns rather than rows, which allows for more efficient querying and aggregation of large amounts of data.

In Cassandra, the data model is based on a keyspace, which is a namespace that contains one or more column families. Each column family is a collection of rows, where each row is identified by a unique key. Each row in a column family can have multiple columns, where each column has a name, a value, and a timestamp.

For example, suppose you are building a social media application, and you want to store user posts in a database. In Cassandra, you could represent each post as a row in a column family, where each column represents a different attribute of the post, like this:

```
```

```
CREATE TABLE posts (
    user_id uuid,
    post_id timeuuid,
    title text,
    body text,
    tags set<text>,
    created_at timestamp,
    PRIMARY KEY ((user_id), created_at, post_id)
);
```

```
```

In this example, the `posts` table has a composite primary key consisting of the `user_id`, `created_at`, and `post_id` columns. The `user_id` column is used as the partition key, which determines the node on which the data is stored. The `created_at` and `post_id` columns are used as clustering keys, which determine the order of the rows within each partition.

You can then use **Cassandra Query Language (CQL)**, to retrieve or manipulate these rows based on their columns and values. For example, you can use the `SELECT` statement to retrieve all posts by a specific user, or the `UPDATE` statement to update the title or body of a specific post.

Graph databases

Graph databases store data in a graph structure, with nodes representing entities and edges representing relationships between them. Graph databases are highly efficient for querying complex relationships between data points, making them popular for use cases such as social networks and recommendation engines.

Examples: Neo4j, ArangoDB, Amazon Neptune, Azure Cosmos DB.

The pros are as follows:

- **Efficient relationship queries**: Graph databases are optimized for querying complex relationships between data points, which makes them well suited for applications that require efficient relationship queries

- **Flexible schema**: Graph databases allow for flexible and dynamic schema design, which makes it easier to handle unstructured or semi-structured data

- **High performance**: Graph databases can provide high performance and low latency because they store related data in a single graph structure, which reduces the need for joins and other complex queries

The cons are as follows:

- **Limited scalability**: Graph databases can be challenging to scale horizontally because they require complex data partitioning and replication strategies to maintain data consistency

- **Limited query flexibility**: Graph databases are optimized for querying relationships between data points, which can make it challenging to perform complex queries that involve multiple types of entities or relationships

- **Limited data modeling**: Graph databases require careful consideration of the data model, which can make them challenging to use for applications with complex relationships between data points

> **Fun fact**
>
> One example of a graph database is Neo4j. In a graph database, data is stored as nodes and edges, where nodes represent entities and edges represent the relationships between them. Graph databases are particularly useful for modeling complex relationships and performing graph-based queries, such as pathfinding and recommendation algorithms.
>
> For example, suppose you are building a social network application, and you want to store information about users and their relationships. In Neo4j, you could represent each user as a node, and each relationship between users as an edge, like this:
>
> ```
> ```
>
> ```
> (:User {id: "1234", name: "Alice"})-[:FRIENDS_WITH]->(:User
> {id: "5678", name: "Bob"})
> (:User {id: "1234", name: "Alice"})-[:FRIENDS_WITH]->(:User {id:
> "9012", name: "Charlie"})
> (:User {id: "5678", name: "Bob"})-[:FRIENDS_WITH]->(:User {id:
> "9012", name: "Charlie"})
> ```
>
> ```
> ```
>
> In this example, each node represents a user with a unique id and name value. Each relationship between users is represented as an edge with a type of FRIENDS_WITH. The direction of the edge indicates the direction of the relationship (for example, Alice is friends with Bob, but Bob is also friends with Alice).
>
> You can then use Neo4j's query language, Cypher, to retrieve or manipulate these nodes and edges based on their properties and relationships. For example, you can use the MATCH statement to find all the friends of a specific user, or the CREATE statement to add a new user or relationship to the graph.

In summary, NoSQL databases come in different paradigms, each with its own strengths and weaknesses. Document-oriented databases are flexible and highly scalable but may have limited query flexibility and transaction support. Key-value databases are simple and fast but may have limited query support and data modeling capabilities. Column-family databases are optimized for large-scale data processing but may have limited query support and complex data modeling requirements. Graph databases are highly efficient for querying complex relationships between data points but may have limited scalability and query flexibility. It's important to consider the specific requirements of your application when choosing a NoSQL database paradigm.

Data warehouses

A data warehouse is a large, centralized repository of data that is used for storing and analyzing data from multiple sources. It is designed to support **business intelligence** (**BI**) activities, such as reporting, data mining, and **online analytical processing** (**OLAP**). In this overview, we will discuss the technical aspects of data warehouses, including their architecture, data modeling, and integration.

Architecture

The architecture of a data warehouse can be divided into three layers: the data source layer, the data storage layer, and the data access layer.

The data source layer consists of all the systems that provide data to the data warehouse. These systems can include transactional databases, operational data stores, and external data sources. Data from these sources is **extracted, transformed, and loaded** (ETL) into the data warehouse.

The data storage layer is where data is stored in a way that is optimized for reporting and analysis. The data in a data warehouse is organized into a dimensional model, which is designed to support OLAP queries. The dimensional model consists of fact tables and dimension tables, which are organized into a star schema or a snowflake schema.

The data access layer is where the end user interacts with the data warehouse. This layer consists of reporting tools, OLAP tools, and other applications that allow users to query and analyze the data in the data warehouse.

Data modeling

Data modeling is the process of designing the structure of the data in a data warehouse. The goal of data modeling is to create a model that is optimized for reporting and analysis.

The dimensional model is the most common data modeling technique used in data warehouses. It consists of fact tables and dimension tables, which are organized into a star schema or a snowflake schema.

A fact table contains the measures or metrics that are being analyzed, such as sales revenue or customer count. Each row in the fact table represents a specific event, such as a sale or a customer interaction. The fact table also contains foreign keys that link to dimension tables.

Dimension tables contain the attributes that describe the data in the fact table. For example, a customer dimension table might contain attributes such as customer name, address, and phone number. The dimension tables are linked to the fact table through foreign keys.

The star schema is a simple and intuitive data model that is easy to understand and use. In a star schema, the fact table is at the center of the model, with the dimension tables radiating out from it like the points of a star. This makes it easy to query the data and perform OLAP analysis.

The snowflake schema is a more complex version of the star schema, where the dimension tables are normalized into multiple tables. This can make the schema more flexible and easier to maintain, but it can also make queries more complex and slower to execute.

Integration

Integrating data from multiple sources is a key function of a data warehouse. The ETL process is used to extract data from the source systems, transform it into a format that is suitable for analysis, and load it into the data warehouse.

There are several challenges involved in integrating data from multiple sources. One challenge is dealing with differences in data structure and format. For example, different systems may use different data types or have different naming conventions for the same data.

Another challenge is dealing with data quality issues. The data in the source systems may contain errors, duplicates, or missing values, which can affect the accuracy of the analysis.

To address these challenges, the ETL process may include data cleansing, data transformation, and data enrichment steps. Data cleansing involves identifying and correcting errors in the data, such as removing duplicates or fixing formatting issues. Data transformation involves converting the data into a format that is suitable for analysis, such as aggregating data at a higher level or creating new variables based on existing data. Data enrichment involves adding new data to the existing data, such as demographic data or geographic data.

In summary, a data warehouse is a large, centralized repository of data that is used for storing and analyzing data from multiple sources. The architecture of a data warehouse consists of three layers: the data source layer, the data storage layer, and the data access layer. Data modeling is the process of designing the structure of the data in the data warehouse, and the most common data modeling technique used in data warehouses is the dimensional model. Integrating data from multiple sources is a key function of a data warehouse, and the ETL process is used to extract, transform, and load the data into the data warehouse.

Data warehouses are suitable for businesses of all sizes and industries that need to store and analyze large amounts of data from multiple sources. Here are some specific scenarios where a data warehouse can be particularly beneficial:

- **Large enterprises**: Large enterprises often have massive amounts of data generated from various sources, such as customer interactions, sales transactions, and operational systems. A data warehouse can help these enterprises store and analyze this data efficiently, enabling them to make well-informed business decisions.

- **Data-driven organizations**: Organizations that rely heavily on data to make decisions can benefit from a data warehouse. By centralizing data from multiple sources, a data warehouse can provide a **single source of truth** (**SSOT**) for data analysis, which can help organizations avoid inconsistencies and inaccuracies in their data.

- **Businesses with complex data structures**: Businesses with complex data structures, such as those with multiple **business units** (**BUs**) or locations, can benefit from a data warehouse. By organizing data into a dimensional model, a data warehouse can simplify the process of querying and analyzing data, enabling businesses to gain insights into their operations more easily.

- **Businesses with a need for real-time data**: While data warehouses are not designed for real-time data processing, they can be useful for businesses that need to store and analyze large amounts of data in near real time. By using technologies such as **change data capture** (**CDC**), businesses can continuously update their data warehouse with new data, enabling them to analyze data more quickly.

- **Businesses with regulatory requirements**: Businesses that are subject to regulatory requirements, such as financial institutions, can benefit from a data warehouse. By storing data in a centralized location, a data warehouse can help these businesses comply with regulations that require them to maintain historical data for a certain period.

Any business that needs to store and analyze large amounts of data from multiple sources can benefit from a data warehouse. By centralizing data, organizing it into a dimensional model, and enabling efficient querying and analysis, a data warehouse can help businesses make well-informed decisions and gain a competitive edge.

Data lakes

Data lakes have become an increasingly popular way for organizations to store and manage large amounts of structured, semi-structured, and unstructured data. In this overview, we'll dive deep into the technical aspects of data lakes, including their architecture, data ingestion and processing, storage and retrieval, and security considerations.

Architecture

At its core, a data lake is an architectural approach to storing data that allows for the aggregation of large volumes of disparate datasets in their original formats. This means that data can be ingested from a wide range of sources, including databases, data warehouses, streaming data sources, and even unstructured data such as social media posts or log files. The data is typically stored in a centralized repository that spans multiple servers or nodes and is accessed using a distributed filesystem such as **Hadoop Distributed File System** (**HDFS**), **Amazon Simple Storage Service** (**Amazon S3**), or Microsoft Azure Data Lake Storage.

Data ingestion and processing

Data ingestion is the process of bringing data into the data lake from various sources. This process can be automated using tools such as Apache NiFi, StreamSets, or Apache Kafka, which allow for the creation of pipelines that can ingest data from a wide range of sources, transform it as needed, and load it into the data lake. Once the data is ingested, it can be processed and analyzed using a variety of tools and frameworks, such as Apache Spark, Apache Hive, or Apache Flink.

One of the key benefits of data lakes is the ability to process data at scale using distributed computing frameworks such as Apache Spark. These frameworks allow for the parallel processing of large datasets across multiple nodes, which can significantly reduce processing times and enable real-time analysis of streaming data. Additionally, data can be processed using ML algorithms to uncover patterns and insights that may not be immediately apparent.

Storage and retrieval

Data lakes use a variety of storage technologies, including HDFS, Amazon S3, and Azure Data Lake Storage, to store data in a distributed, fault-tolerant manner. The data is typically stored in its original format, or a lightly structured format such as Parquet or ORC, which allows for efficient querying and analysis. Additionally, data can be partitioned and bucketed to further optimize query performance.

Data retrieval from a data lake can be performed using a variety of tools and frameworks, including Apache Hive, Apache Spark SQL, or Presto. These tools allow for the creation of SQL-like queries that can be executed across large volumes of data in a distributed manner. Additionally, data can be accessed using APIs, which can be used to retrieve specific datasets or perform more complex operations using programming languages such as Python or Java.

Security considerations

As data lakes often contain sensitive and valuable information, security is a critical consideration. Access to the data should be tightly controlled, and authentication and authorization mechanisms should be put in place to ensure that only authorized users and applications can access the data. Additionally, encryption should be used to protect the data at rest and in transit.

Data governance is another important aspect of data lake security. Organizations should establish policies and procedures for data classification, access controls, data retention, and data lineage. They should also monitor user activity and audit logs to detect and prevent unauthorized access or data breaches.

Conclusion

In summary, data lakes provide an architectural approach for storing and processing large volumes of data from diverse sources. They use distributed computing frameworks and storage technologies to enable scalable data processing and analysis. While data lakes offer many benefits, including flexibility, scalability, and cost-effectiveness, they also come with security and governance challenges that must be carefully managed to ensure the integrity and confidentiality of the data. As organizations continue to generate and collect ever-increasing amounts of data, data lakes are likely to remain a critical component of modern data architectures.

Data lakes can benefit a wide range of organizations and industries that need to store, manage, and analyze large volumes of data. Specifically, data lakes can be useful for the following:

- **Enterprises with large and complex data environments**: Data lakes can help enterprises consolidate and manage their data from multiple sources, including structured, semi-structured, and unstructured data. This can help improve data accessibility and enable more efficient and effective data processing and analysis.

- **Data-driven organizations**: Organizations that rely heavily on data to drive their business decisions and operations can benefit from data lakes. With a data lake, organizations can store and process large volumes of data, enabling them to quickly and easily access the data they need to make informed decisions.

- **Data scientists and analysts**: Data lakes can provide data scientists and analysts with a centralized repository of data that they can use to perform data exploration, analysis, and modeling. This can help them uncover insights and patterns that can inform business decisions and drive innovation.

- **Marketing and advertising companies**: Marketing and advertising companies can use data lakes to store and analyze vast amounts of customer data, including social media data, web analytics data, and advertising data. This can help them gain a better understanding of their target audiences, optimize their advertising campaigns, and improve customer engagement.

In short, any organization that needs to store, manage, and analyze large volumes of data from multiple sources can benefit from a data lake.

A realistic scenario

Imagine a nationwide retail giant that has been efficiently utilizing a data warehouse to consolidate and examine various types of data, such as sales figures, stock levels, and customer profiles. This data warehouse has been instrumental in enabling the company to make informed choices regarding inventory control, store design, and promotional strategies.

However, the organization recognizes that it's missing out on potential insights from unstructured data, such as social media interactions and customer feedback. To address this gap, it opts to introduce a data lake into its data strategy.

The data lake enables the organization to house both structured and unstructured data in one central repository. This unified storage makes it easier to conduct comprehensive analyses that include insights from diverse data streams such as social media sentiment and customer comments. By applying ML models, the company can even forecast future sales patterns based on past data.

By integrating the data warehouse with the data lake, the retail company achieves a more holistic understanding of its data landscape. This enriched view equips it to make better decisions, thereby gaining a competitive edge in the retail sector.

Summary

In this chapter, we've dived deep into the fascinating realm of large-scale data-persistent systems, covering everything from their historical origins to their modern-day complexities. We kicked things off with a stroll down memory lane, providing a brief history of how data persistence has evolved from rudimentary filesystems to sophisticated databases. We pondered the ever-changing needs of businesses and organizations that catalyzed this progression, establishing a solid foundation for understanding the subject.

Then, we shifted our focus to database evolution, focusing on the technical intricacies and the multifaceted growth databases have undergone over the years. From the days of hierarchical and network databases to the era of relational databases and their SQL foundations, we saw how the need to manage structured data led to the development of advanced systems capable of complex queries, indexing, and data integrity.

The chapter then took a significant turn to explore data warehouses, which act as centralized repositories where businesses store their cleaned, transformed, and cataloged data. Data warehouses have been instrumental for companies that rely on comprehensive data analytics and reporting. They have shaped inventory management, marketing strategies, and much more by enabling data-driven decision-making processes.

Finally, we delved into the realm of data lakes. Unlike their data warehouse counterparts, data lakes provide storage for raw, unstructured data. This is the arena where ML algorithms and advanced analytics are unleashed to dig deeper for insights that are not readily apparent in structured data. Data lakes have made it easier to make sense of disparate data types—ranging from customer reviews and social media sentiment to intricate sensor data—by housing them under a single, centralized platform.

So, what have we learned? We've learned that data persistence is not merely about storing data; it's about evolving to meet the multifaceted demands of modern enterprises. From traditional databases to data warehouses, and now to data lakes, each system has its unique strengths and applications. In a world increasingly driven by data, understanding these systems isn't just useful—it's essential. Knowing how and when to use these technologies can mean the difference between simply storing data and turning it into actionable insights that can drive real-world changes. Thus concludes our exploration for this chapter; I hope it's left you not just informed but also inspired.

In the next chapter, we will learn about the evolving role of **database administrators** (**DBAs**) in the changing landscape of technology and data management.

3

DBAs in the World of DevOps

In this chapter, we will take a closer look at the evolving role of **Database Administrators** (**DBAs**) in the changing landscape of technology and data management. We will begin by exploring what the "early days" of database management were like when the DBA was primarily a gatekeeper of structured data, responsible for backups, data integrity, and query optimization. While those days may feel nostalgic, make no mistake, the profession has undergone significant transformations.

We'll then delve into how cloud computing and big data are set to revolutionize the expectations of a DBA. Cloud computing is used to unshackle databases from on-premises limitations, offering scalability and flexibility like never before. Big data will be used to expand the types and volumes of data that DBAs interact with. It will no longer just be about SQL queries; it will be about managing and making sense of a torrent of structured and unstructured data flowing in real time.

This will lead us to the next part of the chapter, where we will discuss the future role of DBAs within DevOps-conscious teams. With the rise of DevOps practices, DBAs will find themselves at the intersection of development, operations, and quality assurance. They will contribute to automating pipelines and implementing schema changes, and may even get involved in application development to some extent. The DevOps culture will encourage DBAs to be more proactive than reactive, and the benefits will be significant—faster deployment cycles, improved communication, and higher quality of software deployments.

So, to sum it all up, the future role of the DBA will not be how it used to be; it will become richer, more multidimensional, and continually evolve. DBAs will emerge as critical players in making data not only accessible but also insightful. As data continues to grow in importance and complexity, the DBA will transition from being a background figure to a key enabler in transforming data into actionable intelligence. There you have it; that is the essence of this chapter. We hope it will offer you not only knowledge but also a perspective on how the tech world will shape, and be shaped by, these unsung heroes of the data world.

The following topics will be covered in this chapter:

- The continuously evolving role of the DBA
- The emergence of cloud computing and big data
- DevOps and DBAs
- The role of database experts in a DevOps-conscious team
- A proven methodology with quantifiable benefits

The continuously evolving role of the DBA

The role of the DBA has evolved significantly since the early days of computing, reflecting changes in technology, business needs, and the increasing importance of data management. In this section, we will explore the evolution of the DBA role, from its early beginnings to its current state, and discuss some of the key trends and challenges that are shaping the role today.

In the early days of computing, databases were simple and relatively small, and it was often possible for a single person to handle all aspects of database management. Databases were typically managed using flat files or hierarchical structures, and the role of the DBA was focused on basic data storage and retrieval. DBAs were responsible for designing and implementing database systems, and for ensuring that data was stored securely and could be retrieved quickly and efficiently.

As databases grew in size and complexity, however, the role of the DBA became more specialized. In the 1970s and 1980s, the introduction of **relational database management systems** (**RDBMSs**) such as Oracle, IBM Db2, and Microsoft SQL Server changed the way databases were managed and expanded the role of the DBA to include more complex tasks, such as performance tuning, backup and recovery, and database security.

Performance tuning is the practice of optimizing database performance by tweaking various database parameters and settings. In the early days of RDBMSs, performance tuning was a critical aspect of DBA work, as databases were often slow and inefficient. DBAs would spend hours or even days tweaking database settings to get the best possible performance, often using trial and error to find the optimal configuration. As databases became more complex, however, performance tuning became a more specialized skill, and many organizations began hiring dedicated performance-tuning experts to handle this task.

Backup and recovery is the practice of creating backups of database data and restoring data in the event of a system failure or data loss. In the early days of computing, backup and recovery was a relatively simple process, as databases were small and could be backed up using tape drives or other simple storage devices. As databases grew in size, however, backup and recovery became a more complex and time-consuming process, requiring specialized tools and expertise. DBAs became responsible for creating backup and recovery plans, testing backup and recovery procedures, and ensuring that data was recoverable in the event of a disaster.

Database security is the practice of protecting sensitive or confidential data from unauthorized access or theft. In the early days of computing, database security was a relatively simple matter, as databases were typically stored on-premises and access was limited to a small number of authorized users. As databases became more complex and distributed, however, database security became a critical concern for organizations. DBAs became responsible for implementing security policies, managing user access, and securing data against external threats such as hacking and malware.

The rise of data architecture and integration

In the 1990s and 2000s, the role of the DBA began to expand beyond basic database management tasks, as organizations began to recognize the strategic importance of data management. With the rise of **enterprise resource planning** (**ERP**) systems and other large-scale applications, the need for data integration and data architecture became increasingly important.

Data architecture is the practice of designing and implementing data structures and systems that support an organization's business objectives. As databases became more complex and distributed, DBAs became responsible for designing data architectures that could support multiple applications and data sources. This involved developing data models, defining data standards, and creating data integration strategies that could help organizations to streamline their data management processes.

Data integration is the process of combining data from multiple sources and applications to create a unified view of an organization's data. As businesses began to rely more heavily on data for decision-making, the need for data integration became increasingly important. DBAs became responsible for managing data integration tools and technologies, developing data mapping and transformation strategies, and ensuring that data was integrated across multiple systems and applications.

The emergence of cloud computing and big data

In the last decade, the role of the DBA has continued to evolve, as new technologies and trends have emerged. Two of the most significant trends that are shaping the role of the DBA today are cloud computing and big data.

Cloud computing has changed the way that databases are managed and deployed, and has presented new challenges and opportunities for DBAs. With the rise of cloud-based databases such as **Amazon Web Services** (**AWS**), Microsoft Azure, and Google Cloud Platform, DBAs are increasingly responsible for managing databases in the cloud, and for working with cloud-based tools and technologies.

Cloud-based databases offer many benefits, including scalability, flexibility, and cost-effectiveness. However, they also present new challenges, such as security and compliance concerns, and the need to manage databases across multiple cloud providers and platforms.

Big data refers to the large and complex datasets that are generated by organizations today. With the rise of social media, mobile devices, and the **Internet of Things** (**IoT**), the amount of data that organizations are generating is increasing exponentially. This presents new challenges for DBAs, who must develop new skills and strategies to manage and analyze this data.

Big data technologies such as Hadoop, Spark, and NoSQL databases have emerged to help organizations manage and analyze large datasets. DBAs are increasingly responsible for working with these technologies and developing strategies to integrate big data with existing databases and applications.

In addition to managing big data technologies, DBAs are also responsible for implementing data governance policies and procedures to ensure that data is accurate, reliable, and secure. This involves developing data quality standards, creating data lineage and metadata management strategies, and monitoring data access and usage to ensure compliance with regulatory requirements.

The shift to DevOps

Another trend that is shaping the role of the DBA today is the shift to DevOps, a methodology that emphasizes collaboration and automation between development and operations teams. DevOps has changed the way that software is developed and deployed, and has led to a new approach to database management.

In a DevOps environment, DBAs are no longer responsible for manually deploying database changes or managing database scripts. Instead, they work closely with developers to ensure that database changes are made in a controlled and automated way, using tools such as database version control, continuous integration, and continuous delivery.

This shift to DevOps has led to a new set of skills and responsibilities for DBAs, including the ability to work with agile development methodologies, write code, and use automation tools and scripts. DBAs must also be able to collaborate effectively with developers and operations teams and communicate technical concepts to non-technical stakeholders.

Conclusion

In conclusion, the role of the DBA has evolved significantly over time, reflecting changes in technology, business needs, and the increasing importance of data management. From its early beginnings as a basic data storage and retrieval role, the DBA has expanded to include more complex tasks, such as performance tuning, backup and recovery, database security, data architecture, and data integration.

Today, DBAs are responsible for managing databases in the cloud, working with big data technologies, implementing data governance policies and procedures, and collaborating with developers and operations teams in a DevOps environment. As technology and business needs continue to evolve, the role of the DBA is likely to continue to change, presenting new challenges and opportunities for those who work in this field.

DevOps and DBAs

As previously established, DevOps is a software development methodology that emphasizes collaboration between development and operations teams to streamline the software development life cycle. It involves automating the entire software delivery process, from code development to deployment and maintenance. One area where DevOps has had a particularly significant impact is database management practices.

In traditional software development, database management was often seen as a separate task from the rest of the development process. DBAs would typically work in isolation from the development team, making it difficult to ensure that the database met the needs of the application. This siloed approach often resulted in delays and errors, as changes to the database schema were not always properly communicated to the development team.

DevOps has changed this approach by promoting collaboration and communication between development and operations teams. By bringing DBAs into the development process earlier, DevOps teams can ensure that the database is designed to meet the needs of the application from the outset. This helps to reduce the risk of errors and delays later in the development process.

One of the key ways that DevOps has improved database management practices is through the use of automation. In traditional software development, many tasks related to database management were performed manually. This was a time-consuming process that was prone to errors. DevOps teams have automated many of these tasks, making the process faster and more reliable.

For example, DevOps teams can use automated scripts to generate database schema changes. These scripts can be version-controlled, which helps to ensure that changes are made in a consistent and repeatable way. This makes it easier to track changes to the database over time and roll back changes if necessary.

Another way that DevOps has improved database management practices is through the use of **continuous integration and continuous deployment (CI/CD)** pipelines. These pipelines automate the process of building, testing, and deploying software, including changes to the database schema.

CI/CD pipelines can be used to automatically test changes to the database schema, ensuring that they work as expected before they are deployed to production. This helps to reduce the risk of errors and downtime caused by database changes.

In addition to automation and CI/CD pipelines, DevOps has also improved database management practices by promoting a culture of collaboration and communication. DevOps teams typically work in cross-functional teams that include developers, operations staff, and DBAs. This helps to ensure that everyone is working together toward a common goal and that everyone has a shared understanding of the requirements and constraints of the database.

By working together, DevOps teams can identify and address issues with the database early in the development process. This reduces the risk of delays and errors later in the development cycle, as issues can be addressed before they become critical.

DevOps also promotes a culture of continuous improvement. By monitoring and analyzing performance metrics, DevOps teams can identify areas for improvement in their database management practices. This helps to ensure that the database remains optimized and performant over time, even as the application grows and evolves.

Another way that DevOps has improved database management practices is through the use of **infrastructure as code** (**IaC**). IaC involves writing code to automate the deployment and configuration of infrastructure resources, including databases. By treating infrastructure as code, DevOps teams can apply the same principles of version control, testing, and automation to their infrastructure as they do to their application code.

Using IaC, DevOps teams can ensure that their database infrastructure is consistent and repeatable across different environments, from development to production. This reduces the risk of errors caused by differences between environments and makes it easier to troubleshoot issues when they arise.

DevOps has also made it easier to manage databases in the cloud. Cloud providers offer a range of database services, including managed database services that handle many of the tasks related to database management automatically. DevOps teams can use these services to offload many of the tasks related to database management, freeing up time and resources to focus on other areas of the application.

Cloud providers also offer tools and services that integrate with DevOps workflows, making it easier to automate tasks related to database management. For example, cloud providers may offer APIs that allow DevOps teams to automate tasks like database backups and scaling.

To summarize, DevOps has had a significant impact on database management practices. By promoting collaboration, automation, and a culture of continuous improvement, DevOps teams can ensure that their databases are designed to meet the needs of the application and that changes to the database are made in a consistent and repeatable way. This reduces the risk of errors and downtime caused by database changes and helps to ensure that the database remains optimized and performant over time.

DevOps has also made it easier to manage databases at scale. As applications grow and evolve, the demands placed on the database can increase significantly. DevOps teams can use automation and infrastructure as code to manage databases at scale, ensuring that the database remains performant even as the application grows.

For example, DevOps teams can use automation to scale the database infrastructure up or down based on demand. This helps to ensure that the application remains responsive even during periods of high traffic.

DevOps teams can also use monitoring and analytics tools to identify performance bottlenecks and other issues with the database. By analyzing performance metrics, DevOps teams can identify areas for improvement and make changes to the database infrastructure to optimize performance.

Another way that DevOps has improved database management practices is through the use of security automation. Security is a critical concern for any database, as even a single security breach can have significant consequences. DevOps teams can use automation to ensure that their databases are configured securely from the outset and to monitor security issues on an ongoing basis.

For example, DevOps teams can use automated scripts to configure database security settings, such as access controls and encryption. They can also use automated tools to scan the database for vulnerabilities and identify potential security risks.

By using automation to manage database security, DevOps teams can ensure that their databases remain secure over time, even as the application evolves and new security threats emerge.

Finally, DevOps has improved database management practices by promoting a culture of experimentation and innovation. DevOps teams are encouraged to try new approaches and technologies and to continually look for ways to improve their processes.

By experimenting with new database technologies and approaches, DevOps teams can identify new ways to optimize performance, improve scalability, and enhance security. This helps to ensure that the database remains up to date and capable of meeting the evolving needs of the application.

In conclusion, DevOps has had a significant impact on database management practices, transforming the way that databases are designed, deployed, and maintained. By promoting collaboration, automation, and a culture of continuous improvement, DevOps teams can ensure that their databases are optimized for performance, scalability, and security and that they remain so over time. As applications continue to evolve and grow, DevOps will continue to play a critical role in ensuring that databases remain a reliable and integral part of the technology stack.

The role of the database expert in a DevOps-conscious team

A DevOps-practicing team is responsible for building and deploying software applications in a fast and efficient manner. The team's goal is to deliver high-quality software that meets business requirements while reducing the time to market. To achieve this goal, the team employs various DevOps practices, including continuous integration, continuous delivery, and continuous deployment.

The role of a database expert in a DevOps-practicing team is to ensure that the database infrastructure is reliable, scalable, secure, and performing optimally. The database is a critical component of any application, and its performance and availability directly impact the application's performance and availability. Therefore, a database expert's role is crucial in ensuring that the database infrastructure meets the team's requirements and the business's goals.

Designing and implementing databases

One of the primary responsibilities of a database expert in a DevOps-practicing team is to design and implement databases that are efficient, scalable, and easy to maintain. The database expert works closely with the application developers and infrastructure engineers to understand the application's requirements and the infrastructure's capabilities. Based on this understanding, the database expert designs and implements a database that meets the application's needs and the infrastructure's requirements.

The database expert must consider various factors while designing and implementing the database, such as data modeling, indexing, partitioning, and replication. The database design should be optimized for performance, scalability, and availability. The database expert should also ensure that the database schema is flexible enough to accommodate future changes without causing significant disruptions to the application.

Ensuring high availability and disaster recovery

Another critical responsibility of a database expert in a DevOps-practicing team is to ensure high availability and disaster recovery. The database is a critical component of the application, and any downtime can cause significant disruptions to the business. Therefore, the database expert must ensure that the database is highly available and can recover quickly in case of failures or disasters.

The database expert can achieve high availability by setting up database replicas and implementing load balancing. The replicas can be used to handle read requests, while the primary database handles write requests. The replicas can also be used to provide failover capability in case of a primary database failure. The database expert must ensure that the replicas are synchronized and that data consistency is maintained across all replicas.

The database expert should also implement a disaster recovery plan to ensure that the database can recover quickly in case of disasters such as hardware failures, data corruption, or natural disasters. The disaster recovery plan should include regular backups, data replication, and failover procedures. The database expert should test the disaster recovery plan regularly to ensure that it is effective and can be executed quickly in case of a disaster.

Performance tuning

Performance is a critical factor in the success of any application. The performance of the database directly impacts the performance of the application. Therefore, a database expert in a DevOps-practicing team must ensure that the database is performing optimally.

The database expert can achieve optimal performance by monitoring the database and identifying bottlenecks. They should monitor various performance metrics, such as CPU usage, memory usage, disk I/O, and network I/O. The database expert should analyze the performance metrics and identify the areas of the database that are causing performance issues.

The database expert can optimize the database performance by tuning the queries, optimizing the database parameters, and indexing the database. They should also ensure that the database statistics are up to date and the database is not fragmented.

Security and compliance

Security and compliance are critical factors in any application. The database contains sensitive data, and the database expert must ensure that the database is secure and compliant with regulations.

The database expert can ensure database security by implementing access controls, encryption, and auditing. They should ensure that only authorized users can access the database and that the data is encrypted in transit and at rest. The database expert should also implement auditing to track the changes made to the database.

The database expert should ensure that the database is compliant with regulations such as HIPAA, PCI-DSS, and GDPR. They should ensure that the database is audited regularly to ensure compliance with regulations.

Automation

Automation is a critical factor in the success of any DevOps-practicing team. The database expert can help automate database deployment, patching, and scaling using tools such as Ansible, Chef, or Puppet. Automation can reduce the time to market and ensure that the database is deployed consistently across all environments.

The database expert can also automate database backup and recovery procedures. Automation can ensure that backups are taken regularly and that the backups are stored in a secure location. Automation can also ensure that the backup and recovery procedures are tested regularly.

> **Note**
>
> One example of database automation is the use of scripts or tools to automate routine tasks such as database backups, schema changes, or data migrations.
>
> For instance, you could use a tool such as Jenkins to automate the execution of scripts that perform regular database backups at predefined intervals. You could also use a tool such as Flyway to automate the application of database schema changes across different environments, such as moving from development to production.
>
> Another example is the use of chatbots or other conversational interfaces to automate database queries and updates. These tools can allow users to interact with databases using natural language, reducing the need for manual data entry and improving the efficiency of data retrieval and analysis.
>
> Overall, database automation can help reduce manual labor, increase efficiency, and improve the accuracy and consistency of database operations.

A proven methodology with quantifiable benefits

DevOps has brought significant benefits to database management, enabling organizations to deliver high-quality software faster and more reliably. The following are some of the quantifiable benefits that DevOps has brought to database management.

Faster time to market

One of the primary benefits of DevOps is faster time to market. By automating processes and improving collaboration between teams, DevOps has enabled organizations to deliver database changes faster, reducing the time to market and increasing business agility.

In traditional database management, database changes were often made manually, which was a slow and error-prone process. DevOps practices such as CI/CD have enabled teams to automate the build, test, and deployment of database changes, reducing the time required to deliver changes to production.

For example, instead of manually creating database instances and running scripts to apply changes, teams can use automated tools such as Jenkins or TeamCity to run tests and deploy changes to multiple environments. This has enabled organizations to release changes more frequently, with shorter feedback loops and faster time to market.

Good to know – why a faster time to market is important

A faster time to market can be critical in today's fast-paced business environment for several reasons:

- **Competitive advantage**: Getting a product to market quickly can give a company a competitive advantage over its rivals. This is especially true in industries where product life cycles are short, and new products are constantly being introduced.

- **Revenue generation**: The faster a product is launched, the sooner a company can start generating revenue from it. This is important because revenue is the lifeblood of any business, and the sooner a new product can start generating revenue, the better it is for the company's bottom line.

- **Customer satisfaction**: In many cases, customers are eagerly waiting for new products or features. By delivering a product to market faster, a company can meet this demand and keep its customers satisfied.

- **Reduced development costs**: The longer a product takes to develop, the more it costs. By shortening the development cycle, a company can reduce the costs of the development cycle, which can help improve profitability.

A faster time to market allows companies to respond more quickly to changes in the market and customer demands, stay ahead of the competition, and generate revenue more quickly.

Improved quality

Another benefit of DevOps is improved quality. By using automated testing and CI/CD pipelines, DevOps has enabled teams to catch errors and defects earlier in the development cycle, reducing the risk of bugs and defects in production.

In traditional database management, database changes were often tested manually, which was a time-consuming and error-prone process. With DevOps, teams can use automated testing tools, such as Selenium or JMeter, to run tests and validate changes, catching errors early in the development cycle.

By catching errors earlier in the development cycle, teams can reduce the risk of bugs and defects in production, improving the quality of database changes. This has enabled organizations to deliver software with fewer defects, resulting in higher customer satisfaction and lower support costs.

Good to know – why improved code quality is important

The reasons improved code quality is important are as follows:

- **Reduced errors and bugs**: High-quality code is less likely to contain errors and bugs, which can cause crashes, security vulnerabilities, and other issues. By improving code quality, businesses can reduce the risk of these issues occurring, which can improve the overall reliability and stability of their software.

- **Improved maintainability**: High-quality code is typically easier to maintain and update, as it is well organized and well documented and adheres to established coding standards. This can reduce the time and effort required to make changes to the code base, which can lead to cost savings and improved productivity.

- **Faster development cycles**: Improved code quality can also lead to faster development cycles, as it reduces the time required to identify and fix errors and bugs. This can help businesses get new features and products to market more quickly, improving their competitive advantage.

- **Better user experience**: High-quality code can also improve the user experience, as it can reduce the likelihood of crashes, errors, and other issues that can frustrate users. By improving the user experience, businesses can improve customer satisfaction and retention.

Improved code quality can lead to reduced errors and bugs, improved maintainability, faster development cycles, and a better user experience. These benefits can improve the overall reliability, stability, and competitiveness of businesses that rely on software.

Reduced downtime

DevOps practices such as continuous monitoring and automated backups have helped to reduce downtime caused by database failures or maintenance activities. By monitoring databases in real time and detecting issues proactively, teams can prevent downtime caused by database failures.

Additionally, by automating backups and disaster recovery processes, organizations can reduce the time required to recover from database failures, minimizing the impact on business operations. This has enabled organizations to maintain high levels of uptime, improving business continuity and reducing the risk of revenue loss.

Good to know: Why improved availability is important

The reasons improved availability is important are as follows:

- **Meeting customer demand**: Availability refers to the ability of a product or service to be accessible and ready for use when needed. If a product or service is not available when customers need it, it can lead to dissatisfaction and lost sales. By improving availability, businesses can meet customer demand and improve customer satisfaction.

- **Maximizing revenue**: Improved availability can also lead to increased revenue. If a product or service is consistently available, it can help generate revenue continuously. Conversely, if a product or service is frequently unavailable, it can lead to lost revenue and missed opportunities.

- **Optimal resource utilization**: Improved availability can also help businesses better utilize their resources. If a product or service is consistently available, it can reduce the need for additional resources to compensate for downtime or delays. This can help businesses operate more efficiently and reduce costs.

- **Competitive advantage**: Availability can also be a competitive advantage. If a business can consistently provide a product or service that is available when competitors cannot, it can help differentiate the business and attract customers.

Improved availability can help businesses meet customer demand, maximize revenue, optimize resource utilization, and gain a competitive advantage.

Increased scalability

DevOps has enabled organizations to scale their database infrastructure more effectively by automating the provisioning and deployment of database instances and using cloud-based infrastructure that can be rapidly provisioned and scaled up or down as needed. With DevOps, teams can automate the creation and configuration of database instances, enabling them to rapidly provision new instances as needed.

For example, if an organization experiences a sudden increase in traffic or user demand, DevOps practices such as IaC and automated scaling can be used to quickly provision additional database resources to handle the increased load. This has enabled organizations to scale their database infrastructure more effectively, reducing the risk of performance issues and downtime caused by resource constraints.

Good to know – why improved scalability is important

The reasons improved scalability is important are as follows:

- **Handling variable workloads**: The cloud allows businesses to handle variable workloads by scaling resources up or down as needed. This means businesses can quickly respond to changes in demand, ensuring that they have the resources they need to operate efficiently without overprovisioning or wasting resources.

- **Cost-effective**: Scalability in the cloud can be cost-effective as it allows businesses to pay only for the resources they need at any given time. This means they can avoid the cost of overprovisioning and can scale down when demand is low, saving money on unused resources.

- **Improved performance**: Scalability can also improve the performance of applications and services by ensuring that they have sufficient resources to operate efficiently. This can help businesses meet performance requirements and deliver a better user experience.

- **Business agility**: The ability to scale quickly and easily in the cloud can improve business agility, allowing businesses to respond more quickly to changing market conditions and customer demands. This can help businesses stay competitive and adapt to new opportunities.

Scalability is especially important in the cloud because it allows businesses to handle variable workloads, operate cost-effectively, improve performance, and improve business agility. By leveraging the scalability of the cloud, businesses can optimize their operations, reduce costs, and deliver better services to their customers.

Improved security

By integrating security testing and validation into the development process, DevOps has helped to improve the security of database environments, reducing the risk of data breaches and other security incidents. DevOps practices such as automated security testing, vulnerability scanning, and compliance validation can be used to detect and address security issues early in the development cycle.

Additionally, by automating the deployment of security updates and patches, organizations can reduce the time required to address security vulnerabilities, minimizing the risk of data breaches and other security incidents.

DevOps has also enabled organizations to implement security best practices such as least-privilege access and separation of duties, reducing the risk of security incidents caused by human error or malicious intent. This has helped organizations to improve the security of their database environments, protecting sensitive data and reducing the risk of reputational damage and regulatory fines.

The merging of these two worlds has brought significant benefits to database management, enabling organizations to deliver high-quality software faster and more reliably. The quantifiable benefits of DevOps in database management include a faster time to market, improved quality, reduced downtime, increased scalability, and improved security. These benefits have enabled organizations to improve business agility, reduce costs, and improve customer satisfaction, making DevOps an essential practice for modern software development.

> **Good to know – why improved software security is important**
>
> The reasons improved software security is important are as follows:
>
> - **Protection of sensitive data**: Many software applications handle sensitive user data, such as personal information, financial information, and intellectual property. Improved software security ensures that this data is protected from unauthorized access or theft.
>
> - **Prevention of cyber-attacks**: Cyber-attacks are becoming more sophisticated and frequent, and the damage they cause can be severe. Improved software security measures can prevent these attacks from happening, or at least reduce their impact.
>
> - **Compliance with regulations**: Many industries are subject to regulations that require specific security measures to be in place. Improved software security can help ensure compliance with these regulations.
>
> - **Reputation management**: If a software application is compromised and user data is stolen, the reputation of the company responsible for the software can be damaged. Improved software security measures can help prevent these types of incidents and protect a company's reputation.
>
> **Cost savings**: Improving software security can help reduce the cost of dealing with security breaches and other related incidents. The cost of fixing security vulnerabilities and dealing with the aftermath of a breach can be significant, so investing in improved security up front can lead to significant cost savings in the long run.

Summary

Database experts play a critical role in a DevOps-practicing team by ensuring that the database infrastructure is reliable, scalable, secure, and performing optimally. The database expert's responsibilities include designing and implementing databases, ensuring high availability and disaster recovery, performance tuning, security and compliance, and automation. The database expert works closely with the application developers and infrastructure engineers to ensure that the database meets the application's needs and the infrastructure's requirements.

By working closely with the DevOps-practicing team, the database expert can help ensure that the application is deployed quickly and reliably and that the application meets the business's requirements. The database expert's in-depth technical knowledge is critical in ensuring that the database infrastructure is optimized for performance, scalability, and availability and that the database is secure and compliant with regulations.

In conclusion, the role of a database expert in a DevOps-practicing team is crucial in ensuring the success of the application. The database expert's knowledge of database design, administration, and optimization can help the team deliver high-quality software that meets business requirements while reducing the time to market.

In the next chapter, we will dissect the complex yet essential subject of cloud migration.

Part 2:
Persisting Data in the Cloud

This part will provide an overview of the evolution of how different database technologies had to evolve from static data centers to remain relevant in the modern, dynamic world of the cloud. Different types of databases reacted and changed differently. We will review the most common technologies, starting from traditional SQL to modern data lakes. We will detail each evolutionary step with data structure examples, implementation best practices, architectural designs, and the most common use cases, highlighting its relevance to day-to-day work.

This part comprises the following chapters:

- *Chapter 4, Data(base) Evolution*
- *Chapter 5, Relational Databases*
- *Chapter 6, Non-Relational Databases*
- *Chapter 7, AI, ML, and Big Data*

4

Cloud Migration and Modern Data(base) Evolution

In this chapter, we will dissect the complex yet essential subject of cloud migration. By the time you finish this chapter, you will understand not only what cloud migration is but also why an increasing number of companies are choosing to make this significant move. We will spell out the critical financial and operational advantages that are compelling businesses to adopt cloud services, allowing you to grasp the urgency of this transformation.

As we navigate through this intricate landscape, you'll be led through the key milestones that characterize a typical cloud migration process. Learning about these milestones is pivotal, as they will serve as your guideposts for where you are and what lies ahead in your cloud journey. Understanding these milestones will offer you a structured roadmap for migration, which is crucial for avoiding pitfalls and ensuring a smooth transition.

We will then highlight the various types of cloud migrations—from the basic "lift-and-shift" models to more intricate "application refactoring" techniques. This knowledge will equip you to make well-informed decisions tailored to your specific organizational needs, thereby optimizing cost and performance.

Subsequently, the focus will shift to the procedural aspects involved in cloud migration. You'll learn about the step-by-step processes, from initial planning and assessment to the actual migration and post-migration optimization. This information will fill in the operational gaps, giving you a holistic view of what it takes to execute a successful migration.

Lastly, the chapter will underscore the crucial role that data migration strategies play, particularly when moving databases to the cloud. You'll come to understand why a robust data migration strategy isn't optional but mandatory, how it integrates with wider cloud migration plans, and how it safeguards data integrity and security.

By covering these facets, this chapter aims to provide you with a comprehensive toolkit for your own cloud migration endeavor. Whether you're a decision-maker pondering the strategic direction or a technical professional engaged in the details, understanding these elements will be invaluable for informed decision-making, risk mitigation, and ultimately, leveraging cloud migration as a competitive advantage in your industry.

The following topics will be covered in this chapter:

- What is cloud migration (and why are companies doing it)?

- Types of cloud migrations

- The process of cloud migration

- What can a database expert help with during cloud migration?

- Data migration strategies and their types

- Why are data migration strategies important during a database cloud migration project?

What is cloud migration (and why are companies doing it)?

Cloud migration refers to the process of moving an organization's IT infrastructure, data, applications, and services from on-premises data centers to cloud computing environments. The cloud migration process can be complex and requires careful planning and execution to ensure a smooth transition and minimize disruption to business operations.

Cloud migration has become increasingly popular in recent years as more organizations adopt cloud computing to take advantage of its scalability, cost-effectiveness, flexibility, and other benefits. Cloud migration can involve moving workloads to public, private, or hybrid cloud environments, depending on the organization's needs and requirements.

The importance of cloud migration

There are several factors that can drive an organization to consider cloud migration. These include the following:

- **Cost savings**: Cloud computing can offer cost savings by eliminating the need for on-premises hardware and reducing IT staff and maintenance costs

- **Scalability and flexibility**: Cloud computing can scale up or down quickly to meet changing business needs and can provide the flexibility to easily add or remove resources as needed

- **Improved performance and reliability**: Cloud computing can offer improved performance and reliability compared to on-premises data centers, due to the use of advanced technologies such as load balancing, auto-scaling, and data replication

- **Security and compliance**: Cloud providers typically have advanced security measures and compliance certifications that can help organizations meet their security and compliance requirements

- **Innovation and agility**: Cloud computing can provide organizations with access to new technologies and services that can help them innovate and stay competitive

Despite the potential benefits of cloud migration, there are also several challenges and risks that need to be considered:

- **Complexity**: Cloud migration can be complex and require significant planning and preparation, as well as careful execution to ensure a successful transition

- **Data security and privacy**: Cloud providers may have different security and privacy policies and controls than on-premises data centers, which can create new risks and challenges

- **Application compatibility**: Some applications may not be compatible with cloud environments or may require modification or re-architecting to work properly in the cloud

- **Connectivity and latency**: Cloud migration can require changes to network connectivity and can introduce new latency and performance issues that need to be addressed

- **Vendor lock-in**: Cloud providers may use proprietary technologies or services that can make it difficult to switch providers or move data and applications back to on-premises data centers

Steps to keep in mind before cloud migration

To mitigate these challenges and risks, organizations need to plan their cloud migration carefully and take a phased approach to the migration process. This typically involves several key steps:

1. **Assessing the current IT environment**: This involves assessing the organization's current IT infrastructure, applications, and services, as well as identifying the business drivers and requirements for cloud migration. This information can be used to develop a migration strategy and roadmap.

2. **Selecting a cloud provider and environment**: Once the organization has identified its requirements and goals for cloud migration, it can evaluate different cloud providers and environments to determine which one meets its needs best. The organization should consider factors such as pricing, security, compliance, performance, scalability, and **service-level agreements (SLAs)**.

3. **Planning the migration**: This involves developing a detailed migration plan that includes timelines, resource requirements, testing and validation procedures, and contingency plans in case of issues or disruptions.

4. **Preparing the workloads**: This involves preparing the applications and data for migration, which may include assessing their compatibility with the cloud environment, making necessary modifications or upgrades, and testing their performance and functionality.

5. **Executing the migration**: This involves moving the workloads to the cloud environment, which may be done using various migration tools and techniques, such as **virtual machine (VM)** migration, containerization, or database migration.

6. **Validating and testing**: Once the migration is complete, the organization should validate and test the migrated workloads to ensure that they are functioning properly and meeting their performance and security requirements.

7. **Optimizing and managing the environment**: After the migration is complete, the organization should continue to monitor and optimize the cloud environment to ensure that it is meeting its performance, security, and cost objectives. This may involve implementing cloud management tools, monitoring and analyzing usage and performance data, and making ongoing adjustments and improvements.

Cloud migration is a complex and challenging process that requires careful planning, execution, and management. By following a phased approach and addressing key challenges and risks, organizations can successfully migrate their IT infrastructure, applications, and services to the cloud and take advantage of its many benefits.

Key milestones through cloud migration

Migrating to the cloud can be a complex process that requires careful planning and execution. The following are some key milestones to consider when migrating to the cloud:

1. **Define your cloud migration strategy**: Before you begin your cloud migration, you need to define your cloud migration strategy. This involves identifying your business goals, assessing your current IT infrastructure, determining which workloads and applications to migrate, and selecting the appropriate CSP.

2. **Assess your current IT infrastructure**: The next step is to assess your current IT infrastructure. This includes identifying your current hardware, software, and network infrastructure, as well as determining which applications and workloads are essential to your business. You should also consider your current security and compliance requirements.

3. **Determine your CSP**: Once you have assessed your current IT infrastructure, you should determine which CSP best meets your needs. Factors to consider include the provider's reputation, the services offered, pricing, and support.

4. **Choose your cloud deployment model**: The next step is to choose your cloud deployment model. You can choose from public, private, or hybrid cloud deployment models. Public clouds are hosted by third-party providers, while private clouds are hosted by an organization's own data center. Hybrid clouds combine elements of both public and private clouds.

5. **Develop a cloud migration plan**: With your cloud deployment model chosen, you can now develop a cloud migration plan. This involves creating a step-by-step plan for migrating your applications, data, and infrastructure to the cloud.

6. **Assess application compatibility**: Before migrating your applications to the cloud, you need to assess their compatibility with the cloud environment. This involves identifying any dependencies on specific hardware or software, as well as any potential performance issues.

7. **Test your migration plan**: Once you have developed your cloud migration plan, you should test it to ensure that it works as expected. This involves performing a trial migration of a small number of applications or workloads to the cloud.

8. **Migrate your applications and data**: With your migration plan tested and refined, you can now begin migrating your applications and data to the cloud. This involves following the steps outlined in your migration plan, such as creating new infrastructure in the cloud, transferring data to the cloud, and configuring applications to work in the cloud environment.

9. **Monitor and optimize your cloud environment**: After migrating to the cloud, you should regularly monitor your cloud environment to ensure that it is performing as expected. This involves monitoring performance metrics, identifying and resolving any issues, and optimizing your cloud infrastructure to ensure maximum performance and cost efficiency.

10. **Train your team**: As you migrate to the cloud, you'll need to train your team on the new cloud environment. This includes training on CSP tools and services, as well as new deployment and management processes.

11. **Implement security and compliance measures**: As with any IT infrastructure, security and compliance are critical considerations when migrating to the cloud. You should implement appropriate security measures, such as firewalls, encryption, and access controls, as well as ensuring compliance with relevant regulations and standards.

12. **Establish DR and business continuity plans**: Cloud environments are not immune to disasters or outages, so it's important to establish DR and business continuity plans. This involves developing plans for data backup and recovery, as well as procedures for maintaining business operations in the event of an outage or disaster.

13. **Optimize costs**: Finally, it's important to optimize costs in your cloud environment. This involves monitoring spending and identifying areas where costs can be reduced, such as through the use of reserved instances or by optimizing resource utilization.

14. **Establish governance and management processes**: Cloud environments can be complex and dynamic, so it's important to establish governance and management processes to ensure that your cloud environment remains secure, compliant, and well managed. This involves developing policies and procedures for managing cloud resources, as well as implementing tools and processes for monitoring and controlling access to cloud resources.

15. **Consider application refactoring or redesign**: Migrating to the cloud provides an opportunity to optimize your applications for the cloud environment. This may involve refactoring or redesigning your applications to take advantage of cloud-native features such as auto-scaling and serverless computing. This can help improve performance, reduce costs, and enhance flexibility.

16. **Develop a cloud security strategy**: Security is a critical consideration when migrating to the cloud, and it's important to develop a comprehensive cloud security strategy that includes both preventive and detective measures. This involves identifying potential security risks, developing strategies to mitigate those risks, and implementing appropriate security controls.

17. **Establish performance and availability metrics**: Cloud environments can be highly dynamic, with resources being added or removed as demand fluctuates. To ensure that your cloud environment is performing optimally and is available when needed, it's important to establish performance and availability metrics that can be monitored and managed in real time.

18. **Consider data migration strategies**: Migrating data to the cloud can be a complex process, and it's important to develop a data migration strategy that minimizes disruption and downtime. This may involve using tools and services provided by the CSP or developing custom migration scripts to move data to the cloud.

19. **Develop a cloud backup and recovery strategy**: Cloud environments are not immune to data loss or corruption, so it's important to develop a backup and recovery strategy that ensures that your data is protected and can be recovered in the event of an outage or disaster.

20. **Plan for ongoing optimization and innovation**: Finally, it's important to plan for ongoing optimization and innovation in your cloud environment. This involves regularly reviewing and optimizing your cloud infrastructure to ensure maximum performance and cost efficiency, as well as exploring new cloud services and features that can help drive innovation and competitive advantage.

21. **Conduct a post-migration review**: Once your migration to the cloud is complete, it's important to conduct a post-migration review to assess the success of the migration and identify any areas for improvement. This involves reviewing performance metrics, analyzing costs, and soliciting feedback from stakeholders.

22. **Develop a cloud governance framework**: As your cloud environment grows and evolves, it becomes increasingly important to establish a cloud governance framework that provides oversight and control over cloud resources. This involves developing policies, procedures, and controls that ensure the security, compliance, and cost-effectiveness of your cloud environment.

23. **Leverage automation and orchestration tools**: Cloud environments can be highly dynamic and complex, so it's important to leverage automation and orchestration tools that can help you manage and optimize your cloud resources. This may involve using tools provided by your CSP or developing custom scripts and tools.

24. **Implement a cloud cost management strategy**: Cloud environments can be highly cost-effective, but they can also be expensive if not managed properly. To ensure that you're getting the most value from your cloud environment, it's important to implement a cloud cost management strategy that includes monitoring and optimizing costs, leveraging cost-effective pricing models, and identifying areas for cost reduction.

25. **Consider multi-cloud and hybrid cloud strategies**: While many organizations choose to migrate to a single CSP, others may choose to adopt a multi-cloud or hybrid cloud strategy that leverages multiple CSPs or combines on-premises and cloud environments. This can provide additional flexibility, redundancy, and cost savings.

26. **Plan for cloud-native application development**: As you migrate to the cloud, it's important to plan for cloud-native application development that takes advantage of the unique features and capabilities of the cloud environment. This involves developing applications that are designed to run in the cloud, and that can take advantage of cloud-native features such as auto-scaling and serverless computing.

27. **Develop a cloud talent strategy**: Finally, it's important to develop a cloud talent strategy that ensures that you have the skilled personnel needed to manage and optimize your cloud environment. This may involve training existing staff, hiring new personnel with cloud expertise, or partnering with third-party providers for cloud management and optimization services.

Migrating to the cloud is a complex process that requires careful planning, execution, and ongoing management. By following these key milestones, you can ensure a successful migration to the cloud that meets your business needs and provides maximum benefits in terms of performance, scalability, and cost efficiency.

Types of cloud migrations

By now we have learned that cloud migration is the process of moving an organization's data, applications, and other business elements from an on-premises data center to a cloud-based infrastructure. There are different types of cloud migrations, each with its own advantages and challenges. In this section, we will explore the five types of cloud migrations:

- Lift-and-shift migration

- Lift-and-reshape migration

- Refactor migration

- Hybrid migration

- Multi-cloud migration

Lift-and-shift migration

The lift-and-shift migration model, also known as rehosting, is a popular cloud migration strategy. This model involves moving an application from an on-premises infrastructure to a cloud infrastructure without making any changes to the application architecture. The primary goal of lift-and-shift migration is to reduce the operational cost of running an application by taking advantage of the benefits that cloud computing offers.

Lift-and-shift migration is an attractive option for businesses that have invested in legacy applications that are tightly coupled with the underlying infrastructure. As an example, a financial institution that relies on legacy software for transaction processing, which is intricately linked with its existing hardware, might opt for a lift-and-shift migration to transition seamlessly to cloud infrastructure without disrupting its critical daily operations. By moving such applications to the cloud without making any changes, businesses can benefit from the scalability, availability, and agility that the cloud provides while continuing to use the same application architecture.

Lift-and-shift migration typically involves four steps:

1. **Inventory of the existing application**: The first step is to create an inventory of the existing application and its dependencies. This includes identifying the hardware, software, and network infrastructure that the application uses.

2. **Determine the cloud infrastructure**: The second step is to determine the cloud infrastructure that the application will be moved to. This includes selecting the cloud provider, the region, and the type of infrastructure that the application will run on.

3. **Migrate the application**: The third step is to migrate the application to the cloud infrastructure. This typically involves creating a VM image of the application and its dependencies and then deploying the image to the cloud.

4. **Test and validate the application**: The final step is to test and validate the application on the new cloud infrastructure to ensure that it is working as expected.

Pros and cons of the lift-and-shift migration model

Some of the advantages of the lift-and-shift migration model are as follows:

- **Reduced operational costs**: One of the primary benefits of lift-and-shift migration is reduced operational costs. By moving to the cloud, businesses can avoid the cost of maintaining their own data center and infrastructure, and instead, pay for the cloud infrastructure on a pay-as-you-go basis.

- **Faster time-to-market**: Lift-and-shift migration allows businesses to quickly move their applications to the cloud without making any changes to the application architecture. This reduces the time-to-market for new applications and features.

- **Scalability**: The cloud provides businesses with the ability to scale their infrastructure up or down based on demand. Lift-and-shift migration allows businesses to take advantage of this scalability without making any changes to the application architecture.

- **High availability**: The cloud provides businesses with the ability to achieve high availability for their applications by replicating data across multiple availability zones. Lift-and-shift migration allows businesses to take advantage of this high availability without making any changes to the application architecture.

Some of the disadvantages of lift-and-shift migration are as follows:

- **Limited cost savings**: While lift-and-shift migration can reduce operational costs, it may not provide significant cost savings in the long run. This is because the application architecture remains the same, and businesses may not be able to take advantage of cloud-native services that can provide greater cost savings.

- **Limited agility**: Lift-and-shift migration does not provide businesses with the ability to quickly adapt to changing market conditions. This is because the application architecture remains the same, and businesses may not be able to take advantage of cloud-native services that can provide greater agility.

- **Limited performance optimization**: Lift-and-shift migration does not provide businesses with the ability to optimize the performance of their applications. This is because the application architecture remains the same, and businesses may not be able to take advantage of cloud-native services that can provide greater performance optimization.

Examples of lift-and-shift migration

Some examples of lift-and-shift migration are as follows:

- **Migration of a legacy application to Amazon Web Services (AWS)**: A company has a legacy application that is tightly coupled with the underlying infrastructure. The application is currently running on a data center that the company owns and operates. The company has decided to move the application to AWS to reduce operational costs and take advantage of the scalability and availability that AWS provides.

  The company performs a lift-and-shift migration of the application to AWS. The application is migrated to EC2 instances, and the company uses **Elastic Load Balancing** (**ELB**) to distribute traffic across multiple instances. The company also uses Amazon RDS to manage the application's database.

  After the migration, the company experiences cost savings and improved availability for the application. However, the company realizes that it is not taking advantage of the full potential of AWS and decides to re-architect the application to take advantage of cloud-native services.

- **Migration of a web application to Azure**: A company has a web application that is running on an on-premises infrastructure. The company has decided to move the application to Azure to take advantage of the scalability and availability that Azure provides.

  The company performs a lift-and-shift migration of the application to Azure. The application is migrated to VMs in Azure, and the company uses Azure Traffic Manager to distribute traffic across multiple instances. The company also uses Azure SQL Database to manage the application's database.

  After the migration, the company experiences cost savings and improved availability of the application. However, the company realizes that it is not taking advantage of the full potential of Azure and decides to re-architect the application to take advantage of cloud-native services.

When is lift-and-shift migration recommended and not recommended?

Lift-and-shift migration is recommended for businesses that have legacy applications that are tightly coupled with the underlying infrastructure. In such cases, moving the application to the cloud without making any changes to the application architecture can provide cost savings and other benefits. Additionally, lift-and-shift migration is recommended for businesses that have a limited budget and need to move their applications to the cloud quickly.

Another scenario where lift-and-shift migration may be recommended is when the business is looking to achieve **disaster recovery** (**DR**) capabilities. Moving the application to the cloud can provide businesses with the ability to replicate their data across multiple availability zones and regions, ensuring that their application remains available even in the event of a disaster.

Lift-and-shift migration may not be recommended for businesses that are looking to take advantage of the full potential of cloud computing. If the business has the budget and time, it may be more beneficial to re-architect the application to take advantage of cloud-native services, such as serverless computing, containers, and microservices. This can provide greater cost savings, agility, and performance optimization.

Another scenario where lift-and-shift migration may not be recommended is when the application is not a good fit for the cloud infrastructure. For example, if the application requires high-performance computing, such as for scientific simulations, it may be more beneficial to keep the application on-premises.

In conclusion, lift-and-shift migration is a popular cloud migration strategy that involves moving an application to the cloud without making any changes to the application architecture. This model can provide cost savings, scalability, and high availability for businesses that have legacy applications that are tightly coupled with the underlying infrastructure. However, lift-and-shift migration may not provide significant cost savings in the long run and may not provide businesses with the agility and performance optimization that they need. Businesses should carefully evaluate their application and infrastructure requirements before deciding to perform a lift-and-shift migration.

Lift-and-reshape migration

The lift-and-reshape migration model is a data migration strategy that is often used when transitioning from one database platform to another. This approach involves lifting data out of the source database and then reshaping it to fit the target database's schema. In this section, we will discuss the technical details of this approach, its pros and cons, and when it is appropriate to use it.

Technical details

The lift-and-reshape migration model involves several steps:

1. **Extraction of data from the source database**: The first step is to extract data from the source database. This can be done using a variety of methods, such as using a data integration tool or writing custom scripts to extract the data.

2. **Transformation of data**: The extracted data may not fit the schema of the target database, so it needs to be transformed. This can include modifying data types, renaming columns, and splitting or combining columns.

3. **Loading of data into the target database**: The transformed data is then loaded into the target database. This can be done using a variety of methods, such as using a data integration tool or writing custom scripts.

4. **Verification of data**: Finally, the data in the target database needs to be verified to ensure that it has been correctly migrated. This can involve running queries to compare the data in the source and target databases or manually checking the data.

Pros and cons of lift-and-reshape migration

The advantages of lift-and-reshape migration are as follows:

- **Flexibility**: The lift-and-reshape migration model is a flexible approach that can be used with any source and target databases. It allows for customization and modification of the data during the migration process, making it easier to fit the target database's schema.

- **Reduced downtime**: The lift-and-reshape migration model can be used to migrate data without taking the source database offline. This allows for a seamless migration process, reducing the downtime of the application.

- **Data quality**: This approach ensures that the data is migrated accurately. By transforming the data, it ensures that the data fits the schema of the target database, improving data quality.

The disadvantages of lift-and-reshape migration are as follows:

- **Complexity**: The lift-and-reshape migration model can be complex and time-consuming, especially for large databases. It requires significant planning and coordination to ensure a smooth migration process.

- **Cost**: This approach can be costly, especially if custom scripts are required to extract, transform, and load the data.

Examples of the lift-and-reshape migration model

Some examples of the lift-and-reshape migration model are as follows:

- **Example 1**: A company is migrating from a MySQL database to a PostgreSQL database. The MySQL database has several tables with columns that do not exist in the PostgreSQL database. The lift-and-reshape migration model can be used to extract data from the MySQL database, transform it to fit the PostgreSQL schema, and load it into the new database.

- **Example 2**: A company is migrating from an Oracle database to a Microsoft SQL Server database. The Oracle database has several tables with different column names and data types than the Microsoft SQL Server database. The lift-and-reshape migration model can be used to extract data from the Oracle database, transform it to fit the Microsoft SQL Server schema, and load it into the new database.

When is it recommended and not recommended?

The lift-and-reshape migration model is appropriate when the source and target databases have significantly different schemas, and when data quality is a priority. However, it is not recommended when time and budget constraints are tight. In such cases, simpler migration approaches may be more appropriate.

This model is a flexible and accurate data migration approach that can be used when transitioning from one database platform to another. However, due to the complexity and time and budget constraints, it is essential to consider the specific requirements and constraints of the migration project before deciding on the migration approach.

When using the lift-and-reshape migration model, it is crucial to plan and coordinate the migration process carefully. The transformation of the data can be a complex process that requires a deep understanding of both the source and target databases. Custom scripts may be required to extract, transform, and load the data, which can increase the cost and complexity of the migration.

It is also important to test and verify the data in the target database after the migration. This can involve running queries to compare the data in the source and target databases or manually checking the data. Verification ensures that the data has been correctly migrated and that the target database is functioning correctly.

In conclusion, the lift-and-reshape migration model is an effective approach for data migration when the source and target databases have significantly different schemas. It offers flexibility and accuracy, but it can be complex and time-consuming. It is important to consider the specific requirements and constraints of the migration project and plan and coordinate the migration process carefully. Verification of the data in the target database is also crucial to ensure that the migration has been successful.

Refactoring migration

Refactoring is the process of restructuring code while preserving its external behavior. Refactoring helps to improve code quality, readability, and maintainability. Migration, on the other hand, is the process of moving code from one environment to another, such as from one language to another or from one framework to another. Refactoring migration, therefore, involves restructuring code to fit into a new environment.

The main objective of refactoring migration is to improve code quality, readability, and maintainability while also updating the code to work within a new environment. Refactoring migration is often used when an existing code base needs to be updated to work with new technologies, such as when migrating from a legacy system to a modern one.

Pros and cons of refactoring migration

The advantages of using refactoring migration are as follows:

- **Improved code quality**: Refactoring migration can help improve the quality of code by restructuring it to follow best practices and coding standards. This can lead to fewer bugs and easier maintenance in the long run.

- **Reduced technical debt**: Technical debt refers to the cost of maintaining code that is not up to current standards. Refactoring migration can help reduce technical debt by bringing code up to current standards.

- **Easier to maintain**: Refactored code is generally easier to maintain than legacy code. This is because it follows current best practices and is easier to understand.

- **Increased scalability**: Refactored code can be designed to be more scalable than legacy code. This can lead to improved performance and better handling of increased traffic.

The disadvantages of refactoring migration are as follows:

- **Time-consuming**: Refactoring migration can be a time-consuming process. Depending on the size of the code base, it may take several months to complete.

- **Risk of introducing bugs**: Refactoring code can introduce new bugs into the code base. This risk can be mitigated by thorough testing.

- **Cost**: Refactoring migration can be expensive, especially if it requires the services of external consultants.

Examples of refactoring migration

Some examples of refactoring migration are as follows:

- **Example 1: Migrating a legacy application to the cloud**

  A company has a legacy application that was built using a proprietary language and framework. The application has become increasingly difficult to maintain, and the cost of maintaining the code base is becoming unsustainable. The company wants to migrate the application to the cloud using a modern language and framework.

  Refactoring migration would be an appropriate solution in this scenario. The code base would need to be refactored to fit into the new environment, but this would also provide an opportunity to improve the code quality and reduce technical debt. The refactored code would be easier to maintain, more scalable, and designed to work with modern technologies. Thorough testing would be required to ensure that the refactored code is free of bugs and that it works as expected.

- **Example 2: Updating an existing application to a newer version of a framework**

  A company has an existing web application built using a popular framework. The framework has released a new version, and the company wants to update the application to use the new version.

  Refactoring migration would be an appropriate solution in this scenario. The code base would need to be refactored to work with the new version of the framework. This would provide an opportunity to improve the code quality and reduce technical debt. The refactored code would be easier to maintain and would be designed to work with the latest version of the framework. Thorough testing would be required to ensure that the refactored code is free of bugs and that it works as expected.

When is it recommended and not recommended?

Refactoring migration is recommended when an existing code base needs to be updated to work with new technologies or to improve its maintainability. Refactoring migration is also recommended when technical debt is high and the cost of maintaining the code base is becoming unsustainable. These are recommended best practices when performing refactoring migration:

- **Plan the migration**: It is important to plan the refactoring migration carefully. This includes identifying the areas of the code base that need to be refactored and developing a roadmap for the migration.

- **Thoroughly test the refactored code**: Refactoring migration can introduce new bugs into the code base. Thorough testing is required to ensure that the refactored code is free of bugs and that it works as expected.

- **Consider the cost**: Refactoring migration can be expensive, especially if it requires the services of external consultants. It is important to consider the cost of the migration and weigh it against the benefits.

- **Evaluate the benefits**: Refactoring migration can improve code quality, readability, and maintainability. It is important to evaluate the benefits of refactoring migration and determine whether it is worth the investment.

- **Use tools and best practices**: Refactoring migration can be a complex process. It is important to use tools and best practices to ensure that the migration is successful. This includes using version control, automated testing, and code analysis tools.

However, refactoring migration is not recommended when the code base is small and relatively simple or when the cost of the migration outweighs the benefits.

As a conclusion, refactoring migration is a process that involves restructuring code to fit into a new environment. It can help improve code quality, readability, and maintainability while also updating the code to work within a new environment. Refactoring migration is recommended when an existing code base needs to be updated to work with new technologies or to improve its maintainability. It is important to plan the refactor migration carefully, thoroughly test the refactored code, consider the cost, evaluate the benefits, and use tools and best practices to ensure that the migration is successful.

Hybrid cloud migration

The hybrid cloud migration model refers to a cloud migration approach that involves the use of both on-premise and cloud-based infrastructure. In the hybrid cloud migration model, some workloads, applications, or data remain on-premises, while others are moved to the cloud. This approach allows organizations to take advantage of the benefits of both on-premise and cloud-based infrastructure, which makes it one of the most popular cloud migration models today.

Technical details of the hybrid cloud migration model

The hybrid cloud migration model is a complex process that involves a combination of on-premise and cloud-based infrastructure. The technical details of the hybrid cloud migration model can vary depending on the specific needs of an organization. However, some common technical details of the hybrid cloud migration model include the following:

- **Network integration**: One of the most important technical details of the hybrid cloud migration model is network integration. Organizations need to establish a seamless and secure connection between their on-premise infrastructure and cloud-based infrastructure. This involves the use of **virtual private networks** (**VPNs**), dedicated circuits, or other connectivity options.

- **Data integration**: Data integration is another critical technical detail of the hybrid cloud migration model. Organizations need to ensure that data can flow seamlessly between their on-premise and cloud-based infrastructures. This requires data integration solutions such as **Extract, Transform, Load** (**ETL**) tools, data pipelines, or data synchronization tools.

- **Application integration**: Application integration is also a crucial technical detail of the hybrid cloud migration model. Organizations need to ensure that their applications can function seamlessly across both on-premise and cloud-based infrastructure. This involves the use of **Application Programming Interfaces** (**APIs**), microservices architecture, or containerization.

- **Security integration**: Security integration is another critical technical detail of the hybrid cloud migration model. Organizations need to ensure that their security policies and procedures apply to both their on-premise and cloud-based infrastructure. This requires the use of **Identity and Access Management** (**IAM**) solutions, encryption, or other security measures.

- **Cost optimization**: Cost optimization is also an essential technical detail of the hybrid cloud migration model. Organizations need to ensure that they are utilizing their on-premise and cloud-based infrastructure in the most cost-effective way possible. This requires the use of cloud cost management tools, optimization strategies, or automation.

Pros and cons of the hybrid cloud migration model

The hybrid cloud migration model has several advantages and disadvantages. Understanding these pros and cons is essential for organizations considering a hybrid cloud migration model.

Pros of the hybrid cloud migration model are as follows:

- **Scalability**: The hybrid cloud migration model allows organizations to scale their infrastructure as needed. This is particularly useful for organizations with unpredictable or rapidly changing workloads.

- **Flexibility**: The hybrid cloud migration model allows organizations to choose the infrastructure that best suits their needs. This provides flexibility and ensures that organizations can take advantage of the benefits of both on-premise and cloud-based infrastructure.

- **Cost-effectiveness**: The hybrid cloud migration model allows organizations to optimize their infrastructure costs. By utilizing on-premise infrastructure for workloads with low utilization or high predictability and cloud-based infrastructure for workloads with high variability or unpredictable demand, organizations can reduce their overall infrastructure costs.

- **Disaster recovery**: The hybrid cloud migration model provides organizations with a DR solution that is both cost-effective and reliable. By replicating critical data and applications to the cloud, organizations can ensure that they have a backup solution in case of a disaster.

- **Compliance**: The hybrid cloud migration model allows organizations to comply with regulatory and compliance requirements. By utilizing on-premise infrastructure for workloads that require strict regulatory compliance and cloud-based infrastructure for workloads that are less sensitive to compliance requirements, organizations can meet their compliance obligations without sacrificing the benefits of cloud infrastructure.

Cons of the hybrid cloud migration model are as follows:

- **Complexity**: The hybrid cloud migration model is a complex process that involves integrating on-premise and cloud-based infrastructure. This complexity can increase the risk of errors and downtime.

- **Security**: The hybrid cloud migration model requires organizations to implement security measures across both on-premise and cloud-based infrastructure. This can increase the complexity and cost of security measures and may increase the risk of security breaches.

- **Skill gap**: The hybrid cloud migration model requires specialized skills and expertise. Organizations may need to invest in additional training or hire new personnel with the required skills.

- **Maintenance**: The hybrid cloud migration model requires ongoing maintenance and management of both on-premise and cloud-based infrastructure. This can increase the complexity and cost of infrastructure management.

- **Dependence on connectivity**: The hybrid cloud migration model is dependent on the reliability and speed of connectivity between on-premise and cloud-based infrastructure. A disruption in connectivity can cause downtime and impact business operations.

Examples of the hybrid cloud migration model

Some examples of hybrid cloud migration are as follows:

- **Example 1: Retail industry**

   Retail organizations often have varying workloads due to seasonal changes or promotional events. For example, a retailer may experience a significant increase in website traffic during the holiday season. By utilizing cloud-based infrastructure for these peak workloads, the retailer can scale its infrastructure as needed. At the same time, the retailer can utilize on-premise infrastructure for less sensitive workloads such as inventory management.

- **Example 2: Healthcare industry**

   Healthcare organizations often have strict regulatory compliance requirements. For example, electronic medical records must comply with **Health Insurance Portability and Accountability Act (HIPAA)** regulations. By utilizing on-premise infrastructure for sensitive workloads such as electronic medical records and cloud-based infrastructure for less sensitive workloads such as email, healthcare organizations can meet their compliance obligations without sacrificing the benefits of cloud infrastructure. Additionally, healthcare organizations can use cloud-based infrastructure for DR solutions, ensuring that critical data and applications are backed up in case of a disaster.

When is the hybrid cloud migration model recommended and not recommended?

The hybrid cloud migration model is recommended for organizations that want to take advantage of both on-premise and cloud-based infrastructure. The hybrid cloud migration model is recommended for the following:

- **Varying workloads**: Organizations with workloads that are unpredictable or rapidly changing can benefit from the hybrid cloud migration model. By utilizing cloud-based infrastructure for workloads with high variability or unpredictable demand, organizations can scale their infrastructure as needed.

- **Compliance requirements**: Organizations with workloads that require strict regulatory compliance can benefit from the hybrid cloud migration model. By utilizing on-premise infrastructure for sensitive workloads and cloud-based infrastructure for less sensitive workloads, organizations can meet their compliance obligations without sacrificing the benefits of cloud infrastructure.

- **Cost considerations**: Organizations that want to optimize their infrastructure costs can benefit from the hybrid cloud migration model. By utilizing on-premise infrastructure for workloads with low utilization or high predictability and cloud-based infrastructure for workloads with high variability or unpredictable demand, organizations can reduce their overall infrastructure costs.

- **Disaster recovery**: Organizations that require a reliable and cost-effective DR solution can benefit from the hybrid cloud migration model. By replicating critical data and applications to the cloud, organizations can ensure that they have a backup solution in case of a disaster.

However, the hybrid cloud migration model is not recommended for organizations that have strict security requirements or limited resources. This model is not recommended when the following apply:

- **Strict security requirements**: Organizations with strict security requirements may find it challenging to implement security measures across both on-premise and cloud-based infrastructure. This can increase the complexity and cost of security measures and may increase the risk of security breaches.

- **Limited resources**: Organizations with limited resources may find it challenging to manage both on-premise and cloud-based infrastructure. This can increase the complexity and cost of infrastructure management.

In conclusion, the hybrid cloud migration model is a popular cloud migration approach that involves the use of both on-premise and cloud-based infrastructure. This model provides organizations with the flexibility and scalability of cloud infrastructure while also allowing them to meet regulatory compliance requirements, optimize infrastructure costs, and provide a reliable DR solution. However, the hybrid cloud migration model also comes with some challenges, including increased complexity, security concerns, and ongoing maintenance requirements.

Organizations considering a hybrid cloud migration model should carefully evaluate their workloads, compliance requirements, cost considerations, and resources before making a decision. If the benefits of the hybrid cloud migration model outweigh the challenges, this model can provide organizations with a flexible, scalable, and cost-effective cloud migration solution.

Multi-cloud migration

Multi-cloud migration is the process of moving data, applications, and other IT resources from one **cloud service provider** (**CSP**) to another, or even between different types of clouds. It has become increasingly popular in recent years as organizations look to reduce vendor lock-in, improve DR and optimize cost and performance. In this section, we will explore the multi-cloud migration model with in-depth technical details, including its pros and cons, and provide recommendations on when it is right for you and when it is not recommended.

Phases of multi-cloud migration

The multi-cloud migration model is a complex and challenging process that involves moving workloads, data, and applications across multiple CSPs. It is typically broken down into three phases: planning, migration, and post-migration.

The planning phase

The planning phase is the first and most critical phase of multi-cloud migration. It involves assessing the current state of the IT infrastructure, identifying the goals and objectives of the migration, and creating a comprehensive migration plan. The following are some key factors that need to be considered during the planning phase:

- **Cost**: Multi-cloud migration can be expensive, so it is important to carefully evaluate the cost of moving to multiple clouds versus sticking with a single CSP. It is important to consider the cost of the migration itself, as well as ongoing costs such as maintenance and support.

- **Security**: Security is a critical concern when moving data and applications between CSPs. It is essential to ensure that all data is encrypted during migration and that access controls are in place to protect sensitive data.

- **Compliance**: Organizations need to comply with various regulations and standards, including GDPR, HIPAA, and PCI DSS. It is important to ensure that all data and applications comply with these regulations during migration.

- **Performance**: Multi-cloud migration can impact application performance, so it is important to ensure that applications perform as expected after migration.

- **Workload placement**: It is important to understand the characteristics of each workload, including its resource requirements and data dependencies, and to choose the best CSP for each workload.

The migration phase

The migration phase involves executing the migration plan created in the planning phase. It typically involves the following steps:

- **Data migration**: Data migration involves copying data from one CSP to another. This can be done using a variety of methods, including network-based transfer, physical transfer, and third-party tools.

- **Application migration**: Application migration involves moving applications from one CSP to another. This can be done using a variety of methods, including re-architecting, lift-and-shift, and containerization.

- **Testing**: After migration, it is important to test the applications to ensure that they are functioning as expected. This includes testing application performance, security, and compliance.

The post-migration phase

The post-migration phase involves monitoring and optimizing the new multi-cloud environment. It typically involves the following steps:

- **Monitoring**: It is important to monitor the performance and availability of the applications in the new multi-cloud environment to ensure that they are meeting the desired service levels.

- **Optimization**: Multi-cloud environments are complex, and it is important to optimize them for cost and performance. This can include adjusting resource allocation, load balancing, and network configuration.

- **Governance**: It is important to establish governance policies and procedures for managing the new multi-cloud environment. This includes policies for resource allocation, access control, and compliance.

Pros and cons of the multi-cloud migration model

The multi-cloud migration model offers several benefits, including the following:

- **Vendor lock-in reduction**: Multi-cloud migration allows organizations to avoid vendor lock-in by distributing workloads across multiple CSPs

- **Improved DR**: Multi-cloud migration can improve DR by providing redundancy across multiple CSPs

- **Cost optimization**: Multi-cloud migration can help organizations optimize costs by choosing the best CSP for each workload based on cost and performance requirements

- **Performance optimization**: Multi-cloud migration can improve application performance by selecting the best CSP based on workload characteristics and data dependencies

- **Security and compliance**: Multi-cloud migration can improve security and compliance by distributing workloads across multiple CSPs and ensuring compliance with various regulations and standards

However, the multi-cloud migration model also has some drawbacks, including the following:

- **Complexity**: Multi-cloud migration is a complex process that requires expertise in multiple CSPs and a deep understanding of the organization's IT infrastructure

- **Increased management overhead:** Multi-cloud migration can increase management overhead as organizations need to manage multiple CSPs and ensure that they are meeting service-level agreements

- **Data synchronization**: Multi-cloud migration can make it challenging to synchronize data across multiple CSPs, which can impact application performance and availability

- **Potential for increased costs**: Multi-cloud migration can be expensive, particularly if the organization does not have the expertise to optimize cost and performance across multiple CSPs

Examples of multi-cloud migration

Some examples of multi-cloud migration include the following:

- **Example 1: Retail industry**

  A retail company with a large customer base decided to migrate its e-commerce platform to a multi-cloud environment to optimize cost and performance. They selected one CSP for their database management system, another for their content delivery network, and a third for their payment gateway. By distributing workloads across multiple CSPs, they were able to improve application performance and reduce costs by choosing the best CSP for each workload.

- **Example 2: Healthcare industry**

  A healthcare organization needed to improve DR and ensure compliance with HIPAA regulations. They migrated their **Electronic Health Records (EHR)** system to a multi-cloud environment that included a public CSP for their primary data center and a private CSP for their secondary data center. By distributing workloads across multiple CSPs, they were able to provide redundancy and improve DR while ensuring compliance with HIPAA regulations.

When is multi-cloud migration recommended and not recommended?

Multi-cloud migration is recommended when organizations have the following requirements:

- **Vendor lock-in reduction**: Multi-cloud migration is recommended for organizations that want to reduce vendor lock-in by distributing workloads across multiple CSPs

- **Disaster recovery**: Multi-cloud migration is recommended for organizations that want to improve DR by providing redundancy across multiple CSPs

- **Cost optimization**: Multi-cloud migration is recommended for organizations that want to optimize costs by choosing the best CSP for each workload based on cost and performance requirements

- **Performance optimization**: Multi-cloud migration is recommended for organizations that want to improve application performance by selecting the best CSP based on workload characteristics and data dependencies

- **Security and compliance**: Multi-cloud migration is recommended for organizations that want to improve security and compliance by distributing workloads across multiple CSPs and ensuring compliance with various regulations and standards

However, multi-cloud migration is not recommended for organizations that have the following requirements:

- **Simplicity**: Multi-cloud migration is not recommended for organizations that prioritize simplicity and want to avoid the complexity of managing multiple CSPs

- **Limited expertise**: Multi-cloud migration is not recommended for organizations that do not have the expertise to optimize cost and performance across multiple CSPs

- **Limited budget**: Multi-cloud migration can be expensive, and it is not recommended for organizations that have a limited budget

- **Small workloads**: Multi-cloud migration is not recommended for organizations that have small workloads that can be efficiently managed by a single CSP

The process of cloud migration

To ensure a successful cloud migration, organizations should follow a well-defined process that includes the following steps:

1. **Assessment**: The first step in cloud migration is to assess the existing infrastructure, applications, and data to determine the best migration strategy. This involves identifying the dependencies between applications, evaluating the current and future workload requirements, and assessing the security and compliance requirements.

2. **Planning**: The planning phase involves developing a detailed migration plan that outlines the steps involved in the migration, the timelines, the roles and responsibilities of the team members, and the budget. The plan should also include a backup and DR strategy.

3. **Preparation**: The preparation phase involves setting up the cloud environment, such as creating the necessary network connections and security configurations. It also involves preparing the data for migration, such as cleaning up the data, transferring it to the cloud, and testing the data integrity.

4. **Migration**: The migration phase involves moving the applications, data, and other business elements to the cloud environment. This can be done using automated tools or manual processes, depending on the complexity of the application.

5. **Testing**: The testing phase involves verifying that the applications and data are functioning as expected in the new cloud environment. This includes testing the performance, availability, and security of the application and data.

6. **Optimization**: The optimization phase involves fine-tuning the cloud environment to improve performance, reduce costs, and optimize resource utilization. This includes using cloud-native services, such as auto-scaling, load balancing, and serverless computing, to improve the application's performance and reduce costs.

7. **Monitoring and maintenance**: The final phase involves monitoring the cloud environment and performing regular maintenance tasks, such as updating the applications and patching the security vulnerabilities. It also involves monitoring the cloud environment for any performance issues or security threats and taking appropriate actions to address them.

To summarize, cloud migration is a complex process that requires careful planning, execution, and monitoring. Organizations should carefully evaluate their options and choose the best migration strategy based on their business goals, application complexity, and data requirements. Following a well-defined process and leveraging cloud providers' offerings can help ensure a successful cloud migration and maximize the benefits of cloud computing, such as increased scalability, flexibility, and cost savings. It's also essential to have a skilled team with expertise in cloud computing, data migration, and application development to ensure a smooth transition to the cloud.

Moreover, it's important to note that cloud migration is not a one-time event but an ongoing process. As the business needs and technology landscape evolve, organizations may need to migrate additional applications and data to the cloud or make changes to the existing cloud environment. Therefore, it's critical to have a well-defined cloud migration strategy and a continuous improvement process to ensure that the cloud environment remains optimized and aligned with the business goals.

There are different types of cloud migrations, each with its own advantages and challenges. Organizations must carefully evaluate their options and choose the best migration strategy for their needs. Following a well-defined process that includes assessment, planning, preparation, migration, testing, optimization, and monitoring can help ensure a successful cloud migration and maximize the benefits of cloud computing.

Monolithic or distributed database systems?

When considering cloud migration, the choice between a monolithic and distributed database approach depends on a variety of factors, including the size and complexity of the application, the scalability and availability requirements, and the performance needs of the system. Here are some pros and cons of each approach:

Monolithic database approach

Pros:

- **Simplicity**: A monolithic database approach can be simpler to design, deploy, and manage than a distributed database approach

- **Data consistency**: A monolithic database approach ensures data consistency since there is only one database to manage

- **Easier to maintain**: With a single database, it is easier to maintain the data schema and ensure data integrity

Cons:

- **Scalability**: Monolithic databases can become a bottleneck as the application grows, and scaling them can be challenging
- **Availability**: A single point of failure can bring down the entire system, making it less available
- **Performance**: As the application grows, a monolithic database can become slower due to increased data access and processing

Distributed database approach

Pros:

- **Scalability**: Distributed databases can scale horizontally by adding more nodes to the cluster
- **Availability**: Distributed databases can provide high availability by replicating data across multiple nodes, reducing the risk of a single point of failure
- **Performance**: Distributed databases can provide better performance by distributing data and processing across multiple nodes

Cons:

- **Complexity**: A distributed database approach can be more complex to design, deploy, and manage than a monolithic database approach
- **Data consistency**: Ensuring data consistency across multiple nodes can be challenging, and additional measures need to be taken to ensure data integrity
- **Cost**: A distributed database approach can be more expensive than a monolithic database approach due to the need for additional infrastructure and maintenance costs

Choosing between a monolithic or distributed database approach for cloud migration depends on the specific requirements of your application. Both approaches have their pros and cons, and the decision should be based on the needs of your application.

In general, a distributed database approach is better suited for large-scale applications that require high scalability, availability, and performance. A distributed database can scale horizontally by adding more nodes to the cluster, providing better performance and availability. Additionally, a distributed database can replicate data across multiple nodes, reducing the risk of a single point of failure.

However, a distributed database approach can be more complex and expensive to design, deploy, and manage than a monolithic database approach. Ensuring data consistency across multiple nodes can be challenging, and additional measures need to be taken to ensure data integrity. Additionally, a distributed database approach can be more expensive due to the need for additional infrastructure and maintenance costs.

On the other hand, a monolithic database approach can be simpler to design, deploy, and manage than a distributed database approach. With a single database, it is easier to maintain the data schema and ensure data integrity. However, a monolithic database can become a bottleneck as the application grows, and scaling it can be challenging. Additionally, a monolithic database approach can be less available, as a single point of failure can bring down the entire system.

In conclusion, there is no one-size-fits-all answer to whether a monolithic or distributed database approach is better for cloud migration. The decision should be based on the specific requirements of your application, considering factors such as scalability, availability, performance, complexity, and cost.

What can a database expert help with during cloud migration?

As a member of a DevOps team, a database expert, or **database administrator** (**DBA**), can play a critical role in ensuring the success of a cloud migration project. Here are some of the ways a DBA can help:

- **Planning the migration strategy**: A DBA can help the team in planning the migration strategy by understanding the existing database structure, identifying the dependencies, and defining the scope of the migration. The DBA can help in selecting the right cloud database service and the architecture that best fits the needs of the application.

- **Data migration**: Data migration is a critical phase in any cloud migration project. A DBA can help in identifying the data that needs to be migrated, validating the data, and ensuring that the data is migrated accurately and securely. The DBA can also help in designing and implementing data migration scripts or tools.

- **Performance optimization**: A DBA can help in optimizing the performance of the database after the migration. This can include tuning the database parameters, optimizing queries, and ensuring that the database is configured to take full advantage of the cloud infrastructure.

- **Security**: A DBA can help in ensuring that the database is secure during and after the migration. This can include implementing access control policies, encryption, and auditing mechanisms. The DBA can also help in identifying and mitigating security risks during the migration.

- **Disaster recovery**: A DBA can help in designing and implementing a DR strategy for the database in the cloud. This can include setting up backups, replication, and failover mechanisms to ensure that the database is highly available and resilient.

- **Automation**: A DBA can help in automating repetitive tasks such as database backups, schema validation, and performance monitoring. This can help reduce the workload for the DevOps team and ensure that the database is always up to date and running smoothly.

- **Monitoring and alerting**: A DBA can help in setting up monitoring and alerting mechanisms to detect and respond to issues with the database. This can include setting up performance metrics, log analysis, and alerting rules to notify the team of any issues that need to be addressed.

- **Documentation**: A DBA can help in documenting the database structure, schema changes, and migration process. This can help ensure that the team has a clear understanding of the database and its dependencies and can help in troubleshooting any issues that arise.

- **Understanding the existing database structure**: A DBA can help the team understand the existing database structure, including the schema, tables, indexes, and relationships. This understanding can help in designing the migration strategy and identifying any potential issues or dependencies that need to be addressed.

- **Identifying and resolving performance issues**: A DBA can help in identifying and resolving performance issues that may arise during or after the migration. This can include optimizing the database queries, tuning the database parameters, and ensuring that the database is configured for maximum performance.

- **Optimizing database design**: A DBA can help in optimizing the database design for the cloud environment. This can include reorganizing the database schema, eliminating redundant data, and optimizing data access patterns.

- **Testing and validation**: A DBA can help in testing and validating the migrated database to ensure that it is functioning correctly and is compatible with the application. This can include verifying that the data is migrated correctly, testing the performance of the database, and ensuring that the database is functioning as expected.

- **Compliance**: A DBA can help ensure that the database is compliant with relevant regulations and standards, such as GDPR or HIPAA. This can include implementing data encryption, access control policies, and audit logging.

- **Database backup and recovery**: A DBA can help in designing and implementing a backup and recovery strategy for the database in the cloud. This can include setting up regular backups, testing the recovery process, and ensuring that the backup data is stored securely.

- **Cost optimization**: A DBA can help in optimizing the cost of running the database in the cloud. This can include selecting the right cloud database service and configuration, using cost-effective storage options, and optimizing the database performance to minimize resource usage.

- **Collaboration with developers**: A DBA can collaborate with developers to help them understand how the database works and how to optimize their code to work well with the database. This can include providing guidance on database design, query optimization, and best practices for accessing and manipulating data.

- **Monitoring performance**: A DBA can use performance monitoring tools to track the performance of the database and identify any issues that may be affecting its performance. This can include monitoring CPU utilization, memory usage, disk I/O, and network traffic, as well as identifying slow queries and other performance bottlenecks.

- **Capacity planning**: A DBA can help with capacity planning by analyzing the current and future usage of the database and determining the resources needed to support that usage. This can include estimating the growth of the database over time, predicting peak usage periods, and ensuring that the database is configured to handle the expected load.

- **DR testing**: A DBA can help with DR testing by simulating various disasters, such as server failures or data center outages, and testing the recovery procedures to ensure that they work correctly. This can help ensure that the database is resilient to unexpected events and can be quickly restored in the event of a disaster.

- **Knowledge transfer**: A DBA can help with knowledge transfer by documenting the migration process, the database structure and configuration, and any best practices or guidelines that are developed during the migration. This can help ensure that the knowledge and expertise gained during the migration are retained within the organization and can be leveraged for future projects.

DBAs or database experts can make a significant contribution to a cloud migration project by bringing their expertise in database management, performance optimization, security, DR automation, monitoring, and documentation. By working closely with the DevOps team and other stakeholders, a DBA can help ensure that the database is migrated smoothly and efficiently and that it is optimized for performance, security, and availability in the cloud environment.

Data migration strategies and their types

A database cloud migration project involves moving data from an on-premise database to a cloud-based database. This migration process can be complex, and it requires careful planning and execution to ensure that the data is migrated accurately and with minimal disruption to the business. One critical aspect of the migration process is the data migration strategy. In this section, we'll discuss the various data migration strategies to consider during a database cloud migration project, their benefits, and why they are essential.

The Big Bang migration strategy

The Big Bang migration strategy is a data migration approach that involves moving all data from a legacy system to a new system in a single, comprehensive transfer. This method is often used when the legacy system is no longer sustainable, and there is a pressing need to migrate all data to a new system quickly.

The key advantage of the Big Bang strategy is that it minimizes the risk of data discrepancies or inconsistencies that can occur when migrating data in stages. Since all data is moved at once, there is less opportunity for data loss, duplication, or corruption.

However, this approach presents several challenges that organizations should be aware of before deciding to adopt it. The biggest challenge is the potential for downtime or service disruption during the migration process. If data transfer encounters unexpected problems, this could lead to system downtime, loss of productivity, and a potential loss of revenue.

To mitigate the risk of downtime, organizations must carefully plan, test, and coordinate the migration process to ensure that all data is transferred correctly, and the new system is fully functional after migration. It is essential to establish clear communication channels, document procedures, and allocate resources to ensure that the migration process goes smoothly.

Another potential challenge of the Big Bang approach is that it can be more complex and expensive than other migration strategies. Since all data is moved at once, the process requires careful planning and execution to ensure that data is correctly transferred, and the new system is fully functional after migration.

In summary, the Big Bang migration strategy is a data migration approach that involves transferring all data from a legacy system to a new system in a single, comprehensive transfer. While it can offer advantages in terms of reduced risk of data discrepancies, it also presents challenges such as potential downtime and higher costs. Organizations should carefully consider the trade-offs before deciding whether this approach is the best fit for their migration needs.

The phased migration strategy

The phased migration strategy is a data migration approach that involves moving data in stages or phases. This method is often used when the legacy system is complex or the dataset is large, and a complete migration all at once would be too disruptive.

The phased migration strategy allows organizations to break down the migration process into smaller, manageable phases. This can reduce the potential risk of downtime, data loss, or corruption that could occur if all data is moved at once. Each phase of the migration is carefully planned, executed, and tested before moving on to the next phase.

One of the advantages of the phased migration strategy is that it allows organizations to prioritize data migration based on importance or urgency. For example, critical data may be migrated first, while less essential data can be migrated later. This approach can help minimize the impact on operations and allow organizations to maintain continuity during the migration process.

However, the phased migration strategy can also present some challenges. One of the main challenges is that the migration process may take longer than other migration strategies since data is moved in stages. This can result in a prolonged period of coexistence between the old and new systems, which can add complexity and cost to the migration process.

Another challenge of the phased migration strategy is that it requires careful planning and coordination to ensure that each phase of the migration process is executed correctly. Any mistakes or problems in one phase can impact the subsequent phases, leading to potential data loss or downtime.

In summary, the phased migration strategy is a data migration approach that involves moving data in stages or phases. This approach can help organizations minimize the risk of downtime or data loss and allows for the prioritization of critical data migration. However, it can also result in a prolonged migration process and requires careful planning and coordination to ensure successful execution.

The parallel migration strategy

The parallel migration strategy is a data migration approach that involves running the old and new systems in parallel while the migration process takes place. This method allows for a gradual transition to the new system, reducing the risk of downtime and minimizing the impact on operations.

In the parallel migration strategy, both the old and new systems run simultaneously, and data is migrated in real time or near-real time. This approach can allow organizations to test the new system while still using the old system, identify and resolve any issues that arise during the migration process, and ensure that the new system meets all operational requirements.

One of the significant advantages of the parallel migration strategy is that it reduces the risk of downtime or service disruption during the migration process. Since both the old and new systems are running in parallel, if any issues occur during the migration process, the organization can continue to use the old system until the issue is resolved.

Another advantage of the parallel migration strategy is that it allows organizations to gradually transition to the new system, reducing the risk of data loss or corruption. Since data is migrated in real time or near-real time, the organization can ensure that all data is correctly transferred and that the new system is fully functional before decommissioning the old system.

However, the parallel migration strategy can also present some challenges. One of the main challenges is the need for a robust and reliable data integration solution that can support real-time or near-real-time data transfer between the old and new systems. This can be complex and require significant resources to implement.

Another challenge of the parallel migration strategy is that it can be more expensive than other migration strategies. Since both the old and new systems are running in parallel, the organization must bear the cost of maintaining and supporting two systems simultaneously during the migration process.

In summary, the parallel migration strategy is a data migration approach that involves running the old and new systems in parallel while the migration process takes place. This method allows for a gradual transition to the new system, reducing the risk of downtime and minimizing the impact on operations. However, it can be complex and require significant resources to implement and maintain.

The hybrid migration strategy

The hybrid migration strategy is a data migration approach that combines elements of both the Big Bang and phased migration strategies. This method involves migrating critical or urgent data in a Big Bang fashion while moving the remaining data in phases.

The hybrid migration strategy is often used when there is a need to migrate critical data quickly to a new system while less critical data can be moved gradually over time. This approach can help minimize disruption to operations and reduce the risk of downtime or data loss.

In the hybrid migration strategy, critical data is identified and migrated first using the Big Bang approach, while less critical data is migrated in phases. This can help ensure that the critical data is available on the new system, allowing organizations to maintain continuity while the migration process continues.

One of the significant advantages of the hybrid migration strategy is that it allows organizations to prioritize data migration based on importance or urgency. This can help minimize the impact on operations and ensure that critical data is available on the new system as soon as possible.

Another advantage of the hybrid migration strategy is that it can reduce the risk of downtime or data loss during the migration process. By migrating critical data first, organizations can ensure that critical operations can continue, even if other data migration is ongoing.

However, the hybrid migration strategy can also present some challenges. One of the main challenges is that it requires careful planning and coordination to ensure that both the Big Bang and phased migration components of the strategy are executed correctly. Any mistakes or problems in one component can impact the other, leading to potential data loss or downtime.

Another challenge of the hybrid migration strategy is that it can result in a prolonged migration process. Since critical data is migrated first using the Big Bang approach, the migration of less critical data in phases can take longer than other migration strategies.

In summary, the hybrid migration strategy is a data migration approach that combines elements of both the Big Bang and phased migration strategies. This method involves migrating critical data in a Big Bang fashion while moving the remaining data in phases. This approach can help organizations prioritize data migration based on importance or urgency while minimizing the risk of downtime or data loss. However, it can also present challenges that require careful planning and coordination to execute migration correctly.

The reverse migration strategy

The reverse migration strategy is a data migration approach that involves moving data from a new system back to the legacy system. This method is often used when a new system is not functioning as expected or is not meeting the operational requirements.

In the reverse migration strategy, data is migrated from the new system back to the legacy system in a reverse process. This can be a complex and time-consuming process that requires careful planning and execution to ensure that all data is correctly transferred and that the legacy system is fully functional after migration.

One of the significant advantages of the reverse migration strategy is that it allows organizations to minimize the risk of downtime or data loss during the migration process. Since data is migrated back to the legacy system, the organization can continue to use the legacy system while any issues with the new system are resolved.

Another advantage of the reverse migration strategy is that it can provide organizations with valuable insights into the reasons why the new system is not meeting the operational requirements. By identifying and resolving issues with the new system, organizations can improve the effectiveness of the migration process and ensure that the new system meets all operational requirements.

However, the reverse migration strategy can also present some challenges. One of the main challenges is that it requires careful planning and coordination to ensure that data is correctly transferred from the new system back to the legacy system. Any mistakes or issues during the migration process can result in data loss or corruption.

Another challenge of the reverse migration strategy is that it can be costly and time-consuming. Since data is migrated twice, the organization must bear the cost of maintaining and supporting both the new and legacy systems during the migration process.

In summary, the reverse migration strategy is a data migration approach that involves moving data from a new system back to the legacy system. This method can help organizations minimize the risk of downtime or data loss and provide valuable insights into the reasons why the new system is not meeting the operational requirements. However, it can also be complex, costly, and time-consuming, requiring careful planning and coordination to execute it correctly.

The ETL strategy

The ETL strategy is a data migration approach that involves three main processes: **Extract**, **Transform**, and **Load**. In this approach, data is extracted from the legacy system, transformed into a format suitable for the new system, and loaded into the new system. This strategy involves three steps:

1. The first step in the ETL strategy is Extract, where data is extracted from the legacy system. This process involves identifying the data to be migrated, selecting the appropriate tools for extracting data, and performing data validation to ensure data consistency and completeness.

2. The second step in the ETL strategy is Transform, where the extracted data is transformed into a format that can be loaded into the new system. This process involves data cleaning, data normalization, data mapping, and data conversion. Data transformation can be a complex process that requires careful planning, testing, and validation to ensure that data is transformed accurately.

3. The final step in the ETL strategy is Load, where the transformed data is loaded into the new system. This process involves selecting the appropriate tools for data loading, performing data validation, and ensuring that the data is correctly loaded into the new system.

One of the significant advantages of the ETL strategy is that it allows organizations to perform data validation and transformation, reducing the risk of data loss or corruption during the migration process. The ETL process also allows organizations to transform data to suit the new system's requirements, ensuring that data is fully functional and usable after migration.

Another advantage of the ETL strategy is that it allows for flexibility in the migration process. Organizations can migrate data in batches or incrementally, reducing the impact on operations and allowing for testing and validation of the migration process at each step.

However, the ETL strategy can also present some challenges. One of the main challenges is that it can be a complex and time-consuming process that requires careful planning, testing, and validation. This can result in a prolonged migration process that can impact operations and incur higher costs.

Another challenge of the ETL strategy is that it requires expertise in data management, transformation, and migration. Organizations must have access to skilled data professionals to execute the ETL process successfully.

In summary, the ETL strategy is a data migration approach that involves three main processes: Extract, Transform, and Load. This approach allows organizations to perform data validation and transformation, reducing the risk of data loss or corruption during the migration process. However, it can be a complex and time-consuming process that requires careful planning and expertise in data management, transformation, and migration.

The replication strategy

The replication strategy is our final data migration approach, which involves copying data from a legacy system to a new system in near-real time. This method is often used when organizations need to maintain two systems in parallel or require a backup of the data.

In the replication strategy, data is replicated from the legacy system to the new system continuously, ensuring that the new system always has up-to-date data. This process is usually performed using replication software or tools that capture changes made to the data in the legacy system and apply those changes to the new system.

One of the significant advantages of the replication strategy is that it allows for continuous data migration, reducing the risk of data loss or inconsistency. Organizations can ensure that the new system always has the latest data, allowing for uninterrupted operations during the migration process.

Another advantage of the replication strategy is that it can provide organizations with a backup of the data in case of a disaster or failure. Since data is replicated continuously, organizations can quickly restore data in case of a system failure, ensuring that critical operations can continue without interruption.

However, the replication strategy can also present some challenges. One of the main challenges is that it can be complex and require significant resources to implement and maintain. Replication software and tools can be expensive, and the process requires careful planning and coordination to ensure that data is correctly replicated.

Another challenge of the replication strategy is that it can lead to potential data consistency issues. Since data is replicated continuously, any issues with data in the legacy system can be replicated in the new system, leading to potential data inconsistencies. Organizations must have appropriate controls and validation processes in place to ensure that data consistency is maintained during the replication process.

In summary, the replication strategy is a data migration approach that involves copying data from a legacy system to a new system in near-real time. This approach allows for continuous data migration and provides a backup of the data. However, it can be complex and require significant resources to implement and maintain, and can lead to potential data consistency issues.

Why are data migration strategies important during a database cloud migration project?

Data migration strategies are essential during a database cloud migration project for the following reasons:

- **Minimizing downtime**: Data migration strategies can help minimize downtime during the migration process. The phased migration and parallel migration strategies, for example, allow for a more controlled migration process and minimize the risk of downtime.

- **Ensuring data integrity**: Data migration strategies can help ensure that the data is migrated accurately and with minimal data loss or corruption. The ETL strategy, for example, allows for the data to be transformed and validated before being loaded into the new database, ensuring data integrity.

- **Reducing risk**: Data migration strategies can help reduce the risk of data loss or corruption during the migration process. The parallel migration and hybrid migration strategies, for example, allow for a fallback option if any issues arise during the migration process, reducing the risk of data loss or corruption.

- **Optimizing performance**: Data migration strategies can help optimize the performance of the new cloud-based database. The replication strategy, for example, allows for the data to be replicated in real time, ensuring that the data on the cloud-based database is always up to date with the existing database.

- **Cost reduction**: Data migration strategies can help reduce the cost of the migration process. The phased migration and hybrid migration strategies, for example, allow for a more flexible migration process, allowing the migration team to prioritize which parts of the data to migrate first, which can help reduce costs.

- **Meeting business requirements**: Data migration strategies can help ensure that the new cloud-based database meets the business requirements. The ETL strategy, for example, allows for the data to be transformed to fit the structure of the new database, ensuring that the business requirements are met.

Data migration strategies are essential during a database cloud migration project. They can help minimize downtime, ensure data integrity, reduce risk, optimize performance, reduce costs, and ensure that the new cloud-based database meets the business requirements. When planning a database cloud migration project, it is essential to carefully consider the various data migration strategies and choose the one that best fits the specific needs and requirements of the organization.

> **Best practices**
>
> The following are the steps to be followed when executing a data migration:
>
> 1. **Plan ahead**: Develop a comprehensive data migration plan that outlines the scope, timeline, budget, and resources required for the project. Identify potential risks and develop contingency plans to address them.
>
> 2. **Cleanse and validate data**: Ensure that the data being migrated is accurate, complete, and up to date. This may involve data profiling, data cleansing, and data enrichment activities.
>
> 3. **Set up a test environment**: Create a test environment that replicates the production environment as closely as possible, and test the migration process thoroughly before performing the actual migration.
>
> 4. **Use automated tools**: Utilize automated tools to assist with data migration tasks such as data extraction, transformation, and loading. These tools can help reduce errors and improve efficiency.
>
> 5. **Establish data security protocols**: Implement security protocols to protect sensitive data during the migration process, and ensure compliance with data privacy regulations.
>
> 6. **Train personnel**: Train personnel involved in the migration process, including data analysts, developers, and end users, to ensure they understand the migration process and their roles and responsibilities.
>
> 7. **Monitor progress**: Monitor the migration process closely to identify and address any issues that arise. Have a plan in place to roll back the migration if necessary.
>
> 8. **Document the process**: Document the migration process thoroughly, including the steps taken, the tools used, and any issues encountered. This documentation can be used to improve future migrations and to troubleshoot any problems that may arise.

Taking your migration journey one step further

Cloud migration is the process of moving an organization's IT infrastructure, data, and applications from on-premises servers to a cloud-based infrastructure. The primary reason for cloud migration is to take advantage of the numerous benefits that come with cloud computing, such as increased flexibility, scalability, cost savings, and improved security. However, cloud migration is just the beginning of the cloud journey, and there are several potential next steps that organizations can take to optimize their cloud environment and further enhance their business operations. Let's explore the potential next steps after cloud migration and why they are important:

- **Cloud optimization** refers to the process of fine-tuning an organization's cloud environment to improve its performance and reduce costs. After cloud migration, it's important to regularly assess and optimize the cloud environment to ensure that it's running efficiently and cost-effectively. For example, organizations can use tools such as **AWS** Trusted Advisor or Microsoft Azure Advisor to analyze their cloud infrastructure and identify areas for optimization. These tools can provide recommendations on areas such as cost optimization, performance, security, and fault tolerance.

• **Containerization** is the process of packaging software into standardized units called containers, which can run consistently across different computing environments. Containerization provides several benefits, including improved application portability, scalability, and agility. After cloud migration, organizations can consider containerizing their applications to make them more flexible and easier to manage. For example, companies can use Docker to package their applications into containers and deploy them to a Kubernetes cluster running in the cloud.

• **Microservices** is an architectural approach to building applications as a collection of small, independent services that work together to deliver a specific business function. Microservices architecture provides several benefits, including improved scalability, agility, and resilience. After cloud migration, organizations can consider adopting a microservices architecture to improve the performance and flexibility of their applications. For example, companies can use AWS Lambda or Azure Functions to build serverless microservices that can scale automatically and are billed based on usage.

• **Serverless computing** is a cloud computing model where the cloud provider manages the infrastructure and automatically provisions and scales resources as needed to run an application. With serverless computing, organizations only pay for the actual usage of the application and do not have to manage any servers or infrastructure. After cloud migration, organizations can consider using serverless computing to improve the scalability and cost-effectiveness of their applications. For example, companies can use AWS Lambda or Azure Functions to build serverless applications that can scale automatically and are billed based on usage.

• **Cloud security** is a critical aspect of cloud computing, and organizations need to ensure that their cloud environment is secure from potential cyber threats. After cloud migration, organizations can consider implementing additional security measures to enhance their cloud security posture. For example, companies can use AWS WAF or Azure Firewall to protect their applications from web attacks or use AWS Shield or Azure DDoS Protection to protect against DDoS attacks.

• **Cloud governance** refers to the process of managing and controlling an organization's cloud environment to ensure that it aligns with business objectives and complies with regulatory requirements. After cloud migration, organizations can consider implementing cloud governance processes to improve the management and control of their cloud environment. For example, companies can use AWS CloudFormation or Azure Resource Manager to automate the deployment and management of cloud resources or use AWS Config or Azure Policy to enforce compliance with organizational policies and regulatory requirements.

• **Cloud analytics** refers to the process of analyzing data stored in the cloud to gain insights and make informed business decisions. After cloud migration, organizations can consider using cloud analytics tools to analyze their data and gain insights that can help improve their business operations. For example, companies can use AWS Redshift or Azure Synapse Analytics to analyze large volumes of data stored in the cloud or use AWS QuickSight or Azure Power BI to create interactive visualizations and dashboards.

- **Cloud-native development** is an approach to building applications that are designed specifically for the cloud environment. Cloud-native applications are typically built using microservices, containers, and serverless computing, and are optimized for cloud scalability and flexibility. After cloud migration, organizations can consider adopting cloud-native development practices to build applications that are more scalable, resilient, and cost-effective. For example, companies can use the Kubernetes platform to build and manage cloud-native applications or use AWS Elastic Beanstalk or Azure App Service to deploy and manage applications in a **platform-as-a-service** (**PaaS**) environment.

- **Multi-cloud and hybrid cloud** refer to the use of multiple cloud providers or a combination of cloud and on-premises infrastructure to support an organization's IT needs. After cloud migration, organizations can consider adopting a multi-cloud or hybrid cloud approach to improve the resilience, flexibility, and cost-effectiveness of their IT infrastructure. For example, companies can use AWS, Azure, and **Google Cloud Platform** (**GCP**) together to achieve high availability and reduce vendor lock-in or use a hybrid cloud approach to leverage the benefits of both on-premises and cloud infrastructure.

- **Cloud-native security** is a security approach that is specifically designed for cloud-native applications and environments. Cloud-native security solutions provide protection for applications and data in the cloud and are optimized for the scalability and agility of cloud computing. After cloud migration, organizations can consider implementing cloud-native security solutions to improve the security posture of their cloud environment. For example, companies can use AWS Security Hub or Azure Security Center to gain visibility of their cloud security posture and identify potential security threats or use AWS **Key Management Service** (**KMS**) or Azure Key Vault to securely manage encryption keys in the cloud.

To summarize, cloud migration is just the first step in a long journey toward optimizing an organization's IT infrastructure and operations. After cloud migration, organizations can take several next steps to further enhance their cloud environment and achieve additional benefits. These potential next steps include cloud optimization, containerization, microservices, serverless computing, cloud security, cloud governance, cloud analytics, cloud-native development, multi-cloud and hybrid cloud, and cloud-native security. By taking these steps, organizations can continue to improve their IT infrastructure and operations and stay ahead of the curve in the rapidly evolving world of cloud computing.

Summary

In this chapter, we delved deeply into the intricate subject of cloud migration. We began by defining what cloud migration is and explained why an ever-growing number of companies have been making the strategic move to the cloud. We established that it's not merely a tech buzzword but rather an essential move for achieving cost efficiency, scalability, and business continuity.

We then journeyed through key milestones that typically mark a cloud migration path, providing guideposts for businesses to chart their own robust roadmaps. Each milestone was accompanied by its own set of tasks, expectations, and potential roadblocks, furnishing a comprehensive overview of what companies could anticipate.

We also outlined the different types of cloud migrations, ranging from lifting and shifting applications to the cloud to complete application refactoring. We emphasized that these categories aren't one-size-fits-all solutions, urging the importance of understanding their nuances for informed decision-making.

Transitioning from types to processes, we detailed the critical steps involved in cloud migration. This portion was the nuts and bolts of the chapter—the methodology, the planning, the execution, and the follow-up. A step-by-step walk-through ensured you grasped not just the "what," but also the "how" of migrating to the cloud.

Finally, we turned our attention to an often-overlooked yet crucial aspect—data migration strategies during a database cloud migration project. We highlighted the indispensability of a well-thought-out strategy for data migration, exploring best practices, common pitfalls, and the significance of aligning your data migration strategy with your overall cloud migration goals.

To sum up, this chapter offered a 360-degree view of cloud migration, aiming to equip you with the knowledge and tools you need for your own migration journey.

In the next chapter, we will delve into the intricate yet rewarding relationship between **Relational Database Management Systems** (**RDBMSs**) and DevOps.

5
RDBMS with DevOps

In this chapter, we'll delve into the intricate yet rewarding relationship between **relational database management systems** (**RDBMSs**) and DevOps. As you traverse this chapter, you will gain a deep understanding of how modern DevOps practices can be intertwined with RDBMS to create a streamlined, efficient, and secure IT environment. This combination offers numerous advantages, and learning how to exploit them is pivotal for any organization aiming to stay competitive in today's fast-paced digital landscape.

One of the first critical aspects we will explore is provisioning and configuration management. Understanding how to automate these tasks for databases in a DevOps culture is essential for rapid deployments and scaling. You'll discover how to implement IaC approaches that enable frictionless environment setup and configuration changes.

Next, we'll move on to monitoring and alerting, which serve as the eyes and ears of any robust system. You'll learn the latest tools and techniques for real-time database monitoring and how to set up automated alerting mechanisms. This knowledge will allow you to identify and fix issues before they escalate, thus ensuring continuous uptime and operational efficiency.

Following this, this chapter will guide you through the vital areas of backup and disaster recovery. Here, you'll find out how to integrate these critical strategies seamlessly into your DevOps pipeline, ensuring that your data is safe and that your systems are resilient against unforeseen calamities.

Performance optimization is another key theme. You'll learn the best practices for making your RDBMS run as efficiently as possible, from indexing and query optimization to caching and beyond. We'll show you how to identify bottlenecks and improve database performance, all within the framework of a DevOps culture.

Last but not least, we'll touch upon DevSecOps, the practice that integrates security into DevOps. You'll understand why security can't be an afterthought and how to embed security measures right into your DevOps workflows and RDBMS configurations.

By addressing these essential components, this chapter will serve as a comprehensive guide to melding RDBMS and DevOps, replete with actionable insights. For system administrators, database administrators, and DevOps engineers alike, the knowledge you will acquire here will be indispensable in leveraging the full power of integrating RDBMS with DevOps.

The following topics will be covered in this chapter:

- Embracing DevOps
- Provisioning and configuration management
- Monitoring and alerting
- Backup and disaster recovery
- Performance optimization
- DevSecOps

Embracing DevOps

In a DevOps team, several activities are involved in managing and maintaining relational databases. Some of the main activities and challenges include the following:

- Provisioning and configuration management
- Monitoring and alerting
- Backup and disaster recovery
- Performance optimization
- Security and access management

In the following sections, we will discuss each of these activities in detail and provide examples of how they can be implemented using various tools.

Provisioning and configuration management

One of the primary activities of a DevOps team is to provision and configure relational databases. This includes creating database instances, configuring database settings, and managing database users and permissions. Here are some examples of how this can be accomplished:

- Creating a MySQL database instance using Terraform
- Configuring PostgreSQL settings using Ansible
- Managing Oracle users and permissions using Puppet

Let's look at these examples in detail.

Creating a MySQL database instance using Terraform

Creating a MySQL database instance in **Amazon Web Services** (**AWS**) using Terraform involves several steps, including setting up the necessary infrastructure, configuring the database, and launching the instance. In this example, we will use Terraform to automate the process of creating a MySQL database instance in AWS.

Architecture overview

The architecture we'll use in this example involves the following components:

- **Virtual Private Cloud** (**VPC**): A VPC is a virtual network that you can configure to host your AWS resources. It provides an isolated environment for your resources and enables you to control network access.

- **Subnet**: A subnet is a range of IP addresses in your VPC that you can use to launch your resources.

- **Security group**: A security group acts as a virtual firewall for your instances to control inbound and outbound traffic. You can specify rules for inbound and outbound traffic to and from the instances.

- **A Relational Database Service** (**RDS**) **instance**: Amazon RDS is a managed database service that makes it easier to set up, operate, and scale a relational database in the cloud. In this example, we will use RDS to create a MySQL database instance.

Terraform is a tool for building, changing, and versioning infrastructure safely and efficiently. It uses a declarative approach to **Infrastructure as Code** (**IaC**), meaning that you define the desired state of your infrastructure and Terraform will figure out how to create it.

Step 1 – setting up the necessary infrastructure

The first step in creating a MySQL database instance using Terraform is to set up the necessary infrastructure. We will create a VPC, a subnet, and a security group for the RDS instance. Here's some example Terraform code for setting up the infrastructure:

VPC

```
provider "aws" {
  region = "us-west-2"
}

resource "aws_vpc" "example" {
  cidr_block = "10.0.0.0/16"
}

resource "aws_subnet" "example" {
```

```
  vpc_id      = aws_vpc.example.id
  cidr_block = "10.0.1.0/24"
}

resource "aws_security_group" "rds" {
  name_prefix = "rds"
  vpc_id      = aws_vpc.example.id

  ingress {
    from_port   = 3306
    to_port     = 3306
    protocol    = "tcp"
    cidr_blocks = ["0.0.0.0/0"]
  }
}
```

This code sets up a VPC with a CIDR block of 10.0.0.0/16 and a subnet with a CIDR block of 10.0.1.0/24. It also creates a security group for the RDS instance with an ingress rule that allows traffic on port 3306 from any IP address.

Step 2 – configuring the database

The next step is to configure the MySQL database. We will create a parameter group and a database instance with the necessary settings. Here's some example Terraform code for configuring the database:

SQL

```
resource "aws_db_parameter_group" "example" {
  name_prefix = "example"
  family      = "mysql5.7"

  parameter {
    name  = "innodb_buffer_pool_size"
    value = "256M"
  }

  parameter {
    name  = "max_connections"
    value = "1000"
  }
}

resource "aws_db_instance" "example" {
  allocated_storage   = 20
```

```
  storage_type         = "gp2"
  engine               = "mysql"
  engine_version       = "5.7"
  instance_class       = "db.t2.micro"
  name                 = "example"
  username             = "admin"
  password             = "password"
}
```

The preceding code creates a parameter group for the MySQL database instance with two parameters – innodb_buffer_pool_size and max_connections. The innodb_buffer_pool_size parameter sets the size of the InnoDB buffer pool to 256 MB, and the max_connections parameter sets the maximum number of connections to 1000.

This code also creates an RDS instance with the following configuration:

- Allocated storage of 20 GB

- A storage type of gp2

- MySQL engine version 5.7

- An instance class of db.t2.micro

- An instance name of example

- A database username of admin

- A database password of password

Step 3 – launching the instance

The final step is to launch the RDS instance. Here's some example Terraform code for launching the instance:

RDS

```
resource "aws_db_instance" "example" {
  # ... other configuration ...

  vpc_security_group_ids = [
    aws_security_group.rds.id,
  ]

  db_subnet_group_name = aws_db_subnet_group.example.name
}
```

```
resource "aws_db_subnet_group" "example" {
  name        = "example"
  subnet_ids = [aws_subnet.example.id]
}
resource "aws_db_instance" "example" {
  # ... other configuration ...

  vpc_security_group_ids = [
    aws_security_group.rds.id,
  ]

  db_subnet_group_name = aws_db_subnet_group.example.name
}

resource "aws_db_subnet_group" "example" {
  name        = "example"
  subnet_ids = [aws_subnet.example.id]
}
```

This code launches the RDS instance and associates it with the security group and subnet we created in *Step 1*. The vpc_security_group_ids parameter specifies the ID of the security group we created earlier, and the db_subnet_group_name parameter specifies the name of the subnet group we created in this step.

The subnet group is created to specify the subnet where the database instance will be launched. In this example, we are only using one subnet, but you can create multiple subnets in different availability zones for high availability and disaster recovery.

Conclusion

In conclusion, creating a MySQL database instance in AWS using Terraform involves setting up the necessary infrastructure, configuring the database, and launching the instance. The infrastructure includes a VPC, a subnet, and a security group for the RDS instance. The database is configured using a parameter group and an RDS instance with the necessary settings. Finally, the RDS instance is launched and associated with the security group and subnet group. Terraform simplifies this process by allowing you to automate the creation and management of your IaC.

Configuring PostgreSQL settings using Ansible

Configuring PostgreSQL settings using Ansible in AWS involves automating the configuration of PostgreSQL database settings using Ansible, a popular automation tool. In this example, we will use Ansible to install PostgreSQL on an EC2 instance in AWS, create a database and user, and configure various settings such as memory allocation, connection settings, and logging.

Architecture overview

The architecture used in this example consists of an AWS EC2 instance running Ubuntu 20.04 LTS as the operating system. Ansible will be used to provision the instance with PostgreSQL, create a database and user, and configure PostgreSQL settings.

To get started, we will assume that Ansible is already installed and configured on the local machine. We will also assume that an AWS EC2 instance has been launched and that we have the necessary credentials to access it via SSH.

Step 1 – creating an Ansible playbook

The first step is to create an Ansible playbook that will define the tasks to be performed. We will create a file called `postgres.yml` in the `playbooks` directory with the following contents:

YAML

```yaml
- name: Install PostgreSQL
  hosts: db
  become: yes
  become_user: root
  tasks:
    - name: Install PostgreSQL
      apt: name=postgresql state=present
      notify:
        - Restart PostgreSQL

- name: Create database and user
  hosts: db
  become: yes
  become_user: postgres
  tasks:
    - name: Create database
      postgresql_db: name=mydb
    - name: Create user
      postgresql_user: name=myuser password=mypassword priv=ALL
db=mydb

- name: Configure PostgreSQL
  hosts: db
  become: yes
  become_user: postgres
  tasks:
    - name: Set shared memory
```

```
        lineinfile:
          path: /etc/sysctl.conf
          line: "kernel.shmmax = 134217728"
        notify:
          - Reload sysctl
    - name: Set max connections
      lineinfile:
        path: /etc/postgresql/13/main/postgresql.conf
        regexp: '^max_connections'
        line: "max_connections = 100"
      notify:
        - Restart PostgreSQL
    - name: Set logging settings
      lineinfile:
        path: /etc/postgresql/13/main/postgresql.conf
        regexp: '^log_'
        line: "log_destination = 'csvlog'"
      notify:
        - Restart PostgreSQL

- name: Restart PostgreSQL
  hosts: db
  become: yes
  become_user: postgres
  tasks:
    - name: Restart PostgreSQL
      service: name=postgresql state=restarted

- name: Reload sysctl
  hosts: db
  become: yes
  become_user: root
  tasks:
    - name: Reload sysctl
      command: sysctl -p
```

This playbook defines four main tasks:

1. Install PostgreSQL.

2. Create a database and user.

3. Configure PostgreSQL.

4. Restart PostgreSQL.

The playbook is divided into several sections, each containing a list of tasks to be executed. Each task specifies the name of the module to be used, the parameters to be passed, and any notifications that should be triggered upon completion.

Step 2 – creating an inventory file

The next step is to create an inventory file that defines the hosts that will be targeted by the playbook. We will create a file called hosts in the inventory directory with the following contents:

hosts

```
[db]
ec2-instance ansible_host=<ec2-instance-ip> ansible_user=ubuntu
```

This inventory file defines a single host group called db that contains the IP address of the EC2 instance and the username to be used for SSH access.

Step 3 – running the playbook

Now that we have created the playbook and inventory file, we can run the playbook using the following command:

Bash

```
ansible-playbook -i inventory/hosts playbooks/postgres.yml
```

This command tells Ansible to use the hosts file in the inventory directory and the postgres.yml file in the playbooks directory.

Upon execution, Ansible will perform the following actions:

1. Install PostgreSQL on the EC2 instance.
2. Create a database called mydb and a user called myuser with a password of mypassword.
3. Set the shared memory to 134217728.
4. Set the maximum number of connections to 100.
5. Configure logging to write logs to a CSV file.
6. Restart PostgreSQL.

Step 4 – verifying the configuration

To verify that the PostgreSQL configuration was successful, we can SSH into the EC2 instance and use the psql command to connect to the mydb database using the myuser user:

```
psql -d mydb -U myuser
```

If the connection is successful, we can run the following command to view the current PostgreSQL settings:

PSQL

```
show all;
```

This command will display a list of all the current PostgreSQL settings, including the values that we set in the Ansible playbook.

Conclusion

In conclusion, configuring PostgreSQL settings using Ansible in AWS involves automating the installation, configuration, and management of a PostgreSQL database on an EC2 instance in AWS. The architecture used in this example consists of an EC2 instance running Ubuntu 20.04 LTS as the operating system, Ansible as the automation tool, and a playbook that defines the tasks to be performed. By using Ansible to automate the configuration of PostgreSQL, we can reduce the time and effort required to set up and manage a PostgreSQL database, while also ensuring consistency and accuracy in the configuration.

Managing Oracle users and permissions using Puppet

Managing Oracle users and permissions in AWS using Puppet is a complex process that requires a thorough understanding of both Puppet and Oracle database management. This example will cover the architecture used in such a setup and provide some sample code to illustrate the implementation.

Architecture overview

The architecture used in this example comprises four components:

- **AWS EC2 instances**: These are virtual machines that host the Oracle database and the Puppet master. The EC2 instances are launched from an **Amazon Machine Image** (**AMI**) that has an Oracle database and Puppet pre-installed.

- **Puppet master**: This is the central point of control for all Puppet agents that are responsible for managing the Oracle database. The Puppet master contains the Puppet manifests and modules that define the desired state of the Oracle database.

- **Puppet agents**: These are the EC2 instances running the Oracle database that are managed by the Puppet master. The agents run the Puppet client, which communicates with the Puppet master to retrieve and apply the configuration changes.

- **Oracle database**: This is the database instance that is being managed by Puppet. The Oracle database is installed on the EC2 instances and is managed using Puppet manifests.

Let's look at an example that demonstrates how to manage Oracle users and permissions using Puppet in AWS.

Step 1 – defining Oracle users and permissions in Puppet manifests

The following Puppet manifest defines a user named user1 with a home director and a .profile file containing environment variables, and grants the user connect and resource privileges in the Oracle database:

Puppet

```
class oracle::users {
    user { 'user1':
        ensure     => present,
        home       => '/home/user1',
        managehome => true,
    }

    file { '/home/user1/.profile':
        ensure => file,
        content => "export ORACLE_SID=ORCL\nexport ORACLE_HOME=/u01/
app/oracle/product/12.2.0/dbhome_1\nexport PATH=$PATH:$ORACLE_HOME/
bin\n",
        owner => 'user1',
        group => 'dba',
        mode => '0600',
        require => User['user1'],
    }

    exec { 'create_user1':
        command => '/u01/app/oracle/product/12.2.0/dbhome_1/bin/
sqlplus / as sysdba <<EOF\nCREATE USER user1 IDENTIFIED BY password;\
nGRANT CONNECT, RESOURCE TO user1;\nEXIT;\nEOF\n',
        onlyif  => '/u01/app/oracle/product/12.2.0/dbhome_1/bin/
sqlplus / as sysdba @/tmp/user1_exists.sql | grep -q "0 rows
selected"',
        require => File['/home/user1/.profile'],
    }
}
```

Step 2 – assigning the Oracle user manifest to the Oracle database agent node

The following Puppet manifest assigns the oracle::users class to the Oracle database agent node named oracle-db-agent. This means that the user and permission settings defined in the oracle::users class will be applied to the Oracle database on the oracle-db-agent node:

Puppet

```
node 'oracle-db-agent' {
    include oracle::users
}
```

Step 3 – running Puppet on the Oracle database agent node

To apply the user and permission changes to the Oracle database, run the following command on the Oracle database agent node:

```
sudo puppet agent -t
```

This command instructs the Puppet client to retrieve the configuration changes from the Puppet master and apply them to the Oracle database.

Managing Oracle users and permissions using Puppet in AWS is a powerful and efficient way to manage the database infrastructure. The architecture used in this example leverages the power of AWS EC2 instances, Puppet, and Oracle database management to automate the process of managing users and permissions. The provided code examples demonstrate how to use Puppet to manage Oracle users and permissions in AWS, and can be extended to cover other areas of Oracle database management.

In addition to managing users and permissions, Puppet can be used to automate other database administration tasks such as database configuration, backups, and monitoring. The Puppet manifests and modules can be customized to suit specific database environments and requirements, making it a flexible and powerful tool for managing Oracle databases in AWS.

Conclusion

In summary, using Puppet to manage Oracle users and permissions in AWS involves defining the desired state of the database in Puppet manifests, assigning the manifests to the appropriate agent nodes, and running Puppet to apply the configuration changes. The architecture used in this example leverages the power of AWS EC2 instances, Puppet, and Oracle database management to provide a robust and efficient way of managing Oracle databases in AWS.

Monitoring and alerting

Another important activity for a DevOps team is to monitor and alert on the performance and availability of relational databases. This includes monitoring database metrics, setting up alarms and notifications, and investigating and resolving issues. Let's look at some examples of how this can be accomplished.

Monitoring MySQL metrics using Datadog

Monitoring database performance is an essential aspect of managing any application's infrastructure. Datadog is a popular cloud-based monitoring tool that provides insights into system metrics, application metrics, logs, and more. In this example, we will explore how to monitor MySQL metrics using Datadog in **Google Cloud Platform** (**GCP**).

Architecture overview

The architecture for monitoring MySQL metrics using Datadog in GCP involves the following components:

- **MySQL Server**: This is the database server that needs to be monitored. In this example, we will use a MySQL instance running on a Compute Engine VM in GCP.

- **Datadog Agent**: The Datadog Agent is a lightweight daemon that collects and sends system and application metrics to Datadog. It is installed on the MySQL server in this example.

- **Datadog API**: The Datadog API is used to create dashboards, alerts, and other monitoring features in Datadog.

- **GCP Stackdriver**: GCP Stackdriver is a monitoring and logging platform provided by Google. It is used to collect logs and metrics from the MySQL instance.

- **Pub/Sub**: Pub/Sub is a messaging service provided by GCP. It is used to send Stackdriver logs to Datadog.

Step 1 – setting up Datadog

To use Datadog for monitoring MySQL metrics, you need to create a Datadog account and set up the Datadog Agent. The Datadog Agent can be installed on MySQL Server using the following command:

Bash

```bash
DD_API_KEY=<YOUR_API_KEY> bash -c "$(curl -L https://raw.
githubusercontent.com/DataDog/datadog-agent/master/cmd/agent/install_
script.sh)"
```

Replace <YOUR_API_KEY> with your Datadog API key.

Once the Datadog Agent has been installed, you can configure it to collect MySQL metrics by adding the following to the Datadog Agent configuration file (/etc/datadog-agent/datadog.yaml):

YAML

```yaml
logs:
  - type: file
    path: /var/log/mysql/error.log
    service: mysql
    source: mysql
    sourcecategory: database
    log_processing_rules:
```

```
- type: multi_line
  name: new_log_start_with_date
  pattern: \d{4}\-\d{2}\-\d{2}
```

This configuration tells the Datadog Agent to collect MySQL error logs and send them to Datadog with the `database` source category.

Step 2 – setting up Stackdriver

To collect metrics from the MySQL instance, you need to set up Stackdriver on the Compute Engine VM. You can do this by following the instructions in the GCP documentation.

Once Stackdriver has been set up, you can create a custom metric for MySQL metrics by adding the following to the MySQL configuration file (`/etc/mysql/my.cnf`):

INI file

```ini
[mysqld_exporter]
user = root
password = <YOUR_PASSWORD>
```

Replace `<YOUR_PASSWORD>` with your MySQL root password.

This configuration tells `mysqld_exporter` to expose MySQL metrics for Stackdriver to collect.

Step 3 – sending Stackdriver logs to Datadog

To send Stackdriver logs to Datadog, you need to set up a Pub/Sub topic and subscription. You can do this by following the instructions in the GCP documentation.

Once the Pub/Sub topic and subscription have been set up, you can configure Stackdriver to send logs to Pub/Sub by adding the following to the Stackdriver log sink configuration:

Bash

```bash
destination: pubsub.googleapis.com/projects/<PROJECT_ID>/
topics/<TOPIC_NAME>
```

Replace `<PROJECT_ID>` with your GCP project ID and `<TOPIC_NAME>` with the name of your Pub/Sub topic.

Next, you need to configure Datadog to receive logs from Pub/Sub. To do this, create a new log pipeline in Datadog and configure it to receive logs from the Pub/Sub subscription.

Step 4 – creating a Datadog dashboard

With the MySQL metrics collected and sent to Datadog, you can now create a dashboard to monitor them. To create a new dashboard in Datadog, go to the **Dashboards** page and click **New Dashboard**.

On the **New Dashboard** page, select a layout and add widgets to display the MySQL metrics you want to monitor. For example, you can add a MySQL overview widget to display the total number of queries, connections, and other important metrics.

You can also add widgets to display specific MySQL metrics, such as the number of slow queries or the percentage of CPU usage.

Step 5 – setting up alerts

In addition to monitoring MySQL metrics with a dashboard, you can also set up alerts to notify you when specific metrics exceed a certain threshold. To create a new alert in Datadog, go to the **Alerts** page and click **New Monitor**.

On the **New Monitor** page, select the MySQL metrics you want to monitor and configure the alert settings, such as the threshold and notification method.

For example, you can create an alert to notify you when the number of slow queries exceeds a certain threshold or when the percentage of CPU usage is above a certain level.

Conclusion

In this example, we explored how to monitor MySQL metrics using Datadog in GCP. By setting up the Datadog Agent, Stackdriver, Pub/Sub, and a Datadog dashboard, we were able to collect, visualize, and monitor MySQL metrics with ease. With alerts set up, we can also receive notifications when important metrics exceed a certain threshold, allowing us to quickly identify and resolve any issues with the MySQL instance.

Setting up PostgreSQL alarms using Prometheus

PostgreSQL is a powerful open source RDBMS. Prometheus is a monitoring and alerting toolkit that collects metrics from monitored targets, stores them, and makes them available for querying and alerting. GCP provides a scalable infrastructure for deploying and managing applications.

Architecture overview

To set up PostgreSQL alarms using Prometheus in GCP, we will follow the following architecture:

1. **Deploy PostgreSQL on GCP**: We will deploy PostgreSQL on GCP using Google Cloud SQL, a managed SQL database service that makes it easy to set up, manage, and administer PostgreSQL databases.

2. **Export PostgreSQL metrics**: We will use the pg_prometheus extension to export PostgreSQL metrics to Prometheus. pg_prometheus is an open source PostgreSQL extension that exports PostgreSQL metrics in the Prometheus format.

3. **Collect PostgreSQL metrics**: We will use Prometheus to collect PostgreSQL metrics from the pg_prometheus extension. Prometheus can scrape metrics from targets using HTTP(S) endpoints. We will expose the PostgreSQL metrics using an HTTP endpoint.

4. **Set up Prometheus alerts**: We will use Prometheus to set up alerts based on the collected PostgreSQL metrics. Prometheus alerts are rules that specify conditions for triggering an alert. When an alert is triggered, Prometheus sends a notification to an alert manager.

5. **Send alerts to a notification channel**: We will use Alertmanager to send alerts to a notification channel, such as email or Slack.

Here's the step-by-step guide on how to set up PostgreSQL alarms using Prometheus in GCP.

Step 1 – deploying PostgreSQL on GCP

We will use Google Cloud SQL to deploy PostgreSQL on GCP. Follow these steps to deploy PostgreSQL on GCP:

1. Create a new Cloud SQL instance in the GCP console.

2. Choose PostgreSQL as the database engine.

3. Choose the desired region and configure the instance.

4. Create a new user and database for the application.

5. Set up the connection to the PostgreSQL instance.

Step 2 – exporting PostgreSQL metrics

We will use the pg_prometheus extension to export PostgreSQL metrics to Prometheus. Follow these steps to export PostgreSQL metrics:

1. Install the pg_prometheus extension on the PostgreSQL instance.

2. Enable the pg_prometheus extension in the PostgreSQL instance.

3. Configure the pg_prometheus extension to expose the PostgreSQL metrics using an HTTP endpoint.

Here's an example of how to enable the pg_prometheus extension:

SQL

```sql
CREATE EXTENSION pg_prometheus;
```

Here's an example of how to configure the `pg_prometheus` extension to expose the PostgreSQL metrics:

```
pg_prometheus.listen_addresses = 'localhost'
pg_prometheus.port = 9187
```

Step 3 – collecting PostgreSQL metrics

We will use Prometheus to collect PostgreSQL metrics from the `pg_prometheus` extension. Follow these steps to collect PostgreSQL metrics:

1. Install Prometheus on GCP.

2. Configure Prometheus to scrape metrics from the `pg_prometheus` extension using an HTTP endpoint.

Here's an example of how to configure Prometheus to scrape metrics from the `pg_prometheus` extension:

YAML

```yaml
scrape_configs:
  - job_name: 'postgresql'
    scrape_interval: 10s
    static_configs:
      - targets: ['localhost:9187']
```

Step 4 – setting up Prometheus alerts

We will use Prometheus to set up alerts based on the collected PostgreSQL metrics. Follow these steps to set up Prometheus alerts:

1. Define alert rules in Prometheus.

2. Reload the Prometheus configuration to apply the new alert rules.

Here's an example of how to define an alert rule in Prometheus:

YAML

```yaml
groups:
  - name: 'PostgreSQL alerts'
    rules:
      - alert: High CPU usage
        expr: postgresql_cpu_usage > sum(rate(postgresql_cpu_
usage[5m])) by (instance) > 0.8
        for: 5m
        labels:
          severity: warning
```

```
        annotations:
            summary: High CPU usage on PostgreSQL {{ $labels.instance }}
            description: '{{ $labels.instance }} has high CPU usage ({{
$value }}).'
```

In this example, we are defining an alert rule named `High CPU usage` that triggers a warning when the sum of the rate of CPU usage for PostgreSQL instances is greater than 80% over a 5-minute window. The alert has a severity label of `warning` and includes annotations for the alert summary and description.

To reload the Prometheus configuration, run the following command:

Bash

```bash
curl -X POST http://localhost:9090/-/reload
```

Step 5 – sending alerts to a notification channel

We will use Alertmanager to send alerts to a notification channel, such as email or Slack. Follow these steps to set up Alertmanager:

1. Install Alertmanager on GCP.

2. Configure Alertmanager to send alerts to a notification channel.

Here's an example of how to configure Alertmanager to send alerts to an email address:

YAML

```yaml
route:
  group_by: ['alertname', 'severity']
  group_wait: 30s
  group_interval: 5m
  repeat_interval: 12h
  routes:
    - match:
        severity: warning
      receiver: email-alerts

receivers:
  - name: email-alerts
    email_configs:
      - to: 'youremail@example.com'
        from: 'alertmanager@example.com'
        smarthost: smtp.gmail.com:587
```

```
auth_username: 'youremail@example.com'
auth_password: 'yourpassword'
starttls_require: true
```

In this example, we are configuring Alertmanager to send alerts with a severity label of `warning` to an email address. We are specifying the email address to send the alerts to, as well as the email address and credentials to use for authentication.

Conclusion

In conclusion, setting up PostgreSQL alarms using Prometheus in GCP requires deploying PostgreSQL on GCP, exporting PostgreSQL metrics using the `pg_prometheus` extension, collecting PostgreSQL metrics using Prometheus, setting up Prometheus alerts based on the collected PostgreSQL metrics, and sending alerts to a notification channel using Alertmanager. With this architecture, you can monitor and alert on PostgreSQL metrics in real time, ensuring the availability and performance of your PostgreSQL database.

Investigating Oracle Database issues using Jenkins

Investigating Oracle Database issues can be a challenging task for database administrators. It involves monitoring and analyzing the database's performance, identifying bottlenecks, and taking corrective actions to optimize the system. One way to automate this process is by using Jenkins, an open source automation server that enables developers to automate tasks related to building, testing, and deploying software.

In this example, we will explore how to use Jenkins to investigate Oracle Database issues by setting up a Jenkins pipeline that performs the following tasks:

1. Connects to Oracle Database using JDBC
2. Executes a SQL query to retrieve performance data
3. Analyzes the data and generates a report
4. Sends an email notification to the database administrator if any issues are found

Architecture

The architecture of the solution involves several components:

*   **Jenkins server**: This is where the Jenkins pipeline is executed. It runs on a separate machine from Oracle Database to avoid interfering with the database's performance.

*   **Oracle Database**: This is the database being monitored for performance issues.

*   **JDBC driver**: This is the driver that's used by the pipeline to connect to the Oracle Database.

- **SQL query**: This is the query that's executed by the pipeline to retrieve performance data from the database.

- **Python script**: This is a script that analyzes the data retrieved by the SQL query and generates a report.

- **Email server**: This is the server that's used by the pipeline to send email notifications to the database administrator.

The pipeline is triggered either manually or automatically by a scheduler. When it runs, it first connects to Oracle Database using the JDBC driver. Then, it executes the SQL query to retrieve performance data. The data is then analyzed by the Python script, which generates a report. If any issues are found, the pipeline sends an email notification to the database administrator.

Jenkins pipeline code

The Jenkins pipeline code is written in Groovy, a scripting language that runs on Java Virtual Machine. Here is an example of what the code might look like:

Groovy

```groovy
pipeline {
  agent any
  stages {
    stage('Connect to Oracle Database') {
      steps {
        script {
          def jdbcUrl = 'jdbc:oracle:thin:@localhost:1521:orcl'
          def dbUser = 'system'
          def dbPassword = 'oracle'

          def driver = Class.forName('oracle.jdbc.driver.
OracleDriver').newInstance()
          DriverManager.registerDriver(driver)

          def conn = DriverManager.getConnection(jdbcUrl, dbUser,
dbPassword)
          // Save connection for later stages
          env.DB_CONN = conn
        }
      }
    }

    stage('Retrieve Performance Data') {
      steps {
```

```
      script {
        def sqlQuery = 'SELECT * FROM performance_data'

        def stmt = env.DB_CONN.createStatement()
        def rs = stmt.executeQuery(sqlQuery)
        // Save result set for later stages
        env.PERF_DATA = rs
      }
    }
  }

  stage('Generate Performance Report') {
    steps {
      script {
        def perfData = env.PERF_DATA
        def report = generateReport(perfData)
        // Save report for later stages
        env.REPORT = report
      }
    }
  }

  stage('Send Email Notification') {
    steps {
      script {
        def report = env.REPORT
        if (report.hasIssues()) {
          sendEmailNotification(report)
        }
      }
    }
  }
}

post {
  always {
    script {
      // Close the database connection
      env.DB_CONN.close()
    }
  }
}
}
```

This pipeline consists of four stages, each of which has one or more steps. The agent any directive specifies that the pipeline can run on any available agent (machine).

The first stage, Connect to Oracle Database, sets up the JDBC connection to Oracle Database. The jdbcUrl, dbUser, and dbPassword variables are used to specify the connection details. The DriverManager class is used to register the JDBC driver and obtain a connection to the database. The resulting connection object is saved as an environment variable for later stages to use.

The second stage, Retrieve Performance Data, executes a SQL query to retrieve performance data from the database. The sqlQuery variable specifies the query to be executed. The resulting result set is saved as an environment variable for later stages to use.

The third stage, Generate Performance Report, uses a Python script to analyze the performance data and generate a report. The perfData variable is used to pass the result set to the generateReport function. The resulting report is saved as an environment variable for later stages to use.

The final stage, Send Email Notification, checks if the report has any issues and sends an email notification to the database administrator if it does. The hasIssues function is used to determine if the report has any issues. If it does, the sendEmailNotification function is called to send an email notification.

The post section contains a cleanup step that always runs, regardless of the outcome of the pipeline. In this case, it closes the database connection that was opened in the first stage.

Python script

The Python script that's used to analyze the performance data and generate a report might look like this:

Python

```python
import pandas as pd

def generateReport(perfData):
    df = pd.DataFrame(perfData, columns=['timestamp', 'cpu_usage',
'memory_usage', 'disk_usage'])
    df['timestamp'] = pd.to_datetime(df['timestamp'])
    df.set_index('timestamp', inplace=True)

    report = {}

    # Check CPU usage
    cpuMax = df['cpu_usage'].max()
    if cpuMax > 90:
        report['cpu'] = f"CPU usage is {cpuMax}%, which is higher than the
recommended maximum of 90%."
```

```
  # Check memory usage
  memMax = df['memory_usage'].max()
  if memMax > 80:
      report['memory'] = f"Memory usage is {memMax}%, which is higher
than the recommended maximum of 80%."

  # Check disk usage
  diskMax = df['disk_usage'].max()
  if diskMax > 70:
      report['disk'] = f"Disk usage is {diskMax}%, which is higher than
the recommended maximum of 70%."

  return report
```

This script uses the `pandas` library to load the performance data into a `DataFrame` object. The `timestamp` column is converted into a datetime object and used as the index. The script then analyzes the data and generates a report if any issues are found. In this example, the script checks for high CPU, memory, and disk usage.

Email notification

The email notification is sent using the Jenkins Email Extension plugin, which allows emails to be sent with customizable content and attachments. Here is an example of what the email notification might look like:

Groovy

```groovy
def sendEmailNotification(report) {
  emailext body: reportToString(report),
    recipientProviders: [
      [$class: 'DevelopersRecipientProvider']
    ],
    subject: 'Oracle Database Performance Issues',
    attachmentsPattern: '**/*.csv'
}
def reportToString(report) {
  if (report.empty) {
    return "No performance issues found."
  } else {
    StringBuilder sb = new StringBuilder()
    for (entry in report.entrySet()) {
      sb.append(entry.getValue()).sb.append("\n\n")
    }
```

```
    return sb.toString()
  }
}
```

This code uses the `emailext` function to send an email notification to the developer's recipient provider, which is defined in the Jenkins configuration. The `subject` parameter specifies the subject of the email, and the `attachmentsPattern` parameter specifies a file pattern that matches the CSV report file generated by the Python script.

The `reportToString` function is used to convert the report generated by the Python script into a string that can be used as the body of the email. If no issues are found, it returns a message indicating that no performance issues were found. If issues are found, it formats the report as a list of bullet points.

In this example, we have seen how Jenkins can be used to automate the process of investigating Oracle Database issues. The pipeline connects to the database using JDBC, retrieves performance data using a SQL query, analyzes the data using a Python script, and sends email notifications to the database administrator if any issues are found. The architecture consists of several components, including the Jenkins server, the Oracle Database, the JDBC driver, the SQL query, the Python script, and the email server. The pipeline code is written in Groovy, and the email notification is sent using the Jenkins Email Extension plugin. By automating this process, database administrators can save time and improve the performance of their Oracle databases.

Backup and disaster recovery

Ensuring that relational databases are backed up and can be recovered in the event of a disaster is another critical activity for a DevOps team. This includes setting up backup and recovery processes, testing backups, and performing disaster recovery exercises. Let's look at examples of how this can be accomplished.

Creating MySQL backups using Ansible

Before we dive into the technical details and code, let's discuss the architecture that we'll be using in this example. The basic architecture consists of three components: the MySQL database, the backup server, and the Ansible controller.

The MySQL database is the data source that we want to back up. We assume that it's already installed and configured properly on its own server.

The backup server is where we'll store the backup files. It should have enough disk space to accommodate the backups.

The Ansible controller is the machine from which we'll execute Ansible playbooks. This machine should have Ansible installed and configured to connect to the MySQL database server and the backup server.

With this architecture in place, we can proceed to create a playbook that performs MySQL backups.

Here is an example playbook that you can use:

YAML

```yaml
---
- name: Create MySQL backups
  hosts: mysql_servers
  become: yes

  vars:
    backup_dir: "/var/backups/mysql"
    mysql_user: "backupuser"
    mysql_password: "backuppassword"
    mysql_databases:
      - "db1"
      - "db2"

  tasks:
    - name: Create backup directory
      file:
        path: "{{ backup_dir }}"
        state: directory
        owner: root
        group: root
        mode: 0700

    - name: Create MySQL backup
      mysql_db_backup:
        login_user: "{{ mysql_user }}"
        login_password: "{{ mysql_password }}"
        db: "{{ item }}"
        backup_dir: "{{ backup_dir }}"
        backup_type: "database"
      with_items: "{{ mysql_databases }}"

    - name: Compress backup files
      command: "tar -czvf {{ item }}.tar.gz {{ item }}/"
      args:
        chdir: "{{ backup_dir }}"
      with_items: "{{ mysql_databases }}"
```

Let's go through this playbook step by step:

1. The first section defines some basic information about the playbook.

2. The `hosts` variable specifies the hosts that we want to run the playbook on. In this case, we assume that we have a group called `mysql_servers` that contains the MySQL database server(s).

3. The `become` variable tells Ansible to run the playbook as the root user.

4. The `vars` section defines some variables that we'll use later in the playbook.

5. The `backup_dir` variable specifies the directory where we want to store the backups.

6. The `mysql_user` and `mysql_password` variables specify the username and password that Ansible will use to connect to the MySQL database.

7. Finally, the `mysql_databases` variable lists the databases that we want to back up.

The first task creates the backup directory if it doesn't already exist. We use the `file` module to create the directory with the appropriate permissions.

The second task performs the actual backup. We use the `mysql_db_backup` module to connect to the MySQL database and create a backup of each database in the `mysql_databases` variable. We specify the backup directory using the `backup_dir` variable, and we set the backup type to `database`.

The third task compresses the backup files using the `tar` command. We use the `command` module to execute the `tar` command with the appropriate arguments. The `chdir` argument tells `tar` to change to the backup directory before compressing the files. We use the `with_items` variable to loop over each database in the `mysql_databases` variable and compress the corresponding backup file.

Now that we have a playbook, we need to create an inventory file that tells Ansible about our servers. Here is an example inventory file:

Inventory

```
[mysql_servers]
mysql.example.com

[backup_servers]
backup.example.com
```

In this example, we have one MySQL database server called `mysql.example.com` and one backup server called `backup.example.com`. You can modify this file to match your own server names and IP addresses.

Next, we need to create a configuration file for Ansible. Here is an example configuration file:

Configuration file

```
[defaults]
inventory = /path/to/inventory/file
remote_user = root
```

This file specifies the location of our inventory file and sets the remote user to `root`.

Now that we have our playbook, inventory file, and configuration file, we can run the playbook using the `ansible-playbook` command:

`ansible-playbook backup_mysql.yml`

This command tells Ansible to run the `backup_mysql.yml` playbook. Ansible will connect to the MySQL database server and back up the databases specified in the playbook. The backups will be stored on the backup server in the directory specified in the playbook.

Overall, this example architecture and playbook should be sufficient for creating MySQL backups using Ansible. Of course, you can modify the playbook to match your own needs and specifications. For example, you might want to modify the backup retention policy, add email notifications, or include additional databases in the backup. With Ansible's flexibility and powerful modules, the possibilities are endless!

Testing PostgreSQL backups using Chef

Testing backups is an essential part of any database administration task. One way to automate this process is by using Chef, a popular configuration management tool, to create recipes that test the integrity of PostgreSQL backups. In this example, we will walk through a deep technical example of how to test PostgreSQL backups using Chef.

First, let's consider the architecture used in this example. We will use Chef to automate the testing of PostgreSQL backups stored in AWS S3 buckets. Our Chef recipe will run a series of checks to ensure that the backups are valid and can be used to restore the database in the event of a disaster.

The following diagram illustrates the high-level architecture used in this example:

Lua

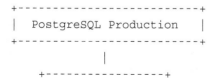

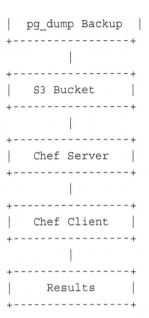

```
|  pg_dump Backup  |
+------------------+

         |

+------------------+
|   S3 Bucket      |
+------------------+

         |

+------------------+
|   Chef Server    |
+------------------+

         |

+------------------+
|   Chef Client    |
+------------------+

         |

+------------------+
|     Results      |
+------------------+
```

In this architecture, we have a PostgreSQL production database that is backed up using pg_dump. The backups are stored in an S3 bucket, which is accessible by a Chef server. A Chef client is configured to run the backup testing recipe, which checks the integrity of the backups and reports the results to the Chef server. The results are then available for analysis and action.

Now, let's take a closer look at the Chef recipe that we will use to test our PostgreSQL backups.

We will start by creating a new Chef cookbook called postgresql-backup-testing. Inside this cookbook, we will create a recipe called default.rb. This recipe will perform the following steps:

1. **Install the** aws-sdk-s3 **gem**: We will use this gem to interact with the S3 bucket that contains our backups.

2. **Download the latest backup from the S3 bucket**: We will use the aws-sdk-s3 gem to download the latest backup file from the S3 bucket.

3. **Verify the integrity of the backup**: We will use the pg_restore command to verify the integrity of the backup file. This command will check that the backup file is valid and can be used to restore the database.

4. **Report the results to the Chef server**: We will use the chef_handler gem to report the results of the backup testing to the Chef server.

Here's the code for the `default.rb` recipe:

Ruby

```ruby
# Install the aws-sdk-s3 gem
chef_gem 'aws-sdk-s3' do
  compile_time true
end


# Download the latest backup from the S3 bucket
s3 = Aws::S3::Client.new(region: 'us-west-2')
bucket_name = 'my-backup-bucket'
backup_prefix = 'postgresql-backups/'
latest_backup = s3.list_objects_v2(bucket: bucket_name, prefix:
backup_prefix).contents.sort_by(&:last_modified).last.key
local_backup_path = "/tmp/#{File.basename(latest_backup)}"
FileUtils.mkdir_p(File.dirname(local_backup_path))
File.open(local_backup_path, 'wb') do |file|
  s3.get_object(bucket: bucket_name, key: latest_backup) do |chunk|
    file.write(chunk)
  end
end
```

Next, we will verify the integrity of the backup using the `pg_restore` command:

Ruby

```ruby
# Verify the integrity of the backup
cmd = "pg_restore --list #{local_backup_path} > /dev/null"
system(cmd)
if $?.exitstatus != 0
  Chef::Log.error("Backup file #{local_backup_path} is invalid!")
  raise "Backup file #{local_backup_path} is invalid!"
else
  Chef::Log.info("Backup file #{local_backup_path} is valid.")
end
```

In this code, we run the `pg_restore --list` command on the backup file to check that it is valid. If the command returns a non-zero exit status, we log an error and raise an exception. Otherwise, we log a success message.

Finally, we will report the results of the backup testing to the Chef server using the `chef_handler` gem:

Ruby

```ruby
# Report the results to the Chef server
chef_gem 'chef-handler-sns' do
  compile_time true
end


require 'chef/handler/sns'
Chef::Config[:s3_backup_test_topic_arn] = 'arn:aws:sns:us-west-
2:123456789012:s3-backup-test-results'
Chef::Config[:s3_backup_test_subject] = "PostgreSQL backup test
results for #{node['hostname']}"
Chef::Config[:s3_backup_test_body] = "Backup file #{local_backup_path}
is valid."
Chef::Config[:s3_backup_test_aws_access_key_id] = 'my-access-key'
Chef::Config[:s3_backup_test_aws_secret_access_key] = 'my-secret-key'
Chef::Config[:s3_backup_test_aws_region] = 'us-west-2'


chef_handler 'Chef::Handler::SNS' do
  source 'chef/handler/sns'
  arguments [Chef::Config[:s3_backup_test_topic_arn], {
    subject: Chef::Config[:s3_backup_test_subject],
    message: Chef::Config[:s3_backup_test_body],
    access_key_id: Chef::Config[:s3_backup_test_aws_access_key_id],
    secret_access_key: Chef::Config[:s3_backup_test_aws_secret_access_
key],
    region: Chef::Config[:s3_backup_test_aws_region],
  }]
  action :enable
end
```

In this code, we use the `chef-handler-sns` gem to create an SNS topic and publish the results of the backup testing to that topic. We set various configuration variables, such as the topic ARN and the access keys, and then enable the `Chef::Handler::SNS` handler.

With this recipe in place, we can now run it on our Chef client to test the integrity of our PostgreSQL backups. The results will be reported to the Chef server, where we can analyze them and take appropriate action if necessary.

In summary, using Chef to test PostgreSQL backups stored in AWS S3 buckets is a powerful way to automate an essential task in database administration. By creating a Chef recipe that checks the integrity of the backups and reports the results to the Chef server, we can ensure that our backups are always valid and ready to use in the event of a disaster.

Performing Oracle disaster recovery exercises using Puppet

Oracle databases are critical to the operation of many organizations. When a disaster occurs, restoring a database to a previous state is often necessary to minimize downtime and prevent data loss. Disaster recovery exercises are important to ensure that databases can be restored quickly and accurately in the event of a disaster.

Puppet is an open source configuration management tool that can be used to automate disaster recovery exercises for Oracle databases. In this example, we will demonstrate how to use Puppet to automate the disaster recovery exercise process for an Oracle database.

Architecture

The architecture used in this example consists of three components: the production database server, the disaster recovery database server, and the Puppet master server.

The production database server is where the Oracle database is hosted and is responsible for serving production workloads. The disaster recovery database server is a standby database that is used to restore the production database in the event of a disaster. The Puppet master server is responsible for managing the Puppet agents running on both the production and disaster recovery servers.

To automate the disaster recovery exercise process, we will use Puppet to do the following:

1. Stop the production database server.
2. Create a backup of the production database.
3. Copy the backup to the disaster recovery database server.
4. Restore the backup on the disaster recovery database server.
5. Test the disaster recovery process.
6. Start the production database server again.

Puppet modules

To perform these tasks, we will create two Puppet modules: one for the production server and one for the disaster recovery server.

The production server module will contain the following Puppet manifests:

- A manifest to stop the production database server
- A manifest to create a backup of the production database
- A manifest to copy the backup to the disaster recovery database server
- A manifest to start the production database server again

The disaster recovery server module will contain the following Puppet manifests:

- A manifest to stop the disaster recovery database server
- A manifest to restore the backup on the disaster recovery database server
- A manifest to start the disaster recovery database server again

Here is an example of the Puppet manifest for stopping the production database server:

Puppet

```
class oracle_production {
  service { 'oracle':
    ensure => stopped,
  }
}
```

This manifest stops the Oracle service running on the production server.

Here is an example of the Puppet manifest for creating a backup of the production database:

Puppet

```
class oracle_production {
  exec { 'backup':
    command => '/usr/local/bin/backup.sh',
  }
}
```

This manifest executes a backup script that creates a backup of the production database.

Here is an example of the Puppet manifest for copying the backup to the disaster recovery server:

Puppet

```
class oracle_production {
  file { '/mnt/backups':
    ensure => directory,
  }

  file { '/mnt/backups/backup.tar.gz':
    source => '/path/to/backup.tar.gz',
  }

  exec { 'copy_backup':
```

```
    command => '/usr/bin/scp /mnt/backups/backup.tar.gz user@disaster-
recovery:/mnt/backups/',
  }
}
```

This manifest creates a directory for backups, copies the backup to that directory, and then uses SCP to copy the backup to the disaster recovery server.

In this example, we have shown how to use Puppet to automate the disaster recovery exercise process for an Oracle database. By using Puppet to automate these tasks, we can ensure that the disaster recovery process is tested regularly and that the database can be restored quickly and accurately in the event of a disaster.

Performance optimization

Optimizing the performance of relational databases is another important activity for a DevOps team. This includes tuning database settings, optimizing queries, and identifying and resolving performance bottlenecks. Some examples of how this can be accomplished are covered in the following sections.

Tuning MySQL settings using Terraform

In this example, we will use Terraform to provision a MySQL instance on AWS and configure some of its settings. We will use the AWS RDS service to provision a MySQL instance, and then use Terraform to configure some of the settings. Specifically, we will set the `innodb_buffer_pool_size` parameter to optimize the use of memory, and the `max_connections` setting to control the maximum number of concurrent connections.

Code example

First, we will define our AWS provider and RDS instance resources in the Terraform configuration file:

SQL

```
provider "aws" {
  region = "us-west-2"
}

resource "aws_db_instance" "mysql" {
  allocated_storage    = 100
  engine               = "mysql"
  engine_version       = "5.7"
  instance_class       = "db.t2.micro"
  name                 = "mydb"
  username             = "admin"
```

```
    password              = "password"
    parameter_group_name = "default.mysql5.7"
}
```

In this code, we are specifying the region for the AWS provider and then defining our RDS instance resource. We are specifying the storage allocation, engine and version, instance class, and other configuration options. We are also specifying a default parameter group that includes some MySQL settings.

Next, we will define a custom parameter group that includes our desired MySQL settings:

SQL

```sql
resource "aws_db_parameter_group" "mysql" {
  name_prefix = "mysql-"
  family      = "mysql5.7"
  parameter {
    name  = "innodb_buffer_pool_size"
    value = "5368709120" # 5 GB
  }
  parameter {
    name  = "max_connections"
    value = "100"
  }
}
```

In this code, we are defining a new parameter group that includes two settings: innodb_buffer_pool_size and max_connections. We are setting innodb_buffer_pool_size to 5 GB and max_connections to 100.

Finally, we will associate our RDS instance with the custom parameter group:

RDS

```
resource "aws_rds_cluster_instance" "mysql" {
  count                 = 1
  identifier            = "mydb-${count.index + 1}"
  db_subnet_group_name  = "${aws_db_subnet_group.mysql.name}"
  cluster_identifier    = "${aws_rds_cluster.mysql.id}"
  instance_class        = "db.t2.micro"
  engine                = "mysql"
  engine_version        = "5.7"
  db_parameter_group_name = "${aws_db_parameter_group.mysql.name}"
}
```

In this code, we are creating an RDS instance and associating it with the custom parameter group we created earlier. We are also specifying the instance class, engine and version, and other configuration options.

This example demonstrates how Terraform can be used to provision and configure a MySQL instance on AWS, including tuning some of its settings for optimal performance. By using IaC, we can easily manage and update our MySQL settings as needed, and ensure that our instance is always configured correctly.

Let's take a closer look at the specific settings we configured in this example:

- `innodb_buffer_pool_size`: This setting controls the size of the `InnoDB` buffer pool, which is where `InnoDB` stores data and indexes. By increasing the buffer pool size, we can improve query performance by reducing the need for disk I/O. The value we set here (5 GB) is just an example; the appropriate value will depend on the amount of available memory and the size of the database.

- `max_connections`: This setting controls the maximum number of concurrent connections to the MySQL instance. By limiting the number of connections, we can avoid overloading the server and ensure that each connection has sufficient resources. Again, the value we set here (`100`) is just an example; the appropriate value will depend on the usage patterns of the application.

It's worth noting that many other MySQL settings can be tuned for optimal performance, depending on the specific workload and hardware configuration. In addition to using Terraform to configure these settings, there are many other tools and techniques available for monitoring and optimizing MySQL performance, including profiling, query optimization, and hardware upgrades.

In summary, we have shown how Terraform can be used to provision and configure a MySQL instance on AWS, including tuning some of its settings for optimal performance. While this example is relatively simple, it demonstrates the power of IaC and the flexibility of cloud-based services such as AWS RDS. By using Terraform to manage our MySQL settings, we can ensure that our database is always configured correctly and optimized for our specific workload.

Optimizing PostgreSQL queries using Ansible

PostgreSQL is a powerful open source RDBMS that is widely used by developers and enterprises for storing and managing large amounts of data. One of the key challenges in working with PostgreSQL is optimizing the performance of SQL queries, which can be complex and time-consuming.

Ansible is an open source automation tool that can be used to manage and automate various IT infrastructure tasks, including provisioning, configuration management, and application deployment. In this example, we will explore how Ansible can be used to optimize PostgreSQL queries.

The architecture used in this example includes a PostgreSQL database server and an Ansible control machine. The control machine is used to manage the configuration and deployment of the PostgreSQL server, as well as to run automated optimization tasks on the database.

The PostgreSQL server is installed on a dedicated server or virtual machine, and the Ansible control machine is installed on a separate machine. The control machine communicates with the PostgreSQL server using SSH, and the Ansible playbook is used to configure and optimize the database.

Example code

The following example code demonstrates how Ansible can be used to optimize PostgreSQL queries using a variety of techniques:

YAML

```yaml
---
- name: Optimize PostgreSQL Queries
  hosts: dbserver
  become: yes
  vars:
    database_name: mydatabase
    database_user: myuser
    database_password: mypassword
  tasks:
    - name: Install PostgreSQL client
      apt:
        name: postgresql-client
        state: present

    - name: Check query execution time
      shell: |
        psql -d {{ database_name }} -U {{ database_user }} -c "EXPLAIN
ANALYZE SELECT * FROM mytable WHERE id = 1234;"
      register: query_output

    - name: Show query plan
      debug:
        var: query_output.stdout_lines

    - name: Create index on id column
      shell: |
        psql -d {{ database_name }} -U {{ database_user }} -c "CREATE
INDEX ON mytable (id);"

    - name: Check query execution time with index
      shell: |
        psql -d {{ database_name }} -U {{ database_user }} -c "EXPLAIN
ANALYZE SELECT * FROM mytable WHERE id = 1234;"
```

```
        register: query_output_index

    - name: Show optimized query plan
      debug:
        var: query_output_index.stdout_lines

    - name: Vacuum analyze the table
      shell: |
          psql -d {{ database_name }} -U {{ database_user }} -c "VACUUM
ANALYZE mytable;"

    - name: Show table statistics
      shell: |
          psql -d {{ database_name }} -U {{ database_user }} -c "SELECT
relname, n_live_tup, n_dead_tup, last_vacuum, last_autovacuum, last_
analyze, last_autoanalyze FROM pg_stat_user_tables WHERE relname =
'mytable';"
        register: table_stats

    - name: Show table statistics output
      debug:
        var: table_stats.stdout_lines
```

In this example, the Ansible playbook includes several tasks that are used to optimize a PostgreSQL query. The first task installs the PostgreSQL client on the Ansible control machine. The second task executes the query and registers the output.

The third task shows the query plan to help identify potential optimization opportunities. The fourth task creates an index on the id column to improve query performance. The fifth task checks the query execution time with the index and registers the output.

The sixth task vacuums and analyzes the table to reclaim space and update statistics. The seventh task shows the table statistics, including the number of live and dead tuples, and the last vacuum and analyze timestamps.

Overall, this Ansible playbook demonstrates how various optimization techniques can be used to improve the performance of PostgreSQL queries. By creating an index on the id column, the query execution time is significantly reduced. Additionally, vacuuming and analyzing the table helps to reclaim space and update statistics, which can further improve query performance.

Utilizing Ansible to optimize PostgreSQL queries can help automate the optimization process and save time and effort for developers and administrators. By implementing various optimization techniques such as index creation, query planning, and table vacuuming, it is possible to improve the performance of SQL queries and ensure that PostgreSQL databases are running at optimal levels.

Identifying Oracle performance issues using Datadog

Oracle database is one of the most widely used relational database management systems in the world, powering many mission-critical applications. However, ensuring that an Oracle database is performing optimally can be a challenging task. In this article, we will explore how Datadog, a popular monitoring and observability platform, can be used to identify performance issues in an Oracle database.

Before we dive into the technical details, let's briefly discuss the architecture used in this example. Datadog is a cloud-based monitoring and observability platform that collects data from various sources, such as servers, databases, and applications, and provides real-time insights and alerts. In this example, we will use Datadog's Oracle integration to collect metrics from an Oracle database. The Oracle integration uses Oracle's **Dynamic Performance Views** (**DPV**) to collect a wide range of performance metrics, such as CPU usage, memory usage, and disk I/O. These metrics are then sent to Datadog, where they can be visualized, analyzed, and alerted on.

Now that we understand the architecture, let's move on to the technical details.

Identifying performance issues

The first step in identifying performance issues is to understand what to look for. Some common performance issues in Oracle databases include slow queries, high CPU usage, high memory usage, and slow I/O. Let's take a closer look at each of these issues and how they can be identified using Datadog.

Slow queries

Slow queries are one of the most common performance issues in databases. They can be caused by a variety of factors, such as suboptimal query plans, missing indexes, or inefficient SQL. Datadog's Oracle integration provides several metrics that can help identify slow queries, such as the following:

- `oracle.sql.query.elapsed_time`: The total elapsed time for executing SQL statements in the database
- `oracle.sql.query.cpu_time`: The CPU time used by SQL statements in the database
- `oracle.sql.query.buffer_gets`: The number of buffers that are required by SQL statements in the database

By monitoring these metrics over time, it is possible to identify queries that are consistently slow or that have a sudden spike in performance.

High CPU usage

High CPU usage can be an indication of inefficient queries, too many active sessions, or insufficient hardware resources. Datadog's Oracle integration provides several metrics that can help identify high CPU usage:

- `oracle.cpu.usage`: The percentage of CPU usage taken up by the Oracle database
- `oracle.process.cpu.usage`: The percentage of CPU usage taken up by Oracle processes

By monitoring these metrics over time, it is possible to identify periods of high CPU usage and correlate them with specific events or queries.

High memory usage

High memory usage can be an indication of inefficient queries, too many open connections, or insufficient memory resources. Datadog's Oracle integration provides several metrics that can help identify high memory usage:

- `oracle.memory.sga.used`: The amount of SGA memory used by the database
- `oracle.memory.pga.used`: The amount of PGA memory used by the database

By monitoring these metrics over time, it is possible to identify periods of high memory usage and correlate them with specific events or queries.

Slow I/O

Slow I/O can be caused by a variety of factors, such as slow disks, high disk usage, or inefficient queries. Datadog's Oracle integration provides several metrics that can help identify slow I/O:

- `oracle.disk.reads`: The number of disk reads performed by the database
- `oracle.disk.writes`: The number of disk writes performed by the database
- `oracle.disk.read.time`: The amount of time spent on disk reads by the database
- `oracle.disk.write.time`: The amount of time spent on disk writes by the database

By monitoring these metrics over time, it is possible to identify periods of slow I/O and correlate them with specific events or queries.

Alerting

Once performance issues have been identified, it is important to be notified immediately when they occur. Datadog provides a powerful alerting system that can be configured to send alerts via email, Slack, PagerDuty, or other channels. Alerts can be triggered based on a variety of conditions:

- A threshold being crossed for a particular metric.
- A metric exhibiting anomalous behavior compared to its historical values
- A metric exhibiting anomalous behavior compared to other related metrics

For example, an alert could be configured to trigger if the `oracle.cpu.usage` metric exceeds a certain threshold for more than 5 minutes. This would allow operations teams to respond quickly and investigate the cause of the high CPU usage.

In this section, we explored how Datadog's Oracle integration can be used to identify performance issues in an Oracle database. By monitoring metrics such as query performance, CPU usage, memory usage, and I/O performance, it is possible to quickly identify and resolve issues that can impact the performance and availability of critical applications. With Datadog's powerful alerting system, operations teams can be notified immediately when performance issues occur, allowing them to respond quickly and minimize the impact on users.

DevSecOps

Finally, ensuring the security and access management of relational databases is an important activity for a DevOps team. This includes setting up authentication and authorization mechanisms, managing database users and permissions, and securing database connections. Let's look at some examples of how this can be accomplished.

Securing MySQL connections using Ansible

Securing MySQL connections is a crucial step in ensuring the confidentiality, integrity, and availability of data stored in MySQL databases. Ansible is a powerful tool that allows for the automation of various IT tasks, including the deployment and configuration of security measures for MySQL connections. In this example, we will explore how to use Ansible to secure MySQL connections by configuring SSL/TLS encryption and mutual authentication.

The architecture for securing MySQL connections using Ansible involves the following components:

- **Ansible control machine**: This is the machine where Ansible is installed and from where the configuration tasks are executed
- **MySQL server**: This is the machine that hosts the MySQL database and where SSL/TLS encryption and mutual authentication will be configured

- **Ansible-managed nodes**: These are the machines that will be managed by Ansible to configure the MySQL server

- **OpenSSL**: OpenSSL is a library that provides cryptographic functions that will be used to generate SSL/TLS certificates and keys

- **Certbot**: Certbot is a tool that automates the process of obtaining and renewing SSL/TLS certificates from Let's Encrypt

The Ansible playbook for securing MySQL connections involves the following tasks:

1. **Installing the necessary packages**: The first task is to install the necessary packages on MySQL Server to support SSL/TLS encryption and mutual authentication. This includes installing OpenSSL and Certbot:

YAML

```yaml
- name: Install packages
  become: true
  apt:
    name:
      - openssl
      - python3-certbot
      - python3-certbot-apache
    state: present
```

2. **Generating SSL/TLS certificates and keys**: The next task is to generate SSL/TLS certificates and keys using OpenSSL. This involves creating a self-signed CA certificate, a server certificate signed by the CA, and a client certificate signed by the CA:

YAML

```yaml
- name: Generate SSL/TLS certificates and keys
  become: true
  openssl_certificate:
    path: /etc/mysql/ssl/ca.pem
    privatekey_path: /etc/mysql/ssl/ca.key
    common_name: "My CA"
    owner: root
    group: root
    mode: 0600
    self_signed: yes
    type: CA
  register: ca_cert
```

```
- openssl_certificate:
    path: /etc/mysql/ssl/server.pem
    privatekey_path: /etc/mysql/ssl/server.key
    common_name: "{{ inventory_hostname }}"
    owner: root
    group: root
    mode: 0600
    ca_path: /etc/mysql/ssl/ca.pem
    ca_privatekey_path: /etc/mysql/ssl/ca.key
    ca_common_name: "My CA"
    type: server
  register: server_cert

- openssl_certificate:
    path: /etc/mysql/ssl/client.pem
    privatekey_path: /etc/mysql/ssl/client.key
    common_name: "MySQL Client"
    owner: root
    group: root
    mode: 0600
    ca_path: /etc/mysql/ssl/ca.pem
    ca_privatekey_path: /etc/mysql/ssl/ca.key
    ca_common_name: "My CA"
    type: client
  register: client_cert
```

3. **Configuring MySQL to use SSL/TLS encryption and mutual authentication**: The next task is to configure MySQL to use SSL/TLS encryption and mutual authentication. This involves adding the SSL/TLS configuration options to the MySQL configuration file and setting the necessary permissions for the SSL/TLS certificates and keys:

YAML

```
- name: Configure MySQL to use SSL/TLS encryption and mutual
  authentication
  become: true
  template:
    src: templates/my.cnf.j2
    dest: /etc/mysql/my.cnf
  notify: restart mysql

- name: Set permissions for SSL/TLS certificates and keys
  become: true
  file:
```

```
        path: "{{ item.path }}"
        owner: root
        group: root
        mode: 0600
      with_items:
        - "{{ ca_cert }}"
        - "{{ server_cert }}"
        - "{{ client_cert }}"
```

4. **Obtaining and renewing SSL/TLS certificates with Certbot**: The final task is to configure Certbot to obtain and renew SSL/TLS certificates from Let's Encrypt. This involves configuring the Certbot Apache plugin and running the `Certbot` command to obtain the initial certificate:

YAML

```
- name: Configure Certbot to obtain and renew SSL/TLS
  certificates
  become: true
  template:
    src: templates/certbot.ini.j2
    dest: /etc/letsencrypt/cli.ini

- name: Obtain SSL/TLS certificate from Let's Encrypt
  become: true
  shell: certbot certonly --non-interactive --agree-tos --email
admin@example.com --apache --domain example.com --domain www.
example.com
```

In this example, we saw how to use Ansible to secure MySQL connections by configuring SSL/TLS encryption and mutual authentication. We also saw how to use OpenSSL to generate SSL/TLS certificates and keys, and how to use Certbot to obtain and renew SSL/TLS certificates from Let's Encrypt. By following these steps, you can ensure that your MySQL connections are secure and that your data is protected from unauthorized access.

Managing PostgreSQL users and permissions using Chef

PostgreSQL is a popular open source RDBMS that is widely used for building applications. Chef is a popular configuration management tool that is used to automate the deployment and management of applications and infrastructure. In this example, we will look at how Chef can be used to manage PostgreSQL users and permissions.

The architecture used in this example consists of three main components:

- **Chef workstation**: This is the machine on which Chef is installed and from where Chef recipes and cookbooks are managed

- **Chef server**: This is the central repository where Chef clients register themselves and from where they retrieve the configuration data
- **PostgreSQL server**: This is the machine on which PostgreSQL is installed and where the database is hosted

In this architecture, Chef is used to manage the configuration of the PostgreSQL server. The Chef workstation is used to author and manage the Chef cookbooks and recipes. The Chef server is used to store the configuration data and the PostgreSQL server is managed by the Chef client.

Managing PostgreSQL users and permissions

PostgreSQL uses a role-based authentication system to manage users and permissions. In this example, we will look at how Chef can be used to manage PostgreSQL users and their permissions.

Step 1 – installing PostgreSQL on the server

Before we can manage PostgreSQL users and permissions, we need to ensure that PostgreSQL is installed on the server. This can be done using Chef by writing a recipe that installs PostgreSQL on the server:

Chef

```
# Recipe to install PostgreSQL on the server
#
package 'postgresql'
```

Step 2 – creating a PostgreSQL user

To create a PostgreSQL user, we can use the `psql` command-line tool. In Chef, we can execute shell commands using the `execute` resource. The following code snippet shows how to create a PostgreSQL user using Chef:

Chef

```
# Recipe to create a PostgreSQL user
#
execute 'create_postgres_user' do
  user 'postgres'
  command "psql -c \"CREATE USER #{node['postgresql']['user']} WITH
PASSWORD #{node['postgresql']['password']};\""
end
```

In this code snippet, we are executing the `psql` command to create a PostgreSQL user. The `user` parameter is set to `postgres`, which is the default user for PostgreSQL. The `command` parameter is set to the SQL statement that creates the user. The `node['postgresql']['user']` and `node['postgresql']['password']` attributes are used to set the username and password for the PostgreSQL user.

Step 3 – granting permissions to the user

Once the user has been created, we can grant them permissions using the GRANT command. In Chef, we can use the `execute` resource to execute the GRANT command:

Chef

```
# Recipe to grant permissions to a PostgreSQL user
#
execute 'grant_postgres_user_permissions' do
  user 'postgres'
  command "psql -c \"GRANT ALL PRIVILEGES ON DATABASE
#{node['postgresql']['database']} TO #{node['postgresql']['user']};\""
end
```

In this code snippet, we are executing the `psql` command to grant permissions to the PostgreSQL user. The `user` parameter is set to `postgres`, which is the default user for PostgreSQL. The `command` parameter is set to the SQL statement that grants permissions to the user. The `node['postgresql']` `['database']` and `node['postgresql']['user']` attributes are used to set the name of the database and the name of the user, respectively.

Step 4 – revoking permissions from the user

If we want to revoke permissions from a PostgreSQL user, we can use the REVOKE command. In Chef, we can use the `execute` resource to execute the REVOKE command:

Chef

```
# Recipe to revoke permissions from a PostgreSQL user
#
execute 'revoke_postgres_user_permissions' do
  user 'postgres'
  command "psql -c \"REVOKE ALL PRIVILEGES ON DATABASE
#{node['postgresql']['database']} FROM #{node['postgresql']
['user']};\""
end
```

In this code snippet, we are executing the `psql` command to revoke permissions from the PostgreSQL user. The `user` parameter is set to `postgres`, which is the default user for PostgreSQL. The `command` parameter is set to the SQL statement that revokes permissions from the user. The `node['postgresql']['database']` and `node['postgresql']['user']` attributes are used to set the name of the database and the name of the user, respectively.

Step 5 – deleting the user

To delete a PostgreSQL user, we can use the DROP ROLE command. In Chef, we can use the execute resource to execute the DROP ROLE command:

Chef

```
# Recipe to delete a PostgreSQL user
#
execute 'delete_postgres_user' do
  user 'postgres'
  command "psql -c \"DROP ROLE IF EXISTS #{node['postgresql']
['user']};\""
end
```

In this code snippet, we are executing the psql command to delete the PostgreSQL user. The user parameter is set to postgres, which is the default user for PostgreSQL. The command parameter is set to the SQL statement that deletes the user. The node['postgresql']['user'] attribute is used to set the name of the user.

In this example, we looked at how Chef can be used to manage PostgreSQL users and their permissions. We saw how to create a PostgreSQL user, grant permissions to the user, revoke permissions from the user, and delete the user. Chef provides a powerful and flexible way to manage PostgreSQL users and permissions, and this example demonstrates how this can be achieved using Chef recipes and resources.

Securing Oracle databases using Puppet

Securing Oracle databases is critical for organizations as databases contain sensitive information and are often targeted by attackers. Puppet is a popular configuration management tool that can be used to automate the process of securing Oracle databases. In this example, we will discuss the architecture used to secure Oracle databases using Puppet and provide sample code to demonstrate the process.

The architecture that's used to secure Oracle databases using Puppet involves several components, including Puppet itself, the Oracle database, and the server hosting the database. The following is a high-level overview of the architecture:

- **Puppet master:** The Puppet master is the central server that manages and controls the configuration of the Oracle database servers. It contains the Puppet code that defines the desired state of the Oracle database servers.

- **Puppet agent:** The Puppet agent is installed on the Oracle database servers and communicates with the Puppet master to retrieve configuration data and apply it to the servers.

- **Oracle database:** The Oracle database is the system being secured. It runs on one or more servers and stores data in a structured format.

- **Server**: The server is the physical or virtual machine that hosts the Oracle database. It runs the operating system and provides the resources required by the database.

Now, let's take a look at how we can use Puppet to secure an Oracle database.

Step 1 – installing the Puppet agent

The first step is to install the Puppet agent on the Oracle database server. This can be done by following the instructions on the Puppet website. Once the agent has been installed, it will automatically communicate with the Puppet master to retrieve configuration data.

Step 2 – creating the Puppet manifest

The next step is to create a Puppet manifest that defines the desired state of the Oracle database server. The manifest is written in the Puppet language, which is a declarative language that allows you to define the desired state of a system.

Here's an example of a Puppet manifest that installs the latest security patches for Oracle:

Puppet

```
class oracle_security {
  package { 'oracle_security_patches':
    ensure => latest,
    provider => 'yum',
  }
}
```

This manifest defines a class called `oracle_security` that installs the latest security patches for Oracle using the `yum` package provider.

Step 3 – applying the Puppet manifest

Once the manifest has been created, it needs to be applied to the Oracle database server using the Puppet agent. This can be done by running the following command on the server:

```
sudo puppet agent -t
```

This command tells the Puppet agent to retrieve the latest configuration data from the Puppet master and apply it to the server.

Step 4 – verifying the configuration

Once the manifest has been applied, it's important to verify that the configuration has been applied correctly. This can be done by checking the logs generated by Puppet and verifying that the desired state of the system has been achieved.

Here's an example of a Puppet log that shows that the security patches were successfully installed:

Bash

```
Info: Applying configuration version '1474461465'
Notice: /Stage[main]/Oracle_security/Package[oracle_security_patches]/
ensure: ensure changed '1.0.0-1' to '1.1.0-1'
```

This log shows that Puppet applied the `oracle_security_patches` package and updated it from version `1.0.0-1` to `1.1.0-1`.

In this example, we discussed how to use Puppet to secure Oracle databases. We looked at the architecture that's used and provided sample code to demonstrate the process. By using Puppet to automate the process of securing Oracle databases, organizations can ensure that their databases are always up- to- date with the latest security patches and configuration settings. This helps reduce the risk of data breaches and other security incidents.

Summary

In this chapter, we embarked on a journey through the complex yet rewarding world of integrating RDBMS with DevOps. As we navigated the intricacies of each section, we gathered invaluable insights that can be directly applied in real-world scenarios.

First, we dived into provisioning and configuration management, grasping how automation can simplify these otherwise tedious tasks. We came to understand that IaC is not just a trend, but a crucial strategy for rapidly setting up and modifying environments.

Next, we explored monitoring and alerting, becoming familiar with the tools and best practices that help with establishing real-time database monitoring and setting up automated alerts. The importance of these proactive steps in pre-empting system issues cannot be overstated.

We then turned our attention to backup and disaster recovery. The importance of integrating solid backup and recovery plans into our DevOps pipeline was highlighted, reinforcing the notion that this is not just a contingency but a business imperative.

Our learning curve continued upward as we examined performance optimization. We found out how applying these methods can significantly improve system performance while simultaneously reducing operational costs.

Finally, this chapter culminated in an enlightening discussion on DevSecOps, which taught us that security is not an afterthought but an integral part of the DevOps framework.

So, what can we do with these insights? Armed with this newfound knowledge, we are now in a position to enhance the efficiency, security, and performance of our systems. By putting what we've learned into practice, we're not just adapting to the current landscape; we're staying ahead of it, granting ourselves and our organizations a competitive advantage.

In the next chapter, we will navigate the intricate yet fascinating landscape of integrating non-RDBMSs (NoSQL) with DevOps.

6

Non-Relational DMSs with DevOps

In this chapter, we will navigate the intricate yet fascinating landscape of integrating non-relational database management systems (also known as NoSQL) with DevOps. We will begin by examining the pivotal role that data modeling plays in NoSQL databases, shedding light on how it differs from its counterpart in relational databases.

Then, we will explore schema management. As NoSQL databases offer flexible schemas, we'll delve into how this flexibility can be both an asset and a challenge when managed within a DevOps framework. From there, we'll move on to the crucial topic of deployment automation, where we will discuss how automated tools and workflows can greatly streamline the deployment process.

Performance tuning will also command our attention. As the scale of data grows exponentially, we'll learn how to fine-tune our NoSQL databases to meet the demanding performance criteria that modern applications require. Subsequently, data consistency in a distributed, NoSQL environment will come under the lens, and we'll learn strategies to maintain it effectively.

Security, an ever-pressing concern, will not be left out of our discussion. We'll scrutinize the best practices and mechanisms that can safeguard our data and infrastructure, aligning them seamlessly with DevOps protocols.

Lastly, but just as importantly, we'll look at anti-patterns, or what not to do when combining NoSQL and DevOps. This section will serve as a cautionary tale, guiding us away from common pitfalls and steering us toward successful implementation.

Throughout this chapter, you will gain actionable insights and real-world applications of each key milestone. The aim is not just to inform but also to equip you with practical knowledge that you can readily apply to your own systems. Let's embark on this educational journey to discover how non-relational Database Managements Systems (DMSs) and DevOps can work in harmony to create robust, scalable, and efficient systems.

In this chapter, we will cover the following main topics:

- Activities and challenges

- Data modeling

- Schema management

- Deployment automation

- Performance tuning

- Data consistency

- Security

- Anti-patterns (what not to do…)

Activities and challenges

As part of the DevOps team, some of the main activities and challenges when working with non-relational databases include data modeling, schema management, and deployment automation, as detailed here, along with other examples:

- **Data modeling**: When working with non-relational databases, data modeling requires a different approach compared to traditional relational databases. One example of this is choosing the right data structure for the type of data being stored. For instance, if storing hierarchical data, a document-based database such as MongoDB may be more suitable than a relational database. In a relational database, this could be handled using a recursive query, but this would be less efficient and more complicated.

- **Schema management**: Unlike relational databases, non-relational databases don't require a fixed schema, which can make schema management more challenging. One example of this is handling schema migrations, which can be trickier to manage when there isn't a predefined schema to work with. In a relational database, schema migrations can be handled through SQL scripts that update the schema, but in a non-relational database, you may be required to write custom code or use third-party tools.

- **Deployment automation**: Automating the deployment of non-relational databases can be more complex than for relational databases. One example of this is configuring the database for high availability and disaster recovery. In a relational database, this can be achieved using replication, but in a non-relational database, it may require setting up a distributed system or using a cloud-based service.

- **Performance tuning**: Non-relational databases often require specific performance tuning, depending on the use case. For example, in a document-based database, indexes need to be optimized based on the data access patterns. In contrast, a relational database typically relies on query optimization and table design to achieve optimal performance.

- **Data consistency**: Unlike relational databases, non-relational databases may not enforce strict data consistency across multiple nodes in a distributed system. For example, in a document-based database, data may be replicated asynchronously, which could result in data inconsistencies. To address this challenge, non-relational databases often provide mechanisms to maintain eventual consistency, such as conflict resolution algorithms or read-after-write consistency.

- **Security**: Non-relational databases may have different security concerns than relational databases, such as preventing unauthorized access to specific documents or collections. For example, in a graph database, access control may need to be implemented at the node or edge level. In contrast, a relational database typically uses role-based access control at the database or table level.

Let's dive deeper into each of these points.

Data modeling

Let's review together three unique challenges around data modeling that are specific to non-relational databases.

Denormalization

In non-relational databases, it's common to use denormalized data models where data is duplicated across multiple documents or collections. This is done to improve query performance and avoid expensive joins. In contrast, relational databases emphasize normalization, where data is organized into separate tables to avoid duplication and maintain data integrity.

Denormalization can introduce unique challenges around data consistency and update anomalies. When data is denormalized, it can lead to redundant or inconsistent data, which can be difficult to manage. For example, if a customer's address is stored in multiple documents, updating the address in one document may not propagate to all the other documents, leading to inconsistent data.

Here's an example of a denormalized data model in MongoDB:

MongoDB

```
{
  _id: ObjectId("616246f4cc84d137c857ff03"),
  title: "The Hitchhiker's Guide to the Galaxy",
  author: "Douglas Adams",
  genres: ["Science Fiction", "Comedy"],
  reviews: [
    { user: "Alice", rating: 4 },
    { user: "Bob", rating: 5 },
```

```
        { user: "Charlie", rating: 3 }
    ]
}
```

In this example, the book's title and author are duplicated across multiple documents, and the book's genres and reviews are stored as arrays within the same document. This makes it easier to retrieve all the relevant information about a book in a single query, but it also introduces the risk of inconsistent data if one of the reviews is updated or deleted.

Nested and dynamic data

Non-relational databases are designed to handle nested and dynamic data structures, such as JSON or XML documents. This makes it easier to store and retrieve complex data structures, but it also introduces unique challenges around indexing and querying. In contrast, relational databases have fixed column definitions, which makes it more difficult to store and query nested or dynamic data.

Nested data structures are common in non-relational databases, where data is stored as a hierarchical tree-like structure. Here's an example of a nested document in MongoDB:

MongoDB

```
{
  _id: ObjectId("6162486dcc84d137c857ff06"),
  name: {
    first: "John",
    last: "Doe"
  },
  email: "johndoe@example.com",
  address: {
    street: "123 Main St",
    city: "Anytown",
    state: "CA",
    zip: "12345"
  }
}
```

In this example, the name and address fields are nested within the document, which makes it easier to query and update data as a single entity. However, querying nested data can be challenging, as it requires traversing the entire tree to find the desired data. To address this, non-relational databases often use indexes to speed up queries on nested data.

Dynamic data structures are also common in non-relational databases, where data can have varying types and properties. For example, a document-based database such as MongoDB can store documents with different structures in the same collection. Here's an example of a dynamic document in MongoDB:

MongoDB

```
{
  _id: ObjectId("61624c0fcc84d137c857ff0a"),
  name: "Alice",
  age: 30,
  email: "alice@example.com",
  phone: "+1 555-1234",
  address: {
    street: "456 Elm St",
    city: "Anycity",
    state: "NY"
  }
}
```

In this example, the `address` field is optional, and the document can contain any combination of the `name`, `age`, `email`, `phone`, and `address` fields. This flexibility can make it easier to store and retrieve data, but it also introduces challenges around data validation and indexing.

Data denormalization

Non-relational databases often use data denormalization to avoid expensive joins and improve query performance. Data denormalization involves duplicating data across multiple documents or collections so that related data can be retrieved together, without having to perform a join operation.

However, denormalization can introduce unique challenges around data consistency and update anomalies.

Here's an example of data denormalization in a document-based database:

MongoDB

```
{
  _id: ObjectId("61624919cc84d137c857ff08"),
  title: "The Catcher in the Rye",
  author: "J.D. Salinger",
  genre: "Fiction",
  year: 1951,
  tags: ["coming of age", "isolation", "alienation"],
  similar_books: [
```

```
    { title: "The Bell Jar", author: "Sylvia Plath" },
    { title: "To Kill a Mockingbird", author: "Harper Lee" },
    { title: "The Great Gatsby", author: "F. Scott Fitzgerald" }
  ]
}
```

In this example, the `similar_books` field is denormalized, with the title and author of related books stored within the same document. This makes it easier to retrieve related data without performing a separate join operation, but it also introduces the risk of inconsistent data if one of the related books is updated or deleted.

To address these challenges, non-relational databases offer several features and techniques, such as schemaless design, document validation, indexing, and sharding.

Schemaless design means that non-relational databases do not require a predefined schema, which makes it easier to store and retrieve data with varying structures. Document validation can be used to ensure that data conforms to a specific schema, preventing inconsistencies and improving data quality.

Indexing can be used to speed up queries on nested and dynamic data, by creating indexes on specific fields or sub-fields. Sharding can be used to scale non-relational databases horizontally across multiple nodes, improving performance and availability.

In summary, non-relational databases offer unique advantages and challenges around data modeling, compared to relational databases. While non-relational databases offer more flexibility and scalability, they also require a different approach to data modeling and management. DevOps teams working with non-relational databases need to be familiar with these unique challenges and techniques, ensuring that their infrastructure is stable and scalable.

Schema management

Let's review together three unique challenges around schema management that are specific to non-relational databases.

Schemaless data modeling

One of the main characteristics of non-relational databases is that they offer a schemaless data modeling approach. This means that they don't enforce a fixed schema on the data and allow for flexible and dynamic data structures. While this can provide many benefits, such as faster iteration and easier scalability, it can also present some challenges in schema management.

In a schemaless database, there may not be a standard way to define or enforce the structure of data. This can make it difficult to ensure data consistency and quality across different documents. Additionally, it can be challenging to maintain compatibility and manage schema changes over time.

For example, in a document-oriented database such as Couchbase, data can be stored in JSON documents with any arbitrary structure. Here's an example of a JSON document:

JSON

```json
{
  "type": "person",
  "name": "Alice",
  "age": 25,
  "address": {
    "street": "123 Main St",
    "city": "Anytown",
    "state": "NY",
    "zip": "12345"
  },
  "interests": ["reading", "traveling", "hiking"]
}
```

In this example, the document has a top-level field called `type` that denotes the type of document, as well as a nested `address` field that represents a complex structure.

To address the challenges of schemaless data modeling, non-relational databases provide features such as schema validation, which allows developers to define and enforce the structure of data. This can help ensure data consistency and quality across different documents.

Dynamic schema evolution

Non-relational databases also often allow for dynamic schema evolution, which means that a schema can change over time to adapt to new requirements or data models. This can present some challenges in schema management, especially if the schema changes are not carefully planned and managed.

In a dynamically evolving schema, the structure of the data can change frequently, which can make it challenging to maintain backward and forward compatibility. Additionally, it can be difficult to ensure that all documents conform to the latest schema version.

For example, in a graph database such as Neo4j, the structure of data can change over time as new nodes and relationships are added. Here's an example of schema evolution in Neo4j:

Neo4j

```
// Create an initial schema for a social network
CREATE (u:User {name: 'Alice'})
CREATE (p:Post {title: 'Hello World'})
```

```
CREATE (u)-[:POSTED]->(p)

// Add a new field to the User node
ALTER (u:User) SET u.email = 'alice@example.com'

// Add a new label to the Post node
MATCH (p:Post)
SET p:Article
REMOVE p:Post
```

In this example, an initial schema is created for a social network, with a `User` node and a `Post` node connected by a `POSTED` relationship. The `User` node does not have an `email` field.

To evolve the schema, a new `email` field is added to the `User` node, using the `ALTER` command. Additionally, a new label called `Article` is added to the `Post` node, and the `Post` label is removed using the `CREATE LABEL` and `REMOVE` commands.

To address the challenges of dynamic schema evolution, non-relational databases provide features such as versioning and migration tools. These tools can help manage changes to the schema and ensure that all documents conform to the latest schema version.

Consistency and concurrency control

Another challenge in non-relational schema management is ensuring consistency and concurrency control in a distributed environment. Non-relational databases often use distributed architectures to achieve scalability and availability, which can create challenges in ensuring that data is consistent across different nodes.

In a distributed database environment, different nodes may have different versions of the same data, which can lead to conflicts and inconsistency. Additionally, concurrency control can be challenging in a distributed environment, as multiple nodes can access and update the same data simultaneously.

For example, in a key-value store such as Redis, concurrency control can be achieved through the use of optimistic locking. Here's an example of optimistic locking in Redis:

JavaScript

```javascript
// Get the current value of the counter
var counter = await redis.get('counter');

// Increment the counter using optimistic locking
while (true) {
  var tx = redis.multi();
```

```
  tx.watch('counter');
  var current = await tx.get('counter');
  var next = parseInt(current) + 1;
  tx.multi();
  tx.set('counter', next);
  var result = await tx.exec();
  if (result !== null) {
    counter = next;
    break;
  }
}

console.log('Counter is now', counter);
```

In this example, the value of a counter is retrieved from Redis using the `get` method. The counter is then incremented using optimistic locking, which involves using the `watch` method to monitor the `counter` key for changes. If the `counter` key is modified by another process, the optimistic locking loop retries the transaction.

To address the challenges of consistency and concurrency control, non-relational databases provide features such as distributed locking, versioning, and conflict resolution. These features can help ensure that data is consistent and up to date across different nodes in a distributed environment.

Non-relational databases present unique challenges around schema management compared to relational databases. These challenges include schemaless data modeling, dynamic schema evolution, and consistency and concurrency control in a distributed environment. To address these challenges, non-relational databases provide features such as schema validation, versioning, migration tools, and distributed locking. DevOps teams working with non-relational databases need to be familiar with these unique challenges and techniques, ensuring that their infrastructure is stable and scalable.

Deployment automation

Deployment automation is an important aspect of DevOps for both relational and non-relational databases, but there are some unique challenges around deployment automation for non-relational databases. Here are three challenges specific to non-relational databases, along with explanations and code snippets.

Deployment of multiple database engines

Non-relational databases often have different database engines, each with its own set of deployment and management requirements. For example, a NoSQL database such as Cassandra may have different deployment requirements than a document-oriented database such as MongoDB.

Deploying and managing multiple database engines can be challenging, as it requires specialized knowledge and expertise for each engine. Additionally, it can be difficult to maintain consistency across different database engines, especially if they have different APIs and query languages.

To address this challenge, DevOps teams may use configuration management tools such as Ansible or Chef to automate the deployment and management of different database engines. These tools allow for the automation of tasks such as installing software, configuring servers, and deploying databases.

Here's an example of deploying Cassandra using Ansible:

YAML

```yaml
- hosts: cassandra
  become: true
  tasks:
    - name: Add Cassandra repo to APT
      apt_repository:
        repo: "deb http://www.apache.org/dist/cassandra/debian 40x
main"
        keyserver: pgp.mit.edu
        state: present
    - name: Install Cassandra
      apt:
        name: cassandra
        state: latest
    - name: Start Cassandra service
      service:
        name: cassandra
        state: started
```

In this example, Ansible is used to add the Cassandra repository to the APT package manager, install the Cassandra package, and start the Cassandra service.

Backup and disaster recovery

Non-relational databases often require specialized backup and disaster recovery strategies, due to the different data structures and distributed architectures used by these databases. For example, a key-value store, such as Redis, may use a distributed architecture that requires different backup and recovery strategies than a document-oriented database, such as Couchbase.

Backing up and restoring data in a non-relational database can be complex, as it often involves managing data across multiple nodes and ensuring that it is consistent and up to date. Additionally, disaster recovery can be challenging in a distributed environment, as different nodes may have different versions of the same data.

To address this challenge, DevOps teams may use specialized backup and recovery tools for non-relational databases, such as the AWS Backup service for Amazon DynamoDB. These tools allow for the automated backup and recovery of data across different nodes, and they can help ensure data consistency and up-to-date backups.

Here's an example of backing up and restoring data in DynamoDB using the AWS Backup service:

AWS CLI

```
// Create a backup of the DynamoDB table
aws dynamodb create-backup --table-name MyTable --backup-name MyBackup

// Restore the backup to a new DynamoDB table
aws dynamodb restore-table-from-backup --target-table-
name MyRestoredTable --backup-arn arn:aws:dynamodb:us-west-
2:123456789012:backup:MyBackup
```

In this example, the AWS CLI is used to create a backup of a DynamoDB table using the `create-backup` command. The backup is then restored to a new DynamoDB table, using the `restore-table-from-backup` command.

Capacity planning and scaling

Non-relational databases often require specialized capacity planning and scaling strategies, due to the distributed architecture used by these databases. Scaling a non-relational database can be complex, as it often involves adding or removing nodes from a distributed cluster, as well as managing data across different nodes.

Capacity planning and scaling in a non-relational database can also be challenging, as it can be difficult to predict how much storage and processing power will be required as the database grows. Additionally, scaling a non-relational database can involve different strategies than scaling a relational database, as non-relational databases often use horizontal scaling, where more nodes are added to a cluster to increase capacity.

To address this challenge, DevOps teams can use specialized tools for capacity planning and scaling in non-relational databases, such as the Kubernetes autoscaler for scaling clusters. These tools allow for the automated scaling of clusters based on metrics such as CPU usage and network traffic, and they can help ensure that the database infrastructure is always right-sized.

Here's an example of scaling a cluster in Cassandra using the Kubernetes autoscaler:

YAML

```
apiVersion: autoscaling/v2beta2
kind: HorizontalPodAutoscaler
```

```
metadata:
  name: cassandra
spec:
  scaleTargetRef:
    apiVersion: apps/v1
    kind: StatefulSet
    name: cassandra
  minReplicas: 3
  maxReplicas: 10
  metrics:
  - type: Resource
    resource:
      name: cpu
      target:
        type: Utilization
        averageUtilization: 70
```

In this example, the Kubernetes autoscaler is used to scale a Cassandra cluster based on CPU usage. The `minReplicas` and `maxReplicas` fields define the minimum and maximum number of nodes in the cluster, respectively, and the `metrics` field defines the metric used to scale the cluster (in this case, CPU utilization).

To summarize, deployment automation is an important aspect of DevOps for both relational and non-relational databases, but there are some unique challenges around deployment automation for non-relational databases. These challenges include deploying multiple database engines, backup and disaster recovery, and capacity planning and scaling. To address these challenges, DevOps teams can use configuration management tools, specialized backup and recovery tools, and capacity planning and scaling tools designed for non-relational databases.

Performance tuning

Performance tuning is a critical aspect of DevOps for both relational and non-relational databases. However, there are some unique challenges around performance tuning for non-relational databases. Here are three challenges specific to non-relational databases, along with explanations and code snippets.

Data modeling for performance

One of the unique challenges of performance tuning for non-relational databases is data modeling for performance. Unlike relational databases, non-relational databases often have flexible schema models that can be optimized for different types of queries and access patterns. However, this also means that performance tuning may require specialized knowledge of the data model and how it maps to the underlying storage and retrieval mechanisms.

To address this challenge, DevOps teams may use specialized tools and techniques for data modeling and query optimization in non-relational databases. For example, graph databases such as Neo4j can use indexing and caching techniques to optimize queries, while key-value stores such as Redis can use data sharding and replication techniques to optimize storage and retrieval.

Here's an example of data modeling for performance in a graph database such as Neo4j:

Neo4j

```
// Create an index on the Person node's name property
CREATE INDEX ON :Person(name)

// Query for all people with the name "Alice"
MATCH (p:Person {name: 'Alice'})
RETURN p
```

In this example, an index is created on the `name` property of the `Person` node in Neo4j. This allows for faster querying of people with the name `Alice` by using the index to find matching nodes.

Distributed query optimization

Non-relational databases often use distributed architectures to achieve scalability and availability. However, this can present unique challenges around query optimization, as queries may need to be optimized across multiple nodes in the cluster.

Distributed query optimization in non-relational databases requires specialized knowledge of the database architecture and how queries are executed across different nodes. Additionally, it can be challenging to maintain consistency and performance across different nodes in the cluster, especially if there are network latency or data transfer issues.

To address this challenge, DevOps teams can use specialized tools and techniques for distributed query optimization in non-relational databases. For example, distributed databases such as Cassandra can use techniques, such as partitioning and clustering, to optimize queries across multiple nodes in the cluster.

Here's an example of distributed query optimization in Cassandra:

CQL

```
// Create a table with a partition key and clustering columns
CREATE TABLE users (
  id UUID PRIMARY KEY,
  name TEXT,
  email TEXT,
  created_at TIMESTAMP
```

```
) WITH CLUSTERING ORDER BY (created_at DESC)

// Query for all users with a specific email address
SELECT * FROM users WHERE email = 'example@example.com'
```

In this example, a table is created in Cassandra with a partition key and clustering columns. This allows for efficient querying of data across multiple nodes in the cluster. The SELECT statement queries for all users with a specific email address by using the email column as the partition key.

Network latency and data transfer

Non-relational databases often use distributed architectures that require data to be transferred across the network between different nodes in the cluster. This can create unique challenges around performance tuning, as network latency and data transfer speeds can impact query performance and overall database throughput.

To address this challenge, DevOps teams can use specialized tools and techniques to optimize network latency and data transfer in non-relational databases. For example, database caching and load balancing can be used to reduce the amount of data transferred over a network and improve query performance.

Here's an example of database caching in Redis:

JavaScript

```javascript
// Get a value from the cache
var cachedValue = await redis.get('key');

// If the value is not in the cache, fetch it from the database and
store it in the cache
if (cachedValue === null) {
  var result = await db.query('SELECT * FROM my_table WHERE id = ?',
[id]);
  if (result.length > 0) {
    cachedValue = result[0];
    await redis.set('key', JSON.stringify(cachedValue), 'EX', 600);
  }
}

console.log('Result is', cachedValue);
```

In this example, Redis is used as a caching layer to store the result of a database query. The get method is used to retrieve the value from the cache. If the value is not in the cache, the query is executed against the database, and the result is stored in Redis using the set method, with a TTL of 10 minutes (600 seconds). The result is then returned to the calling function.

By using a cache layer such as Redis, the database can be queried less frequently, reducing the amount of data transferred over the network and improving query performance.

In summary, performance tuning is an important aspect of DevOps for both relational and non-relational databases, but there are some unique challenges around performance tuning for non-relational databases. These challenges include data modeling for performance, distributed query optimization, and network latency and data transfer. To address these challenges, DevOps teams can use specialized tools and techniques for data modeling, query optimization, and network optimization in non-relational databases.

Data consistency

Data consistency is a critical aspect of any database, both relational and non-relational. However, non-relational databases present some unique challenges around data consistency. Here are three challenges specific to non-relational databases, along with explanations and code snippets.

Lack of transactions

Unlike relational databases, non-relational databases cannot support transactions, or – to be more precise – they can only support limited forms of transactions. Transactions are critical to ensure data consistency, as they allow for multiple database operations to be treated as a single unit of work. Without transactions, data consistency can be compromised if one operation fails and others are left incomplete.

To address this challenge, DevOps teams may need to implement custom transaction-like mechanisms in non-relational databases, such as conditional updates or two-phase commit protocols. These mechanisms can help ensure that data modifications are atomic and consistent.

Here's an example of a conditional update in MongoDB:

MongoDB

```
// Update the user's email address if the current email address
matches the expected value
db.users.update(
  { _id: '123' },
  { $set: { email: 'newemail@example.com' } },
  { multi: false, upsert: false, writeConcern: { w: 'majority' } },
  function(err, result) {
    if (err) {
      console.log(err);
    } else if (result.n === 0) {
      console.log('User not found');
    } else if (result.nModified === 0) {
      console.log('Update failed - email address did not match
expected value');
```

```
    } else {
      console.log('Update successful');
    }
  }
);
```

In this example, an update is performed on a user's email address in MongoDB using the `update` method. The `multi` option is set to `false` to ensure that only one document is updated, and the `upsert` option is set to `false` to prevent the creation of new documents. The `writeConcern` option is used to ensure that the write operation is durable and consistent.

Eventual consistency

Non-relational databases often use eventual consistency models, where data modifications cannot be immediately reflected in all replicas of the data. This can create challenges around data consistency, as queries may return stale or outdated data if they are performed on replicas that have not yet received the latest modifications.

To address this challenge, DevOps teams may need to implement custom techniques to manage eventual consistency in non-relational databases, such as conflict resolution or quorum-based consistency. These techniques can help ensure that data modifications are propagated and consistent across all replicas.

Here's an example of quorum-based consistency in Cassandra:

CQL

```
// Create a Cassandra table with a quorum-based consistency level
CREATE TABLE users (
  id UUID PRIMARY KEY,
  name TEXT,
  email TEXT,
  created_at TIMESTAMP
) WITH read_repair_chance = 0.2 AND dclocal_read_repair_chance = 0.1
AND CL = QUORUM

// Query for all users with a specific email address using a quorum-
based consistency level
SELECT * FROM users WHERE email = 'example@example.com' AND CL =
QUORUM
```

In this example, a Cassandra table is created with a quorum-based consistency level, which ensures that at least a majority of replicas must respond to a read or write operation before it is considered successful. The `read_repair_chance` and `dclocal_read_repair_chance` options are used to repair inconsistencies in the database, and the `CL` option is set to QUORUM to ensure quorum-based consistency.

Data sharding

Non-relational databases often use data-sharding techniques to distribute data across multiple nodes in a cluster. However, data sharding can create challenges around data consistency, as queries may need to be executed across multiple shards, and ensuring consistency across shards can be difficult.

To address this challenge, DevOps teams may need to implement custom techniques to manage data sharding in non-relational databases, such as consistent hashing or virtual nodes. These techniques can help ensure that data is distributed evenly across shards and that queries are executed efficiently and consistently.

Here's an example of consistent hashing in Riak:

Riak

```
// Create a Riak bucket with consistent hashing enabled
curl -XPUT http://localhost:8098/buckets/my_bucket/props \
  -H 'Content-Type: application/json' \
  -d '{ "props": { "consistent_hashing": true } }'

// Store a value in the Riak bucket with a key
curl -XPUT http://localhost:8098/buckets/my_bucket/keys/my_key \
  -H 'Content-Type: application/json' \
  -d '{ "value": "my_value" }'

// Retrieve the value from the Riak bucket using consistent hashing
curl -XGET http://localhost:8098/buckets/my_bucket/keys/my_key \
  -H 'Content-Type: application/json' \
  -H 'X-Riak-Consistent-Hashing: true'
```

In this example, a Riak bucket is created with consistent hashing enabled, which ensures that data is distributed evenly across shards. A value is stored in the bucket with a key, and the value is retrieved using consistent hashing by setting the X-Riak-Consistent-Hashing header to true.

Data consistency is critical for any database, but there are some unique challenges around data consistency for non-relational databases. These challenges include a lack of transactions, eventual consistency, and data sharding. To address these challenges, DevOps teams may need to implement custom techniques to manage data consistency in non-relational databases, such as conditional updates, conflict resolution, and consistent hashing.

Security

Security is a critical aspect of any database, both relational and non-relational. However, non-relational databases present some unique challenges around security. Here are three challenges specific to non-relational databases, along with explanations and code snippets.

Limited access control

Non-relational databases may not support the same level of access control as relational databases. This can create challenges around securing sensitive data and preventing unauthorized access.

To address this challenge, DevOps teams may need to implement custom access control mechanisms in non-relational databases, such as role-based access control or custom authentication mechanisms. These mechanisms can help ensure that data is accessed only by authorized users and that sensitive data is protected.

Here's an example of role-based access control in MongoDB:

MongoDB

```
// Create a user with a specific role in MongoDB
db.createUser({
  user: 'myuser',
  pwd: 'mypassword',
  roles: [ { role: 'readWrite', db: 'mydatabase' } ]
});

// Authenticate with MongoDB using the created user
db.auth('myuser', 'mypassword');

// Query for data in MongoDB using the authenticated user
db.my_collection.find({});
```

In this example, a user is created in MongoDB with the `readWrite` role for a specific database. The user is then authenticated with the database using the created credentials, and data is queried using the authenticated user.

Distributed denial of service attacks

Non-relational databases often use distributed architectures that may be vulnerable to **distributed denial of service (DDoS)** attacks. DDoS attacks can overwhelm a database with traffic, rendering it unavailable and compromising data security.

To address this challenge, DevOps teams may need to implement custom DDoS prevention mechanisms in non-relational databases, such as load balancing or rate limiting. These mechanisms can help ensure that a database is protected from excessive traffic and that data security is maintained.

Here's an example of rate limiting in Redis:

Lua

```lua
// Configure Redis to use a maximum memory limit of 1GB
maxmemory 1gb

// Enable Redis rate limiting for incoming requests
redis.config set lua-time-limit 1000
redis.config set maxmemory-samples 10
redis.eval("local c=redis.call('incr',KEYS[1]);if tonumber(c)==1
then redis.call('expire',KEYS[1],ARGV[1]) end;return c",{1,"rate_
limiter"},1)
```

In this example, Redis is configured to use a maximum memory limit of 1 GB, which helps protect against DDoS attacks that attempt to overload a database with excessive traffic. Rate limiting is also enabled for incoming requests, which helps ensure that the database is not overwhelmed with too many requests.

Lack of encryption

Non-relational databases may not support the same level of encryption as relational databases. This can create challenges around protecting sensitive data and ensuring data privacy.

To address this challenge, DevOps teams may need to implement custom encryption mechanisms in non-relational databases, such as application-level encryption or network-level encryption. These mechanisms can help ensure that data is protected both at rest and in transit.

Here's an example of network-level encryption in Cassandra:

YAML

```yaml
// Enable network-level encryption for Cassandra
server_encryption_options:
  internode_encryption: all
  keystore: /path/to/keystore.jks
  keystore_password: password
  truststore: /path/to/truststore.jks
  truststore_password: password
client_encryption_options:
  enabled: true
```

```
optional: false
keystore: /path/to/keystore.jks
keystore_password: password
```

In this example, network-level encryption is enabled for Cassandra by setting the `internode_encryption` option to `all`, which ensures that all communication between nodes is encrypted. Keystores and truststores are also specified to provide authentication and encryption key management. Client-level encryption is also enabled to ensure that data is encrypted in transit between clients and nodes.

In conclusion, security is critical for any database, but there are some unique challenges around security for non-relational databases. These challenges include limited access control, DDoS attacks, and lack of encryption. To address these challenges, DevOps teams may need to implement custom access control mechanisms, DDoS prevention mechanisms, and encryption mechanisms in non-relational databases, such as role-based access control, rate limiting, and network-level encryption.

Anti-patterns (what not to do...)

There are several anti-patterns/wrong practices that should be avoided when working with NoSQL systems. Let's review some obvious examples of what not to do.

Overusing or misusing denormalization

Overusing or misusing denormalization can lead to inconsistent or redundant data, making it difficult to maintain data integrity.

For example, consider a hypothetical e-commerce application that uses a NoSQL database to store order and product data. The database uses a denormalized data model, where each order document contains product information as embedded documents. However, the application team decides to denormalize further and embed order data within each product document as well, simplifying querying. This leads to redundant data and inconsistent order data, as changes to order data will need to be updated in multiple places.

Here's an example of overusing denormalization in MongoDB:

JSON

```
// Example of overusing denormalization in MongoDB
// Embedding order data within each product document

{
  "_id": "product123",
  "name": "iPhone",
  "description": "Apple iPhone 12 Pro",
```

```
  "price": 999,
  "orders": [
    {
      "_id": "order456",
      "customer_id": "customer789",
      "quantity": 2,
      "price": 1998
    },
    {
      "_id": "order789",
      "customer_id": "customer123",
      "quantity": 1,
      "price": 999
    }
  ]
}
```

In this example, each product document contains order data as embedded documents. However, this leads to redundant data and inconsistent order data, as changes to order data will need to be updated in multiple places.

Ignoring or underestimating data consistency

Ignoring or underestimating data consistency can lead to data inconsistencies and loss of data integrity.

For example, consider a hypothetical social media application that uses a NoSQL database to store user profiles and posts. The database uses eventual consistency, and the application team underestimates the complexity of managing consistency across nodes. This leads to inconsistent post data, as users may see different versions of the same post on different devices.

Here's an example of underestimating data consistency in Cassandra:

CQL

```
// Example of underestimating data consistency in Cassandra
// Using low consistency levels for reads and writes

CREATE TABLE posts (
  post_id UUID PRIMARY KEY,
  user_id UUID,
  text TEXT
);

INSERT INTO posts (post_id, user_id, text) VALUES (
```

```
    uuid(), uuid(), 'Hello, world!'
) USING CONSISTENCY ONE;

SELECT * FROM posts WHERE post_id = uuid() USING CONSISTENCY ONE;
```

In this example, Cassandra is used to store post data, but low consistency levels are used for reads and writes. This can lead to data inconsistencies, as users can see different versions of the same post on different devices.

Failing to secure a database

Failing to secure a database can lead to data breaches and data loss.

For example, consider a hypothetical healthcare application that uses a NoSQL database to store patient data. The database is not secured properly, and a hacker gains access to the database, compromising sensitive patient data.

Here's an example of failing to secure a database in Elasticsearch:

Elasticsearch

```
// Example of failing to secure the database in Elasticsearch
// Using default settings without authentication

curl -XPUT 'http://localhost:9200/my_index/my_type/1' -d '
{
  "name": "John Doe",
  "age": 35,
  "email": "john.doe@example.com"
}'
```

In this example, Elasticsearch is used to store patient data, but default settings are used without authentication. This can lead to data breaches, as unauthorized users can gain access to the database.

Overlooking performance tuning

Overlooking performance tuning can lead to slow queries and poor database performance.

For example, consider a hypothetical logistics application that uses a NoSQL database to store shipping information. The database is not tuned properly for the application's workload, leading to slow queries and poor performance.

Here's an example of overlooking performance tuning in Couchbase:

N1QL

```
// Example of overlooking performance tuning in Couchbase
// Using default settings without optimization

// Query for all shipments
SELECT * FROM shipments;

// Query for shipments with a specific status
SELECT * FROM shipments WHERE status = "delivered";
```

In this example, Couchbase is used to store shipping data, but the default settings are used without optimization. This can lead to slow queries, as the database is not optimized for the application's workload.

Neglecting to plan for growth

Neglecting to plan for growth can lead to scalability issues and poor performance.

For example, consider a hypothetical gaming application that uses a NoSQL database to store user data. The database is not designed to handle the application's growing user base, leading to scalability issues and poor performance.

Here's an example of neglecting to plan for growth in Amazon DynamoDB:

JSON

```
// Example of neglecting to plan for growth in DynamoDB
// Using a single partition key for all users

{
  "user_id": "1234567890",
  "name": "John Doe",
  "score": 1000,
  "level": 5
}
```

In this example, DynamoDB is used to store user data, but a single partition key is used for all users. This can lead to scalability issues, as the database may not be able to handle the growing number of users.

DevOps teams should avoid overusing or misusing denormalization, ignoring or underestimating data consistency, failing to secure a database, overlooking performance tuning, and neglecting to plan for growth. By avoiding these anti-patterns and wrong practices, teams can ensure that NoSQL databases are used effectively and efficiently, with optimal performance, data consistency, and data security.

Summary

In this chapter, we discussed the main activities and challenges involved in working with non-relational databases as part of a DevOps team. We covered five areas of concern – data modeling, schema management, deployment automation, performance tuning, and security. For each of these areas, we identified three unique challenges that are specific to non-relational databases and explained why they exist. We provided in-depth explanations and code snippets for each challenge to illustrate the complexities involved. Overall, we emphasized that working with non-relational databases requires specialized knowledge and skills, as well as that DevOps teams may need to use custom tools and techniques to ensure that data is managed effectively and securely.

In summary, working with non-relational databases as part of the DevOps team involves specific challenges that differ from those of relational databases. Non-relational databases offer greater flexibility and scalability but require a different approach to data modeling, schema management, deployment automation, performance tuning, data consistency, and security.

Data modeling in non-relational databases involves selecting the appropriate data structure for the type of data being stored. For example, document-based databases such as MongoDB may be more suitable for hierarchical data. Schema management in non-relational databases can be more challenging, since there is no fixed schema, and schema migrations can be more difficult to manage. Deployment automation for non-relational databases may require configuring a database for high availability and disaster recovery, which can be more complex than in relational databases.

Performance tuning in non-relational databases requires optimizing indexes based on data access patterns. Data consistency is also a challenge, since non-relational databases may not enforce strict data consistency across multiple nodes in a distributed system. Security in non-relational databases may require implementing access control at a granular level, such as nodes or edges.

In contrast, relational databases offer a structured approach to data modeling and schema management, making it easier to manage data and schema changes. However, relational databases can be less flexible and more complex to scale. Performance tuning in relational databases typically relies on query optimization and table design. Data consistency is also easier to achieve, since relational databases enforce strict consistency across all nodes. Security in relational databases typically uses role-based access control at the database or table level.

Understanding and addressing these differences is essential to achieving optimal results in managing non-relational databases in a DevOps environment. DevOps teams must be familiar with the specific challenges of non-relational databases and develop customized solutions to address them. With the right approach, DevOps teams can effectively manage and optimize non-relational databases, providing scalable and reliable data solutions for their organizations.

In the next chapter, we will provide a brief overview of **artificial intelligence** (**AI**), **machine learning** (**ML**), and **big data** technologies and how they relate to one another.

7

AI, ML, and Big Data

Artificial intelligence (**AI**), **machine learning** (**ML**), and **big data** are three of the most talked-about technologies in the modern world. While they are distinct from one another, they are often used together to create powerful solutions that can automate complex tasks, extract insights, and improve decision-making. In this chapter, we will provide a brief overview of each of these technologies and how they relate to one another.

The following topics will be covered in this chapter:

- The definitions and application of AI, ML, and big data
- A deep dive into big data as a DevOps data expert
- A deep dive into ML as a DevOps data expert
- A deep dive into AI as a DevOps data expert

Definitions and applications of AI, ML, and big data

AI is a branch of computer science that focuses on creating intelligent machines that can perform tasks that would typically require human intelligence. AI systems can analyze data, recognize patterns, and make decisions based on that analysis. Some examples of AI applications include speech recognition, computer vision, natural language processing, robotics, and expert systems.

ML is a branch of AI that concentrates on creating algorithms that can learn from given data and enhance their efficiency as time progresses. ML algorithms can automatically identify patterns in data and use them to make predictions or decisions. Some examples of ML applications include predictive analytics, fraud detection, recommender systems, image recognition, and autonomous vehicles.

Big data refers to the large and complex sets of data that are generated by modern technology. This data is often unstructured, diverse, and difficult to process using traditional methods. Big data technologies are used to store, manage, and analyze these large datasets. Some examples of big data applications include social media analytics, customer profiling, supply chain optimization, and cybersecurity.

The relationship between AI, ML, and big data

AI, ML, and big data are all closely related and often used together to create powerful solutions. Big data provides the fuel for AI and ML algorithms, which are used to extract insights and make predictions from the data. AI and ML, in turn, can be used to automate the processing of large datasets, making it possible to analyze and extract insights from massive amounts of data quickly and accurately.

One of the most common use cases for AI, ML, and big data is in the field of predictive analytics. **Predictive analytics** is the practice of using data, statistical algorithms, and ML techniques to identify the likelihood of future outcomes, based on historical data. In this context, big data provides the raw data that is used to train ML models, while AI is used to develop predictive models that can analyze the data and make accurate predictions.

Another use case for AI, ML, and big data is in the field of **natural language processing** (**NLP**). NLP is a subset of AI that focuses on analyzing and understanding human language. Big data is used to train NLP models on large datasets of text data, while ML is used to develop algorithms that can recognize patterns in language and extract meaning from text. NLP applications include chatbots, sentiment analysis, and language translation.

AI, ML, and big data are also used in the field of computer vision, which is the study of how computers can interpret and understand visual data from the world around them. Computer vision applications include facial recognition, object detection, and self-driving cars. In this context, big data is used to train ML models on large datasets of images, while AI is used to develop algorithms that can recognize patterns in visual data and make decisions based on that analysis.

The role of DevOps and engineering in AI, ML, and big data

The development of AI, ML, and big data solutions requires a high degree of collaboration between different teams, including data scientists, software engineers, and DevOps professionals. DevOps is a methodology that emphasizes collaboration, automation, and communication between software development and IT operations teams. In the context of AI, ML, and big data, DevOps is used to streamline the development, deployment, and maintenance of these solutions.

Engineering teams are responsible for the design and development of the underlying infrastructure that supports AI, ML, and big data solutions. This includes building data pipelines, developing software frameworks, and managing cloud infrastructure. Engineering teams also work closely with data scientists and software developers to ensure that AI, ML, and big data solutions are deployed and scaled correctly.

DevOps teams play a critical role in the development and deployment of AI, ML, and big data solutions. DevOps practices such as **continuous integration and continuous delivery** (**CI/CD**) are used to automate the deployment and testing of these solutions, ensuring that they are delivered quickly and with high quality. DevOps also helps to ensure that AI, ML, and big data solutions are highly available and scalable, allowing them to handle large volumes of data and traffic.

Another critical aspect of DevOps in the context of AI, ML, and big data is security. As these technologies become increasingly important in various industries, ensuring the security and privacy of the data they handle is of paramount importance. DevOps teams must work closely with security teams to implement robust security measures, including encryption, access controls, and monitoring.

Challenges of AI, ML, and big data

In the contemporary digital era, AI, ML, and big data stand out as transformative technologies, rendering unparalleled advantages in various sectors such as healthcare, finance, and e-commerce. However, the utilization of these sophisticated technologies is also entwined with a multitude of challenges that demand meticulous attention and comprehensive strategies.

A prominent challenge that has been conspicuous in the deployment of AI, ML, and big data solutions is the persistent issue of data quality. While big data solutions are inherently dependent on processing vast datasets to derive insightful analytics and predictions, the efficacy of these solutions is invariably tethered to the quality of the data being processed. Suboptimal data quality, characterized by inconsistencies, errors, or incompleteness, can severely undermine the precision and reliability of models developed through AI and ML. Therefore, ensuring the veracity and accuracy of data becomes imperative to safeguard the credibility of outcomes obtained through these technologies.

Complexity and skill scarcity in the domain of AI, ML, and big data also stand out as formidable challenges. The effective development, deployment, and maintenance of solutions harnessing these technologies mandate a nuanced understanding of diverse fields, including data science, software engineering, and DevOps practices. Skilled professionals who embody expertise in these domains are not only scarce but also increasingly sought after, thereby engendering a competitive environment where organizations vie to secure top talent. This emphasizes the importance of not only focusing on talent acquisition but also on nurturing and developing in-house expertise, through training and development initiatives.

Simultaneously, the surge in the implementation of AI, ML, and big data technologies has catapulted ethical considerations into the spotlight, warranting earnest deliberation. Ethical challenges encompass diverse aspects such as privacy implications, potential biases in algorithmic decision-making, and overarching fairness. The ubiquitous infusion of these technologies into everyday life raises legitimate concerns regarding data privacy and the ethical dimensions of automated decisions, especially in critical areas such as healthcare and criminal justice. Ensuring that algorithms are free from biases and function in a manner that upholds fairness and justice necessitates a collaborative effort involving DevOps, engineering teams, data scientists, and ethical compliance specialists.

In a similar way, regulatory compliance emerges as a critical aspect, necessitating adherence to a myriad of legal frameworks and guidelines that govern the utilization of AI, ML, and big data across various jurisdictions. Ensuring that solutions conform to regulatory stipulations, such as the GDPR in Europe and the CCPA in California, is imperative to mitigate legal risks and uphold organizational repute.

Conclusively, AI, ML, and big data, while heralding an era of technological advancements and innovative solutions, concurrently present a landscape fraught with challenges that demand deliberate, ethical, and strategic responses. The role of DevOps and engineering teams, in concert with data scientists and compliance specialists, is pivotal in navigating through these challenges and ensuring the responsible, ethical, and effective deployment of these technologies. It's undeniable that the potential boons offered by AI, ML, and big data are colossal, but they must be pursued with a steadfast commitment to quality, ethical considerations, and continuous improvement, in order to truly harness their transformative power in the future.

A deep dive into big data as a DevOps data expert

Big data refers to extremely large, complex, and diverse datasets that are generated at a high velocity and require advanced tools and techniques to process and analyze effectively. The amount of data being generated by businesses, organizations, and individuals is increasing exponentially, and this data can come from a variety of sources, including sensors, social media, and mobile devices.

The key characteristics of big data are commonly referred to as the **3Vs** – **volume**, **velocity**, and **variety**:

- **Volume**: Big data involves extremely large datasets, often in the petabyte or even exabyte range. These datasets can include both structured and unstructured data.

- **Velocity**: Big data is generated at a high velocity, meaning that it is constantly being created and updated in real time. This requires tools and techniques that can handle the fast pace of data ingestion and processing.

- **Variety**: Big data includes a variety of data types and formats, including text, audio, video, and images. This requires tools and techniques that can handle a diverse range of data formats and structures.

To process and analyze big data, advanced tools and techniques are required. Some of the key technologies used in big data include the following:

- **Distributed computing**: This involves breaking up the processing of large datasets into smaller tasks that can be distributed across a network of computers, allowing for faster processing and analysis.

- **Hadoop**: Hadoop is an open source framework that enables distributed storage and processing of large datasets. It is based on the MapReduce programming model and the **Hadoop Distributed File System** (**HDFS**).

- **NoSQL databases**: NoSQL databases are designed to handle unstructured data and are often used in big data applications. Examples of NoSQL databases include MongoDB, Cassandra, and Couchbase.

- **Data mining and ML**: These techniques are used to extract insights and patterns from big data. They can be used for tasks such as predictive modeling, anomaly detection, and clustering.

- **Data visualization**: Data visualization tools are used to present the results of big data analysis in a way that is easy to understand and interpret.

Big data is being used in a variety of industries and applications, from healthcare and finance to marketing and social media. By effectively processing and analyzing big data, organizations can gain insights and make data-driven decisions that can improve their operations and competitiveness.

At the infrastructure level, big data relies on a combination of hardware and software components to store, process, and analyze data. As a DevOps engineer, it is important to understand how big data works at the infrastructure level and the common challenges you may encounter.

Big data infrastructure

Big data infrastructure typically includes a combination of the following components:

- **Storage**: Big data requires large-scale storage solutions that can store terabytes, petabytes, or even exabytes of data. Popular storage solutions include HDFS, Amazon S3, and Google Cloud Storage.

- **Processing**: Big data processing involves parallel processing of data across multiple servers. Distributed processing frameworks such as Apache Spark and Apache Hadoop are popular solutions to process big data.

- **Compute**: Big data workloads require significant compute resources to process and analyze data. Compute resources can be provided by on-premises servers or cloud-based solutions, such as Amazon EC2 and Google Compute Engine.

- **Networking**: Big data workloads often involve moving large amounts of data across networks. High-speed networks and low-latency connections are essential for efficient big data processing.

Challenges with big data

As a DevOps engineer working with big data, you may encounter several challenges. Here are some of the most common challenges and how to address them:

- **Data integration**: Big data often comes from multiple sources and in different formats. Integrating and processing data from multiple sources can be challenging. To address this, you can use data integration tools such as Apache NiFi, Talend, or Apache Beam.

  Here is an example of using Apache NiFi for data integration:

XML

```xml
<?xml version="1.0" encoding="UTF-8" ?>
<flow>
<source name="GenerateFlowFile" type="GenerateFlowFile">
```

```
<property name="batchSize" value="1"/>
</source>
<processor name="SplitText" type="SplitText">
<property name="LineSplit" value="\n"/>
</processor>
<destination name="LogAttribute" type="LogAttribute"/>
</flow>
```

- **Data security**: Big data can contain sensitive information that requires protection. To address this, you can implement security measures such as access control, encryption, and monitoring.

Here is an example of using encryption with Amazon S3:

PYTHON

```python
import boto3
# create an S3 client
s3 = boto3.client('s3')

# create a bucket and enable encryption
bucket_name = 'my-bucket'
s3.create_bucket(Bucket=bucket_name)
s3.put_bucket_encryption(
Bucket=bucket_name,
ServerSideEncryptionConfiguration={
'Rules': [
        {
'ApplyServerSideEncryptionByDefault': {
'SSEAlgorithm': 'AES256',
            },
        },
    ],
    },
)
```

- **Performance**: Big data processing can be computationally intensive and require significant resources. To address this, you can use techniques such as distributed processing and caching.

Here is an example of using caching with Redis:

PYTHON

```python
import redis
# create a Redis client
client = redis.Redis(host='my-redis-host', port=6379)
```

```
# cache a value
client.set('my-key', 'my-value')

# retrieve a cached value
value = client.get('my-key')
```

- **Monitoring**: Big data processing can be complex, and monitoring is essential to ensure that the processing is running smoothly. To address this, you can use monitoring tools such as Nagios, Zabbix, or Grafana.

  Here is an example of using Nagios for monitoring:

SHELL

```
# create a Nagios service check
define service{
    use                     generic-service
    host_name               my-host
    service_description     my-service
    check_command           check_bigdata
}

# create a Nagios check command
define command{
    command_name            check_bigdata
    command_line            /usr/lib/nagios/plugins/check_bigdata.sh
}
```

Big data is a complex and diverse field that involves processing and analyzing large and complex datasets. At the infrastructure level, big data relies on a combination of hardware and software components to store, process, and analyze the data. As a DevOps engineer, it is important to understand how big data works on the infrastructure level and the common challenges you may encounter.

Common challenges with big data include data integration, data security, performance, and monitoring. To address these challenges, DevOps engineers can use a combination of tools and techniques, such as data integration tools, encryption, caching, and monitoring tools.

By understanding the common challenges with big data and implementing robust processes and tools, DevOps engineers can build effective and reliable big data solutions that deliver accurate and actionable results.

A deep dive into ML as a DevOps data expert

ML is a subset of AI that involves building systems that can automatically learn and improve from data without being explicitly programmed. ML algorithms are designed to identify patterns and relationships in data, using these patterns to make predictions or take actions.

From a DevOps point of view, ML can be viewed as a software application that can learn and improve over time. This requires a different approach to software development and deployment than traditional applications. In this section, we will discuss how ML works and how it differs from traditional software applications.

How ML works

ML involves several key steps:

1. **Data collection**: The first step in ML is to collect data that can be used to train a model. This data can come from a variety of sources, including sensors, social media, or user interactions.

2. **Data preprocessing**: Once the data is collected, it needs to be preprocessed to ensure that it is in a suitable format to train the ML model. This may involve tasks such as data cleaning, data normalization, and feature engineering.

3. **Model training**: The next step is to train the ML model on the preprocessed data. This involves selecting an appropriate algorithm, setting hyperparameters, and training the model on the data.

4. **Model evaluation**: Once the model is trained, it needs to be evaluated to determine its accuracy and performance. This may involve testing the model on a separate dataset or using cross-validation techniques.

5. **Model deployment**: The final step is to deploy the model in a production environment, where it can make predictions or take actions based on new data.

How ML differs from traditional software applications

ML differs from traditional software applications in several ways:

- **ML applications are data-driven**: Unlike traditional software applications, which are designed to execute a predefined set of instructions, ML applications are designed to learn from data and improve over time.

- **ML applications require continuous training and improvement**: ML models need to be continuously trained and improved over time to maintain their accuracy and reliability. This requires a different approach to software development and deployment than traditional applications.

- **ML applications require a different infrastructure**: ML applications often require complex infrastructure and specific hardware and software configurations. This requires a different approach to infrastructure management than traditional applications.

- **ML applications require different testing and validation techniques**: ML models require different testing and validation techniques than traditional software applications. This may involve techniques such as cross-validation, confusion matrix analysis, and A/B testing.

In conclusion, ML is a subset of AI that involves building systems that can automatically learn and improve from data. From a DevOps point of view, ML can be viewed as a software application that requires a different approach to development, deployment, infrastructure management, and testing and validation. By understanding the unique challenges and requirements of ML, DevOps teams can build effective and reliable ML solutions that deliver accurate and actionable results.

Challenges with ML for a DevOps data expert

As a DevOps data expert, there are several challenges and technical aspects that you need to know about when working with ML. These include data preparation, model training, model deployment, monitoring, and maintenance. In this section, we will discuss these challenges and technical aspects, providing examples with code snippets to help you better understand them.

Data preparation

Data preparation is the process of collecting, cleaning, and transforming data to make it suitable for use in ML models. This is a critical step, as the quality of the data used to train ML models has a direct impact on their accuracy and performance.

One of the challenges of data preparation is dealing with missing data. There are several ways to handle missing data, including imputation, deletion, and using models that can handle missing values. Here is an example of how to handle missing data using Pandas in Python:

PYTHON

```
import pandas as pd
import numpy as np

# create a dataframe with missing values
df = pd.DataFrame({'A': [1, 2, np.nan, 4], 'B': [5, np.nan, np.nan, 8]})
# fill missing values with mean
df.fillna(df.mean(), inplace=True)
```

This code imports the `pandas` and `numpy` libraries to handle and manipulate data. It then creates a DataFrame (`df`), with some missing values indicated by `np.nan`. Subsequently, it fills the missing values in the dataframe with the mean of each respective column.

Another challenge of data preparation is dealing with categorical variables. ML algorithms typically work with numerical data, so categorical variables must be encoded in some way. There are several encoding methods, including one-hot encoding, label encoding, and binary encoding. Here is an example of one-hot encoding using Scikit-Learn in Python:

PYTHON

```
from sklearn.preprocessing import OneHotEncoder
# create a one-hot encoder
encoder = OneHotEncoder()
# encode categorical variables
encoded_data = encoder.fit_transform(data)
```

Model training

Model training is the process of using data to train an ML model. This involves selecting an appropriate algorithm, setting hyperparameters, and training the model on the data. One of the challenges of model training is **overfitting**, which occurs when a model is too complex and fits the training data too closely, resulting in poor generalization to new data.

To address overfitting, several regularization techniques can be used, including L1 regularization, L2 regularization, and dropout. Here is an example of L2 regularization, using Keras in Python:

PYTHON

```
from keras.models import Sequential
from keras.layers import Dense
from keras.regularizers import l2

# create a neural network with L2 regularization
model = Sequential()
model.add(Dense(32, input_shape=(input_dim,), activation='relu',
kernel_regularizer=l2(0.01)))
model.add(Dense(16, activation='relu', kernel_regularizer=l2(0.01)))
model.add(Dense(output_dim, activation='softmax'))
```

Another challenge of model training is hyperparameter tuning. Hyperparameters are parameters that are set before training and determine the behavior of the algorithm. These include the learning rate, the batch size, and the number of hidden layers. Hyperparameter tuning involves selecting the best combination of hyperparameters for a given problem. Here is an example of hyperparameter tuning, using `GridSearchCV` in Scikit-Learn:

PYTHON

```python
from sklearn.model_selection import GridSearchCV
from sklearn.ensemble import RandomForestClassifier
# define hyperparameters
params = {'n_estimators': [10, 100, 1000], 'max_depth': [None, 10,
50]}
# create a random forest classifier
rfc = RandomForestClassifier()


# perform grid search
grid_search = GridSearchCV(rfc, params, cv=3)
grid_search.fit(X_train, y_train)
# print best parameters
print(grid_search.best_params_)
```

Model deployment

Model deployment is the process of making ML models available for use in production environments. This involves creating an infrastructure that can support the model, such as a server or cloud environment, and integrating the model into an application or service.

One of the challenges of model deployment is scalability. As the number of users or requests increases, the infrastructure supporting the model must be able to handle the load. This can be addressed by using techniques such as load balancing, caching, and auto-scaling. Here is an example of using **Amazon Web Services (AWS)** to deploy an ML model with auto-scaling:

PYTHON

```python
import boto3
# create an AWS client
client = boto3.client('autoscaling')


# create an auto-scaling group
response = client.create_auto_scaling_group(
AutoScalingGroupName='my-auto-scaling-group',
LaunchConfigurationName='my-launch-config',
MinSize=1,
MaxSize=10,
DesiredCapacity=2
)
```

Another challenge of model deployment is versioning. As models are updated and improved, it is important to keep track of different versions and ensure that the correct version is used in production.

This can be addressed by using version control systems and implementing versioning in the model deployment process.

Monitoring and maintenance

Once an ML model is deployed, it is important to monitor its performance and maintain its accuracy. One of the challenges of monitoring is detecting drift, which occurs when the distribution of the data used to train the model changes over time. Drift can result in degraded performance and inaccurate predictions.

To detect drift, several techniques can be used, including statistical tests, divergence measures, and anomaly detection. Here is an example of using the Kolmogorov-Smirnov test to detect drift in Scikit-Learn:

PYTHON

```
from scipy.stats import ks_2samp
# calculate the Kolmogorov-Smirnov statistic
statistic, p_value = ks_2samp(x_train, x_new)
# check for drift
if p_value < alpha:
print('Drift detected')
```

Another challenge of monitoring and maintenance is retraining the model. As data changes or model performance degrades, it may be necessary to retrain the model on new data. This can be automated using techniques such as online learning and active learning.

In conclusion, there are several challenges and technical aspects to consider when working with ML as a DevOps data expert. These include data preparation, model training, model deployment, monitoring, and maintenance. By understanding these challenges and using the appropriate techniques and tools, DevOps data experts can create effective ML solutions that deliver accurate and reliable results.

A deep dive into AI as a DevOps data- expert

AI services are a type of cloud service that provides access to pre-trained models and algorithms, for use in ML and other AI applications. From a DevOps and infrastructure point of view, AI services can be a powerful tool to accelerate the development and deployment of AI applications.

Here are some examples of AI services and how they can be used.

Amazon SageMaker

Amazon SageMaker is a fully managed service that provides developers and data scientists with the ability to build, train, and deploy ML models at scale.

Here is an example of using Amazon SageMaker to train an ML model:

PYTHON

```python
import boto3
import sagemaker

# create a SageMaker session
session = sagemaker.Session()

# create an S3 bucket for storing training data
bucket_name = 'my-bucket'
bucket = session.default_bucket()
s3_input = sagemaker.s3_input(s3_data=f's3://{bucket_name}/training_
data.csv', content_type='csv')
# create a training job
estimator = sagemaker.estimator.Estimator('my-container', role='my-
role', train_instance_count=1, train_instance_type='ml.m5.large',
output_path=f's3://{bucket_name}/output')
estimator.fit({'training': s3_input})
```

This code interfaces with AWS's SageMaker and S3 services to facilitate ML training. Firstly, it establishes a SageMaker session and creates an S3 bucket for data storage, specifying a CSV file for training. Then, it defines a training job with specified parameters, including the machine instance type and container image, and initiates the training using the provided data.

Google Cloud AI platform

The Google Cloud AI platform is a cloud-based service that provides tools and infrastructure to develop and deploy ML models.

Here is an example of using Google Cloud AI platform to train an ML model:

PYTHON

```python
import google.auth
from google.cloud import aiplatform

# authenticate with Google Cloud
creds, project = google.auth.default()
client_options = {"api_endpoint": "us-central1-aiplatform.googleapis.
com"}
client = aiplatform.gapic.JobServiceClient(
    client_options=client_options, credentials=creds
)
```

```
# create a training job
job_spec = {
    "worker_pool_specs": [
        {
            "machine_spec": {
                "machine_type": "n1-standard-4",
            },
            "replica_count": 1,
            "container_spec": {
                "image_uri": "my-image",
                "command": ["python", "train.py"],
                "args": [
                    "--input-path=gs://my-bucket/training_data.csv",
                    "--output-path=gs://my-bucket/output",
                ],
            },
        }
    ],
}
parent = f"projects/{project}/locations/us-central1"
response = client.create_custom_job(parent=parent, custom_job=job_
spec)
```

This code interacts with Google Cloud's AI platform to launch a custom training job. Using the provided credentials, it establishes a connection to AI Platform in the us-central1 region and specifies a job that utilizes a Docker image named my-image to execute a Python script, train.py, with designated input and output paths in a Google Cloud Storage bucket. Once the job specification is set, it's submitted to the platform for execution.

Microsoft Azure Machine Learning

Microsoft Azure Machine Learning is a cloud-based service that provides tools and infrastructure to build, train, and deploy ML models.

Here is an example of using Microsoft Azure Machine Learning to train an ML model:

PYTHON

```
import azureml.core
from azureml.core import Workspace, Experiment, Datastore, Dataset,
Environment, ScriptRunConfig

# authenticate with Azure
workspace = Workspace.from_config()
```

```
# create a training experiment
experiment = Experiment(workspace, 'my-experiment')
datastore = Datastore.get(workspace, 'my-datastore')
dataset = Dataset.File.from_files(datastore.path('training_data.csv'))
environment = Environment.get(workspace, 'my-environment')
config = ScriptRunConfig(
    source_directory='.',
    script='train.py',
    arguments=['--input-path', dataset.as_named_input('training').as_
mount(), '--output-path', datastore.path('output').as_mount()],
    environment=environment
)
run = experiment.submit(config)
```

AI services are a powerful tool to accelerate the development and deployment of AI applications. From a DevOps and infrastructure point of view, AI services provide access to pre-trained models and algorithms, as well as tools and infrastructure to build, train, and deploy machines.

Challenges with AI for a DevOps data expert

As a DevOps engineer responsible for AI services, there are several challenges that you may encounter on a day-to-day basis. These challenges can include managing infrastructure, managing ML models, ensuring security and compliance, and optimizing performance and scalability. Let's review some examples of the most common challenges and suggest ways to overcome them.

Managing infrastructure

One of the primary challenges of managing AI services is managing the infrastructure required to support ML workflows. This can include setting up and configuring cloud-based resources such as virtual machines, databases, and storage solutions.

Example – provisioning infrastructure with AWS CloudFormation

To automate the process of setting up and managing infrastructure, you might use a tool such as AWS CloudFormation. **CloudFormation** is an infrastructure-as-code tool that allows you to define and manage AWS resources, using a high-level JSON or YAML configuration file.

Here is an example of using CloudFormation to create an Amazon SageMaker notebook instance:

YAML

```
AWSTemplateFormatVersion: '2010-09-09'
Resources:
  NotebookInstance:
```

```
Type: AWS::SageMaker::NotebookInstance
Properties:
InstanceType: ml.t2.medium
RoleArn: !Sub "arn:aws:iam::${AWS::AccountId}:role/MySageMakerRole"
NotebookInstanceName: MyNotebookInstance
DirectInternetAccess: Enabled
```

This CloudFormation template creates an Amazon SageMaker notebook instance with the specified instance type and IAM role.

To overcome the challenge of managing infrastructure, I recommend using infrastructure-as-code tools such as CloudFormation or Terraform to automate the provisioning and management of cloud resources. By using these tools, you can easily create, update, and delete resources as needed, reducing the risk of manual errors and ensuring consistency across environments.

Managing ML models

Another significant challenge of managing AI services is managing ML models. This can include building and training models, deploying models to production, and monitoring model performance.

Example – building and training an ML model with TensorFlow

To build and train an ML model, I might use a popular deep learning framework such as TensorFlow. **TensorFlow** provides a range of tools and infrastructure to build and train ML models.

Here is an example of using TensorFlow to build and train a convolutional neural network for image classification:

PYTHON

```python
import tensorflow as tf

# load the dataset
(train_images, train_labels), (
    test_images,
    test_labels,
) = tf.keras.datasets.fashion_mnist.load_data()
# preprocess the data
train_images = train_images / 255.0
test_images = test_images / 255.0

# define the model
model = tf.keras.Sequential(
    [
        tf.keras.layers.Flatten(input_shape=(28, 28)),
```

```
        tf.keras.layers.Dense(128, activation="relu"),
        tf.keras.layers.Dense(10),
    ]
)

# compile the model
model.compile(
    optimizer="adam",
    loss=tf.keras.losses.SparseCategoricalCrossentropy(from_
logits=True),
    metrics=["accuracy"],
)
# train the model
model.fit(train_images, train_labels, epochs=10)
# evaluate the model
test_loss, test_acc = model.evaluate(test_images, test_labels,
verbose=2)
print(f"Test accuracy: {test_acc}")
```

This code defines a convolutional neural network for image classification, trains the model on the *Fashion MNIST* dataset, and evaluates the model's performance.

To overcome the challenge of managing ML models, I recommend using a version control system such as **Git** to track changes to model code and configuration. This allows for easy collaboration, experimentation, and tracking of changes over time. Additionally, using automated testing and deployment processes can help ensure that models are working as expected and that changes are properly tested and deployed to production.

Ensuring security and compliance

Security and compliance are critical concerns when managing AI services, especially when dealing with sensitive data such as personal or financial information. As DevOps engineers responsible for AI services, we must ensure that the infrastructure and processes we implement comply with relevant security and data protection regulations.

Example – securing ML models with AWS SageMaker

Amazon SageMaker provides several tools and services to secure ML models. For example, you can use SageMaker's built-in model encryption and data encryption features to ensure that models and data are encrypted both in transit and at rest. You can also use AWS **Key Management Service** (**KMS**) to manage encryption keys and control access to sensitive data.

Here is an example of using SageMaker's encryption features to encrypt an ML model:

PYTHON

```python
import boto3
from botocore.exceptions import ClientError


sagemaker = boto3.client("sagemaker")


# create a model
model_name = "my-model"
primary_container = {"Image": "my-container-image"}
model_response = sagemaker.create_model(
    ModelName=model_name,
    ExecutionRoleArn="my-execution-role",
    PrimaryContainer=primary_container,
)


# encrypt the model
try:
    sagemaker.update_model(
        ModelName=model_name,
        EnableNetworkIsolation=True,
        VpcConfig={
            "SecurityGroupIds": ["sg-1234"],
            "Subnets": ["subnet-1234"]

        },
    )
except ClientError as e:
    print(f"Error encrypting model: {e}")
```

This code creates a SageMaker model and then enables network isolation and VPC configuration, ensuring that the model is encrypted and secured.

To overcome the challenge of ensuring security and compliance, I recommend working closely with security and compliance teams to understand relevant regulations and best practices. Implementing secure infrastructure and processes, such as encrypting data and managing access control with AWS KMS, can help ensure that sensitive data is protected and that regulatory requirements are met.

Optimizing performance and scalability

Finally, as a DevOps engineer responsible for AI services, I must ensure that the infrastructure and processes I implement are performant and scalable. This includes optimizing resource usage, identifying and resolving bottlenecks, and implementing efficient data processing pipelines.

Example – scaling data processing with Apache Spark

Apache Spark is a popular distributed computing framework that can be used to process large datasets in parallel. To optimize performance and scalability, I can use Spark to preprocess and transform data for use in ML workflows.

Here is an example of using Spark to preprocess a dataset for use in an ML pipeline:

PYTHON

```
from pyspark.sql import SparkSession
from pyspark.ml.feature import VectorAssembler
from pyspark.ml import Pipeline
# create a Spark session
spark = SparkSession.builder.appName('preprocessing').getOrCreate()
# load the dataset
df = spark.read.csv('my-dataset.csv', header=True, inferSchema=True)
# preprocess the data
assembler = VectorAssembler(inputCols=['feature1', 'feature2',
'feature3'], outputCol='features')
pipeline = Pipeline(stages=[assembler])
preprocessed_data = pipeline.fit(df).transform(df)
```

This code uses Spark to read in a dataset from a CSV file, assemble the features into a vector, and then apply a preprocessing pipeline to the data.

To overcome the challenge of optimizing performance and scalability, I recommend using tools such as Apache Spark and Amazon EMR to distribute data processing and handle large-scale ML workloads. Additionally, using monitoring and logging tools such as AWS CloudWatch or the ELK Stack can help identify performance bottlenecks and debug issues as they arise.

As a DevOps engineer responsible for AI services, my day-to-day activities involve managing the infrastructure and processes to build, train, and deploy ML models. I face challenges such as managing infrastructure, managing ML models, ensuring security and compliance, and optimizing performance and scalability. However, by using best practices and tools such as infrastructure-as-code, version control, and distributed computing frameworks, I can overcome these challenges and build robust and efficient AI services.

Summary

In summary, AI, ML, and big data are technologies that have revolutionized the way we work with data and automation. They offer a wide range of benefits to organizations, such as improved efficiency, accuracy, and decision-making. However, integrating and managing these technologies can be challenging, particularly for DevOps and engineering teams who are responsible for building, deploying, and maintaining these solutions.

One of the most significant challenges that DevOps engineers face when working with AI, ML, and big data is managing the infrastructure required to support these technologies. For example, building and maintaining cloud-based resources such as virtual machines, databases, and storage solutions can be complex and time-consuming. Infrastructure-as-code tools such as AWS CloudFormation and Terraform can help automate the process of setting up and managing cloud resources. Using these tools, DevOps engineers can easily create, update, and delete resources as needed, reducing the risk of manual errors, and ensuring consistency across environments.

Another challenge that DevOps engineers face when working with AI services is managing ML models. Building and training models, deploying them to production, and monitoring model performance are all complex tasks that require specialized knowledge and expertise. Version control systems such as Git can help track changes to model code and configuration, ensuring that changes are properly tested and deployed to production. Automated testing and deployment processes can also help ensure that models work as expected and that changes are properly tested and deployed to production.

Ensuring security and compliance is another critical concern when managing AI services, especially when dealing with sensitive data such as personal or financial information. DevOps engineers must ensure that the infrastructure and processes they implement comply with relevant security and data protection regulations. Cloud-based services such as Amazon SageMaker provide several tools and services to secure ML models, including built-in model encryption and data encryption features. AWS KMS can also be used to manage encryption keys and control access to sensitive data.

Finally, DevOps engineers must ensure that the infrastructure and processes they implement are performant and scalable. This includes optimizing resource usage, identifying and resolving bottlenecks, and implementing efficient data processing pipelines. Distributed computing frameworks such as Apache Spark can help handle large-scale ML workloads, and monitoring and logging tools such as AWS CloudWatch or the ELK Stack can help identify performance bottlenecks and debug issues as they arise.

To overcome these challenges, DevOps engineers must use best practices such as infrastructure-as-code, version control, and distributed computing frameworks. They must also work closely with other teams, such as data scientists and security teams, to ensure that AI services are delivered quickly, with high quality, and in a secure and ethical manner. DevOps engineers should also stay up to date with the latest developments in AI, ML, and big data and be prepared to adapt their skills and processes as these technologies evolve.

In conclusion, AI, ML, and big data are technologies that have the potential to transform organizations and industries. However, to harness their benefits, it is essential to approach their integration and management strategically, working collaboratively across teams. With the right tools, practices, and mindset, DevOps engineers can play a critical role in realizing the potential of AI services and helping organizations succeed in the years to come.

In the next chapter, we will learn about zero-touch operations.

Part 3:
The Right Tool for the Job

This part will demonstrate the multiple supporting tools you can leverage to build, monitor, test, and optimize or troubleshoot different types of databases in production systems. Choosing the right tools at the beginning can determine your level of success or failure. We will walk through the key characteristics of these tools, provide a baseline for reference, and give practical examples of how to use, build, and operate them alongside your databases.

This part comprises the following chapters:

- *Chapter 8, Zero-Touch Operations*

- *Chapter 9, Design and Implementation*

- *Chapter 10, Tooling for Database Automation*

8

Zero-Touch Operations

In the field of DevOps, **zero-touch operations** refers to a concept or approach where operations and processes related to managing and maintaining *any objects or services* (such as databases) are automated to the extent that they require little to no manual intervention or human interaction.

The goal of zero-touch operations is to minimize human involvement and reduce the risk of errors or inconsistencies that can occur due to manual processes. It involves implementing automation techniques, tools, and workflows that streamline and simplify various tasks associated with database management, deployment, monitoring, scaling, and recovery.

With zero-touch operations, routine and repetitive tasks such as provisioning new database instances, applying patches and updates, monitoring performance, optimizing configurations, and managing backups can be performed automatically through scripts, configuration management tools, or **Infrastructure as Code (IaC)** solutions. This allows for faster and more efficient operations, reduces the chances of human error, and enables teams to focus on higher-value activities.

By leveraging automation, zero-touch operations can help improve reliability, scalability, and consistency across database environments. It also enables teams to adopt **continuous integration and continuous deployment (CI/CD)** practices, where changes to databases can be automatically tested, validated, and deployed without manual intervention.

However, it's important to note that achieving a fully **zero-touch** state may not always be feasible or practical in all scenarios. Certain exceptional cases or critical situations may still require human intervention or decision-making. Nonetheless, the aim is to minimize manual effort and maximize automation wherever possible to streamline database operations.

The following topics will be covered in this chapter:

- Traditional versus zero-touch approaches
- Increased operational efficiency
- Improved reliability and consistency
- Accelerated deployment and time-to-market

- Enhanced scalability and elasticity

- Reduced downtime and faster recovery

- Improved compliance and security

- Sanity-checking our approach

Traditional versus zero-touch approaches

Let's delve into the technical details to understand the differences between the traditional approach and the zero-touch approach.

Automated configuration management

Traditional approach:

- In the traditional approach, configuration management involves manually configuring systems and applications. Configuration changes are performed directly on each system, often through command-line interfaces or configuration files.

- There is a lack of standardized processes and centralized control, leading to variations in configurations across different systems and a higher risk of errors or inconsistencies.

Zero-touch approach:

- The zero-touch approach automates configuration management using tools such as Ansible, Puppet, or Chef

- Configuration settings are defined in code or declarative language, allowing for consistent and repeatable configurations across systems

- Automation tools apply the desired configurations to the target systems, ensuring that they conform to the specified state

Key differences:

- **Traditional approach**: Manual configuration changes on individual systems

- **Zero-touch approach**: Automated configuration management using code or declarative language

Automated release management

Traditional approach:

- In the traditional approach, release management typically involves manual steps for building, testing, and deploying software releases

- These manual steps are often time-consuming and error-prone, relying on manual intervention to initiate and track the release process

- Coordination and communication between various teams is necessary to ensure the proper sequencing of tasks

Zero-touch approach:

- The zero-touch approach automates release management through CI/CD pipelines

- The CI/CD pipeline is configured to automatically trigger build, test, and deployment processes based on events such as code commits or predefined schedules

- Automated testing ensures that the software is thoroughly validated before deployment, reducing the risk of releasing faulty code

Key differences:

- **Traditional approach**: Manual, error-prone release coordination and deployment

- **Zero-touch approach**: Automated release management through CI/CD pipelines

Automated monitoring and alerting

Traditional approach:

- In the traditional approach, monitoring systems and applications often rely on manual checks and log analysis

- Monitoring tools may be configured, but their usage and data interpretation require human intervention

- Alerting systems, if present, may be set up to send notifications for specific events or thresholds, but manual configuration is typically required

Zero-touch approach:

- The zero-touch approach automates monitoring and alerting using tools such as Prometheus, Nagios, and **Elasticsearch, Logstash, and Kibana (ELK)**

- Monitoring metrics and events are collected automatically from various sources, including system logs, application logs, and performance counters

- Automated alerting mechanisms are set up to send notifications when specific conditions or thresholds are met

Key differences:

- **Traditional approach**: Manual monitoring and log analysis

- **Zero-touch approach**: Automated monitoring and alerting through predefined configurations and event-driven notifications

In summary, the key technical differences between the traditional approach and the zero-touch approach lie in the level of automation, standardization, and centralized control achieved. The traditional approach relies on manual intervention, leading to variations, errors, and slower processes. In contrast, the zero-touch approach automates tasks, ensures consistency, and provides centralized control through configuration management tools, CI/CD pipelines, and automated monitoring and alerting systems.

Zero-touch operations have a high potential in the context of DevOps with databases. Let me try to illustrate some of the potential improvements you can expect if you decide to go down this road:

- **Increased operational efficiency**:

  - Automation reduces the time and effort required to perform routine tasks, resulting in increased operational efficiency

  - A study by Forrester Consulting found that organizations implementing automation in database management experienced a 50% reduction in operational costs and a 40% reduction in time spent on manual tasks

- **Improved reliability and consistency**:

  - Automation helps enforce standardization and consistency across database environments, reducing the risk of human errors or configuration inconsistencies

  - A report by Puppet State of DevOps revealed that high-performing organizations with automated release processes experienced 60 times fewer failures and recovered from failures 168 times faster than low-performing organizations

- **Accelerated deployment and time-to-market**:

  - Automating deployment processes enables faster and more frequent releases, reducing time-to-market for new features and enhancements

  - A survey by **DevOps Research and Assessment** (**DORA**) found that organizations with higher levels of automation in software delivery achieved 46 times more frequent deployments and had a lead time for changes that was 440 times faster than their low-performing counterparts

- **Enhanced scalability and elasticity**:

  - Automation enables the dynamic scaling of database resources based on demand, allowing organizations to handle increased workloads without manual intervention

- **Amazon Web Services (AWS)** reported that customers using AWS Database Migration Service, an automated database migration tool, achieved up to 98% reduction in manual effort and scaled database migrations to handle petabytes of data

- **Reduced downtime and faster recovery**:

  - Automated monitoring and proactive alerting help identify and address issues before they cause significant downtime or performance degradation

  - The State of Database DevOps Report by Redgate found that organizations implementing automated monitoring and alerting reduced the **mean time to recovery (MTTR)** by 79%

- **Improved compliance and security**:

  - Automation allows for consistent implementation of security measures, such as access controls, encryption, and patch management, reducing the risk of vulnerabilities

  - A study by IBM reported that organizations using automated security tools achieved a 92% higher **return on investment (ROI)** compared to manual security practices

These examples demonstrate the tangible benefits organizations have realized through the adoption of zero-touch operation principles, including cost savings, faster deployment cycles, improved reliability, and enhanced security.

Let's dive deeper into these topics one by one.

Increased operational efficiency

Zero-touch operations improve increased operational efficiency by automating manual tasks, reducing human effort, and minimizing the risk of errors. In this section, we'll explain how it enhances operational efficiency with clear examples, along with the associated risks and effort required for implementation and maintenance. Based on the risks and effort highlighted, we can draw a conclusion on the ROI.

Automated database provisioning

Let's look at this in further detail:

- **Implementation**:

  - Use IaC tools such as Terraform to define and provision databases automatically

  - Define the desired database configurations, including instance size, storage, and access controls, in the Terraform code

- **Risks**:

  - Misconfigurations in the IaC templates or improper handling of sensitive data may result in security vulnerabilities or operational issues. It is crucial to follow best practices, conduct regular code reviews, and perform thorough testing before deploying the infrastructure.

- **Effort**:

  - The initial implementation effort involves designing the IaC templates, defining configurations, and setting up integration with version control and CI/CD systems

  - Ongoing maintenance requires updating the templates to reflect changes in requirements, performing regular security audits, and staying up to date with new features or changes in the IaC tool

Automated backup and recovery

Let's look at this in further detail:

- **Implementation**:

  - Utilize built-in backup and recovery features of database management systems or use backup automation tools

  - Define backup schedules, retention policies, and recovery procedures to ensure data protection and fast recovery

- **Risks**:

  - Inadequate backup configurations or failure to regularly test the recovery process may result in data loss or extended downtime during recovery. Regular testing and validation of backups and recovery procedures are crucial to mitigate these risks.

- **Effort**:

  - The initial implementation effort involves configuring backup schedules, defining retention policies, and setting up the necessary automation scripts or tools

  - Ongoing maintenance includes monitoring backup operations, regularly testing recovery procedures, and updating configurations as needed

Improved reliability and consistency

Zero-touch operations improve reliability and consistency by automating processes, reducing human errors, and ensuring standardized configurations. In this section, we'll explain how it enhances reliability and consistency with clear examples, along with the associated risks and effort required for implementation and maintenance. Based on the risks and effort highlighted, we can draw a conclusion on the ROI.

Automated configuration management

Let's look at this in further detail:

- **Implementation**:

  - Use configuration management tools such as Ansible, Puppet, or Chef to define and automate the configuration of systems and applications
  - Define desired configurations in code, such as server settings, application configurations, and security policies

- **Risks**:

  - Misconfigurations in the automation scripts or incomplete coverage of configurations may lead to inconsistencies or security vulnerabilities. Thorough testing, code reviews, and periodic audits are crucial to minimize these risks.

- **Effort**:

  - The initial implementation effort involves designing the automation scripts, defining configurations, and integrating them with version control and CI/CD systems
  - Ongoing maintenance requires updating the scripts to reflect changes in requirements, conducting regular reviews, and addressing any configuration drift

Automated release management

Let's look at more details:

- **Implementation**:

  - Utilize CI/CD pipelines to automate the release and deployment processes
  - Define pipelines that automatically build, test, and deploy software releases based on version control commits or trigger events

- **Risks**:

  - Inadequate testing, incomplete automation, or issues in the CI/CD pipeline can lead to faulty releases, downtime, or degraded performance. Rigorous testing, quality assurance, and monitoring are necessary to mitigate these risks.

- **Effort**:

  - The initial implementation effort involves setting up CI/CD pipelines, defining build and deployment scripts, and integrating with testing frameworks and version control systems

  - Ongoing maintenance includes updating the pipelines, addressing any pipeline failures or performance issues, and continuously improving the release process

Accelerated deployment and time-to-market

Zero-touch operation improves accelerated deployment and time-to-market by automating the software release process, reducing manual effort, and enabling faster and more frequent deployments. In this section, we'll explain how it enhances deployment speed and time-to-market with clear examples, along with the associated risks and effort required for implementation and maintenance. I will also highlight the differences between traditional deployment approaches and the zero-touch approach that's used in the examples provided.

CI/CD pipelines

Let's look at this in more detail:

- **Traditional approach**:

  - In the traditional approach, software releases involve manual steps such as building, testing, and deploying code

  - Manual intervention and coordination are required to ensure the proper sequence of tasks, resulting in longer deployment cycles and slower time-to-market

- **Zero-touch approach**:

  - With zero-touch operations, CI/CD pipelines are implemented to automate the software release process

  - Version control systems, such as Git, trigger the CI/CD pipeline when changes are committed, initiating automated building, testing, and deployment

  - Automated testing ensures that the software is thoroughly validated, enabling confidence in the release quality

- **Risks**:

  - Risks in the zero-touch approach include inadequate testing or incomplete automation, which can result in faulty releases or regressions. Proper testing and quality assurance processes are essential to mitigate these risks.

- **Effort**:

  - The initial implementation effort involves setting up the CI/CD pipeline, defining build scripts, and configuring automated testing frameworks

  - Ongoing maintenance includes updating the pipeline as new requirements arise, adding new tests, and continuously improving the release process

IaC and orchestration

Let's look at this in more detail:

- **Traditional approach**:

  - In the traditional approach, infrastructure provisioning and configuration are often manual, leading to delays and inconsistencies

  - Manual intervention is required to set up servers, install dependencies, and configure the infrastructure

- **Zero-touch approach**:

  - Zero-touch operation leverages IaC tools such as Terraform or cloud provider APIs to automate infrastructure provisioning and configuration

  - Infrastructure definitions are written in code, enabling consistent and repeatable deployments

  - Orchestration tools such as Kubernetes or Docker Swarm automate containerized deployments, ensuring consistent environments

- **Risks**:

  - Risks in the zero-touch approach include misconfigurations in the IaC templates or inadequate coverage of deployment scenarios. Rigorous testing and reviews are necessary to mitigate these risks.

- **Effort**:

  - The initial implementation effort involves designing IaC templates, configuring orchestration tools, and integrating with version control and CI/CD systems

  - Ongoing maintenance includes updating infrastructure configurations, addressing changes in requirements, and performing regular audits

In summary, zero-touch operation accelerates deployment and time-to-market by automating the release process and infrastructure provisioning. It reduces manual effort, eliminates coordination overhead, and enables faster and more frequent deployments. While there are risks associated with inadequate testing, incomplete automation, or misconfigurations, proper testing, quality assurance, and continuous improvement efforts help mitigate these risks.

The implementation effort for zero-touch operations involves setting up CI/CD pipelines, defining automated deployment configurations, and integrating with IaC and orchestration tools. Ongoing maintenance requires updating the pipelines, infrastructure definitions, and tests to reflect changes in requirements.

The ROI of zero-touch operations in terms of accelerated deployment and time-to-market is significant as it allows organizations to release software faster, respond to market demands promptly, and gain a competitive edge. While the initial implementation effort and ongoing maintenance should be considered, the long-term benefits and improved efficiency outweigh the risks and effort involved.

Enhanced scalability and elasticity

Zero-touch operations improve enhanced scalability and elasticity by automating the management of resources and enabling dynamic scaling based on demand. In this section, we'll explain how it enhances scalability and elasticity with clear examples, along with the associated risks and effort required for implementation and maintenance. I will also highlight the differences between traditional approaches and the zero-touch approach used in the examples.

Automated resource provisioning

Let's look at this in more detail:

- **Traditional approach**:

  - In the traditional approach, provisioning resources involves manual intervention, such as setting up new servers or allocating additional storage

  - Manual scaling requires human effort and coordination and may lead to delays in responding to increased workloads

- **Zero-touch approach**:

  - With zero-touch operation, resource provisioning is automated using tools such as Terraform or cloud provider APIs

  - IaC templates define the desired resource configurations, allowing for dynamic and consistent provisioning of resources

  - Auto-scaling groups or similar mechanisms automatically adjust resource capacity based on predefined rules or workload metrics

- **Risks:**

  - Risks in the zero-touch approach include misconfigurations in the IaC templates or improper scaling rules, which may lead to resource inefficiencies or unexpected scaling behavior. Thorough testing and validation are necessary to mitigate these risks.

- **Effort:**

  - The initial implementation effort involves designing IaC templates, defining scaling rules, and integrating with auto-scaling mechanisms or cloud provider APIs

  - Ongoing maintenance includes updating scaling rules as per changing requirements, monitoring resource utilization, and optimizing configurations

Container orchestration

Let's look at this in more detail:

- **Traditional approach:**

  - In the traditional approach, scaling applications to handle increased workloads may involve manual intervention and coordination

  - Manually setting up and configuring additional servers or virtual machines to handle increased traffic can be time-consuming and error-prone

- **Zero-touch approach:**

  - Zero-touch operation leverages container orchestration platforms such as Kubernetes and Docker Swarm

  - These platforms automate the scaling of containerized applications based on defined rules, metrics, or workload thresholds

  - The orchestration layer automatically adjusts the number of running containers or replicas to handle changes in demand

- **Risks:**

  - Risks in the zero-touch approach include misconfigurations in the orchestration settings or inadequate monitoring of resource utilization, which may lead to resource wastage or insufficient capacity. Rigorous testing, monitoring, and continuous optimization are essential to mitigate these risks.

- **Effort**:

  - The initial implementation effort involves setting up the container orchestration platform, defining scaling rules, and configuring monitoring and alerting

  - Ongoing maintenance includes adjusting scaling rules, monitoring application performance, and optimizing resource allocation as per changing requirements

In summary, it improves enhanced scalability and elasticity by automating resource provisioning and dynamically scaling based on demand. It reduces manual effort, enables faster response to workload fluctuations, and ensures efficient resource utilization. While there are risks associated with misconfigurations or inadequate monitoring, proper testing, monitoring, and continuous optimization efforts help mitigate these risks.

The implementation effort for zero-touch operation involves designing IaC templates, integrating with auto-scaling mechanisms or container orchestration platforms, and configuring scaling rules. Ongoing maintenance includes updating configurations, monitoring resource utilization, and optimizing scaling parameters.

The ROI of zero-touch operation in terms of enhanced scalability and elasticity is significant as it allows organizations to handle increased workloads without manual intervention, optimize resource usage, and improve overall system performance. While the initial implementation effort and ongoing maintenance should be considered, the long-term benefits and improved scalability outweigh the risks and effort involved.

Reduced downtime and faster recovery

Zero-touch operations improve reduced downtime and faster recovery by automating monitoring, proactive alerting, and streamlined recovery processes. In this section, we'll explain how it enhances reduced downtime and faster recovery with clear examples, along with the associated risks and effort required for implementation and maintenance. I will also highlight the differences between traditional approaches and the zero-touch approach used in the examples.

Automated monitoring and alerting

Let's look at this in more detail:

- **Traditional approach**:

  - In the traditional approach, monitoring systems and applications rely on manual checks or reactive troubleshooting

  - Manual monitoring and response can lead to delays in detecting issues and addressing them, resulting in prolonged downtime

- **Zero-touch approach**:

  - Zero-touch operations automate monitoring using tools such as Prometheus, Nagios, or ELK

  - Automated monitoring systems collect real-time metrics, log data, and perform health checks on systems and applications

  - Proactive alerting mechanisms are configured to notify appropriate teams or individuals when predefined conditions or thresholds are met

- **Risks**:

  - Risks in the zero-touch approach include misconfigurations or inadequate coverage in monitoring configurations, leading to missed alerts or false positives. Thorough testing, proper configuration, and continuous monitoring are necessary to mitigate these risks.

- **Effort**:

  - The initial implementation effort involves setting up the monitoring infrastructure, configuring metrics, and defining alerting rules

  - Ongoing maintenance includes updating monitoring configurations, adjusting alerting thresholds, and addressing any issues or false alarms

Streamlined recovery processes

Let's look at this in more detail:

- **Traditional approach**:

  - In the traditional approach, recovery from failures or data loss often involves manual intervention, complex procedures, and longer downtime

  - The lack of standardized and automated recovery processes can lead to delays in restoring services or data

- **Zero-touch approach**:

  - Zero-touch operations automate recovery processes using predefined and tested recovery procedures

  - Automated recovery mechanisms, such as backups and replication, are implemented to minimize data loss and restore services quickly

  - Orchestration tools such as Kubernetes or database-specific tools provide built-in mechanisms for automating recovery and failover processes

- **Risks**:

  - Risks in the zero-touch approach include inadequate backup configurations, incomplete testing of recovery procedures, or errors in automation scripts, which may result in data loss or extended downtime. Rigorous testing, validation, and continuous improvement are necessary to mitigate these risks.

- **Effort**:

  - The initial implementation effort involves setting up automated backup mechanisms, defining recovery procedures, and configuring failover or replication settings

  - Ongoing maintenance includes regular testing of recovery procedures, updating backup configurations, and addressing any issues or gaps in the automation

In summary, it reduces downtime and faster recovery by automating monitoring, proactive alerting, and streamlined recovery processes. It reduces manual effort, enables faster issue detection and resolution, and minimizes the impact of failures. While there are risks associated with misconfigurations, incomplete automation, or errors in recovery procedures, proper testing, validation, and continuous improvement efforts help mitigate these risks.

The implementation effort for zero-touch operation involves setting up the monitoring infrastructure, configuring alerting rules, and implementing automated recovery mechanisms. Ongoing maintenance includes monitoring, updating configurations, testing recovery procedures, and addressing any issues that arise.

The ROI of zero-touch operation in terms of reduced downtime and faster recovery is significant as it minimizes the impact of failures, reduces downtime, and improves overall system availability. While the initial implementation effort and ongoing maintenance should be considered, the long-term benefits and improved reliability outweigh the risks and effort involved.

Improved compliance and security

Zero-touch operations improve compliance and security by automating security measures, enforcing standardized configurations, and providing auditability. In this section, we'll explain how it enhances compliance and security with clear examples, along with the associated risks and effort required for implementation and maintenance. I will also highlight the differences between traditional approaches and the zero-touch approach used in the examples.

Automated security configurations

Let's look at this in more detail:

- **Traditional approach**:

  - In the traditional approach, security configurations are often manually implemented, leading to inconsistencies and the potential for misconfigurations

- Manual configuration increases the risk of security vulnerabilities and makes it challenging to enforce standardized security measures

- **Zero-touch approach**:

  - Zero-touch operations automate security configurations using tools such as Ansible, Puppet, or Chef

  - Security settings, such as access controls, firewall rules, or encryption configurations, are defined in code or declarative language

  - Automation tools apply the desired security configurations consistently across systems, reducing the risk of misconfigurations

- **Risks**:

  - Risks in the zero-touch approach include misconfigurations in the automation scripts or incomplete coverage of security configurations, which may introduce security vulnerabilities. Rigorous testing, adherence to security best practices, and continuous monitoring are necessary to mitigate these risks.

- **Effort**:

  - The initial implementation effort involves designing and implementing the automation scripts for security configurations, defining security policies, and integrating them with version control and CI/CD systems

  - Ongoing maintenance includes updating the scripts to reflect changes in security requirements, addressing security vulnerabilities, and performing regular security audits

Automated compliance checks

Let's look at this in more detail:

- **Traditional approach**:

  - In the traditional approach, compliance checks are often performed manually, requiring time-consuming inspections and manual documentation

  - Manual checks and documentation can be error-prone, leading to compliance gaps or difficulties in proving compliance

- **Zero-touch approach**:

  - Zero-touch operations automate compliance checks using tools such as OpenSCAP, InSpec, or custom scripts

- Compliance rules or requirements are defined in code, enabling automated checks against desired configurations

- Reports and audit trails are generated automatically, providing documentation and evidence of compliance

- **Risks**:

  - Risks in the zero-touch approach include incomplete coverage of compliance checks, misconfigurations in compliance scripts, or false positives/negatives in the automated checks. Thorough testing, adherence to compliance standards, and regular validation are necessary to mitigate these risks.

- **Effort**:

  - The initial implementation effort involves setting up compliance automation tools, defining compliance rules, and integrating them with monitoring systems

  - Ongoing maintenance includes updating compliance rules, addressing new compliance requirements, and performing regular audits and validations

In summary, it improves compliance and security by automating security configurations and compliance checks. It reduces manual effort, ensures standardized security measures, and provides auditable evidence of compliance. While there are risks associated with misconfigurations, incomplete coverage, or false positives/negatives, proper testing, adherence to security best practices, and continuous improvement efforts help mitigate these risks.

The implementation effort for zero-touch operation involves designing and implementing automation scripts for security configurations, defining compliance rules, and integrating them with relevant systems. Ongoing maintenance includes updating configurations, addressing security vulnerabilities, updating compliance rules, and performing regular audits.

The ROI of zero-touch operations in terms of compliance and security is significant as it reduces manual effort, improves security consistency, and provides evidence of compliance. While the initial implementation effort and ongoing maintenance should be considered, the long-term benefits and improved security posture outweigh the risks and effort involved.

Sanity-checking our approach

To determine if you have implemented zero-touch operations correctly, you can consider the following indicators:

- **Minimal manual intervention**: Zero-touch operations aim to minimize manual intervention and human interaction in routine tasks. Evaluate the level of automation achieved and ensure that most of the operations related to database management, deployment, monitoring, scaling, and recovery are automated. Manually initiated actions should be exceptions rather than the norm.

- **Automated workflows**: Verify that you have established end-to-end automated workflows for database-related processes. For example, database provisioning, configuration management, deployment, and backup/restoration processes should be orchestrated through automated scripts, tools, or IaC solutions.

- **Monitoring and alerting**: Implement automated monitoring and alerting systems to proactively identify issues and notify the appropriate teams. Ensure that the system can detect performance bottlenecks, resource utilization, and potential security vulnerabilities. This helps maintain a proactive approach to managing the databases and minimizes the need for reactive manual intervention.

- **CI/CD**: Evaluate the level of automation that's achieved in the CI/CD pipeline for databases. Verify if changes to the database schema, configurations, or data can be automatically tested, validated, and deployed. CI/CD automation ensures that changes are rapidly and consistently deployed without manual intervention.

- **Metrics and reporting**: Implement automated metrics collection and reporting mechanisms to gather data on database performance, resource utilization, availability, and other relevant metrics. Automated reporting enables teams to monitor the health and performance of the databases without manual effort and helps identify trends and areas for improvement.

- **Efficiency and error reduction**: Measure the impact of zero-touch operations on operational efficiency and error reduction. Assess the time and effort that's saved through automation, as well as the reduction in manual errors and inconsistencies. Compare key performance metrics before and after implementing zero-touch operations to evaluate their effectiveness.

It's important to remind ourselves that achieving a fully "zero-touch" state may not be feasible or necessary for all tasks or situations. Some exceptional cases or critical scenarios may still require human intervention. However, the goal is to minimize manual effort and maximize automation wherever possible to improve operational efficiency and reduce the risk of errors.

Regularly review and refine your automation processes based on feedback, performance metrics, and evolving requirements to continuously improve the implementation of zero-touch operations.

Conclusion on ROI

Implementing zero-touch operations requires an initial investment of time and effort to design, implement, and validate the automated workflows. Additionally, ongoing maintenance efforts are needed to ensure the reliability and consistency of the automated processes.

However, the ROI can be significant in terms of improved reliability and consistency. By automating configuration management and release processes, organizations can reduce human errors, ensure standardized configurations, and achieve faster and more consistent deployments.

The risks associated with misconfigurations or incomplete automation can be mitigated through thorough testing, reviews, and ongoing monitoring. Regular updates and enhancements to the automated processes help maintain their reliability and effectiveness.

Overall, the ROI of implementing zero-touch operations depends on the specific context, the complexity of the systems involved, and the level of automation achieved. Organizations that prioritize reliability and consistency, invest in robust testing and monitoring practices, and continuously improve their automation workflows are likely to realize significant long-term benefits and improved operational stability.

Summary

Implementing zero-touch operations requires an initial investment of time and effort to design, implement, and validate the automated workflows. Additionally, ongoing maintenance efforts are needed to ensure the reliability and consistency of the automated processes.

However, the ROI can be significant in terms of improved reliability and consistency. By automating configuration management and release processes, organizations can reduce human errors, ensure standardized configurations, and achieve faster and more consistent deployments.

The risks associated with misconfigurations or incomplete automation can be mitigated through thorough testing, reviews, and ongoing monitoring. Regular updates and enhancements to the automated processes help maintain their reliability and effectiveness.

Overall, the ROI of implementing zero-touch operations depends on the specific context, the complexity of the systems involved, and the level of automation achieved. Organizations that prioritize reliability and consistency, invest in robust testing and monitoring practices, and continuously improve their automation workflows are likely to realize significant long-term benefits and improved operational stability.

In the next chapter, we will learn about the role of the DevOps DBA through design to production.

Design and Implementation

The role of a DevOps **Database Administrator (DBA)** is a crucial one as it bridges a gap – that between the database and the rest of the application. In traditional environments, changes to the database are often a source of risk and delay in software releases. DBAs are usually seen as gatekeepers, carefully guarding the data and ensuring its integrity, often at the expense of speed.

However, in a DevOps culture, the DBA's role must evolve. Instead of being a gatekeeper, the DevOps DBA becomes a facilitator, helping the development and operations teams to work with the database effectively and efficiently without compromising its reliability, integrity, or security.

A DevOps DBA maintains the database in production environments, troubleshoots any issues, and is actively involved in the design and decision-making processes. They play a vital role in making sure that the database integrates smoothly with the CI/CD pipeline. They use infrastructure as code to create and manage databases, allowing for consistency across all environments and making the creation and teardown of databases quicker and more efficient.

They work with version control systems to track changes to the database schema, just like developers do with application code. They're responsible for automating database tasks wherever possible, reducing the potential for human error and freeing up their own time to focus on higher-value activities.

In performance tuning, a DevOps DBA will use monitoring tools to keep an eye on the database's performance and make the necessary adjustments to ensure it's running as efficiently as possible. When it comes to security, they are in charge of implementing measures to protect the data and ensure the organization is in compliance with relevant laws and regulations.

The DevOps DBA is a communicator and collaborator, working closely with developers, operations staff, and other stakeholders. They help to break down the traditional silos, sharing their knowledge and expertise to enable everyone to work with the database more effectively.

In conclusion, the role of a DevOps DBA in modern software development is vital. With their unique skills and perspective, they are perfectly placed to help bring about a truly cross-functional DevOps culture that values collaboration, shared responsibility, and a focus on delivering value to the end user.

The following are the main topics to be covered in this chapter:

- Designing data-persistence technologies
- Implementing data-persistence technologies
- Database provisioning and Infrastructure as Code
- Database version control and CI/CD
- Database performance tuning
- Security and compliance
- Collaboration and communication

Designing data-persistence technologies

In the ever-evolving landscape of technology, the manner in which data is stored, retrieved, and manipulated plays a pivotal role in determining the efficiency and reliability of systems. At the heart of this is the art and science of database design, which serves as the foundation for many applications, from simple websites to sophisticated machine learning models. Mastering the principles of database design, including understanding, organizing, maintaining, and securing data, is indispensable for anyone aiming to leverage the full potential of modern systems. Moreover, as database technologies evolve and diversify, the choices between RDBMS, NoSQL, and NewSQL become increasingly nuanced, warranting a deeper exploration of their respective strengths and use cases. In this section, we aim to shed light on these crucial facets, guiding you through the labyrinth of database intricacies.

Database design principles

Database design is an integral part of creating an efficient and useful system to store and manipulate data. The core principles revolve around understanding your data, organizing it well, maintaining its integrity, and ensuring its security. We will look at each of the core principles in detail as follows:

- **Understanding your data**: The first step in designing a database is understanding what kind of data you are working with and how it is related. This often involves working closely with stakeholders and potential end users to identify the information that the system needs to store and manipulate.

- **Organizing your data**: Once you have a good understanding of your data, you can start organizing it. Here, you employ techniques such as data normalization and denormalization. Normalization is the process of structuring the data to minimize redundancy and dependency by organizing fields and table relationships. Denormalization is the process of combining tables to improve read performance at the cost of some write performance.

- **Maintaining data integrity**: Data integrity refers to the accuracy and consistency of data. The aim is to prevent data from becoming corrupt or inaccurate. This can be achieved through constraints, such as primary keys, foreign keys, unique, check, and not null constraints.

- **Ensuring data security**: Data security refers to protective measures put in place to keep data safe from unauthorized access or alterations. This involves implementing appropriate user permissions and roles, encrypting data both at rest and in transit, and regularly auditing database activity.

A concrete example of designing a scalable, robust, and secure database is the creation of an e-commerce platform database. It involves understanding the necessary data, including products, customers, orders, and payments, and identifying the relationships between them. A highly normalized schema can be designed to avoid data redundancy. However, to improve read operations, some level of denormalization might be used, such as creating view tables that aggregate product and order data for quick access.

Data integrity can be maintained by setting up primary keys, foreign keys, and other constraints. For instance, a foreign key constraint can be set up between orders and customers, ensuring that every order is always associated with a valid customer.

Data security can be ensured by creating different roles with different access levels. For example, a sales role might have read access to product and order data but no access to payment data. All data can be encrypted using industry-standard protocols to protect it from unauthorized access. Regular audits can also be set up to monitor database activity and identify potential security breaches.

RDBMS versus NoSQL versus NewSQL

When it comes to choosing a database, the decision often depends on the specific needs of the application you're building. The choice is generally among **Relational Database Management System (RDBMS)**, NoSQL, and NewSQL databases:

- **RDBMS**: These databases, such as MySQL, PostgreSQL, and Oracle, are based on a relational model where data is stored in tables, and relationships are formed using primary and foreign keys. RDBMS databases are a great choice for applications that require complex transactions with multiple operations or queries that require aggregation. They're also excellent for maintaining data integrity and supporting SQL for a robust, declarative query language.

- **NoSQL**: NoSQL databases, such as MongoDB, Cassandra, and CouchDB, do not adhere to the traditional relational database structure. Instead, they can store data in several ways: document-based, column-based, graph-based, or key-value pairs. NoSQL databases are ideal for applications with large amounts of data or need to scale horizontally. They're designed to excel in speed and flexibility.

- **NewSQL**: NewSQL databases such as CockroachDB, VoltDB, and MemSQL attempt to combine the best of both worlds. They offer the scalability of NoSQL databases and the ACID transactions of RDBMS. NewSQL databases are designed to overcome the limitations of traditional RDBMSs in distributed environments and provide horizontal scalability while maintaining the strong consistency of traditional databases.

Making a decision among these types of databases depends on various factors such as the data structure, scalability, consistency, and latency requirements of your application.

Consider the case of a large-scale, distributed, write-heavy application such as a real-time analytics system. Here, the primary need is to handle a huge volume of write operations with low latency and to distribute data across multiple nodes for redundancy and availability.

For such an application, a traditional RDBMS such as MySQL might not be the best fit. MySQL follows a strong consistency model that can become a bottleneck when write operations are exceptionally high. Also, while it's possible to distribute a MySQL database across multiple nodes, doing so can be complex and may not offer the same level of performance or ease of scalability as a system designed with distribution in mind.

On the other hand, a NoSQL database such as Apache Cassandra could be a much better fit. Cassandra is designed to handle large amounts of data across many commodity servers, providing high write throughput and low latency. It follows an "eventual consistency" model, which means it prioritizes availability and partition tolerance. This makes it a good choice for write-heavy applications where it's acceptable for data to be slightly out of sync across nodes for a short period.

Cassandra's data model, based on the wide-column store paradigm, is another point of consideration. It allows you to store large amounts of data in a semi-structured manner, offering more flexibility than the rigid schema of an RDBMS.

NewSQL databases could also be a possible choice here, as they attempt to combine the scalability of NoSQL with the ACID transactions of RDBMS. However, given their relative newness in the field, they may not be the best choice for all applications. In a high-volume, write-heavy scenario like our example, Cassandra's proven scalability and performance might make it a safer bet.

In conclusion, the choice between RDBMS, NoSQL, and NewSQL databases depends greatly on the specific requirements of the application. Understanding these different types of databases and their strengths and weaknesses is crucial in making an informed choice.

Implementing data-persistence technologies

In our digital age, the ability to store, access, and manage vast amounts of data swiftly and securely forms the backbone of many essential applications. Central to this is the database system, acting as a repository that not only holds the data but also ensures its seamless integration into the applications that rely on it. Whether you're implementing a traditional RDBMS or venturing into the realms of NoSQL, a successful setup goes beyond mere installation. It demands a holistic approach, encompassing judicious configuration, vigilant management, and foresight into potential pitfalls and recovery mechanisms. Dive into this section to gain insights into the foundational steps of installing, configuring, and effectively managing your database systems.

Installation, configuration, and management of database systems

Database systems are complex software suites that require careful installation and configuration to function optimally. The specific steps for installation, configuration, and management can vary significantly between different types of database systems, be it RDBMSs such as PostgreSQL, MySQL, or Oracle, or NoSQL databases including MongoDB, Cassandra, and Redis.

However, some universal steps need to be taken across most database systems:

- **System requirements**: Before the installation process, ensure that your system meets the minimum requirements to run the database system. These requirements include hardware specifications (CPU, RAM, and disk space), the operating system, and its version.

- **Installation**: Installation steps vary depending on the platform (Windows, Linux, or macOS) and the specific database system. In many cases, installation might involve downloading an installer or package from the official website or using a package manager such as `apt`, `yum`, or `brew`.

- **Configuration**: After installation, you may need to configure the database system to suit your needs. This could include setting memory limits, configuring security settings, setting up user accounts and permissions, setting up network settings, and more.

- **Management**: Database management involves regular tasks such as creating and managing databases and tables, managing users and permissions, monitoring performance, backing up and restoring data, and troubleshooting any issues that arise.

Practical example – PostgreSQL database server installation, configuration, and management

PostgreSQL is a powerful, open source, object-relational database system with a strong emphasis on extensibility and standards compliance. The following are step-by-step instructions for installing, configuring, and managing a PostgreSQL server on a Linux system:

1. **Installation**: You can install PostgreSQL on Ubuntu using the `apt` package manager:

BASH

```
sudo apt-get update
sudo apt-get install postgresql postgresql-contrib
```

This command installs the PostgreSQL server and also includes `contrib`, a package that contains several additional utilities and functionalities.

2. **Accessing PostgreSQL**: By default, PostgreSQL sets up a `postgres` user for basic administration. Switch to the `postgres` account:

BASH

```
sudo -i -u postgres
```

3. Then, you can access the PostgreSQL prompt by typing the following:

BASH

```
psql
```

4. To exit the PostgreSQL prompt, you can type the following:

PSQL

```
\q
```

5. **Configuration**: PostgreSQL's configuration files are stored in the `/etc/postgresql/<version>/main` directory. Key files include the following:

   - `postgresql.conf`: This is the main configuration file for the PostgreSQL database. It includes settings for data directories, connection settings, resource usage, and more.

   - `pg_hba.conf`: This file controls client authentication. You can specify the IP addresses and networks that can connect to the database and what authentication method they must use.

6. To modify these settings, you can open the files in a text editor with root privileges:

BASH

```
sudo nano /etc/postgresql/<version>/main/postgresql.conf
```

7. Once you've made changes, save and close the file. Then, restart PostgreSQL to apply the changes:

BASH

```
sudo systemctl restart postgresql
```

8. **Management**: Managing a PostgreSQL server involves tasks such as creating databases and tables and managing users and permissions. To create a new database, you can use the `createdb` command:

PSQL

```
createdb mydatabase
```

9. To create a new user, you can use the `createuser` command:

PSQL

```
createuser myuser
```

10. Once you've created a user, you can grant them permissions. For example, to give a user access to a database, you can use the GRANT SQL command:

PSQL

```
GRANT ALL PRIVILEGES ON DATABASE mydatabase TO myuser;
```

This command gives `myuser` all permissions on the `mydatabase` database.

11. PostgreSQL provides the `pg_dump` utility for backing up a single database. Here's how to back up the `mydatabase` database to a file:

BASH

```
pg_dump mydatabase > mydatabase.sql
```

12. To restore this backup, you can use the `psql` command:

BASH

```
psql mydatabase < mydatabase.sql
```

For monitoring and performance-tuning purposes, PostgreSQL provides various statistics views that you can query to monitor the database's performance. You can also use the EXPLAIN command to understand how PostgreSQL executes a query, which can be useful for performance tuning.

Security is a crucial aspect of database management. Here are some of the ways to enhance the security of your PostgreSQL server:

- **Updating PostgreSQL**: Keep your PostgreSQL server updated to the latest stable version to get the latest security patches. The command for this is as follows:

BASH

```
sudo apt-get update
sudo apt-get upgrade postgresql
```

- **Managing user roles and privileges**: Don't give more privileges than necessary. Use the GRANT and REVOKE commands to manage user privileges.

- **Encryption**: PostgreSQL supports SSL certificates to encrypt client/server communications. You can generate a certificate and key, then configure PostgreSQL to use them by editing the postgresql.conf and pg_hba.conf files.

- **Firewall**: Use a firewall to restrict which IP addresses can connect to your PostgreSQL server. On Ubuntu, you can use the UFW firewall.

The preceding steps and methods give a broad overview of installing, configuring, and managing a PostgreSQL server. However, PostgreSQL is a powerful and complex system, and fully mastering its features may require more in-depth study or professional training.

Disaster recovery planning

In the context of database management, disaster recovery planning and high availability are paramount for ensuring the robustness and continuity of the applications that rely on your database. Let's examine what this entails in more detail:

- **Disaster recovery**: Disaster recovery planning aims to restore data and resume operation as soon as possible following a disaster. The key aspect of disaster recovery is maintaining backups of the database, which can be used to restore the database to a previous state. The recovery plan should define the **recovery point objective** (**RPO**), which indicates how much data loss is acceptable, and the **recovery time objective** (**RTO**), which indicates how quickly the system should be back online after a disaster.

- **High availability**: High availability aims to ensure that the database remains available at all times, even in the event of a node failure. High availability can be achieved through various strategies, including replication and automatic failover. Replication involves maintaining copies of the database on multiple nodes, while automatic failover involves automatically switching to a backup system if the primary system fails.

Practical example – MongoDB replication and automatic failover

MongoDB offers replication and automatic failover features out of the box, providing a solid foundation for implementing high availability and disaster recovery strategies.

MongoDB replication

Replication in MongoDB is accomplished through replica sets, a group of MongoDB instances that maintain the same dataset. A replica set contains several data-bearing nodes and, optionally, one arbiter node. Of the data-bearing nodes, one is a primary node that receives all write operations, while the others are secondary nodes that replicate the primary node's dataset.

To set up a MongoDB replica set, use the following steps:

1. Start each MongoDB instance in the replica set. Use the `--replset` option to specify the name of the replica set:

BASH

```
mongod --port 27017 --dbpath /data/db1 --replSet rs0
mongod --port 27018 --dbpath /data/db2 --replSet rs0
mongod --port 27019 --dbpath /data/db3 --replSet rs0
```

2. Connect a mongo shell to one of your MongoDB instances:

BASH

```
mongo --port 27017
```

3. Initiate the replica set. In the mongo shell, use the `rs.initiate()` method:

MongoDB

```
rs.initiate()
```

4. Add the remaining instances to the replica set using the `rs.add()` method:

MongoDB

```
rs.add("hostname:27018")
rs.add("hostname:27019")
```

The replica set is now operational. You can check the status of the replica set at any time with the `rs.status()` command in the mongo shell.

MongoDB automatic failover

MongoDB's replica set provides automatic failover support. If the primary node fails, the remaining secondary nodes will hold an election to choose a new primary.

Automatic failover ensures the high availability of your MongoDB system. However, it's important to note that failover is not instantaneous. It usually takes 10-30 seconds to complete. Applications must be able to handle this downtime.

In conclusion, MongoDB's built-in support for replication and automatic failover is a powerful tool for achieving high availability and facilitating disaster recovery. However, these strategies should be part of a broader plan that also includes regular backups and thorough testing to ensure the system can recover from a disaster quickly and efficiently.

Disaster recovery in MongoDB

MongoDB's replication and automatic failover features provide strong mechanisms for disaster recovery, but there are additional steps you should take to ensure that your system can recover from a disaster:

1. **Backups**: Regular backups are an essential part of any disaster recovery plan. MongoDB provides several backup solutions, including `mongodump`, a utility that performs a binary export of the contents of a MongoDB instance. The `mongorestore` utility can be used to restore these backups.

    To back up a MongoDB database using `mongodump`, run the following command:

BASH

```
mongodump --db mydatabase --out /path/to/backup/directory
```

This will create a backup of the `mydatabase` database in the specified directory.

2. To restore the database from the backup, run the following:

BASH

```
mongorestore /path/to/backup/directory
```

3. **Sharding**: Sharding is a method for distributing data across multiple machines. It provides high availability and data redundancy. MongoDB supports sharding through its sharded clusters feature.

4. **Monitoring**: Use MongoDB's built-in Cloud Manager or Ops Manager to monitor the state of your MongoDB systems. These tools provide visibility into your MongoDB deployment and alert you to any issues that could impact system performance or availability.

Testing your disaster recovery plan

It's crucial not only to have a disaster recovery plan but also to test it regularly to ensure it works as expected. Here are some best practices:

- **Regularly simulate disasters**: Regularly shut down a node in your system to simulate a disaster. Verify that failover occurs as expected, and test your application to ensure it handles the failover gracefully.

- **Test your backups**: Regularly restore your backups to a separate system to ensure they work as expected. This can help you catch any issues with your backup process.

- **Document your plan**: Ensure that your disaster recovery plan is thoroughly documented and that your team is familiar with the steps to recover from a disaster.

In conclusion, MongoDB provides robust features for replication, automatic failover, and disaster recovery. However, setting up these features is just one part of building a highly available and resilient system. Regular monitoring, testing, and documentation are crucial for ensuring that your system can recover from a disaster quickly and with minimal data loss.

Database provisioning and Infrastructure as Code

As we discussed in the previous chapter, **Infrastructure as Code** (**IaC**) is a key DevOps practice that involves managing and provisioning data centers through machine-readable definition files, rather than physical hardware configuration or interactive configuration tools. This approach has several advantages, including speed, repeatability, scalability, and reduced human error.

IaC is highly relevant to DevOps DBAs because it can automate many of the tasks involved in setting up and managing databases. For example, instead of manually installing a database server, configuring it, and creating databases and tables, a DevOps DBA can write a script that does all this automatically. The script can be version controlled, tested, and run multiple times to create identical environments.

Furthermore, IaC tools including Terraform, Ansible, Chef, and Puppet allow DBAs to manage infrastructure across different cloud providers and on-premises environments using the same scripts. This consistency across different environments can reduce bugs and streamline the deployment process.

Practical example – using Terraform to script the setup of a SQL Server database

Terraform is a popular IaC tool that can be used to script the setup of a SQL Server database. The following is a step-by-step guide to setting up a SQL Server database on an Azure environment using Terraform:

1. **Installing Terraform**: If you haven't already, download and install Terraform from the official website. Add Terraform to your system's path so you can run it from any command prompt.

2. **Setting up Azure provider**: To manage resources in Azure, you need to set up the Azure provider. Create a file named `provider.tf` with the following contents:

HCL

```
terraform {
  required_providers {
    azurerm = {
      source = "hashicorp/azurerm"
      version = "=2.40.0"
    }
  }
}

provider "azurerm" {
  features {}
}
```

This code tells Terraform to use the Azure Resource Manager provider. Replace the version number with the latest version available.

3. **Creating a SQL Server instance**: To create a SQL Server instance, you need to define the resource in a Terraform script. Create a file named `main.tf` with the following contents:

HCL

```
resource "azurerm_sql_server" "example" {
  name                         = "examplesqlserver"
  resource_group_name          = azurerm_resource_group.example.name
  location                     = azurerm_resource_group.example.location
  version                      = "12.0"
  administrator_login          = "admin"
  administrator_login_password = "password"

  tags = {
    environment = "Example"
  }
}
```

This code tells Terraform to create a SQL Server instance with the specified name, resource group, location, version, and admin credentials. You should replace these values with your own.

4. **Creating a SQL database**: To create a SQL database, add the following code to your `main.tf` file:

HCL

```
resource "azurerm_sql_database" "example" {
    name                 = "examplesqldatabase"
    resource_group_name  = azurerm_resource_group.example.name
    server_name          = azurerm_sql_server.example.name
    location             = azurerm_resource_group.example.
location
    edition              = "Standard"
    collation            = "SQL_Latin1_General_CP1_CI_AS"
    max_size_bytes       = "1073741824"

    tags = {
      environment = "Example"
    }
}
```

This code tells Terraform to create a SQL database with the specified name, resource group, server name, location, edition, collation, and maximum size. Again, replace these values with your own.

5. **Apply the Terraform script**: Finally, to create the SQL Server and database in Azure, run the following command in the directory containing your Terraform files:

BASH

```
terraform apply
```

This is a basic example of how a DevOps DBA can use Terraform to script the setup of a SQL Server database. The actual process might involve more steps and scripts, depending on the complexity of the environment and the specific requirements of the database.

Database version control and CI/CD

As the digital realm evolves, the significance of cohesive workflows becomes ever more apparent. The intersection of software development and databases brings forth challenges, requiring meticulous management. Beyond the realms of managing lines of code lies the vast and intricate world of databases. A slight alteration in the structure can set off a domino effect, impacting an entire application. To ensure the integrity and efficiency of this domain, the principles of version control, a mainstay in software development, are increasingly being applied to databases. Delve into this section to understand the essence of database version control and witness its practical implementation using tools such as Liquibase.

Importance of database version control

Version control systems are fundamental to modern software development, providing a way to track changes, manage code, and coordinate work among multiple developers. However, it's not just source code that can benefit from version control; database schemas and changes can also be version controlled, offering similar advantages.

Database version control is crucial for several reasons:

- **Synchronization**: It ensures that everyone is working with the same database structure, reducing inconsistencies and bugs.

- **Traceability**: It keeps a historical record of all changes, allowing developers to understand why a particular change was made and when.

- **Coordination**: It helps multiple developers work on the same database without overwriting each other's changes.

- **Deployment**: It makes it easier to manage deployments and roll back changes if something goes wrong. You can recreate the exact state of the database at any point in time.

- **Compliance**: In some cases, database version control can help meet compliance requirements by providing an audit trail of changes.

Despite its importance, database version control can be challenging to implement because databases are stateful and because changes can affect existing data. Fortunately, tools such as Liquibase can help manage database changes and provide version control-like capabilities for databases.

Practical example – using Liquibase to manage database schema changes

Liquibase is an open source tool that helps manage database schema changes. It works by applying a series of changesets to a database, which are stored in XML, YAML, JSON, or SQL files. Each changeset contains a change to be made to the database and is identified by a unique ID.

Here's a step-by-step guide to setting up and using Liquibase:

1. **Install Liquibase**: Download the Liquibase installer from the official website and follow the installation instructions for your operating system.

2. **Create a database**: Before you can use Liquibase, you need a database. This example assumes you have a MySQL database named `mydatabase` running on localhost with the username `root` and password `password`.

3. **Create a Liquibase project**: A Liquibase project is simply a directory that contains all your changeset files. You can organize your changesets in any way you want, but a common approach is to create a separate directory for each version of your application, such as the following example:

BASH

```bash
mkdir -p ~/myproject/1.0.0
cd ~/myproject/1.0.0
```

4. **Create a changeset**: A changeset is a file that describes a change to the database. For example, to create a table, you might create a changeset like this:

XML

```xml
<?xml version="1.0" encoding="UTF-8"?>

<databaseChangeLog
    xmlns="http://www.liquibase.org/xml/ns/dbchangelog"
    xmlns:xsi="http://www.w3.org/2001/XMLSchema-instance"
    xsi:schemaLocation="http://www.liquibase.org/xml/ns/
dbchangelog
            http://www.liquibase.org/xml/ns/dbchangelog/
dbchangelog-3.1.xsd">

    <changeSet id="1" author="bob">
      <createTable tableName="person">
        <column name="id" type="int">
          <constraints primaryKey="true" nullable="false"/>
        </column>
        <column name="firstname" type="varchar(50)">
          <constraints nullable="false"/>
        </column>
        <column name="lastname" type="varchar(50)">
          <constraints nullable="false"/>
        </column>
      </createTable>
    </changeSet>

</databaseChangeLog>
```

Save this file as `1.0.0.xml` in your `1.0.0` directory.

5.   **Run the changeset**: To apply the changeset to your database, run the following command:

BASH

```bash
liquibase --driver=com.mysql.cj.jdbc.Driver \
          --classpath=/path/to/mysql-connector-java-8.0.19.jar \
          --url="jdbc:mysql://localhost/mydatabase" \
          --changeLogFile=1.0.0.xml \
          --username=root \
          --password=password \
          update
```

Replace `/path/to/mysql-connector-java-8.0.19.jar` with the path to your MySQL JDBC driver.

6.   **Create more changesets**: As your application evolves, you'll need to make more changes to your database. For each change, create a new changeset file in the appropriate directory, incrementing the changeset ID.

7.   **Roll back changes**: If something goes wrong, you can use Liquibase to roll back changes. For example, to roll back the last change, run the following:

BASH

```bash
liquibase --driver=com.mysql.cj.jdbc.Driver \
          --classpath=/path/to/mysql-connector-java-8.0.19.jar \
          --url="jdbc:mysql://localhost/mydatabase" \
          --changeLogFile=1.0.0.xml \
          --username=root \
          --password=password \
          rollbackCount 1
```

Liquibase provides a robust, flexible way to manage database schema changes and enables database version control. It's a valuable tool in the DevOps DBA's toolkit, enabling you to manage databases in the same systematic, controlled way you manage source code.

Role of the DevOps DBA in CI/CD pipelines

The role of the DevOps DBA in CI/CD pipelines is to ensure that database changes are seamlessly integrated and deployed as part of the software release process. The DevOps DBA collaborates with development, operations, and release management teams to create an automated, efficient, and error-free release pipeline that includes database elements.

Key responsibilities of the DevOps DBA in CI/CD pipelines include the following:

- **Schema management**: Managing database schema changes and ensuring they are version-controlled, tested, and deployed in sync with application code

- **Automated migrations**: Automating database migrations to ensure that schema changes and data updates are applied correctly and consistently across environments

- **Performance testing**: Ensuring that database changes do not degrade performance by incorporating database performance tests into the CI/CD pipeline

- **Security**: Ensuring that database changes comply with security best practices and that sensitive data is protected in all environments

- **Disaster recovery and backups**: Making sure that backups are taken before deployments and that there's a plan in place for quick recovery in case of failure

- **Monitoring and alerts**: Implementing monitoring tools to check the health of the database as changes are deployed, and setting up alerts for any issues

- **Coordination and communication**: Coordinating with various stakeholders involved in the release process to ensure database changes are reviewed and approved before deployment

Practical example – Jenkins pipeline with database migrations using Flyway

Flyway is an open source database migration tool that makes it easy to version control and migrate your database schema. Jenkins is an automation server used for implementing continuous integration and delivery pipelines. The following is an in-depth walk-through of setting up a Jenkins pipeline that includes database migrations using Flyway:

1. **Prerequisites**: Before you start, you will need to have Jenkins and Flyway installed, and a database (such as MySQL) that you want to run migrations against.

2. **Set up Flyway configuration**: Create a Flyway configuration file named `flyway.conf` with your database connection details:

   ```
   flyway.url=jdbc:mysql://localhost:3306/mydatabase
   flyway.user=myuser
   flyway.password=mypassword
   ```

   Also, create a directory named `sql` to store your SQL migration scripts.

3. **Create a Jenkins pipeline**: In Jenkins, create a new pipeline. You can do this by selecting **New Item** from the dashboard, then choosing the **Pipeline** option.

4. **Configure the pipeline:** In the pipeline configuration page, scroll down to the **Pipeline** section. You'll be entering a script here that defines your pipeline.

5. **Write the pipeline script**: In the **Pipeline** section, choose **Pipeline script** and enter a script that defines your pipeline. The following is an example script:

GROOVY

```groovy
pipeline {
    agent any

    environment {
        FLYWAY_HOME = '/path/to/flyway'
    }

    stages {
        stage('Checkout Code') {
            steps {
                // Checkout code from your repository
                git 'https://github.com/your-repo.git'
            }
        }

        stage('Database Migration') {
            steps {
                script {
                    // Run Flyway migrations
                    sh "${FLYWAY_HOME}/flyway
-configFiles=flyway.conf migrate"
                }
            }
        }

        stage('Build') {
            steps {
                // Your build steps go here
            }
        }

        stage('Deploy') {
            steps {
                // Your deployment steps go here


            }
        }
```

```
        }
    }
```

This script defines a pipeline with four stages:

- `Checkout Code`: This stage checks out the code from your repository. Replace the URL with the URL of your repository.

- `Database Migration`: This stage runs Flyway migrations against your database.

- `Build`: This builds your application. Replace the comment with the actual steps for your build process.

- `Deploy`: This deploys your application. Replace the comment with the actual steps for your deployment process.

6. **Run the pipeline**: Save the pipeline and run it. You can do this by clicking **Build Now** on the pipeline page.

This Jenkins pipeline allows for the seamless integration of database migrations into the CI/CD process. When the pipeline is run, Flyway applies any pending migrations to the database, ensuring the database schema is up to date and in sync with the application code.

In conclusion, as a DevOps DBA, working with CI/CD pipelines allows for a smooth, automated, and efficient process, managing database schema changes, automated migrations, and ensuring database performance, security, and disaster recovery in alignment with the application's release process. This elevates the role of the DBA from a background role to a critical part of the development, deployment, and release life cycle.

Database performance tuning

In the intricate world of software applications, speed and efficiency often dictate success. While the user interface, design, and features draw the users in, it's the underlying performance that ensures they stay. Central to this performance is the database – the beating heart that powers most digital platforms. However, like any intricate machinery, databases require fine-tuning to deliver their best. Dive into the nuances of performance tuning in this section, understanding its significance, and unraveling strategies that ensure a seamless software experience.

Importance of performance tuning and common strategies

In a software application, performance plays a crucial role in providing a satisfactory user experience. A well-optimized database not only serves the application faster but also reduces the resources needed to store and retrieve data. Performance tuning is the process of identifying and fixing bottlenecks to improve the system's speed and efficiency.

Database performance tuning is essential to achieve the following:

- **Improved user experience**: A well-optimized database ensures the application runs smoothly and rapidly, which greatly enhances user experience

- **Efficient resource utilization**: By improving query performance, you can make better use of existing hardware and delay costly upgrades

- **Increased system scalability**: A well-optimized database can handle a larger number of users and operations, allowing your application to scale more effectively as it grows

To attain the preceding, the following are some common performance-tuning strategies:

- **Indexing**: Indexes can significantly speed up data retrieval. However, they can slow down data insertion and update operations because the indexes must be updated whenever data changes. Therefore, it's a balance between read and write operations.

- **Partitioning**: This involves dividing a large database table into smaller, more manageable parts, which can improve query performance.

- **Denormalization**: While normalization is key to reducing data redundancy, sometimes data is intentionally denormalized (i.e., certain data is duplicated across tables) to reduce complex joins and improve performance.

- **Caching**: By storing frequently accessed data in memory, you can reduce the need to fetch data from the disk, improving performance.

- **Query optimization**: Queries can often be rewritten or refactored to execute more efficiently. This can include avoiding full table scans, reducing joins, or eliminating unnecessary subqueries.

- **Database design**: A well-designed database can significantly improve performance. This includes proper use of data types, constraints, and relationships.

Practical example – optimizing a poorly performing query in Oracle

Let's consider a simple scenario: you have a query that is running slow in an Oracle database, and you need to optimize it. The query is as follows:

SQL

```sql
SELECT * FROM employees e JOIN departments d ON e.department_id =
d.department_id WHERE d.department_name = 'Sales';
```

This query retrieves all employees in the `Sales` department. Suppose the `employees` table has a million records, and the query is performing a full table scan, making it slow. Here's how you might go about optimizing it:

1. **Identify the problem**: The first step is to identify what is causing the query to run slowly. In Oracle, you can use the `EXPLAIN PLAN` statement to understand the Oracle optimizer's plan for executing your query. Run the following:

SQL

```
EXPLAIN PLAN FOR
SELECT * FROM employees e JOIN departments d ON e.department_
id = d.department_id WHERE d.department_name = 'Sales';
```

2. Then, view the plan using the following command:

SQL

```
SELECT * FROM TABLE(DBMS_XPLAN.DISPLAY);
```

Suppose this shows a full table scan on the `employees` table. That's likely the source of the problem.

3. **Use indexing**: As the `employees` table is large, a full table scan can be expensive. If the `department_id` column in the `employees` table is not already indexed, creating an index can improve performance:

SQL

```
CREATE INDEX idx_department_id ON employees (department_id);
```

4. **Restructure the query**: Instead of using `SELECT *`, specify only the columns you need. Every extra column requires more memory and slows down processing.

5. **Use bind variables**: If your application constructs similar queries with different values, using bind variables can improve performance by allowing Oracle to reuse the execution plan:

SQL

```
SELECT /*+ BIND_AWARE */
    *
FROM employees e
JOIN departments d ON e.department_id = d.department_id
WHERE d.department_name = :department_name;
```

Here, `:department_name` is a bind variable that your application sets to the desired department name.

6. **Re-evaluate the plan**: After making these changes, run `EXPLAIN PLAN` again to see the new execution plan. If it shows that Oracle is using the index and no longer performing a full table scan, your optimization efforts have likely paid off.

Remember, performance tuning is an iterative process. The changes you make should be guided by a thorough understanding of the problem and carefully tested to ensure they produce the desired improvement.

In conclusion, performance tuning plays a pivotal role in software applications. It improves user experience, efficiently utilizes resources, and increases system scalability. By understanding different strategies such as indexing, partitioning, denormalization, caching, query optimization, and robust database design, a DevOps DBA can significantly influence the performance and success of an application.

Security and compliance

In our digital age, data is the new gold. As businesses rely heavily on digital interactions, vast amounts of data are amassed daily, making databases the treasuries of this age. However, with this invaluable resource comes the ever-present shadow of security threats. The digital realm is fraught with dangers, from hackers trying to breach systems for valuable data to inadvertent mistakes that could expose sensitive information. As we dive deeper into the realm of database management, the critical role of security becomes glaringly evident. Through this section, we'll explore the significance of security measures, common threats, mitigation strategies, and practical examples to fortify these data repositories.

Importance of security in database management

The importance of security in database management cannot be overstated. Databases often store sensitive data such as personal user information, financial records, confidential company information, and more. A security breach could lead to catastrophic consequences, including loss of customer trust, legal repercussions, financial losses, and damage to the organization's reputation. Therefore, ensuring that the database is secure is paramount to the health and integrity of any system or organization.

Database security involves protecting the database from intentional or accidental threats, misuse, or malicious attacks. This can involve a wide range of activities, including securing the data itself, securing the database applications, and infrastructure.

There are several common types of threats to databases:

- **Unauthorized access**: This can occur when an unauthorized individual gains access to the database
- **Data breaches**: This involves the release of secure or private/confidential information into an untrusted environment

- **Data loss or corruption**: This could occur due to hardware failure, human error, or a malicious attack

- **Insider threats**: Sometimes, employees or other individuals with legitimate access to the database misuse their privileges and perform unauthorized activities

Common security measures

To mitigate these risks, several security measures are commonly employed:

- **Access controls**: These are used to manage who has the ability to view and use the data. This often involves creating user accounts with passwords and assigning roles and permissions to these accounts.

- **Encryption**: Data encryption translates data into an encoded form so that only people with access to a secret key (formally referred to as a decryption key) or password can read it.

- **Backup and recovery**: Regular backups are crucial for restoring a database to its previous state in case of data loss.

- **Firewalls**: A firewall controls network traffic and can prevent unauthorized access to the database.

- **Auditing**: Regular audits can help identify potential security vulnerabilities, ensure compliance with access policies, and provide a record of who has accessed data.

- **Data masking**: Data masking is used to protect sensitive data by replacing it with fictitious data. This is often used in development and testing environments to protect real data while still allowing operations to be performed on the database.

Practical example – best practices for securing a MySQL database and ensuring GDPR compliance

MySQL, one of the most popular open source RDBMSs, comes with a host of features that can be used to secure your databases. Here are some of the best practices for securing a MySQL database:

- **Secure the MySQL installation**: MySQL comes with a script called `mysql_secure_installation` that helps to secure your MySQL installation by setting a password for the root accounts, removing root accounts that are accessible from outside the localhost, and removing anonymous user accounts.

- **User management**: Limit the number of users who have access to your database. Each user should be given only those privileges that they need to perform their tasks.

- **Encrypt data**: MySQL provides several functions that allow you to encrypt data. Encryption should be used for any sensitive data, such as credit card numbers or personal user information.

- **Regular backups**: Regular backups are crucial to protect your data. If something goes wrong, a backup will allow you to restore your database to its previous state.

- **Keep MySQL up to date**: Regularly update your MySQL installation to ensure that you have the latest security patches.

In addition to these MySQL-specific practices, complying with data protection regulations such as the **General Data Protection Regulation (GDPR)** is critical. The GDPR is a regulation that requires businesses to protect the personal data and privacy of EU citizens for transactions that occur within EU member states.

Here are some steps to ensure GDPR compliance:

1. **Understand what data you have and why you're processing it**: Under GDPR, you should only collect data that you need and have a legitimate reason to process.

2. **Encrypt personal data**: As mentioned earlier, MySQL provides several functions for data encryption.

3. **Ensure right to erasure**: The GDPR includes the right to erasure, also known as the right to be forgotten. This means that individuals can request that their data be deleted. You should have a system in place to handle such requests.

4. **Data breach notification**: In case of a data breach, the GDPR requires you to notify all affected individuals and the supervisory authority within 72 hours of becoming aware of the breach.

In conclusion, ensuring database security and compliance with regulations such as the GDPR is a key responsibility for any organization. By following best practices and regular auditing, you can help to protect both your data and your users' data, and maintain the trust and confidence of your customers.

Collaboration and communication

The heart of DevOps lies in communication and collaboration. These are crucial because, in traditional environments, developers and operations often work in silos, with each group having its own priorities and objectives. This siloed approach often leads to conflicts, inefficiencies, and blame games when issues arise. In contrast, a DevOps environment fosters a culture where multiple teams share responsibilities, collaborate on challenges, and work toward the shared goal of delivering high-quality software rapidly and reliably.

As we just walked through, in a DevOps setting, a DBA's role is much more dynamic and integrated into the development and deployment processes than in traditional settings. Some of the key responsibilities of DBAs in DevOps are as follows:

- **Integrated pipeline**: In DevOps, DBAs are involved in the CI/CD pipeline. They collaborate with developers to ensure that database schemas, configurations, and migrations are integrated into the pipeline.

- **Collaborative database design**: DBAs work closely with development teams in the early stages of product design to ensure that databases are scalable, performant, and meet the application's requirements.

- **Shared responsibility**: In a DevOps culture, DBAs share the responsibility for the system's performance and availability with the rest of the team. They no longer work in isolation but are a part of a collective effort to ensure the reliability and performance of the entire system.

- **Automating database deployment**: Automation is key in DevOps, and this includes database deployment and configuration. DBAs need to work with operations teams to automate the deployment of database changes.

- **Monitoring and feedback loops**: DBAs are often involved in setting up monitoring for databases and creating feedback loops that can help the team understand how database changes affect the application.

These increased responsibilities paired with the correct communication strategies can lead to the following:

- **Accelerating development cycles**: Through effective communication and collaboration, DBAs can provide vital insights during the development phase, helping to create efficient database structures, which in turn can lead to reduced development cycles.

- **Mitigating risks**: Collaboration between DBAs and development teams can facilitate better risk assessment and mitigation strategies, especially concerning database migrations and schema changes, which are often delicate procedures.

- **Enhancing system performance**: DBAs have specialized knowledge regarding query optimization and database performance. Through collaboration, this knowledge can be shared with developers, resulting in a more performant system.

- **Reducing downtime**: Communication between DBAs and operations teams is essential for planning maintenance and updates to minimize downtime.

- **Knowledge sharing**: DBAs have a deep knowledge of database systems. In a collaborative environment, they have the opportunity to share this knowledge with developers, testers, and operations staff, enhancing the team's overall capabilities.

- **Faster issue resolution**: When issues arise, communication and collaboration are crucial for a rapid response. Whether it's a performance issue, a bug, or a failure, having a collaborative environment means that everyone can work together efficiently to solve the problem.

- **Adapting to changes**: The IT landscape is continually evolving, and databases are no exception. DBAs need to keep up to date with new database technologies, practices, and trends. A collaborative culture encourages continuous learning and adaptation to these changes.

It's reasonable to conclude that the DBA role in a DevOps environment involves a high degree of collaboration and communication with other teams. This is vital for speeding up development cycles, mitigating risks, enhancing system performance, reducing downtime, sharing knowledge, enabling faster issue resolution, and adapting to changes. Thus, the traditional image of the DBA as a gatekeeper or a siloed role is no longer relevant. Instead, DBAs are integral members of a cross-functional team that works together to deliver high-quality software rapidly and reliably.

Summary

In today's fast-paced and highly competitive technological landscape, the role of a DevOps DBA holds immense importance in fostering a successful DevOps environment. By combining their expertise in database administration with a deep understanding of DevOps principles, DevOps DBAs play a pivotal role in bridging the gap between development and operations teams, ensuring seamless collaboration and efficient workflows.

The responsibilities undertaken by a DevOps DBA are diverse and impactful. They are responsible for effectively managing databases, from design and implementation to maintenance, with a focus on data integrity, security, and availability. DevOps DBAs optimize database performance, monitor resource utilization, and plan for scalability to ensure that databases can handle increasing workloads without compromising efficiency. Their involvement in database management contributes to the overall reliability, performance, and security of the applications.

Automation and IaC are crucial elements of a successful DevOps environment, and DevOps DBAs are at the forefront of implementing these practices. By leveraging automation tools and frameworks, DevOps DBAs streamline the provisioning, configuration management, and backup/recovery processes for databases. This automation minimizes manual errors, accelerates deployment cycles, and enhances reproducibility across different environments. Additionally, through the use of IaC techniques, DevOps DBAs codify and version control the database infrastructure, enabling consistent and reliable deployments throughout the software development life cycle.

Collaboration is a fundamental aspect of DevOps, and DevOps DBAs excel in fostering effective collaboration between development and operations teams. They actively participate in project planning, offering their expertise and insights on database-related matters. DevOps DBAs ensure that the database schema aligns with application requirements, providing guidance on best practices for data storage, retrieval, and caching. This collaboration between DevOps DBAs and development teams results in enhanced application performance, improved quality, and accelerated development cycles.

The integration of **continuous integration/continuous deployment** (**CI/CD**) practices is a cornerstone of the DevOps methodology. DevOps DBAs play a pivotal role in this process by seamlessly integrating database changes into the automated release pipeline. They employ tools for database migration, version control, and automated testing to ensure that application updates and database changes are synchronized. This integration enables frequent and reliable deployments, ensuring that new features and bug fixes are promptly delivered to end users.

Monitoring and incident management are crucial aspects of maintaining a robust DevOps environment, and DevOps DBAs excel in these areas. They implement comprehensive monitoring solutions to proactively identify and resolve database-related issues. By establishing performance baselines, creating alerts, and conducting capacity planning, DevOps DBAs optimize resource utilization and anticipate capacity needs. In the event of failures or incidents, DevOps DBAs respond promptly to restore service and investigate the root causes, minimizing downtime and ensuring the high availability of database systems.

In summary, the contributions of DevOps DBAs are indispensable in facilitating a successful DevOps environment. They bridge the gap between development and operations teams, enabling effective communication, collaboration, and alignment of priorities. DevOps DBAs efficiently manage databases, ensuring data integrity, security, and performance. They automate processes and utilize IaC techniques to streamline provisioning, configuration, and backup/recovery tasks. Their collaboration with development teams enhances application performance and quality. Additionally, DevOps DBAs integrate database changes seamlessly into the CI/CD pipeline, enabling frequent and reliable deployments. Their monitoring and incident management capabilities ensure the reliability and resilience of the DevOps environment.

Embracing the role of a DevOps DBA is crucial for organizations seeking to optimize their development processes and deliver high-quality applications in a fast-paced, continuously evolving digital landscape. By leveraging their expertise, DevOps DBAs contribute significantly to the success and competitiveness of businesses, empowering them to deliver innovative solutions efficiently and reliably. As technology continues to advance, the role of DevOps DBAs will continue to evolve and adapt, playing an increasingly vital role in the future of software development and operations.

In the next chapter, we will learn about database automation.

10
Database Automation

Apart from DevOps adoption, which we covered in great depth in this book so far, there were some great advancements in the field of database automation! In this chapter, we will have a high-level overview of these, highlighting their impact on today's industry. These are the following:

- **Self-driving databases**: **Database management systems** (**DBMs**) have become more autonomous and capable of managing and tuning themselves. These self-driving databases can automate tasks such as data backup, recovery, tuning, and indexing. They can also proactively repair and prevent faults, reducing the need for human intervention.

- **Artificial intelligence and machine learning enhancements**: **Artificial Intelligence** (**AI**) and **Machine Learning** (**ML**) have been incorporated into database systems to analyze query performance, predict future workloads, and optimize resource allocation accordingly. This has significantly improved the efficiency and speed of databases.

- **Automated data lineage tracking**: New technologies have emerged that can automatically track the lineage of data, providing transparency about how data has been processed and moved around. This helps in understanding the source of data, the transformations it underwent, and its present state.

- **Data privacy automation**: With the increasing focus on data privacy, automated tools for data masking and data anonymization have seen a lot of advancement. They allow companies to use and share data while ensuring compliance with privacy regulations.

- **Automated data discovery and cataloging**: New tools automatically discover and catalog data across various databases and cloud systems, making it easy for businesses to know what data they have and where it's stored.

- **Database as a service (DBaaS)**: The increased adoption and enhancement of DBaaS platforms have allowed businesses to offload the mundane tasks of database setup, maintenance, and scaling to third-party providers. This allows businesses to focus on utilizing data to generate insights and value.

- **Serverless databases**: These are a more recent development in the DBaaS model. Serverless databases can automatically scale up and down to match an application's needs, and businesses are only billed for the resources they use. This provides great flexibility and cost-efficiency.

The significance of these innovations lies primarily in efficiency and cost-effectiveness. They allow for a reduction in routine and manual tasks, free up resources, and allow database administrators to focus more on strategy and less on maintenance. They also lower the barriers to entry for smaller businesses that might not have the resources to employ a full-time database team. The enhancements in AI and ML can lead to smarter systems that can provide businesses with valuable insights, informing strategy and decision-making.

The following main topics are covered in this chapter:

- Autonomous database management

- The revolution of performance tuning – from manual to autonomous

- Automated data lineage tracking – a new era of transparency in data management

- Data privacy automation – advancing the frontier of privacy compliance in the digital age

- Automated data discovery and cataloging – unveiling the hidden treasures in today's data landscape

- The ascendancy of DBaaS – transforming business efficiency and data utilization in the digital age

- The emergence of serverless databases – revolutionizing DBaaS through on-demand scalability and cost efficiency

Autonomous database management

The vast realm of database management, once dominated by the meticulous hands of database administrators, is on the cusp of a transformative shift. Amidst the digital age, where data burgeons at an exponential rate, the traditional methods of database management are being tested and often stretched to their limits. Enter the promising world of self-driving databases – a pioneering approach that merges cutting-edge AI with the intricacies of database management. In this section, we embark on a journey to understand the mechanics, advantages, and potential challenges of this novel horizon in the domain of DBMs.

Self-driving databases – a new horizon in DBMs

Database management has traditionally been a complex, labor-intensive process that requires a high level of expertise in data architecture, SQL scripting, and system performance tuning. However, the digital age's increasing data complexity and volume have made it increasingly difficult to manage databases manually. As a result, the paradigm of self-driving databases has emerged, offering a solution to these challenges.

Understanding self-driving databases

Self-driving databases, also known as autonomous databases, utilize advanced technologies such as AI and ML to automate database administration tasks. These tasks include data backup, recovery, performance tuning, indexing, and fault detection and recovery. The goal of a self-driving database is to reduce the need for human intervention in database administration, making it less error-prone, more efficient, and scalable.

The technological foundations of self-driving databases

The evolution of self-driving databases is rooted in advancements in AI and ML. These technologies are incorporated into database systems, allowing them to learn from patterns in data and a system's operational characteristics. ML algorithms allow these databases to understand typical workloads, predict future performance requirements, and adjust system parameters accordingly.

AI and ML also play a vital role in predictive fault detection and recovery. By analyzing historical system logs and detecting anomalies in real time, the self-driving database can identify potential faults before they affect system performance and initiate preventive measures.

Automation of database administration tasks

The various processes involved in database administration automation are as follows:

- **Data backup and recovery**: Self-driving databases automate the crucial task of data backup and recovery. These systems continuously backup data, reducing the risk of data loss due to system failures or human errors. They also implement automated recovery procedures, restoring the database to its state before a failure without the need for manual intervention.

- **Performance tuning**: Traditional databases require administrators to monitor and adjust system performance manually continually. However, a self-driving database automatically tunes its performance. It adjusts system parameters based on the analysis of workloads and prediction of future performance requirements.

- **Indexing**: Creating and managing database indexes is a complex task that can significantly impact database performance. Self-driving databases can automatically manage indexes, creating, dropping, or modifying them as required, based on the evolving nature of data and queries.

- **Fault detection and recovery**: Self-driving databases use AI and ML algorithms to proactively detect potential system faults. Once a potential issue is detected, the database system can initiate preventive measures, such as rerouting workloads, recovering from backups, or alerting administrators for further action.

The implications of self-driving databases

The emergence of self-driving databases holds significant implications for businesses and database administrators. For businesses, these systems promise lower costs, reduced risk, and improved system performance. They eliminate the need for manual administration, reducing labor costs and the potential for human errors. Continuous data backup and automated recovery also minimize the risk of data loss.

For database administrators, self-driving databases shift their role from routine administration to more strategic tasks. Rather than spending time on performance tuning or backup and recovery, administrators can focus on data architecture, policy management, data security, and other strategic tasks.

Furthermore, self-driving databases facilitate scalability and agility in responding to business needs. They can adjust to changes in data volume or query complexity without the need for manual intervention, making them ideal for businesses with fluctuating data requirements.

Challenges and future directions

While self-driving databases offer significant benefits, they also present new challenges. The reliance on AI and ML algorithms raises questions about data security and privacy. Businesses must ensure that these algorithms do not inadvertently expose sensitive data or violate privacy regulations.

Additionally, while self-driving databases reduce the need for manual administration, they do not eliminate it entirely. Database administrators must oversee these systems, understand their operation, and be able to intervene when necessary.

In the future, the development of self-driving databases will likely focus on addressing these challenges. Researchers and developers will need to enhance data security and privacy features, improve system transparency, and develop tools to help administrators manage these systems effectively.

Conclusion

Self-driving databases represent a significant advance in the field of database management. By automating routine administration tasks, they promise to improve system performance, reduce costs, and allow database administrators to focus on strategic tasks. However, as with any new technology, they also present new challenges that must be addressed. As these databases continue to evolve, they will play an increasingly central role in managing the complex, data-rich environments of the digital age.

The revolution of performance tuning – from manual to autonomous

Performance tuning in traditional databases has been a perpetual and tedious task that requires a keen understanding of data architecture, SQL queries, and the ability to anticipate system usage patterns. However, the growing complexity of data and an increasingly demanding digital environment have given birth to an innovative approach – autonomous or self-driving databases that can automatically tune performance, altering system parameters based on workload analysis and predictions of future requirements.

Understanding performance tuning

Performance tuning is the process of optimizing database performance to meet specific objectives, typically related to processing speed and responsiveness. It involves making adjustments to database configuration, hardware, and SQL queries to improve efficiency and minimize resource use.

In traditional databases, performance tuning is a manual, labor-intensive process. Database administrators must continuously monitor system performance, identify bottlenecks, and make adjustments to system parameters. This process requires a high level of expertise and can be time-consuming and error-prone.

The need for automated performance tuning

The digital age's data landscape has changed drastically, with businesses handling vast amounts of complex data. Moreover, modern applications demand real-time processing and instant insights, placing a significant burden on databases. Manual performance tuning is no longer feasible or efficient in this environment.

Automated performance tuning, facilitated by AI and ML technologies, has become essential. It allows databases to learn from data and system operation patterns and make necessary adjustments automatically. This results in systems that are more efficient, less prone to human error, and able to meet the demands of modern applications.

Technological foundations of automated performance tuning

Automated performance tuning is underpinned by advancements in AI and ML. These technologies enable a system to learn from data, understand system operation patterns, and make predictions. Key aspects of these technologies as applied to performance tuning include the following:

- **Workload analysis**: ML algorithms are employed to analyze workload patterns in the database. This analysis helps a system understand how data is accessed and processed under different conditions and times.

- **Prediction models**: AI models are used to predict future system usage patterns based on historical data. These predictions guide a system in adjusting its parameters to cater to future requirements effectively.

- **Continuous learning**: A system continuously learns from data and its operational characteristics, adjusting its learning models and tuning mechanisms accordingly.

The mechanics of automated performance tuning

Automated performance tuning in self-driving databases involves several steps:

1. **Data collection**: A database continuously collects data about its operation, including system metrics, query execution times, and error logs.

2. **Workload analysis**: A system analyzes this data to understand workload patterns. This helps it identify bottlenecks, understand peak usage times, and discern patterns in query execution.

3. **Predictive modeling**: The database uses AI models to predict future workload patterns based on historical data and system operation characteristics.

4. **Parameter adjustment**: Based on the analysis and predictions, the system adjusts its parameters to improve performance. This could involve altering memory allocation, adjusting query execution plans, or changing indexing strategies.

5. **Performance monitoring**: The system continuously monitors its performance to assess the effectiveness of its tuning actions. If performance does not improve or deteriorates, the system learns from this and adjusts its tuning strategies accordingly.

The implications of automated performance tuning

Automated performance tuning holds several implications for businesses and database administrators. For businesses, it offers the potential for improved system performance, cost savings, and increased agility, as detailed here:

- **Improved performance**: By continuously adjusting to changing workloads and predicting future requirements, self-driving databases can maintain optimal performance levels, resulting in faster query execution and better application responsiveness.

- **Cost savings**: Automated performance tuning reduces the need for manual intervention, leading to cost savings in terms of reduced labor and lower hardware requirements. Optimizing resource usage also helps minimize infrastructure costs.

- **Increased agility**: With automated tuning, databases can quickly adjust to changing business requirements, making it easier to introduce new features or cope with increased data volumes.

For database administrators, automated tuning shifts their role from routine tuning tasks to more strategic activities. Instead of continuously monitoring and tweaking system performance, administrators can focus on data architecture, policy management, data security, and other high-value tasks.

Challenges and future directions

Despite its advantages, automated performance tuning also presents new challenges. One of the main issues is the "black-box" nature of AI and ML algorithms. It can be difficult to understand why a system made specific tuning decisions, leading to a lack of transparency and potential difficulties in troubleshooting.

Moreover, while automated tuning reduces the need for manual intervention, it does not eliminate it. Administrators still need to oversee system operation, understand the basics of the tuning process, and intervene when necessary.

In the future, we can expect developments in automated performance tuning to focus on addressing these challenges. Improved algorithm transparency, enhanced learning models, and tools to help administrators oversee and understand system operations are likely areas of focus.

Conclusion

Automated performance tuning in self-driving databases represents a significant step forward in database management. By leveraging AI and ML technologies, these databases can deliver improved performance, cost savings, and increased agility. However, as with any new technology, they also present new challenges. Looking forward, the evolution of self-driving databases will undoubtedly continue to shape the landscape of data management in the digital age.

Automated data lineage tracking – a new era of transparency in data management

Data lineage, the journey that data takes from its source through various transformations to its current form, has long been a vital yet complex element of data management. Understanding data lineage helps organizations ensure data quality, trace errors, and meet compliance requirements. However, manually tracking data lineage can be challenging, especially as the amount and complexity of data grows. This is where automated data lineage tracking comes in. By leveraging new technologies, it provides a transparent view of how data has been processed and moved, offering a more manageable, accurate, and comprehensive understanding of data sources, transformations, and present states.

Understanding data lineage

Before delving into automated data lineage tracking, it's essential to understand what data lineage is and why it matters. In its most basic sense, data lineage refers to the life cycle of data, from its initial creation to its final state after undergoing various processing stages and transformations. It maps out the data's journey, providing a historical record of data flow, which includes where it originated, where it moves to, what happens to it, and how it ends up in its final form.

Understanding data lineage is crucial for several reasons:

- **Data quality**: Tracking data lineage helps ensure the quality of data. By knowing where data came from and how it has been transformed, organizations can validate its accuracy and consistency.
- **Error tracing**: When anomalies or errors are detected in data, lineage helps trace the root cause of these issues.

- **Regulatory compliance**: Many industries have regulations requiring businesses to provide comprehensive records of their data handling. Data lineage allows organizations to demonstrate compliance by showing exactly how data has been processed and stored.

- **Impact analysis**: Understanding data lineage is essential to assess the potential impact of changes to data or systems. Knowing how data flows and transforms can help predict and mitigate the effects of changes.

The evolution from manual to automated data lineage tracking

Traditionally, data lineage was tracked manually, a process that was time-consuming and prone to errors. As organizations began handling increasingly larger volumes of data and more complex data transformations, manual tracking became less feasible. This led to the advent of automated data lineage tracking.

Automated data lineage tracking leverages technological advancements to track the journey of data automatically. It involves tools and systems that can automatically detect, record, and visualize the lineage of data, providing a clear and comprehensive view of data flow and transformations.

The technological foundations of automated data lineage tracking

Several technologies underpin automated data lineage tracking:

- **Metadata management**: Automated data lineage relies heavily on metadata – data about data. Metadata management tools automatically capture, store, and manage information about data, such as its source, format, and relationships with other data.

- **Data integration tools**: These tools can automatically capture data lineage information as they **extract, transform, and load** (ETL) data from various sources.

- **Data governance platforms**: These platforms provide a comprehensive approach to managing, improving, and utilizing data. Many include features for automated data lineage tracking.

- **AI and ML**: AI and ML algorithms can be used to analyze data lineage information, detect patterns, predict future data flows, and identify potential issues.

The process of automated data lineage tracking

The process of automated data lineage tracking involves several stages:

1. **Data capture**: The system automatically captures information about data as it enters the system, including its source, format, and initial state.

2. **Data transformation tracking**: As data undergoes various transformations (cleaning, aggregation, calculation, etc.), the system records information about these transformations and their results.

3. **Data movement tracking**: The system tracks the movement of data within the system, recording where it goes and when.

4. **Visualization**: The system presents the data lineage information in a visual format, often a flowchart or graph, making it easy to understand the journey of data.

5. **Analysis**: AI and ML algorithms analyze the data lineage information, detecting patterns, predicting future data flows, and identifying potential issues.

The implications of automated data lineage tracking

Automated data lineage tracking has significant implications for businesses:

- **Improved data quality**: By providing a clear view of data flow and transformations, automated data lineage tracking helps organizations ensure data quality. They can validate the accuracy and consistency of data and trace the source of errors or anomalies.

- **Regulatory compliance**: Automated tracking makes it easier for organizations to meet regulatory requirements for data handling. They can provide comprehensive, accurate records of data lineage to demonstrate compliance.

- **Efficiency**: Automated tracking saves time and reduces the potential for error compared to manual tracking. It allows businesses to handle larger volumes of data and more complex transformations, without sacrificing an understanding or control of their data.

Challenges and future directions

While automated data lineage tracking offers significant benefits, it also presents challenges. These include the complexity of implementing automated tracking systems, the need for standardization in lineage information, and concerns about data security and privacy.

As these challenges are addressed, we can expect to see further advancements in automated data lineage tracking. This could include more sophisticated AI and ML algorithms to analyze lineage information, improved visualization tools, and enhanced integration with other data management systems.

Conclusion

Automated data lineage tracking represents a significant advance in data management. By providing a transparent, accurate, and comprehensive view of data lineage, it enables organizations to ensure data quality, trace errors, meet compliance requirements, and perform effective impact analysis. As this field continues to evolve, it will play a central role in helping organizations navigate the increasingly complex landscape of data.

Data privacy automation – advancing the frontier of privacy compliance in the digital age

The exponential growth of data and its increasingly critical role in driving business decisions and digital innovation has elevated data privacy to the forefront of global consciousness. The revelation of high-profile data breaches, along with the implementation of stringent data protection regulations such as **General Data Protection Regulation (GDPR)** and **California Consumer Privacy Act (CCPA)**, have driven an increased focus on data privacy. As a result, tools for data masking and data anonymization have seen substantial advancements, with automation playing a central role. Data privacy automation allows companies to use and share data while ensuring compliance with privacy regulations, thereby navigating the fine line between data utility and data privacy.

Understanding data privacy

Data privacy refers to the practice of ensuring that sensitive information remains safe from unauthorized access and exploitation. It encompasses various aspects, including data protection, regulatory compliance, and user privacy rights. Key to data privacy is understanding that not all data is equal – some data points are sensitive and require higher protection levels.

Sensitive data often includes **personally identifiable information (PII)**, such as names, social security numbers, and addresses, as well as financial information or health records. Unauthorized access or misuse of such data can lead to severe consequences for individuals, including identity theft, financial loss, or violation of personal privacy.

The challenges of data privacy

Maintaining data privacy is not a trivial task and poses several challenges:

- **Scale and complexity**: With organizations collecting and storing vast amounts of data, tracking and managing sensitive data becomes a significant challenge.

- **Regulatory Compliance**: Regulations such as the GDPR in the EU and the CCPA in the US have stringent requirements for data privacy, with severe penalties for non-compliance. Ensuring compliance requires organizations to track all the sensitive data they hold and understand how it is used and protected.

- **Balancing utility and privacy**: One of the major challenges for organizations is finding the balance between data utility and privacy. While data provides crucial insights that can drive business decisions, it must be handled in a way that respects privacy and complies with regulations.

Data masking and anonymization

Two techniques widely used to maintain data privacy are data masking and data anonymization.

- **Data masking** is a process that obscures specific data elements within data stores. It ensures that sensitive data is replaced with fictitious yet realistic data, ensuring that the data remains useful for purposes such as testing and analysis, without exposing sensitive information.

- **Data anonymization** is a technique used to protect private or sensitive information by erasing or encrypting identifiers that link an individual to stored data. Unlike masking, which can often be reversed, anonymization is intended to be irreversible.

The advent of data privacy automation

Given the complexity and scale of data privacy challenges, automation has emerged as a necessity rather than a luxury. Data privacy automation involves using technology to automate tasks associated with data privacy, including the identification of sensitive data, data masking, data anonymization, and compliance reporting.

Automated data privacy tools leverage advanced technologies such as AI and ML to categorize and classify data, understand where sensitive data resides, and apply appropriate masking or anonymization techniques.

Technological underpinnings of data privacy automation

Several key technologies underpin data privacy automation:

- **AI and ML**: These technologies enable a system to learn from data, understand patterns, and make predictions. They can be used to categorize and classify data, identify sensitive information, and understand how data moves and transforms within the system.

- **Natural Language Processing** (**NLP**): NLP is used to analyze text data and understand its context and semantics. This can be particularly useful to identify sensitive information in unstructured data.

- **Data discovery tools**: These tools automatically scan data sources to identify and categorize sensitive data.

- **Encryption and tokenization**: These are techniques used to protect data, either by encoding it in a way that only authorized parties can read it (encryption) or replacing it with a non-sensitive equivalent, known as a token (tokenization).

The process of data privacy automation

Data privacy automation typically involves several stages:

1. **Data discovery**: A system scans data sources to identify and classify data, including recognizing sensitive information. This stage can involve AI and ML algorithms, along with NLP for text data.

2. **Data masking and anonymization**: Once sensitive data has been identified, the system applies data masking or anonymization techniques. This ensures that the sensitive data is protected, while still retaining its utility for analysis and decision-making.

3. **Monitoring and compliance**: The system continuously monitors data privacy measures to ensure they remain effective as data changes or new data is added. It also generates compliance reports to demonstrate to regulators that data privacy regulations are being met.

The benefits and implications of data privacy automation

The benefits of data privacy automation are manifold:

- **Efficiency and accuracy**: Automated processes are generally faster and more accurate than manual ones. They can handle large volumes of data and complex transformations, reducing the chance of human error.

- **Regulatory compliance**: Automation can make it easier to comply with data privacy regulations by ensuring that all data is properly categorized and protected, and by generating necessary compliance reports.

- **Data utility**: By using data masking and anonymization, companies can continue to gain insights from their data without compromising privacy.

However, the rise of data privacy automation also presents new challenges and questions. For instance, who is responsible if an automated system fails and causes a data breach? How can the correctness of automated categorization and masking be ensured? As data privacy automation continues to evolve, these and other questions will need to be addressed.

Conclusion

As the importance of data privacy continues to grow, data privacy automation represents a vital tool for organizations to protect sensitive information, comply with regulations, and continue to extract value from their data. By combining technologies such as AI, ML, and NLP with data masking and anonymization techniques, data privacy automation provides a powerful, efficient, and scalable solution to the challenges of data privacy. As this field continues to advance, it will undoubtedly play a critical role in shaping the future of data management and protection.

Automated data discovery and cataloging – unveiling the hidden treasures in today's data landscape

As the digital revolution rages on, data has risen to become the world's most valuable resource, driving innovation, strategic decisions, and operational efficiencies. However, as data grows in volume, variety, and velocity, businesses grapple with a fundamental challenge – knowing what data they have and where it is stored. Enter automated data discovery and cataloging – a groundbreaking technological innovation that enables businesses to navigate the increasingly complex data landscape effectively.

Understanding data discovery and cataloging

Data discovery refers to the process of finding and understanding patterns and trends in data. In contrast, data cataloging involves creating a comprehensive inventory of data assets and providing details about their source, usage, relationships, and business context. Combined, data discovery and cataloging offer a roadmap to navigate the vast data landscape, enabling businesses to understand what data they have, where it resides, how it's connected, and how it can be used.

The growing need for automation in data discovery and cataloging

Several factors have led to the increasing need for automation in data discovery and cataloging:

- **The scale of data**: The sheer volume of data generated and stored by businesses has grown exponentially, making manual data discovery and cataloging impractical.

- **The complexity of the data landscape**: Data is now distributed across multiple systems and platforms – from on-premises databases to various cloud systems, making it challenging to have a consolidated view of all data assets.

- **The speed of business**: In today's fast-paced business environment, the ability to quickly find and understand relevant data can provide a significant competitive advantage.

- **Regulatory compliance**: Regulations such as GDPR and CCPA require businesses to know where their data is and how it's used. Automated data discovery and cataloging can help ensure compliance by providing a comprehensive view of all data assets and their lineage.

What is automated data discovery and cataloging?

Automated data discovery and cataloging involves using technology to automatically identify, classify, and catalog data across various databases and cloud systems. By leveraging technologies such as ML, AI, and NLP, these tools can parse through vast volumes of structured and unstructured data, identifying patterns, relationships, and metadata.

The key features of automated data discovery and cataloging tools

Automated data discovery and cataloging tools typically provide several key features:

- **Data discovery**: These tools automatically scan various databases and cloud systems to identify and classify data, including sensitive and regulated data.

- **Data cataloging**: After discovering the data, the tools create a centralized data catalog that lists all data assets, along with their metadata, such as source, usage, relationships, and business context.

- **Data lineage**: These tools also provide information on data lineage – the journey of data from its source to its current form, including all the transformations it underwent.

- **Data profiling**: By analyzing data patterns and quality, these tools provide insights into data's health and integrity, helping businesses ensure data accuracy and consistency.

- **Search and collaboration**: With built-in search capabilities, users can easily find relevant data. Collaboration features allow users to share insights, enrich metadata with business context, and foster a data-driven culture.

The process of automated data discovery and cataloging

The process of automated data discovery and cataloging typically involves several steps:

1. **Data scanning**: A tool scans various data sources, identifying and classifying data based on its structure, content, and metadata.

2. **Metadata extraction**: The tool extracts metadata about the data, such as its source, usage, relationships, and business context.

3. **Data cataloging**: The tool creates a centralized data catalog, listing all data assets and their metadata.

4. **Data profiling**: The tool analyzes the data, providing insights into its quality, consistency, and integrity.

5. **Data lineage tracking**: The tool tracks the journey of the data, providing information on its lineage.

6. **Search and collaboration**: Users can search the data catalog, find relevant data, and share insights with their team.

The benefits and implications of automated data discovery and cataloging

Automated data discovery and cataloging offers several significant benefits:

- **Increased efficiency**: By automating the time-consuming process of data discovery and cataloging, businesses can significantly increase efficiency, freeing up time for more valuable tasks

- **Enhanced data understanding**: By providing a comprehensive view of all data assets and their context, these automated data discovery and catloging enhance the understanding of data, facilitating better decision-making

- **Regulatory compliance**: These tools help businesses comply with data regulations by providing a clear view of all data, its usage, and lineage

- **Data democratization**: By making data easily accessible and understandable, these tools promote data democratization, fostering a data-driven culture

Despite its benefits, automated data discovery and cataloging also present challenges, such as the need for proper data governance to ensure data accuracy and consistency, and the potential risk of exposing sensitive data. As the field continues to evolve, it will be essential to address these issues effectively.

Conclusion

As businesses navigate the complex and dynamic data landscape, automated data discovery and cataloging serve as an invaluable compass, guiding them toward informed decision-making, strategic insights, and regulatory compliance. As the volume and complexity of data continue to grow, these tools will become increasingly vital in unlocking the hidden treasures within the vast seas of data. Through their capacity to automatically identify, understand, and organize data assets, they provide businesses with a powerful lever to harness the full potential of their data.

The ascendancy of DBaaS – transforming business efficiency and data utilization in the digital age

The modern era, marked by an accelerating digital transformation and an exponential increase in data generation, has necessitated novel approaches to data management. Among these, DBaaS has emerged as a powerful tool to offload the mundane tasks of database setup, maintenance, and scaling to third-party providers. This transformative model allows businesses to concentrate on the strategic utilization of data for insights and value generation, changing the way they operate and compete.

Understanding DBaaS

DBaaS is a cloud-based approach to database management that enables businesses to leverage the capabilities of a managed database without the complexities and hassles of setting up, maintaining, and scaling an in-house database system. In essence, DBaaS providers offer a fully managed database that is ready for use, allowing businesses to focus on their core functions rather than the intricacies of database management.

Why DBaaS? The rationale behind its growing adoption is as follows:

- **Cost-effectiveness**: DBaaS eliminates the need for upfront capital investments in hardware, software licenses, and infrastructure. Organizations can leverage the pay-as-you-go model, paying only for the resources they consume. This reduces upfront costs, lowers operational expenses, and eliminates the need for dedicated **database administrators** (**DBAs**).

- **Scalability**: DBaaS offers scalability options that allow organizations to scale their database resources up or down based on demand. It enables seamless handling of data growth, ensuring optimal performance during peak times and cost savings during low-demand periods. Scaling can be achieved quickly and efficiently, ensuring that databases can keep up with evolving business needs.

- **Flexibility**: DBaaS provides a wide range of database options, supporting various DBMs such as MySQL, Oracle, and MongoDB. It allows organizations to choose the most suitable database technology for their specific requirements without worrying about infrastructure or software installations. This flexibility fosters innovation and enables organizations to experiment with different database technologies easily.

- **Reduced management burden**: With DBaaS, organizations can offload the management and maintenance of databases to the service provider. This frees up internal IT resources, allowing them to focus on core business activities and strategic initiatives rather than routine database management tasks. Service providers handle backups, software updates, patching, and other administrative tasks, ensuring high availability and the reliability of databases.

- **Enhanced security**: DBaaS providers typically have robust security measures in place to protect data. They employ industry best practices, including encryption, access controls, and regular security audits, ensuring data privacy and compliance with regulations. By leveraging the expertise of DBaaS providers, organizations can benefit from enhanced security without investing heavily in security infrastructure and expertise.

- **Operational efficiency**: DBaaS simplifies and streamlines database management processes. It offers automated provisioning and deployment of databases, reducing the time and effort required to set up new environments. Additionally, DBaaS provides monitoring and performance optimization tools, allowing organizations to identify and address performance bottlenecks proactively. This improves operational efficiency and minimizes downtime.

The mechanics of DBaaS

DBaaS operates on the foundational principles of cloud computing, where resources are provided as a service over the internet. A DBaaS platform involves multiple components:

- **Database software**: This is the software that manages the storage, retrieval, and manipulation of data

- **Hardware infrastructure**: This is the physical servers, storage devices, and network infrastructure where the database software runs

- **Management layer**: This includes the tools and applications used to manage and maintain the database, including performance monitoring, backup and recovery, and security measures

- **User interface**: The platform's user interface, often a web-based dashboard, allows users to interact with a database, perform queries, and manage their data

- **APIs**: These enable integration of the DBaaS platform with other applications or services, allowing data to flow between them

The impact of DBaaS on business operations

By taking over the mundane tasks of database setup, maintenance, and scaling, DBaaS platforms can significantly transform businesses' operations:

- **Focus on core business functions**: By offloading database management to DBaaS providers, businesses can focus more on their core functions, accelerating innovation and growth

- **Accelerated time to market**: DBaaS can significantly reduce the time it takes to set up and launch new applications, as the database component is ready to use

- **Resource optimization**: Instead of tying up resources in managing databases, businesses can redirect them to strategic areas, optimizing resource utilization

- **Enhanced collaboration**: As DBaaS platforms are accessible over the internet, they enable seamless collaboration between teams located in different geographies

- **Data-driven decisions**: With a reliable and high-performance database at their disposal, businesses can focus on utilizing data for insights, leading to more data-driven decision-making

DBaaS – the future of database management

The increased adoption and enhancement of DBaaS platforms signify a paradigm shift in how businesses approach database management. By taking the mundane tasks off businesses' shoulders, DBaaS allows them to focus on data utilization for insights, value generation, and so on:

- **Data utilization and value generation**: DBaaS enables businesses to shift their focus, from routine database management tasks to utilizing data for generating insights and driving value. With DBaaS, handling tasks such as infrastructure management, backups, and updates, businesses can allocate their resources and expertise toward extracting meaningful information from data, making data-driven decisions, and creating innovative solutions.

- **Advanced features and future evolution**: As DBaaS platforms continue to evolve, they are likely to incorporate more advanced features to enhance their capabilities. Automated performance tuning, for example, can optimize database performance by analyzing workload patterns and adjusting resource allocations accordingly. This automation reduces the manual effort required for performance optimization, ensuring efficient and responsive database operations.

  Additionally, AI-based predictive analytics can be integrated into DBaaS platforms, allowing businesses to leverage ML algorithms to gain deeper insights from their data. AI algorithms can identify patterns, detect anomalies, and predict future trends, enabling businesses to make proactive decisions and improve operational efficiency.

- **Tighter integration with cloud services**: DBaaS platforms are expected to provide tighter integration with other cloud services, allowing seamless data exchange and workflow automation. Integration with storage services enables efficient data storage and retrieval, while integration with compute services enables data processing and analytics. This integration enables businesses to leverage the full potential of cloud-based ecosystems, enabling streamlined and integrated data workflows.

- **Edge-based DBaaS solutions**: With the rise of edge computing, we can anticipate the emergence of edge-based DBaaS solutions. Edge computing involves processing data closer to the source or the edge of the network, reducing latency and enabling real-time data processing. Edge-based DBaaS solutions will be optimized for low-latency, high-availability applications that require immediate access to data for real-time decision-making and responsiveness.

  These edge-based solutions can leverage distributed databases, enabling local data storage and processing at the edge devices. By combining the benefits of DBaaS with edge computing, businesses can achieve efficient and reliable data management for applications such as **Internet of Things (IoT)**, autonomous systems, and edge analytics.

In conclusion, the adoption and enhancement of DBaaS platforms are revolutionizing database management by freeing businesses from mundane tasks and enabling them to focus on data utilization for insights and value generation. The future of DBaaS will witness the integration of advanced features such as automated performance tuning, AI-based predictive analytics, and tighter integration with other cloud services. Furthermore, the emergence of edge-based DBaaS solutions will cater to the growing need for low-latency, high-availability applications in the era of edge computing. As businesses continue to embrace DBaaS, they can leverage these advancements to unlock the full potential of their data and drive innovation.

Conclusion

DBaaS represents a significant breakthrough in the field of database management, fundamentally altering how businesses handle their data needs. By transforming the traditionally resource-intensive and complex task of database management into a simplified, scalable, and cost-effective service, DBaaS frees businesses to focus on their core competencies and harness their data for insights and value creation.

The surge in the adoption and evolution of DBaaS platforms is a testament to the value they bring to businesses in the digital age. As we look toward the future, it is evident that DBaaS will continue to play a central role in driving business efficiency, agility, and innovation in an increasingly data-driven world.

The emergence of serverless databases – revolutionizing DBaaS through on-demand scalability and cost efficiency

The surge in digital transformation and data-driven decision-making has escalated the need for effective and efficient database management systems. Traditionally, these systems have required significant investments in infrastructure and skilled personnel to ensure their efficient operation. This scenario is evolving rapidly, with DBaaS and, more recently, the development of serverless databases. These are fundamentally changing the way businesses manage and utilize data. By automatically scaling to match an application's needs, serverless databases provide unprecedented flexibility and cost-efficiency, shifting the paradigms of traditional database management.

Understanding serverless databases

Serverless databases represent a significant advancement in the DBaaS model by abstracting the management of physical servers. Businesses can leverage serverless databases without the burden of provisioning, scaling, and managing the underlying database infrastructure. These databases exhibit automatic scaling capabilities, adjusting resources based on application requirements, while businesses are billed only for the resources consumed. The serverless model offers notable benefits in terms of flexibility and cost savings, particularly for workloads with fluctuating or unpredictable demands.

Serverless databases eliminate the need for businesses to worry about the intricate details of server management. The abstracted infrastructure allows developers and data professionals to concentrate on application logic and data management, enhancing productivity and efficiency. With serverless databases, provisioning and configuring servers, applying patches, and managing backups are handled by the service provider, freeing businesses from these time-consuming tasks.

The automatic scaling feature of serverless databases ensures that resources match an application's needs. As workloads increase, the database dynamically scales up to meet demand, guaranteeing optimal performance. Conversely, during periods of low demand, resources are automatically scaled down, reducing costs by eliminating the need to pay for idle capacity. This elasticity makes serverless databases highly adaptable to changing workloads, ensuring a seamless user experience and cost-effectiveness.

The pay-per-usage pricing model of serverless databases is another significant advantage. Businesses are billed based on the actual resources consumed, aligning costs directly with usage. This eliminates the need to overprovision resources, optimizing budget allocation. The granular billing system charges for specific operations performed, storage utilized, and data transferred, providing transparency and cost savings for businesses, especially those with unpredictable or varying workloads.

Serverless databases revolutionize database management by abstracting away server management tasks, providing automatic scaling, and employing a pay-per-usage pricing model. Businesses can focus on application development and data management, benefitting from increased productivity, flexibility, and cost savings. With serverless databases, organizations can optimize resource allocation, respond effectively to changing demands, and streamline their database operations in a scalable and efficient manner.

Why serverless databases? The driving forces

The adoption of serverless databases is propelled by the following benefits:

- **Zero administration**: With serverless databases, businesses no longer need to worry about server provisioning, maintenance, and scaling, freeing up valuable time and resources for other tasks

- **Auto-scaling**: Serverless databases automatically scale to meet an application's requirements, ensuring optimal performance even during peak demand periods

- **Cost efficiency**: Serverless databases operate on a pay-per-use model, meaning businesses only pay for the resources they consume, leading to significant cost savings

- **High availability and durability**: Serverless databases are typically built to be highly available and durable, with built-in redundancy, automated backups, and failover capabilities to ensure data safety

How serverless databases work

Serverless databases use cloud-native technologies to abstract away a server's management. They are designed to scale automatically based on workload demand. When demand is low, the database can scale down or even pause, reducing or eliminating costs. When demand increases, the database scales up rapidly to ensure continued performance.

The underlying infrastructure of a serverless database typically consists of stateless compute resources and distributed storage. The stateless nature of the compute resources allows them to be quickly created or destroyed based on demand, while the distributed storage ensures data durability and availability.

The impact of serverless databases on business operations

The advent of serverless databases has a profound impact on how businesses handle their data:

- **Resource optimization**: By removing the need for database administration, businesses can allocate their resources to areas that directly contribute to their strategic objectives

- **Cost savings**: The pay-per-use model of serverless databases can result in substantial cost savings, especially for workloads with fluctuating demands

- **Agility and speed**: The automatic scaling of serverless databases enables businesses to quickly respond to changes in demand, ensuring optimal performance at all times

- **Data-driven decisions**: With the assurance of a robust and flexible database, businesses can focus on utilizing their data to derive insights and make data-driven decisions

The future of serverless databases

The future of serverless databases is promising. As more businesses recognize the benefits of serverless databases, their adoption is likely to increase. We can expect to see advancements in serverless database technologies, including improved auto-scaling algorithms, integration with other serverless services, and enhanced security and compliance features.

Furthermore, the growth of edge computing and IoT may also drive the development of serverless databases optimized for these environments. Such databases will need to handle large volumes of data, generated by IoT devices, and provide low-latency responses for edge-computing applications.

Conclusion

The emergence of serverless databases signifies a major milestone in the evolution of database management. By providing on-demand scalability and cost efficiency, serverless databases have made database management more accessible and affordable for businesses of all sizes. As these databases continue to evolve and mature, they will play an increasingly crucial role in powering the data-driven digital economy. Their ability to automatically scale in response to application needs, coupled with a pay-per-use cost model, provides businesses with a powerful tool to efficiently manage their data and harness its value.

Summary

Throughout this chapter, we have explored significant advancements in database automation that have revolutionized the way businesses manage their databases. These innovations have brought about notable improvements in efficiency, cost-effectiveness, and strategic decision-making. Let's highlight these key advancements.

Firstly, self-driving databases have emerged as intelligent systems capable of managing and optimizing themselves. They automate tasks such as data backup, recovery, tuning, and fault prevention. By reducing the need for human intervention, self-driving databases enhance operational efficiency and minimize downtime.

AI and ML technologies have been integrated into database systems, enabling advanced analytics and optimization. AI and ML enhancements analyze query performance, predict future workloads, and optimize resource allocation, leading to improved efficiency and faster response times.

Automation has extended to areas such as data lineage tracking, where new technologies automatically trace and provide transparency regarding how data has been processed and moved. This enhances data governance, compliance, and auditability, offering businesses greater control and visibility over their data.

Data privacy automation tools have also seen significant advancements. They enable companies to protect sensitive information and ensure compliance with privacy regulations through data masking and anonymization techniques. This allows businesses to utilize and share data securely while maintaining privacy.

Automated data discovery and cataloging solutions have emerged, simplifying the process of locating and managing data across diverse databases and cloud systems. These tools provide a centralized view of data assets, facilitating effective data management, governance, and utilization.

The adoption and enhancement of DBaaS platforms have empowered businesses to outsource the routine tasks of database setup, maintenance, and scaling. By leveraging DBaaS, organizations can focus on data utilization to generate insights and value, while service providers handle the underlying infrastructure.

Lastly, the emergence of serverless databases within the DBaaS model has introduced auto-scaling based on application needs. Serverless databases enable businesses to scale resources dynamically, only paying for the resources consumed. This flexibility enhances efficiency and cost-effectiveness.

These advancements in database automation have transformed the way businesses approach database management. By automating mundane tasks, optimizing performance, and ensuring data privacy, organizations can allocate resources strategically, drive productivity, and make data-driven decisions with greater confidence.

In the next chapter, we will look at end-to-end ownership models.

Part 4:
Build and Operate

In this part, you will be introduced to the end-to-end ownership model, which plays a key role in implementing the DevOps strategy correctly. We will dive deep into operational best practices with clear examples of each stage. For different environments (on-premises, cloud, Kubernetes, etc.), we will provide different tooling examples with best-in-class implementation examples to achieve high availability and operational excellence.

This part comprises the following chapters:

11

End-to-End Ownership Model – a Theoretical Case Study

In this chapter, we delve into the practical implementation of end-to-end ownership through an in-depth case study. We'll start by exploring the adoption of the end-to-end ownership model, setting the stage for its application. We'll then take you through each phase of the product life cycle, from design and development to deployment and release, followed by monitoring and **incident management** (**IM**).

We'll also highlight the critical role of feedback and iteration, emphasizing how they contribute to product excellence. Finally, we'll address the challenges and complexities that arise as we scale end-to-end ownership across teams, offering valuable insights for organizations looking to embrace this model.

This chapter will cover the following topics:

- End-to-end ownership – a case study
- Adoption of the end-to-end ownership model
- Setting the stage
- Design and development phase
- Deployment and release
- Monitoring and IM
- Feedback and iteration
- Scaling and challenges

End-to-end ownership – a case study

End-to-end ownership is a model in software engineering with DevOps or **site reliability engineering (SRE)** where a team or an individual takes full responsibility for the entire life cycle of a product or service, from development to deployment and maintenance. It emphasizes accountability, autonomy, and cross-functional collaboration, aiming to streamline processes, increase efficiency, and improve overall product quality. In this model, the team or individual is responsible for everything related to the product or service, including its design, development, testing, deployment, monitoring, and ongoing support.

End-to-end ownership is important for several reasons. Firstly, it fosters a sense of ownership and accountability within the team. When a team is responsible for the entire life cycle of a product, it has a vested interest in its success and is more likely to prioritize quality, reliability, and customer satisfaction. This can lead to higher-quality products and faster delivery times.

Secondly, end-to-end ownership promotes cross-functional collaboration. Since a team is responsible for all aspects of a product, members with different expertise and skills need to work together closely. This collaboration breaks down silos and encourages knowledge sharing, resulting in better communication, more efficient workflows, and improved problem-solving capabilities.

Thirdly, end-to-end ownership enables faster feedback loops. When a team has complete ownership of a product, it can gather feedback from users and stakeholders directly, allowing for faster iterations and quicker responses to issues or changing requirements. This iterative feedback loop helps in delivering value to customers more rapidly and continuously improving the product.

Furthermore, end-to-end ownership encourages innovation and continuous improvement. Since the team has a holistic view of the product, it can identify areas for improvement and implement changes more effectively. It can also experiment with new features or technologies, iterate quickly based on feedback, and learn from failures. This promotes a culture of learning and innovation within the team.

Despite the benefits, implementing end-to-end ownership can present challenges. One of the challenges is the need for a diverse skill set within the team. In traditional models, teams are often specialized, with separate teams handling development, testing, deployment, and maintenance. In an end-to-end ownership model, team members need to have a broader skill set to cover all aspects of the product life cycle. This requires training and upskilling team members, which can be time-consuming and resource-intensive.

Another challenge is managing dependencies. In complex systems, different components may have dependencies on external services or teams. When a team has end-to-end ownership, it is responsible for coordinating and managing these dependencies. This requires effective communication and collaboration with other teams or stakeholders to ensure smooth integration and delivery.

Maintaining a balance between autonomy and alignment can also be challenging. While end-to-end ownership promotes autonomy and decision-making at the team level, it is important to align the team's goals with the overall objectives of the organization. This requires clear communication of expectations, regular feedback and performance reviews, and mechanisms to ensure that the team's work aligns with the broader organizational strategy.

In addition to the aforementioned points, scaling end-to-end ownership can be challenging. As the organization grows and more teams adopt this model, coordination and collaboration between teams become crucial. Sharing best practices, establishing common standards, and creating platforms or tools to support end-to-end ownership at scale are necessary to ensure consistency and efficiency across teams.

End-to-end ownership is a model that promotes accountability, autonomy, and cross-functional collaboration in software engineering, DevOps, and SRE. It has several positive benefits, including a sense of ownership, improved collaboration, faster feedback loops, and a culture of innovation. However, it also comes with challenges such as the need for a diverse skill set, managing dependencies, balancing autonomy and alignment, and scaling the model. Overcoming these challenges requires investment in training, effective communication, coordination, and the establishment of common practices and tools. Despite the challenges, organizations that successfully adopt the end-to-end ownership model can achieve faster delivery, higher quality, and increased customer satisfaction.

This theoretical case study explores the implementation of an end-to-end ownership model in a software development company, highlighting the technical depth of the model throughout the product life cycle. The case study follows a hypothetical project from inception to deployment, emphasizing the benefits and challenges encountered at each stage. By examining the practical application of the end-to-end ownership model, this case study provides valuable insights for organizations considering its adoption.

Adoption of the end-to-end ownership model

The world of software engineering is rapidly evolving, with organizations striving to develop high-quality software products and deliver them to the market faster than ever before. In this pursuit, many companies are adopting new methodologies and approaches to optimize their development processes. One such approach is the implementation of the end-to-end ownership model.

The end-to-end ownership model is a paradigm shift in software development, DevOps, and SRE. It places the responsibility for the entire life cycle of a product or service in the hands of a single team or individual. From conceptualization and design to development, testing, deployment, and ongoing support, the team takes full ownership, accountability, and autonomy over the product.

The objective of this case study is to explore the technical depth of implementing the end-to-end ownership model and to provide insights into its benefits and challenges. By following a hypothetical project from inception to deployment, we will illustrate how the model can be applied in practice and the impact it has on the various stages of the product life cycle.

The implementation of the end-to-end ownership model requires a shift in mindset and a reconfiguration of traditional development processes. It promotes collaboration, knowledge sharing, and cross-functional expertise, empowering teams to deliver high-quality products with speed and efficiency.

Through this case study, we aim to shed light on the technical intricacies of this model and highlight its potential advantages and hurdles.

In this case study, we will focus on a software development company called *Acme Software Solutions*. *Acme* is a mid-sized company specializing in building web and mobile applications for various clients. The company has decided to adopt the end-to-end ownership model to improve the quality of its deliverables, accelerate **time-to-market** (**TTM**), and enhance customer satisfaction.

Throughout the case study, we will explore the different stages of the project life cycle and how the end-to-end ownership model is applied. We will examine the challenges faced by the team, the technical solutions implemented, and the overall impact on the product development process. By diving into the technical details, we aim to provide a comprehensive understanding of the model's implementation and its effects on the organization.

The structure of this case study is as follows:

- **Introduction**: This section provides an overview of the case study, highlighting the objectives and significance of implementing the end-to-end ownership model.

- **Setting the stage**: Here, we delve into the initial stages of the project, including project initiation, the formation of cross-functional teams, and the definition of end-to-end ownership. We explore the motivations behind adopting this model and emphasize the importance of collaboration and shared responsibility.

- **Design and development phase**: This section focuses on the design and development phase, highlighting collaborative design and planning, agile development practices, and the role of **continuous integration** (**CI**) and continuous testing. We provide technical insights into how the team manages the development process under the end-to-end ownership model.

- **Deployment and release**: Here, we explore the deployment and release process, showcasing the use of **infrastructure as code** (**IaC**), **continuous deployment** (**CD**) pipelines, and techniques such as canary releases and feature flags. We outline the benefits of these practices in achieving efficient and reliable deployments.

- **Monitoring and IM**: This section emphasizes the significance of proactive monitoring and alerting in maintaining the health and stability of the deployed application. We cover **incident response** (**IR**) and post-mortems, demonstrating how the end-to-end ownership model facilitates the swift resolution of issues and continuous improvement.

- **Feedback and iteration**: Here, we focus on the gathering of user feedback and the iteration process. We discuss techniques for collecting feedback, prioritizing changes, and conducting A/B testing and experiments to drive continuous product improvement.

- **Scaling and challenges**: This section addresses the challenges faced when scaling the end-to-end ownership model. We explore managing dependencies, balancing autonomy and alignment, and maintaining consistency across multiple teams.

- **Conclusion**: The final section summarizes the key findings of the case study, highlights the main benefits of implementing the end-to-end ownership model, and provides recommendations for organizations seeking to adopt this model.

In the subsequent sections, we will dive deeper into each stage of the project life cycle and explore the technical aspects of implementing the end-to-end ownership model. Through this case study, you will gain insights into the practical application of this model and its potential impact on software development processes.

Setting the stage

In this section, we will explore the initial stages of the project where the end-to-end ownership model is being introduced at *Acme Software Solutions*. We will examine the project initiation, the formation of cross-functional teams, and the definition of end-to-end ownership, setting the foundation for the implementation of this model.

Project initiation

The journey toward adopting the end-to-end ownership model begins with the identification of the need for change within *Acme Software Solutions*. The company recognizes the challenges associated with siloed development processes, slow feedback loops, and lack of ownership and accountability. To address these issues, the executive leadership decides to explore a new approach that empowers teams to take complete ownership of their products.

At this stage, a cross-functional team is assembled, comprising members from different departments such as development, operations, and **quality assurance** (**QA**). This team will be responsible for leading the implementation of the end-to-end ownership model throughout the organization.

Formation of cross-functional teams

One of the key aspects of the end-to-end ownership model is the formation of cross-functional teams. In the case of *Acme Software Solutions*, the existing departmental boundaries are dissolved, and new teams are formed around specific products or projects. These teams consist of individuals with diverse skill sets, including developers, testers, operations engineers, and **user experience** (**UX**) designers.

The formation of cross-functional teams encourages collaboration and knowledge sharing. Each team member brings a unique perspective and expertise, enabling them to collectively address all aspects of the product life cycle. The teams are self-organizing, allowing them to make decisions collectively and take ownership of their products.

Defining end-to-end ownership

With the cross-functional teams in place, the next step is to define and establish the principles of end-to-end ownership. The team leads and management collaborate to create a clear and shared understanding of what it means to have end-to-end ownership.

End-to-end ownership at *Acme Software Solutions* encompasses the following key elements:

- **Responsibility for the entire product life cycle**: The teams take full ownership of their products, from ideation and design to development, testing, deployment, and maintenance. They are accountable for the success of their products and the satisfaction of the end users.

- **Autonomy and decision-making**: The teams have the authority to make decisions related to their products. This autonomy allows them to prioritize tasks, choose appropriate technologies, and define development and deployment processes that work best for their specific context.

- **Collaboration and shared knowledge**: Collaboration is fostered within and across teams. Team members actively share knowledge, best practices, and lessons learned. This collaborative culture encourages continuous learning and improvement.

- **Continuous feedback and iteration**: Feedback loops are established throughout the development process, allowing teams to gather feedback from stakeholders and end users. This feedback is used to iterate and improve the product continuously.

- **Quality and reliability**: The teams have a strong focus on delivering high-quality and reliable products. They are responsible for ensuring thorough testing, robust infrastructure, and proactive monitoring to maintain the health and performance of their applications.

By defining these principles, *Acme Software Solutions* establishes a clear framework for the teams to operate within. It sets the stage for a culture of ownership, collaboration, and continuous improvement.

The implementation of the end-to-end ownership model requires a shift in mindset and the willingness to embrace change. *Acme Software Solutions* recognizes the importance of providing support, training, and resources to the teams as they adapt to this new way of working. Through effective communication and guidance, the organization ensures that everyone is aligned with the objectives and expectations associated with the end-to-end ownership model.

In the next section, we will delve into the design and development phase, exploring how the cross-functional teams at *Acme Software Solutions* collaborate and apply the principles of end-to-end ownership to create innovative and high-quality products.

Design and development phase

In this section, we will explore the design and development phase of the project, highlighting how the cross-functional teams at *Acme Software Solutions* collaborate and apply the principles of end-to-end ownership. We will delve into collaborative design and planning, agile development practices, and the role of CI and continuous testing in ensuring the quality and efficiency of the development process.

Collaborative design and planning

Under the end-to-end ownership model, collaborative design and planning are key components of the development phase. The cross-functional teams at *Acme Software Solutions* come together to discuss and define the requirements of the product. They leverage their diverse expertise and perspectives to brainstorm ideas, identify potential challenges, and propose solutions.

During the design phase, the teams focus on UX, usability, and scalability. UX designers work closely with developers and testers to ensure that the product meets the needs and expectations of the end users. Design prototypes and wireframes are created and shared among team members, allowing for iterative feedback and refinement.

Collaborative planning involves breaking down the project into smaller tasks or user stories, estimating their complexity, and prioritizing them based on business value and technical feasibility. The teams use agile methodologies such as Scrum or Kanban to manage their work, with frequent stand-up meetings and sprint planning sessions to track progress and adjust plans as needed.

The collaborative design and planning process fosters a shared understanding of the product vision and aligns the team members toward a common goal. It promotes effective communication, minimizes misunderstandings, and sets the stage for efficient and coordinated development efforts.

Agile development practices

Agile development practices play a significant role in the design and development phase under the end-to-end ownership model. At *Acme Software Solutions*, the teams embrace agile methodologies to deliver value incrementally and adapt to changing requirements.

The teams work in short development cycles called sprints, typically lasting 1 to 2 weeks. They use tools such as Jira or Trello to manage their tasks and track progress. Daily stand-up meetings are held to provide updates, discuss any blockers or challenges, and ensure everyone is aligned on the goals for the day.

Within each sprint, the development work is organized into user stories or tasks, which are assigned to individual team members based on their skills and availability. The teams follow coding best practices and coding conventions to maintain consistency and ensure the maintainability of the code base.

CI is a crucial aspect of the development process. The teams leverage tools such as Jenkins or GitLab CI to automatically build, test, and integrate their code changes into a shared repository multiple times a day. This approach enables early detection of integration issues, ensures code quality, and facilitates collaboration between developers.

CI and continuous testing

CI is tightly coupled with continuous testing at *Acme Software Solutions*. As the teams frequently integrate their code changes, they also continuously test their applications to maintain a high level of quality.

Automated testing is an integral part of the development process. The teams employ various testing techniques, including unit testing, integration testing, and end-to-end testing. Unit tests are written alongside the code to validate individual components and ensure their correctness. Integration tests focus on verifying the interactions between different components or services. End-to-end tests validate the entire application flow from the user's perspective.

Testing is not limited to the development phase alone. The teams actively engage in exploratory testing and usability testing throughout the project to gather feedback and identify any usability or performance issues. They leverage user feedback, user analytics, and A/B testing to refine and improve the product iteratively.

The CI and continuous testing practices enable the teams to catch issues early in the development process, facilitating rapid feedback and quicker resolution of bugs or defects. By automating the testing process, they reduce the risk of regressions and ensure that the code base remains stable and deployable at all times.

Through collaborative design, agile development practices, and CI and continuous testing, the cross-functional teams at *Acme Software Solutions* embody the principles of end-to-end ownership during the design and development phase. In the next section, we will explore the deployment and release phase, highlighting how the teams leverage IaC, CD pipelines, and deployment strategies to ensure efficient and reliable releases of their products.

Deployment and release

In this section, we will delve into the deployment and release phase of the project, focusing on how the cross-functional teams at *Acme Software Solutions* leverage IaC, CD pipelines, and deployment strategies to ensure efficient and reliable releases of their products. The implementation of the end-to-end ownership model empowers the teams to take full ownership and control over the deployment process.

IaC

IaC is a fundamental concept in the deployment phase under the end-to-end ownership model. At *Acme Software Solutions*, the teams leverage tools such as Terraform and AWS CloudFormation to define their infrastructure in a declarative manner. They codify their infrastructure configuration, including servers, networks, databases, and other resources, using scripts or configuration files.

By treating infrastructure as code, the teams can version, manage, and deploy their infrastructure consistently and reproducibly. Infrastructure changes are tracked using source control systems such as Git, enabling easy collaboration and auditing. The use of IaC ensures that the infrastructure is provisioned accurately and consistently across different environments, reducing the chances of configuration drift and human errors.

CD pipelines

CD pipelines play a vital role in the deployment and release phase at *Acme Software Solutions*. The teams establish automated pipelines using tools such as Jenkins, GitLab CI/CD, and AWS CodePipeline. These pipelines orchestrate the entire deployment process, from code commit to production release.

The pipelines are configured to trigger on each successful code commit or merge to the main branch. The code is built, tested, and packaged automatically, ensuring that the application is in a deployable state. The teams leverage containerization technologies such as Docker to create lightweight, isolated environments for their applications, enhancing portability and consistency across different deployment environments.

The pipelines encompass various stages, including code compilation, unit testing, integration testing, security scanning, and artifact creation. Each stage is executed sequentially, and if any stage fails, the pipeline is halted and the team is notified to address the issue.

Deployment artifacts, such as Docker images or application packages, are generated as part of the pipeline. These artifacts are versioned and stored in artifact repositories or container registries, making them easily accessible for deployment to different environments.

Canary releases and feature flags

To ensure a smooth and reliable release process, the teams at *Acme Software Solutions* employ deployment strategies such as canary releases and feature flags.

Canary releases involve gradually rolling out new versions of the application to a small subset of users or servers before a wider release. By monitoring the performance and stability of the canary deployment, the teams can detect any issues or anomalies and take corrective actions before a full-scale release. This approach minimizes the impact of potential issues and allows for incremental validation of the new release.

Feature flags are another key deployment strategy utilized by the teams. Feature flags allow the teams to selectively enable or disable specific features or functionalities of the application at runtime. This enables them to control the release of new features, gradually exposing them to different user segments or environments. Feature flags provide flexibility and enable easy rollback in case of issues, as the new features can be disabled without the need for redeployment.

Through the adoption of IaC, CD pipelines, and deployment strategies such as canary releases and feature flags, the teams at *Acme Software Solutions* ensure that their deployment and release process is efficient, reliable, and easily controlled. The end-to-end ownership model empowers the teams to have full control over the deployment process, resulting in faster TTM, reduced deployment risks, and improved customer experience.

In the next section, we will explore the monitoring and IM phase, highlighting the teams' proactive monitoring practices, IR procedures, and continuous improvement efforts under the end-to-end ownership model.

Monitoring and IM

In this section, we will focus on the monitoring and IM phase of the project, highlighting the proactive monitoring practices, IR procedures, and continuous improvement efforts undertaken by the cross-functional teams at *Acme Software Solutions*. By implementing the principles of end-to-end ownership, the teams ensure the health, performance, and stability of their deployed applications.

Proactive monitoring and alerting

Under the end-to-end ownership model, proactive monitoring and alerting are critical components of maintaining the reliability and performance of the deployed applications. At *Acme Software Solutions*, the teams implement robust monitoring systems and practices to gain visibility into the application's health and to proactively identify any potential issues.

The teams leverage monitoring tools such as Prometheus, Grafana, and New Relic to collect and analyze metrics, logs, and traces from various components of the application stack. They define relevant **key performance indicators** (**KPIs**) and set up dashboards and alerts to track and notify them of any abnormal behavior or performance degradation.

Additionally, the teams establish proactive monitoring practices by implementing synthetic monitoring and uptime monitoring. Synthetic monitoring involves periodically simulating user interactions with the application to ensure it is functioning correctly and within acceptable response times. Uptime monitoring checks the availability of the application from different geographical locations, promptly notifying the teams of any service disruptions.

By continuously monitoring the application's performance, the teams can proactively address potential bottlenecks, scalability issues, or other performance-related concerns. Early detection of anomalies allows them to investigate and resolve issues promptly, minimizing the impact on end users.

IR and post-mortems

Despite the proactive monitoring efforts, incidents and outages may still occur. Under the end-to-end ownership model, the teams at *Acme Software Solutions* are equipped to respond quickly and effectively to such incidents.

When an incident occurs, the teams follow established IR procedures. They engage in real-time communication channels such as Slack or Microsoft Teams to collaborate and coordinate their efforts. IR playbooks provide a structured approach to resolving the incident, outlining the steps to be taken, key contacts, and escalation paths.

During the IR process, the teams focus on identifying the root cause of the issue and taking necessary actions to mitigate the impact. This may involve rolling back to a previous version, temporarily disabling specific features, or implementing quick fixes to restore service availability. They keep stakeholders informed about the incident's progress, ensuring transparency and managing customer expectations.

Once the incident is resolved, the teams conduct post-mortem reviews to analyze the incident's cause, impact, and the effectiveness of the response. The post-mortem includes a detailed analysis of the incident timeline, contributing factors, and actions taken to mitigate and resolve the issue. The objective is not only to identify the root cause but also to learn from the incident and prevent similar occurrences in the future.

Continuous improvement

Continuous improvement is a core principle of the end-to-end ownership model, and the monitoring and IM phase is no exception. At *Acme Software Solutions*, the teams leverage the insights gained from incidents and monitoring data to drive continuous improvement in their processes, infrastructure, and applications.

The post-mortem analysis serves as a foundation for identifying areas of improvement. The teams document actionable recommendations and lessons learned from each incident, focusing on process enhancements, automation opportunities, and preventive measures. They prioritize these recommendations and incorporate them into their backlog, ensuring that they are addressed in subsequent sprints or iterations.

Additionally, the teams engage in retrospectives at the end of each development cycle or project milestone. Retrospectives provide a dedicated space for the team members to reflect on their work, identify areas for improvement, and propose changes to enhance their collaboration, communication, and efficiency.

Continuous improvement also extends to the monitoring infrastructure itself. The teams regularly review and refine their monitoring setup, adding new metrics, improving alert thresholds, and incorporating new technologies or tools as needed. They keep up with industry best practices and emerging trends to ensure that their monitoring practices remain effective and up to date.

By embracing proactive monitoring, establishing IR procedures, and driving continuous improvement, the cross-functional teams at *Acme Software Solutions* uphold the principles of end-to-end ownership in the monitoring and IM phase. Their efforts result in improved application reliability, faster IR times, and enhanced customer satisfaction.

In the next section, we will explore the feedback and iteration phase, highlighting how the teams gather user feedback, prioritize changes, and continuously improve the product under the end-to-end ownership model.

Feedback and iteration

In this section, we will focus on the feedback and iteration phase of the project, highlighting how the cross-functional teams at *Acme Software Solutions* gather user feedback, prioritize changes, and continuously improve the product under the end-to-end ownership model. This phase emphasizes the importance of customer-centricity and iterative development to deliver a high-quality and user-friendly product.

Gathering user feedback

Under the end-to-end ownership model, the teams at *Acme Software Solutions* actively seek user feedback to gain insights into the UX, identify pain points, and understand evolving user needs. They employ various methods to gather feedback, including the following:

- **User surveys**: The teams create and distribute user surveys to collect quantitative and qualitative data on user satisfaction, feature preferences, and suggestions for improvement. Surveys provide valuable insights into the overall UX and help identify areas for enhancement.

- **User interviews**: To gain deeper insights into user preferences and pain points, the teams conduct one-on-one user interviews. These interviews allow for in-depth discussions, clarification of user needs, and the discovery of usability issues that may not be apparent through other feedback channels.

- **User analytics**: The teams leverage user analytics tools, such as Google Analytics and Mixpanel, to track user behavior within the application. This data helps identify usage patterns, popular features, and areas where users may encounter difficulties or drop-off. User analytics provide quantitative insights that complement qualitative feedback.

- **Customer support and feedback channels**: The teams actively monitor customer support channels, such as email or chat, to gather direct feedback and address customer concerns. They also encourage users to provide feedback through in-app feedback mechanisms or community forums, fostering a continuous feedback loop.

By gathering user feedback from multiple sources, the teams gain a comprehensive understanding of user needs, pain points, and expectations. This feedback serves as a foundation for making informed decisions and driving product improvements.

Prioritizing and implementing changes

Once the teams have collected user feedback, they employ a structured approach to prioritize and implement changes. They use techniques such as user story mapping, impact mapping, or prioritization matrices to evaluate and prioritize the identified enhancements and new features.

The teams collaborate with product owners, stakeholders, and users to refine and validate the requirements. They break down the prioritized changes into actionable user stories or tasks, ensuring that they are well defined and aligned with the product vision. The teams estimate the effort required for each task, considering factors such as complexity, dependencies, and business value.

The prioritized changes are then added to the team's backlog and incorporated into the sprint planning process. The teams leverage agile development methodologies, such as Scrum and Kanban, to manage their work and ensure that the highest-priority items are addressed in each iteration.

CI/CD pipelines facilitate the rapid delivery of changes to production. Once the changes are developed, tested, and integrated, they are deployed using the established deployment pipelines, ensuring that the improvements reach the end users in a timely manner.

A/B testing and experiments

To validate the impact of changes and gather further insights, the teams at *Acme Software Solutions* leverage A/B testing and experiments. A/B testing involves presenting different versions of a feature or design to different segments of users and measuring the impact on key metrics. By comparing the performance of the variations, the teams can make data-driven decisions about the effectiveness of the changes.

The teams use A/B testing tools, such as Optimizely and Google Optimize, to set up and monitor experiments. They define success criteria and KPIs for each experiment, allowing them to evaluate the impact of the changes objectively. A/B testing helps the teams identify the most effective solutions, reduce risks, and avoid unnecessary rework.

In addition to A/B testing, the teams also conduct small-scale experiments to validate hypotheses or test new ideas. These experiments involve launching lightweight features or prototypes to gather user feedback and validate assumptions before committing to full-scale development. This iterative approach allows the teams to learn quickly, iterate rapidly, and deliver features that align with user needs.

By actively seeking user feedback, prioritizing changes, and leveraging techniques such as A/B testing and experiments, the teams at *Acme Software Solutions* ensure that the product is continuously refined and aligned with user expectations. The end-to-end ownership model empowers the teams to make informed decisions based on user feedback and iterative development, resulting in a user-centric and continuously improving product.

In the next section, we will explore the challenges and considerations involved in scaling the end-to-end ownership model and maintaining consistency across multiple teams.

Scaling and challenges

In this section, we will delve into the challenges and considerations involved in scaling the end-to-end ownership model at *Acme Software Solutions*. As the organization grows and multiple teams adopt this model, various challenges need to be addressed to maintain consistency, collaboration, and efficiency across teams.

Scaling the end-to-end ownership model

Scaling the end-to-end ownership model requires careful planning and coordination. As *Acme Software Solutions* expands its team structure and adopts this model across different projects and products, the following considerations come into play:

- **Team structure**: Scaling the model involves forming new cross-functional teams. It is crucial to ensure that the teams are properly structured, with the right mix of skills and expertise. The teams should have clear roles, responsibilities, and areas of ownership, while still maintaining a cohesive and collaborative environment.

- **Knowledge sharing and documentation**: As new teams are formed, it is essential to establish mechanisms for knowledge sharing and documentation. Encouraging cross-team collaboration, organizing regular knowledge-sharing sessions, and maintaining a centralized knowledge repository can help disseminate best practices, lessons learned, and technical documentation.

- **Consistency and standardization**: Ensuring consistency in development processes, tools, and infrastructure becomes more challenging as the number of teams grows. Establishing common standards, coding conventions, and architectural guidelines helps maintain consistency and facilitates collaboration. Regular code reviews and architectural reviews can also serve as **quality control (QC)** mechanisms.

- **Communication and alignment**: Effective communication and alignment become critical when scaling the end-to-end ownership model. As teams become more distributed, it is important to establish clear communication channels, conduct regular team sync-ups, and maintain transparency across teams. Alignment with the overall organizational goals and strategies is essential to ensure that the teams' work contributes to the company's objectives.

Managing dependencies

In complex systems, teams often have dependencies on external services, components, or teams. As the end-to-end ownership model scales, managing these dependencies becomes a challenge. The following approaches can help address this challenge:

- **Cross-team collaboration**: Encouraging cross-team collaboration and communication is essential to manage dependencies effectively. Establishing regular meetings or forums for teams to discuss and align on dependencies, sharing roadmaps and plans, and maintaining open lines of communication can help minimize delays and conflicts.

- **Service-level agreements (SLAs)**: When teams have dependencies on external services or teams, defining clear SLAs becomes important. The SLAs should outline expectations, response times, and responsibilities to ensure that dependencies are managed effectively and the teams can rely on each other for timely support.

- **Dedicated integration and testing environments**: Providing dedicated integration and testing environments can help teams identify and resolve integration issues early on. These environments allow teams to test their components in a controlled setting, ensuring that dependencies are properly integrated and functioning as expected.

Balancing autonomy and alignment

Maintaining a balance between team autonomy and alignment with the overall organizational strategy is another challenge when scaling the end-to-end ownership model. While autonomy empowers teams to make decisions and take ownership, alignment ensures that their work aligns with the broader organizational objectives. The following approaches can help strike a balance:

- **Clear vision and direction**: Communicating a clear vision and direction to the teams is crucial. It provides a framework within which teams can operate autonomously while understanding how their work contributes to the company's goals. Regular communication of the company's vision, objectives, and priorities keeps teams aligned and focused.

- **Feedback and performance reviews**: Establishing feedback loops and conducting regular performance reviews can help align team efforts with organizational expectations. Feedback sessions provide an opportunity to provide guidance, align priorities, and address any misalignments or concerns. Performance reviews can assess individual and team contributions toward the overall organizational goals.

- **Agile governance and oversight**: Implementing agile governance practices can help strike a balance between autonomy and alignment. Establishing mechanisms for periodic reviews, checkpoints, and accountability ensures that teams are on track and aligned with organizational guidelines. This governance should focus on enabling teams rather than imposing strict control.

Scaling the end-to-end ownership model is a complex undertaking that requires careful consideration of team structures, knowledge sharing, communication, and alignment. By addressing these challenges and leveraging the right strategies, *Acme Software Solutions* can successfully scale the model and maintain consistency, collaboration, and efficiency across multiple teams.

Summary

Throughout this case study, we have explored the implementation of the end-to-end ownership model in a software development company, *Acme Software Solutions*. We examined the various stages of the project life cycle, from setting the stage to design and development, deployment and release, monitoring and IM, feedback and iteration, and scaling challenges. By adopting the end-to-end ownership model, *Acme Software Solutions* transformed its development processes, empowered cross-functional teams, and achieved several benefits while also encountering challenges along the way.

The end-to-end ownership model, with its emphasis on collaboration, accountability, and autonomy, brought numerous positive outcomes for *Acme Software Solutions*. By establishing cross-functional teams, the organization fostered collaboration and knowledge sharing, leading to improved communication and a shared understanding of the product vision. Agile development practices, such as collaborative design, CI, and testing, enabled faster development cycles and quicker feedback loops, resulting in higher-quality deliverables. IaC and CD pipelines streamlined the deployment process, ensuring efficient and reliable releases. Proactive monitoring, IR, and continuous improvement efforts enhanced application reliability and performance. Gathering user feedback, prioritizing changes, and leveraging A/B testing and experiments facilitated a user-centric approach and continuous product improvement.

However, the adoption of the end-to-end ownership model also presented challenges. Scaling the model across multiple teams required careful coordination, knowledge sharing, and maintaining consistency. Managing dependencies, both technical and organizational, necessitated effective communication and collaboration between teams. Balancing autonomy and alignment was an ongoing effort to ensure that individual teams were empowered while remaining aligned with the overall organizational strategy.

In conclusion, the implementation of the end-to-end ownership model allowed *Acme Software Solutions* to transform its software development processes and reap several benefits. By embracing collaboration, accountability, and autonomy, the organization achieved faster TTM, improved product quality, enhanced customer satisfaction, and a culture of continuous improvement. The model empowered cross-functional teams to take ownership of the entire product life cycle and enabled them to make informed decisions, respond swiftly to incidents, and iterate based on user feedback.

To successfully implement the end-to-end ownership model, organizations should carefully consider the challenges associated with scaling, managing dependencies, and balancing autonomy and alignment. By addressing these challenges and leveraging effective strategies, organizations can unlock the full potential of the model and create a culture of ownership, collaboration, and innovation.

By examining the technical depth of the end-to-end ownership model in this case study, we hope to inspire organizations to explore and adopt this approach to software development, DevOps, and SRE. The end-to-end ownership model has the potential to revolutionize development practices, empower teams, and drive impactful outcomes in the ever-evolving software industry.

In the next chapter, we will learn about immutable and idempotent logic.

12

Immutable and Idempotent Logic – A Theoretical Case Study

In this chapter, we'll embark on a comprehensive journey through the fundamental principles and practical applications of immutable and idempotent logic in data-persisting technologies. We will begin by laying a solid foundation with an introduction to these critical concepts, emphasizing their role in maintaining data integrity and reliability.

Subsequently, we will explore how immutable logic is harnessed within data-persisting technologies to ensure data immutability and consistency. Alongside this, we will delve into the world of idempotent logic, demonstrating how it facilitates the graceful handling of repeated operations, a crucial aspect of data persistence.

Then, we will transition into the real-world domain, where we will present practical examples and use cases, offering a tangible understanding of how organizations can leverage these concepts to enhance their data persistence strategies. Complementing this, we will provide considerations and best practices to guide professionals and organizations in implementing efficient and reliable data persistence solutions.

As we conclude, our gaze will turn to the horizon of future trends and the challenges that may emerge in the ever-evolving landscape of data-persisting technologies, providing valuable insights for those looking to stay at the forefront of data integrity and reliability.

The following main topics will be covered in this chapter:

- Introduction to immutable and idempotent logic
- Immutable logic in data-persisting technologies
- Idempotent logic in data-persisting technologies

- Practical examples and use cases

- Considerations and best practices

- Future trends and challenges

Introduction to immutable and idempotent logic

Let's define immutable logic.

In software engineering, immutable logic refers to a design principle where once an object or data structure is created, it cannot be modified. Immutable objects are those whose state cannot be changed after they are created. Any operation on an immutable object results in the creation of a new object rather than modifying the existing one.

The significance of immutable logic lies in its benefits for software development. Here are some key advantages:

- **Thread safety**: Immutable objects are inherently thread-safe since they cannot be modified concurrently. Multiple threads can access and use immutable objects without the need for synchronization mechanisms, reducing the chances of race conditions.

- **Simplicity and predictability**: Immutable logic simplifies code by eliminating the need for complex update operations. Developers can reason about the behavior of immutable objects more easily, as their state remains constant throughout their lifetime.

- **Consistency and reliability**: Immutable objects provide a consistent view of data across the system. Once created, they cannot be altered by any part of the application, ensuring data integrity. This consistency contributes to more reliable and bug-free software.

- **Caching and optimization**: Immutable objects can be safely cached and reused as their state is guaranteed not to change. This allows for performance optimizations by reducing redundant computations or database queries.

The concept of immutability is not new and has been widely used in functional programming languages such as Haskell and Scala. However, it has gained significant attention in recent years, particularly in the context of distributed systems and concurrent programming. Immutable data structures and objects are becoming more prevalent in modern software architectures to improve scalability and fault tolerance.

Now, let's focus on idempotent logic.

Idempotent logic refers to a property of an operation or function that can be applied multiple times without changing the result beyond the initial application. In other words, whether the operation is performed once or multiple times, the outcome remains the same.

The significance of idempotent logic in software engineering can be observed in various areas:

- **System stability**: Idempotent operations are crucial for maintaining system stability, especially in distributed and fault-tolerant environments. If an operation can be repeated without adverse effects, it becomes easier to recover from failures or retry operations.

- **Network communication**: In the context of APIs and network protocols, idempotent operations ensure that performing the same request multiple times does not cause unintended side effects or inconsistencies in the system. This property is especially important for operations with potential side effects, such as modifying data on the server.

- **Reliable data processing**: Idempotent functions play a significant role in data processing and transformations. By designing operations to be idempotent, developers can safely rerun data processing pipelines without worrying about duplicating or corrupting data.

Idempotent logic has been a fundamental concept in distributed systems for a long time. With the rise of microservices architectures, cloud computing, and containerization, idempotent operations have become increasingly important. They help ensure the reliability, scalability, and fault tolerance of systems by allowing for repeated and safe execution of critical operations.

Both immutable and idempotent logic promote robustness, scalability, and reliability in software systems. While immutable logic primarily focuses on the immutability of objects and data structures, idempotent logic deals with the stability of operations and functions. The significance of these concepts continues to grow as software engineers strive to build more resilient and distributed systems to meet the demands of modern technology.

Utilizing immutable and idempotent logic with data-persisting technologies can have significant benefits in terms of data integrity, reliability, and scalability. Here are some ways you can apply these principles:

- **Immutable logic with data-persisting technologies**:

  - **Immutable data storage**: Design your data-persisting system to store data in an immutable manner. Instead of allowing modifications to existing records, create new records for every update or change. This approach ensures that previous versions of data remain intact and can be referred to if needed, providing a historical view of changes.

  - **Versioning**: Implement versioning or timestamping mechanisms within your data-persisting technology to track changes over time. By associating each change with a unique identifier or timestamp, you can easily retrieve and analyze different versions of the data.

  - **Immutable data structures**: Utilize immutable data structures, such as immutable lists or trees, when storing complex data. Immutable data structures ensure that any modifications result in the creation of a new structure, preserving the integrity of the original data.

- **Event sourcing**: Employ the event sourcing pattern, where you store a sequence of immutable events that represent state changes in your system. By persisting events rather than the current state, you can reconstruct the system's state at any given point in time, enabling auditing, debugging, and time-traveling capabilities.

- **Idempotent logic with data-persisting technologies**:

  - **Idempotent write operations**: Design write operations in your data-persisting system to be idempotent. If an operation is performed multiple times, it should have the same effect as executing it only once. This ensures that duplicate or repeated writes do not cause unintended side effects or data inconsistencies.

  - **Idempotent APIs**: When exposing APIs for interacting with your data-persisting technology, make sure that the API endpoints that modify data follow idempotent principles. Clients should be able to repeat the same request multiple times without causing data corruption or undesirable effects.

  - **Transactional integrity**: Utilize transactions to ensure atomicity and consistency in write operations. By designing transactions to be idempotent, you can safely retry or replay transactions without introducing inconsistencies or conflicts in the data.

  - **Idempotent data processing**: When processing and transforming data before persisting it, ensure that the operations are idempotent. This allows you to reprocess the same data multiple times without causing data duplication or corruption.

By incorporating immutable and idempotent logic into your data-persisting technologies, you can build systems that are more resilient, scalable, and reliable. These principles help safeguard data integrity, enable efficient versioning, simplify data processing, and provide mechanisms for recovering from failures or retries without compromising data consistency.

Immutable logic in data-persisting technologies

Immutability in data storage refers to the unchanging nature of stored data. Once data is set, it remains constant, ensuring data integrity and protection against unintended or unauthorized alterations. Immutable data storage offers various advantages, including consistent data integrity, enhanced thread safety, and precise auditability. Practical approaches to implementing immutability include event sourcing and write-once, append-only storage systems. These methods are supported by technologies such as immutable databases, versioning, timestamping, and immutable data structures. When utilized effectively, these methodologies provide scalable and trustworthy data storage solutions, which is vital for sectors where data accuracy and traceability are paramount.

Understanding immutability in the context of data storage

Immutability is a fundamental concept in data storage that refers to the property of data being unchangeable once it is created. In the context of data storage, immutability ensures that the state of stored data remains constant and cannot be modified after it is initially stored. This characteristic distinguishes immutable data from mutable data, which can be altered or updated.

Immutability guarantees data integrity and consistency as it prevents accidental or unauthorized modifications. Once data is stored, it remains in its original form, providing a reliable and unchanging source of information. This property is particularly valuable in scenarios where accurate historical data is crucial, such as auditing, compliance, and forensic analysis.

Benefits and use cases of immutable data storage

Immutable data storage offers several benefits and is applicable in various use cases:

- **Data integrity and consistency**: By ensuring that data remains unmodified, immutable data storage guarantees data integrity and consistency. It provides a reliable and immutable source of truth, eliminating the risk of accidental or malicious changes.

- **Thread safety and concurrency**: Immutable data structures are inherently thread-safe as multiple threads can access and use the same data without synchronization or locking mechanisms. This property simplifies concurrency management and reduces the risk of race conditions, enhancing performance and scalability.

- **Auditability and traceability**: Immutable data storage enables comprehensive audit trails and traceability of changes over time. Each version or change to the data is recorded, allowing easy tracking and investigation of data-related issues. This is crucial in compliance-driven industries and for maintaining a transparent data history.

Examples of immutable data storage approaches

Here are some examples of immutable data storage approaches:

- **Event sourcing**:

    Event sourcing is a pattern where the state of an application is determined by a sequence of immutable events. Instead of modifying mutable data, each state change is captured as an immutable event and appended to an event log. The log serves as the source of truth, and the application state is derived by replaying the events.

    Event sourcing provides a complete audit trail of all changes and enables easy rollbacks or rewinds to previous states. It also supports temporal queries, allowing the system to provide an accurate view of data at any given point in time. Event sourcing is widely used in domains such as banking, finance, and supply chain management, where accurate historical data is critical.

The following is a code example:

Python

```python
class Event:
    def __init__(self, event_id, timestamp, data):
        self.event_id = event_id
        self.timestamp = timestamp
        self.data = data

class EventStore:
    def __init__(self):
        self.events = []

    def append_event(self, event):
        self.events.append(event)

    def get_events(self):
        return self.events

# Usage
event_store = EventStore()
event_store.append_event(Event(1, "2023-07-15T10:00:00",
{"data": "example"}))
events = event_store.get_events()
```

- **Write-once, append-only data stores**:

  Write-once, append-only storage systems enforce immutability by allowing data to be written only once and then appended but not modified. These systems are designed for scenarios where preserving data integrity and preventing accidental changes are paramount. Examples include transaction logs, system logs, and compliance records.

  By prohibiting modifications, write-once, append-only data stores ensure the reliability and immutability of the stored data. They provide a reliable audit trail and simplify data validation processes by ensuring that data remains unaltered once validated.

  Here's a code example:

Python

```python
def write_to_log(log_file, data):
    with open(log_file, "a") as file:
        file.write(data + "\n")

# Usage
```

```
write_to_log("app.log", "Log entry 1")
write_to_log("app.log", "Log entry 2")
```

Implementing immutable logic with data-persisting technologies

The steps for implementing immutable logic with data-persisting technologies are as follows:

1. **Immutable databases and data models:**

   Immutable databases are designed to enforce immutability at the database level. This can be achieved through various means, such as constraints, triggers, or specific database features. Immutable data models are built to prevent modifications to stored data, providing a foundation for reliable and immutable data storage.

   Here's an example:

SQL

```sql
CREATE TABLE employee (
    id INT PRIMARY KEY,
    name VARCHAR(50) NOT NULL,
    created_at TIMESTAMP DEFAULT CURRENT_TIMESTAMP
);
```

2. **Versioning and timestamping mechanisms:**

   Versioning and timestamping are commonly used mechanisms to track changes and preserve historical versions of data. Versioning involves associating each change with a unique version identifier, allowing the easy retrieval and querying of specific versions of the data. Timestamping assigns a timestamp to each modification, enabling temporal queries, auditing, and temporal navigation through the data history.

   Here's an example:

Python

```python
class VersionedData:
    def __init__(self, data, version, timestamp):
        self.data = data
        self.version = version
        self.timestamp = timestamp

data = VersionedData({"name": "John Doe"}, 1, "2023-07-
15T10:00:00")
```

3. **Immutable data structures in storage systems:**

    Immutable data structures, such as persistent data structures, play a crucial role in achieving immutability in storage systems. These structures ensure that operations that are performed on them create new versions of the structure while preserving the original versions. Immutable collections, such as lists, sets, or maps, provide thread-safe and efficient ways to store and manipulate data without modifications, supporting immutability at a granular level.

    Here's an example:

Python

```python
from immutables import Map

data = Map({"name": "John", "age": 30})
updated_data = data.set("age", 31)
```

In conclusion, embracing immutable logic in data-persisting technologies offers numerous benefits, including data integrity, thread safety, auditability, and traceability. Approaches such as event sourcing and write-once, append-only data stores exemplify the practical implementation of immutability. By utilizing immutable databases, versioning mechanisms, and immutable data structures, organizations can create reliable, scalable, and auditable data storage solutions.

Idempotent logic in data-persisting technologies

In the intricate web of data operations, the ability to confidently re-execute an action without the fear of unintended consequences or duplications is invaluable. Enter idempotent operations: a seemingly abstract concept but one that, when applied, forms the bedrock of reliability and consistency across data-persisting systems. Whether it's the simple task of adding an entry to a database, making updates via an API, or even using complex data processing pipelines, the philosophy of idempotency ensures that repeated operations maintain the stability and integrity of our data. In this section, we'll dissect the essence of idempotent operations, their varied applications across data persistence scenarios, and the profound significance they hold in ensuring fault-tolerant and resilient systems. Let's dive in and explore the consistent, safe, and repeatable world of idempotent operations.

Introduction to idempotent operations and their significance

Idempotent operations are a fundamental concept in data-persisting technologies. An operation is considered idempotent if performing it multiple times has the same effect as performing it once. In other words, repeating an idempotent operation does not produce any additional changes or side effects beyond the initial execution.

The significance of idempotent operations lies in their ability to ensure reliability, consistency, and fault tolerance in data persistence. By designing operations to be idempotent, developers can safely repeat or retry them without causing unintended consequences, data inconsistencies, or duplicate entries.

Examples of idempotent operations in data persistence

Here are some examples of idempotent operations in data persistence:

- **Idempotent write operations:**

  Idempotent write operations are crucial in data persistence to prevent data corruption and maintain consistency. Here are some examples:

  - **Insert or create**: When creating a new record in a database, an idempotent approach ensures that executing the operation multiple times does not result in duplicate entries. The operation checks whether the record already exists before creating it.

  - **Update**: Idempotent updates guarantee that executing the update operation multiple times does not alter the state beyond the desired change. This is achieved by making the update operation based on the current state of the data, ensuring that subsequent executions do not produce any additional modifications.

  - **Delete**: An idempotent delete operation ensures that executing the operation multiple times has no effect beyond the initial deletion. This is typically achieved by checking whether the record exists before attempting to delete it.

  By designing these write operations to be idempotent, data persistence systems can avoid unintended modifications or deletions, ensuring the integrity of the stored data.

- **Idempotent APIs for data modification:**

  Idempotent APIs are essential when exposing data modification endpoints to external clients or systems. Here are some examples:

  - **PUT or PATCH requests**: RESTful APIs often utilize PUT or PATCH methods for updating resources. An idempotent PUT or PATCH request ensures that repeated requests with the same payload produce the same outcome, without unintended side effects. The request body specifies the desired modifications, and the server applies them consistently.

  - **Idempotent key-based operations**: APIs that allow updates or modifications based on unique identifiers, such as primary keys, can be designed to be idempotent. By ensuring that repeated requests with the same identifier have no additional effects beyond the initial operation, data consistency and correctness are maintained.

  Idempotent APIs simplify error handling, retries, and error recovery in distributed systems. They enable clients to repeat requests without the fear of causing data duplication or corruption.

Ensuring idempotency in data processing and transformations

Idempotent logic is not limited to write operations or APIs; it can also be applied to data processing and transformations. Here are some examples:

- **Idempotent data processing pipelines:**

  Data processing pipelines often involve a series of operations applied to input data. Designing these pipelines to be idempotent ensures consistent and predictable outcomes, even when processing is repeated. Some techniques to achieve idempotency in data processing pipelines are as follows:

  - **Checkpoints**: Introduce checkpoints or markers to track the progress of data processing. By persisting the current state or progress at various stages, the pipeline can be resumed or retried from a specific point without reprocessing the entire dataset.

  - **Idempotent operations**: Ensure that each operation within the pipeline is idempotent. This means that running the operation multiple times produces the same result as running it once. This guarantees that repeating the entire pipeline does not lead to duplicated or inconsistent outputs.

- **Idempotent transactional operations:**

  In transactional systems, idempotent operations are crucial to maintaining data consistency and reliability. Idempotent transactional operations exhibit the following characteristics:

  - **Repeatable reads**: In read operations, the data should remain consistent, even if the operation is executed multiple times within the same transaction. This allows for a consistent view of the data during the entire transaction.

  - **Idempotent writes**: Write operations in a transaction should have no additional effects beyond the initial write, even if the transaction is retried. This ensures that transactional writes do not lead to data duplication or inconsistency.

  - **Transactional rollbacks**: Rollbacks should be idempotent, meaning that executing a rollback operation multiple times does not produce any additional changes beyond the initial rollback. This guarantees that retrying a failed transaction rollback does not lead to undesired changes in the data.

- **Idempotent data transformation functions:**

  Data transformation functions, such as those used in **Extract, Transform, Load** (ETL) processes, can be designed to be idempotent. This ensures consistent and reliable transformations, regardless of how many times they are applied. Here are some key considerations for achieving idempotency in data transformation functions:

- **Stateless transformations**: Stateless functions or transformations guarantee that the output depends solely on the input. Repeating the transformation with the same input produces the same output, regardless of previous executions.

- **Input validation**: Proper input validation is crucial to ensure that the transformation function handles invalid or unexpected data gracefully. By validating the input and handling edge cases, idempotent transformation functions can consistently process data without introducing errors or inconsistencies.

- **Non-destructive updates**: Transformation functions should avoid destructive updates that modify the original input. Instead, they should create new output data structures, preserving the integrity of the original data.

By ensuring idempotency in data processing and transformations, systems can be more resilient, reliable, and fault-tolerant. Idempotent logic simplifies error handling, retries, and error recovery, providing consistency and predictability in data processing workflows.

Idempotent logic plays a vital role in data-persisting technologies. Idempotent write operations and APIs ensure consistency and prevent unintended modifications or duplications. Idempotent data processing pipelines, transactional operations, and data transformation functions guarantee reliable and consistent data processing. By applying idempotent logic, systems can maintain data integrity, improve fault tolerance, and simplify error handling and recovery processes.

Practical examples and use cases

In the realm of data management, the terms "immutable" and "idempotent" often emerge as cornerstones for ensuring robustness, consistency, and fault tolerance. Relational databases, having been the backbone of structured data storage for decades, aren't impervious to the growing demands for these principles. The application of these concepts in relational systems, NoSQL databases, and distributed storage structures offers a transformative approach to data handling. This section unfolds the intricacies of blending immutability and idempotency with these data-persisting technologies. Through practical insights, we will explore how these principles fortify the foundation of data integrity, reliability, and resilience. Whether you're navigating the structured domains of SQL or the dynamic landscapes of NoSQL, or venturing into the vast world of distributed systems, this section serves as a guide to harnessing the power of immutable and idempotent logic in your data operations.

Immutable and idempotent logic in relational databases

Relational databases are a widely used data-persisting technology, and they can benefit from incorporating both immutable and idempotent logic. Here are some practical examples of how these concepts can be applied:

- **Using versioning and audit tables for immutability:**

  One way to introduce immutability in relational databases is by utilizing versioning and audit tables. These tables capture the historical changes made to the data, ensuring data integrity and providing an audit trail. Here's how it works:

  - **Versioning**: By introducing versioning, each modification to a record creates a new version of the data. The new version includes a timestamp or version identifier, allowing for historical data retrieval or point-in-time analysis. This ensures that previous versions of data are preserved and remain immutable.

  - **Audit tables**: Audit tables store information about the changes made to the data, such as the user who made the modification, the timestamp, and the type of operation performed. The audit table captures the before and after values of the data, providing a complete historical record.

  By incorporating versioning and audit tables, relational databases can maintain immutability and ensure data integrity while enabling comprehensive auditing and traceability.

- **Idempotent SQL operations and stored procedures:**

  Relational databases support SQL operations and stored procedures, and they can be designed to be idempotent. Here are some examples:

  - **Idempotent inserts**: When inserting data into a relational database, checks can be performed to ensure that duplicate entries are not created. By verifying the existence of a record before inserting it, the operation can be made idempotent.

  - **Idempotent updates**: Updates in SQL can be made idempotent by performing checks on the current state of the data before applying the modification. By verifying that the data matches the expected state before updating, the operation remains idempotent, even if it's executed multiple times.

  - **Idempotent deletes**: Idempotent delete operations involve checking the existence of the record before deleting it. If the record does not exist, the operation can be considered successful, even when executed multiple times.

By incorporating idempotent SQL operations and stored procedures, relational databases ensure that repeated execution of these operations does not lead to unintended modifications or data inconsistencies.

Immutable and idempotent approaches in NoSQL databases

NoSQL databases provide flexible and scalable data storage solutions. Immutable and idempotent approaches can be applied to enhance their reliability and consistency. Here are some practical examples:

- **Immutable document models in document databases:**

  Document databases, such as MongoDB, store data as flexible JSON-like documents. Immutable document models can be used to ensure data integrity. Here's how it can be implemented:

  - **Immutable documents**: Instead of modifying existing documents, new documents are created for every change. Each document represents a specific version of the data, allowing for historical tracking and analysis.

  - **Versioning or timestamping**: Documents can be associated with version numbers or timestamps to indicate the sequence of changes. By querying the database using specific versions or timestamps, different states of the data can be retrieved.

  - **Immutable collections**: NoSQL databases often support immutable collections, such as lists or maps, as part of the document structure. Immutable collections provide a way to store data in a manner that doesn't allow modification after creation, ensuring immutability at a granular level.

- **Idempotent operations with NoSQL databases:**

  NoSQL databases can also benefit from idempotent operations to maintain data consistency. Here are examples of idempotent operations in the context of NoSQL databases:

  - **Conditional updates**: NoSQL databases often provide mechanisms to perform conditional updates. By specifying conditions that must be met before applying the update, the operation can be made idempotent. For example, updating a document only if a specific field has a certain value ensures that repeated updates with the same value have no additional effects.

  - **Idempotent upserts**: Upserts, which insert or update a record if it exists or creates a new record if it doesn't, can be made idempotent by ensuring that the upsert operation is based on the current state of the data. This guarantees that repeated upserts do not produce additional changes beyond the desired modifications.

Applying these idempotent approaches to NoSQL databases ensures that repeated operations or failures do not introduce data inconsistencies or unintended side effects.

Immutable and idempotent patterns in distributed storage systems

Distributed storage systems, such as those used in microservices architectures, can leverage immutable and idempotent patterns to achieve data consistency and fault tolerance. Here are practical examples:

- **Event sourcing with distributed databases:**

  Event sourcing, as mentioned earlier, can be combined with distributed databases to ensure immutable and consistent data storage. Here's how it can be implemented:

  - **Event logs in distributed databases**: Distributed databases can store event logs that capture immutable events representing state changes. These events are appended to the log, maintaining the order of occurrence.

  - **Distributed event processing**: Distributed systems can process events in a distributed and scalable manner. By replicating and distributing the event log, multiple instances can process events independently, allowing for high throughput and fault tolerance.

  - **State reconstruction from events**: By replaying the events from the event log, the state of the system can be reconstructed at any given point in time. This enables reliable data retrieval and temporal analysis.

- **Immutable and idempotent message queues and event streams:**

  Message queues and event streams are fundamental components of distributed systems. Applying immutability and idempotency to these components enhances their reliability and fault tolerance:

  - **Immutable messages**: Messages in queues or event streams can be made immutable by preventing modifications or deletions after they are published. Immutable messages ensure that the original data remains intact and unchanged.

  - **Idempotent message processing**: Message consumers can be designed to handle messages idempotently. By using message deduplication techniques or maintaining processing checkpoints, consumers can ensure that repeated message processing does not lead to unintended side effects or data inconsistencies.

By combining immutability and idempotency in message queues and event streams, distributed systems can reliably process and communicate data, even in the presence of failures or network disruptions.

Applying immutable and idempotent logic in practical scenarios can enhance the reliability, integrity, and consistency of data-persisting technologies. Relational databases can benefit from versioning and idempotent SQL operations, while NoSQL databases can utilize immutable document models and idempotent operations. In distributed storage systems, event sourcing and immutable message queues enable fault tolerance and data consistency. By leveraging these examples, organizations can build robust and scalable data persistence solutions.

Considerations and best practices

In an age where data is at the heart of nearly all business operations, its effective management and persistence are critical to a system's success. Data persistence encompasses more than just storing data; it involves ensuring data integrity, reliability, and availability, even amid challenges such as system failures, evolving requirements, and scalability demands. Two key concepts that have gained prominence in ensuring effective data persistence are **immutability** and **idempotency**. These approaches promise consistent and fault-tolerant data management. However, like all architectural choices, they come with their set of implications. In this section, we will delve deep into the performance, scalability, consistency, and evolutive considerations of immutable and idempotent data persistence. We will provide insights into their benefits, potential challenges, and best practices, guiding practitioners in making informed decisions to build resilient and efficient data-persisting systems.

Performance and scalability implications of immutable and idempotent approaches

While immutable and idempotent approaches offer numerous benefits in data persistence, it's essential to consider their impact on performance and scalability. Here are some key considerations:

- **Performance overhead**: Immutable and idempotent operations may introduce additional overhead due to the need for creating new data objects or performing validation checks. It's crucial to evaluate the performance impact and ensure that it aligns with the system's performance requirements.

- **Write amplification**: Immutable approaches often involve creating new versions of data or appending new records, which can lead to increased storage requirements. It's important to consider the storage overhead and ensure that the system can handle the increased data volume efficiently.

- **Caching considerations**: Caching mechanisms can significantly improve performance in data-persisting technologies. However, caching mutable data can introduce challenges when using immutable or idempotent logic. It's crucial to design caching strategies that consider the immutability or idempotency of the data to ensure cache consistency.

- **Scalability and concurrency**: Immutable and idempotent approaches can enhance scalability by reducing contention and enabling parallel processing. However, ensuring efficient parallelism and scalability requires careful consideration of concurrency control mechanisms, data partitioning strategies, and distributed processing techniques.

It is important to conduct thorough performance testing, monitor system performance, and optimize the implementation to strike a balance between the benefits of immutability and idempotency and the system's performance requirements.

Data consistency and integrity considerations

Maintaining data consistency and integrity is paramount in data persistence. Immutable and idempotent approaches can help ensure these properties, but careful consideration is required to address potential challenges:

- **Transactional integrity**: When combining immutable and idempotent operations within transactions, it's crucial to ensure that the transactional boundaries encompass all related operations. This ensures that either all operations within a transaction are successfully applied or none at all, maintaining transactional integrity.

- **Synchronization and replication**: In distributed environments, maintaining data consistency across replicas or distributed systems is essential. Immutable and idempotent approaches should consider synchronization mechanisms, such as distributed consensus protocols or replication strategies, to ensure consistency and integrity across multiple nodes.

- **Error handling and rollbacks**: Idempotent logic enables safe error handling and retries. However, it's important to design appropriate error-handling mechanisms and rollbacks to address exceptional scenarios. Rollbacks should ensure that any partially applied operations are reverted to maintain data consistency.

- **Data validation**: Immutable and idempotent approaches rely on data validation mechanisms to ensure the correctness of the operations. Proper data validation should be implemented to prevent invalid or inconsistent data from being persisted. Validation checks should be performed during both input and output to ensure data integrity.

By considering data consistency and integrity concerns and implementing appropriate mechanisms, data-persisting systems can maintain the reliability and accuracy of the stored data.

Handling failures and retries with idempotent logic

Idempotent logic provides a powerful mechanism for handling failures and retries in data persistence. Here are some best practices:

- **Idempotent operations for retries**: Idempotent operations can be retried safely without causing unintended modifications or inconsistencies. When a failure occurs, the system can simply retry the operation, and if the operation was previously executed, it has no additional effects.

- **Exponential backoff and retry policies**: Implementing exponential backoff and retry policies can help manage retries effectively. By gradually increasing the time between retries, the system can handle transient failures and avoid overwhelming the resources.

- **Idempotent request handling**: When processing requests from clients or external systems, idempotent request handling is crucial to prevent unintended side effects. Using request deduplication techniques or request identifiers, the system can identify and discard duplicate requests to ensure idempotency.

- **Failure logging and monitoring**: It's essential to log and monitor failures and retries. This allows for the identification of recurring issues, performance bottlenecks, or potential data inconsistencies. Comprehensive logging and monitoring enable effective troubleshooting and system improvement.

By leveraging idempotent logic for handling failures and retries, data-persisting systems can improve fault tolerance, recoverability, and overall system reliability.

Managing data evolution and schema changes with immutability

As systems evolve and requirements change, managing data evolution and schema changes becomes crucial. Immutability can provide benefits in this context. Consider the following best practices:

- **Immutable schema evolution**: Immutability simplifies schema evolution by ensuring that existing data remains unchanged. Instead of modifying the existing schema, new versions of data structures can be introduced, allowing for backward compatibility and graceful migration.

- **Versioned data structures**: Introducing versioning mechanisms for data structures enables smooth transitions during schema changes. By associating data with specific versions, the system can handle both old and new versions of data during the migration process, ensuring data compatibility and continuity.

- **Data migration strategies**: Immutability allows for the gradual migration of data from one schema version to another. By applying well-defined migration strategies, the system can transform and migrate data incrementally without interrupting normal operations or causing data inconsistencies.

- **Compatibility and deprecation**: As the system evolves, deprecated or obsolete data structures or fields can be marked as such without affecting the existing data. This allows for a controlled deprecation process and ensures backward compatibility during the transition period.

By leveraging immutability in managing data evolution and schema changes, systems can ensure smooth transitions, avoid data corruption, and maintain compatibility with different versions of data structures.

Considerations and best practices in data persistence involve understanding the performance and scalability implications of immutable and idempotent approaches, ensuring data consistency and integrity, handling failures and retries effectively, and managing data evolution and schema changes with immutability. By applying these practices, organizations can design robust and reliable data-persisting systems that provide consistency, scalability, and fault tolerance.

Future trends and challenges

In the dynamic world of technology, grasping the future trends and challenges in data persistence is crucial. As data's volume and importance surge, our storage methods and technologies must progress accordingly. From blockchain's decentralized capabilities to the expansive reach of object storage, numerous innovations are reshaping data storage paradigms. Additionally, the integration of immutable and idempotent logic with cloud-native architectures brings forth both fresh opportunities and intricate challenges. Large-scale data persistence systems confront a host of complexities, necessitating a balance among elements such as consistency, scalability, and security. This section explores these developments and hurdles, shedding light on the impending direction of data persistence.

Emerging technologies and advancements in data persistence

Data persistence technologies are continuously evolving, and several emerging trends and advancements are shaping the future of data storage. Here are some key areas to consider:

- **Distributed ledger technologies (DLTs) and blockchain**: DLTs, including blockchain, offer decentralized and immutable data storage capabilities. These technologies provide tamper-proof data persistence, making them suitable for applications requiring transparent and auditable records.

- **Object storage**: Object storage systems, such as Amazon S3 and Azure Blob Storage, are gaining popularity due to their scalability and cost-effectiveness. Object storage provides a simple and efficient way to store vast amounts of unstructured data, making it ideal for big data analytics and content management systems.

- **In-memory databases**: In-memory databases, which store data in the system's memory for faster access, are becoming increasingly prevalent. Advancements in memory technology and decreasing costs are making in-memory databases more accessible, enabling real-time data processing and analytics.

- **Data lakes and data warehousing**: Data lakes and data warehousing solutions are evolving to handle the growing volumes and varieties of data. These platforms enable the consolidation and storage of structured and unstructured data for advanced analytics, machine learning, and data-driven decision-making.

- **Edge computing and edge storage**: With the rise of **Internet of Things (IoT)** devices and edge computing, there is a growing need for distributed storage solutions at the edge of the network. Edge storage enables data persistence closer to the data source, reducing latency and enabling real-time processing.

Integrating immutable and idempotent logic with cloud-native architectures

Cloud-native architectures, based on containerization, microservices, and serverless computing, provide scalability and agility. Integrating immutable and idempotent logic with these architectures presents both opportunities and challenges:

- **Containerization and immutable infrastructure**: Containerization, facilitated by technologies such as Docker and Kubernetes, supports the deployment of immutable infrastructure. Containers can be treated as immutable units, allowing for easy replication and scaling. Immutable logic aligns well with containerization, ensuring consistency and simplifying infrastructure management.

- **Microservices and idempotent APIs**: Microservices architecture promotes the development of loosely coupled and independently deployable services. Idempotent APIs are well-suited for microservices communication as they enable reliable and fault-tolerant interactions. By designing microservices to handle idempotent requests, systems can achieve resiliency and scalability.

- **Serverless computing and event-driven architectures**: Serverless computing, such as AWS Lambda and Azure Functions, leverages event-driven architectures. Immutable events, combined with idempotent processing, are natural fits for serverless and event-driven systems. Immutable events serve as triggers for functions, ensuring reliable and consistent data processing.

Integrating immutable and idempotent logic with cloud-native architectures can enhance scalability, fault tolerance, and deployment flexibility. However, it requires careful design, implementation, and consideration of the unique characteristics and challenges of these architectures.

Addressing complexities and trade-offs in large-scale data persistence systems

Large-scale data persistence systems often involve complex architectures and face various trade-offs. Here are some challenges to consider:

- **Consistency versus scalability**: Achieving strong data consistency across distributed systems may come at the cost of scalability. Designing data persistence systems to strike a balance between consistency and scalability is crucial. Techniques such as eventual consistency or consistency models tailored to specific use cases can help address these trade-offs.

- **Performance versus durability**: Ensuring high-performance data access and processing can sometimes conflict with durability and data persistence. Balancing performance optimizations with reliable data storage mechanisms is essential. Techniques such as data replication, caching, and intelligent data placement can help mitigate these challenges.

- **Data volume and storage costs**: As data volumes continue to grow exponentially, managing storage costs becomes a significant concern. Identifying cost-effective storage solutions, implementing data life cycle management strategies, and leveraging compression or deduplication techniques can help address the challenges of storing and managing large volumes of data.

- **Security and compliance**: Data persistence systems need to address security and compliance requirements, such as data encryption, access control, and privacy regulations. Integrating immutable and idempotent logic with robust security measures, auditing capabilities, and compliance frameworks ensures data integrity and protects sensitive information.

- **Operational complexity**: Large-scale data persistence systems can be operationally complex. Managing and monitoring distributed storage clusters, data replication, backup and recovery, and data migrations require robust operational tooling and automation. Investing in comprehensive monitoring, orchestration, and management platforms helps simplify system administration and maintenance.

As the scale and complexity of data persistence systems continue to grow, addressing these challenges requires careful architectural planning, leveraging automation and intelligent management tools, and staying informed about emerging technologies and best practices.

The future of data persistence involves emerging technologies such as distributed ledgers, object storage, in-memory databases, and edge computing. Integrating immutable and idempotent logic with cloud-native architectures can enhance scalability and resilience. Addressing complexities and trade-offs in large-scale data persistence systems requires careful consideration of consistency, scalability, performance, storage costs, security, and operational complexity. By embracing future trends and addressing these challenges, organizations can build robust, scalable, and reliable data persistence systems to support their evolving business needs.

Summary

In our exploration of data persistence, we delved into the principles of immutable and idempotent logic. Immutable logic ensures data remains unaltered over time, offering benefits such as auditability and scalability. In contrast, idempotent logic focuses on operations that yield consistent results even when repeated, ensuring reliability and fault tolerance. The integration of these logics into data persistence systems guarantees data integrity, consistency, and enhanced error management.

Selecting appropriate data-persisting technology hinges on specific use cases. Factors such as scalability, data structure, and query needs are pivotal. For instance, while in-memory databases may suit high-performance scenarios, relational databases might be more apt for structured data with complex queries. Compliance and security are equally paramount, making it essential to opt for technologies offering robust encryption, access control, and compliance capabilities.

Looking ahead, the essence of data persistence revolves around the further advancement of immutable and idempotent principles. Technologies such as blockchain and edge computing are set to redefine data storage, emphasizing security and decentralization. Integration with cloud-native solutions will amplify the significance of these logics, offering scalable and resilient data persistence frameworks. Challenges such as data evolution and schema management persist, but immutable logic can streamline data migrations and compatibility. As technology progresses, we expect enhancements in performance, scalability, and tooling, making data persistence more efficient and manageable. Ultimately, by embracing these forward-looking trends and addressing inherent challenges, organizations will be able to craft sturdy and adaptable data persistence systems to meet future business demands.

13

Operators and Self-Healing Data Persistent Systems

This chapter aims to delve into the realm of operators and self-healing data persistent systems, with a particular focus on Kubernetes and containerization technologies. It provides an in-depth exploration of the concept of self-healing, elucidates its benefits and risks, and highlights the factors to consider when implementing self-healing mechanisms in different types of databases. By the end of this chapter, you will have gained a thorough understanding of how self-healing systems can enhance the reliability and resilience of data persistence in modern infrastructure.

Throughout this chapter, we will explore self-healing data persistent systems from various angles, including their definition, core principles, benefits, and risks. We will also discuss the specific factors that come into play when implementing self-healing mechanisms in different types of databases, with a focus on relational, NoSQL, NewSQL, and time-series databases. Additionally, we will highlight the implementation and best practices for self-healing in a Kubernetes environment, showcasing relevant case studies and discussing the challenges and future directions of this technology.

The following main topics will be covered in this chapter:

- Self-healing systems
- Operators in Kubernetes
- Self-healing databases
- Factors influencing self-healing in different databases
- Self-healing in Kubernetes – implementation and best practices
- Case studies – self-healing databases in Kubernetes
- Benefits of self-healing databases in Kubernetes
- Challenges and future directions

Self-healing systems

Self-healing systems refer to autonomous systems capable of detecting, diagnosing, and resolving issues or failures automatically without human intervention. These systems leverage advanced technologies, such as **machine learning** (**ML**), **artificial intelligence** (**AI**), and automation, to continuously monitor their own health and make intelligent decisions to recover from faults or anomalies.

The core principles of self-healing systems can be summarized as follows:

- **Monitoring**: Self-healing systems rely on comprehensive monitoring mechanisms to continuously collect data about the system's health, performance, and state. This monitoring can encompass various aspects, including hardware metrics, software metrics, network traffic, and application-specific metrics.

- **Detection**: By analyzing the collected data, self-healing systems can detect deviations from normal or expected behavior. This detection process involves comparing current system states with predefined thresholds or patterns to identify anomalies or potential issues.

- **Diagnosis**: Once an anomaly or issue is detected, self-healing systems employ diagnostic techniques to identify the root cause. This may involve analyzing log files, correlating events, or applying ML algorithms to pinpoint the underlying problem accurately.

- **Recovery**: After diagnosing the root cause, self-healing systems initiate recovery procedures to restore the system to a healthy state. Recovery mechanisms can vary depending on the nature of the problem, ranging from automated restarts, reconfiguration, and failover to backup systems, or even dynamic scaling of resources.

- **Adaptation**: Self-healing systems exhibit adaptability by dynamically adjusting their behavior or configuration based on changing circumstances. This adaptive capability allows them to respond to evolving conditions, workload fluctuations, and performance requirements.

Components of a self-healing system

Self-healing systems consist of several key components working together to enable automatic fault detection, diagnosis, and recovery. These components include the following:

- **Monitoring agents**: These agents are responsible for collecting and aggregating data from various sources within the system, including hardware sensors, logs, and performance metrics. They transmit this data to the monitoring subsystem for analysis.

- **Monitoring subsystem**: This subsystem receives the data from monitoring agents and processes it using various techniques, such as statistical analysis, anomaly detection algorithms, or ML models. It identifies abnormal patterns, potential failures, or deviations from expected behavior.

- **Decision-making engine**: The decision-making engine receives alerts or notifications from the monitoring subsystem and makes informed decisions regarding the appropriate course of action. It leverages predefined rules, policies, or algorithms to determine the severity of the issue and the most suitable recovery strategy.

- **Recovery mechanisms**: These mechanisms encompass a range of actions that self-healing systems can undertake to restore the system's health. Examples include restarting failed components, reallocating resources, triggering backup systems, or reconfiguring the system to adapt to changing conditions.

- **Feedback loop**: The feedback loop enables continuous improvement by learning from past experiences and adjusting the system's behavior or rules accordingly. It collects feedback on the effectiveness of the recovery actions, the accuracy of diagnosis, and the overall system performance, providing valuable insights for future enhancements.

Importance of self-healing systems

Self-healing systems bring numerous benefits to modern infrastructure and applications:

- **Increased reliability**: By automating fault detection and recovery, self-healing systems minimize downtime and reduce the impact of failures. They enhance the overall reliability and availability of the system, ensuring uninterrupted operation even in the face of unexpected events.

- **Enhanced scalability**: Self-healing systems can dynamically scale resources in response to changing demands. They can automatically provision additional resources or distribute the workload across multiple nodes, enabling efficient utilization and seamless scalability.

- **Improved performance**: Self-healing systems can proactively address performance issues by identifying bottlenecks, resource constraints, or suboptimal configurations. Through automated recovery and adaptive mechanisms, they optimize system performance and maintain optimal service levels.

- **Reduced operational overhead**: With self-healing systems in place, manual intervention for issue resolution becomes less frequent. This leads to a reduction in operational overhead, freeing up human resources to focus on more critical tasks and strategic initiatives.

- **Resilience to failures**: Self-healing systems strengthen the resilience of applications and infrastructure by swiftly recovering from failures. They minimize the impact of faults, maintain service continuity, and provide a robust foundation for mission-critical systems.

- **Proactive issue resolution**: Self-healing systems can identify and resolve potential issues before they manifest as significant problems. By detecting early warning signs and taking corrective measures, they prevent system degradation and preemptively avoid disruptions.

Risks and limitations

While self-healing systems offer numerous advantages, they also pose certain risks and limitations:

- **False positives and negatives**: The automated nature of self-healing systems introduces the possibility of false positives (incorrectly identifying an issue) or false negatives (failing to detect an actual issue). These errors can lead to unnecessary or delayed recovery actions, impacting system performance or availability.

- **Complexity and overhead**: Implementing self-healing mechanisms adds complexity to the system architecture, requiring additional resources and expertise. The design, development, and maintenance of self-healing systems demand careful consideration and ongoing investment.

- **Unpredictable behavior**: The adaptive nature of self-healing systems can sometimes result in unexpected behavior or unintended consequences. The system's autonomous decision-making may not always align with human expectations or predefined rules, requiring careful monitoring and fine-tuning.

- **Security considerations**: Self-healing systems need robust security measures to safeguard against potential exploits or unauthorized actions. Automated recovery mechanisms must be carefully designed to prevent malicious activities and protect sensitive data.

- **Dependency on monitoring**: Self-healing systems heavily rely on accurate and comprehensive monitoring data. Inadequate or inaccurate monitoring can impair their ability to detect anomalies effectively and make informed decisions, compromising the system's self-healing capabilities.

- **Performance impact**: The continuous monitoring, analysis, and recovery processes of self-healing systems can introduce performance overhead. The additional computational and network resources required for self-healing mechanisms may affect the overall system performance.

Despite these risks and limitations, the benefits of self-healing systems often outweigh the challenges, especially in complex and dynamic environments where rapid fault detection and recovery are crucial.

Technical example of each core principle of a self-healing system

We will see a technical example of each core principle of a self-healing system as follows:

- **Monitoring**: Monitoring involves collecting data from various sources to assess the system's health and performance. In the context of self-healing systems, metrics and logs are commonly monitored. Here's an example of using Prometheus, a popular monitoring tool, to collect and monitor metrics in a Kubernetes cluster:

YAML

```
# Define a Prometheus deployment and service
apiVersion: apps/v1
```

```
kind: Deployment
metadata:
  name: prometheus
spec:
  selector:
    matchLabels:
        app: prometheus
  replicas: 1
  template:
    metadata:
      labels:
        app: prometheus
    spec:
      containers:
        - name: prometheus
          image: prom/prometheus
          args:
            - "--config.file=/etc/prometheus/prometheus.yml"
          ports:
            - containerPort: 9090
---
apiVersion: v1
kind: Service
metadata:
  name: prometheus
spec:
  selector:
    app: prometheus
  ports:
    - port: 9090
      targetPort: 9090
```

- **Detection**: Detection involves analyzing collected data to identify anomalies or deviations from expected behavior. ML algorithms can be used to detect patterns and anomalies in system metrics. Here's an example of using the Prophet library in Python to detect anomalies in time-series data:

Python

```python
from fbprophet import Prophet
import pandas as pd

# Load and preprocess time-series data
df = pd.read_csv('metrics.csv')
df['ds'] = pd.to_datetime(df['timestamp'])
```

```
df['y'] = df['value']

# Create and fit the Prophet model
model = Prophet()
model.fit(df)

# Predict future values
future = model.make_future_dataframe(periods=30)
forecast = model.predict(future)

# Identify anomalies in the forecasted values
anomalies = forecast[forecast['yhat_upper'] < df['y']]
```

- **Diagnosis**: Diagnosis involves determining the root cause of detected anomalies or issues. In a self-healing system, diagnostic logs and analysis can provide insights into the underlying problem. Here's an example of using log analysis in Elasticsearch and Kibana to diagnose issues:

Elasticsearch

```
# Query logs related to a specific component or error
GET /logs/_search
{
  "query": {
    "bool": {
      "must": [
          { "match": { "component": "database" }},
          { "match": { "error": "connection error" }}
      ]
    }
  }
}
```

- **Recovery**: Recovery involves taking appropriate actions to restore the system to a healthy state. In a Kubernetes environment, automated recovery mechanisms can be implemented using Kubernetes operators. Here's an example of a basic **Custom Resource Definition (CRD)** for a self-healing Redis database operator:

YAML

```
apiVersion: apiextensions.k8s.io/v1
kind: CustomResourceDefinition
metadata:
  name: redisclusters.mycompany.com
spec:
```

```
group: mycompany.com
versions:
  - name: v1
    served: true
    storage: true
scope: Namespaced
names:
  plural: redisclusters
  singular: rediscluster
  kind: RedisCluster
```

- **Adaptation**: Adaptation involves dynamically adjusting the system's behavior or configuration based on changing conditions. Configuration management tools such as Ansible can be used to automate adaptive changes. Here's an example of an Ansible playbook for dynamically adjusting resource allocation in a Kubernetes cluster:

YAML

```
---
- name: Scale Kubernetes Deployment
  hosts: kubernetes
  tasks:
    - name: Scale Deployment
      k8s:
        api_version: apps/v1
        kind: Deployment
        name: myapp
        namespace: mynamespace
        replicas: 5
```

These examples demonstrate how each core principle of self-healing systems can be implemented using specific technologies and tools. The actual implementation may vary depending on the specific requirements and the technologies employed in the system architecture.

Operators in Kubernetes

In the ever-evolving world of containerization and cloud-native technologies, Kubernetes stands out as a pivotal tool for managing and orchestrating containerized applications. Beyond its fundamental capabilities, the realm of Kubernetes extends into specialized areas, one of which is the concept of operators. Operators are designed to automate, simplify, and enhance the way applications and services run within a Kubernetes environment. Delving into this section, you will gain insights into the basic principles of Kubernetes and containerization, the intricate functionalities of operators, the broader operator ecosystem, and their invaluable benefits and use cases in real-world Kubernetes deployments.

Overview of Kubernetes and containerization

Before diving into operators, let's first understand the fundamentals of Kubernetes and containerization. Kubernetes is an open source container orchestration platform that automates the deployment, scaling, and management of containerized applications. It provides a framework for abstracting away the underlying infrastructure and allows developers to focus on the application logic.

Containerization, on the other hand, is a lightweight virtualization technique that encapsulates an application and its dependencies into isolated and portable units called containers. Containers provide a consistent and reproducible environment, ensuring that applications run consistently across different computing environments.

Kubernetes leverages containerization to create highly scalable and resilient applications. It manages containers in a cluster of nodes, handles load balancing, monitors application health, and facilitates efficient resource allocation.

Understanding operators

Operators are a key concept in Kubernetes that extend its capabilities beyond basic container orchestration. They are Kubernetes-native applications that encode domain-specific knowledge and operational best practices into software. Operators automate complex and repetitive tasks related to managing applications and services within a Kubernetes environment.

An operator typically consists of the following components:

- **CRD**: Operators introduce **Custom Resources** (**CRs**) by defining CRDs. CRDs extend the Kubernetes API and allow users to define and manage higher-level abstractions specific to their applications or services.

- **Controller**: The controller is the core component of an operator. It watches the CRs' state and performs the necessary actions to ensure the desired state is achieved. It reconciles the current state with the desired state and handles tasks such as provisioning, scaling, and configuration management.

- **CR instances**: CR instances are created by users to define the desired state of the resources managed by the operator. For example, an operator for a database might have a CR called "Database" that defines the desired configuration, storage, and replication settings.

- **Operator SDK**: The Operator SDK is a software development framework that assists in building operators. It provides libraries, tools, and scaffolding to simplify the creation and management of operators.

Operator frameworks and ecosystem

The Kubernetes operator ecosystem is vast and diverse, with several operator frameworks available to streamline operator development. Some popular operator frameworks include the following:

- **The Operator Framework**: The Operator Framework, developed by Red Hat, is a collection of tools and utilities that simplifies operator development. It provides a **software development kit (SDK)**, an operator life-cycle manager, and an operator metering framework.

- **Kubebuilder**: Kubebuilder is a framework built on top of the Kubernetes controller-runtime library. It offers a simplified development experience by generating code scaffolding, handling CRD creation, and providing testing utilities.

- **The Operator SDK**: The Operator SDK is an open source project that provides an SDK for building Kubernetes operators. It supports multiple programming languages, including Go, Ansible, and Helm, and offers features such as code generation, testing, and deployment.

- **Helm**: While not a dedicated operator framework, Helm is a package manager for Kubernetes that can be used to package and deploy operators. Helm charts provide a templated way to define and manage complex applications and services.

- **OperatorHub**: OperatorHub is a marketplace for finding and sharing operators. It serves as a central repository of pre-built operators that can be easily deployed into Kubernetes clusters.

The operator framework and ecosystem enable developers to build and share reusable operators, reducing the effort required to manage complex applications and services within Kubernetes.

Benefits of operators in Kubernetes

Operators offer several benefits for managing applications and services in a Kubernetes environment:

- **Automation**: Operators automate tasks that would otherwise require manual intervention, such as provisioning, scaling, and updating applications. They encapsulate domain-specific knowledge and best practices, reducing the burden on administrators and ensuring consistent operations.

- **Declarative management**: Operators enable declarative management of complex applications by defining the desired state of resources. They continuously reconcile the actual state with the desired state, ensuring that the application remains in the desired configuration.

- **Extensibility**: Kubernetes operators allow users to extend the Kubernetes API by defining CRs tailored to their specific applications or services. This extensibility empowers developers to manage higher-level abstractions and automate application-specific operations.

- **Standardization**: Operators promote standardization by encapsulating operational expertise within the operator code. This eliminates manual processes, reduces human error, and ensures consistent deployments and configurations across environments.

- **Portability**: Operators provide a consistent way to manage applications across different Kubernetes clusters and cloud environments. Operators encapsulate application-specific logic and configurations, making it easier to migrate or replicate applications across different infrastructures.

- **Community collaboration**: The operator ecosystem fosters collaboration and knowledge sharing among developers. OperatorHub serves as a platform for sharing and discovering pre-built operators, accelerating the adoption of best practices and reducing development time.

Use cases of operators in Kubernetes

Operators can be applied to various use cases within Kubernetes, extending the platform's capabilities for managing complex applications and services. Some common use cases include the following:

- **Databases**: Operators can manage the life cycle of databases, including provisioning, scaling, backup and restore, and **high availability** (**HA**) configurations. Examples include the `etcd` Operator, PostgreSQL Operator, and MongoDB Operator.

- **ML**: Operators can simplify the deployment and management of ML workloads. They can handle tasks such as model training, serving, and scaling. Kubeflow, an open source project, provides operators for building end-to-end ML pipelines.

- **Observability**: Operators can automate the setup and configuration of observability tools such as Prometheus and Grafana. They ensure that the necessary monitoring, logging, and alerting components are properly deployed and integrated with the application.

- **Networking**: Operators can automate the management of networking components within a Kubernetes cluster. They can handle tasks such as ingress control, load balancing, and service discovery. The NGINX Ingress Controller Operator is an example of a networking operator.

- **Storage**: Operators can simplify the provisioning and management of storage resources in Kubernetes. They can dynamically provision and attach storage volumes, manage snapshots, and handle storage-related configurations. The Rook Operator is an example of a storage operator.

These use cases highlight the versatility and flexibility of operators in managing a wide range of applications and services within Kubernetes.

Operators are a fundamental concept in Kubernetes that extends the platform's capabilities beyond basic container orchestration. They automate complex tasks, encode domain-specific knowledge, and facilitate the management of applications and services within a Kubernetes environment. The operator framework and ecosystem provide tools and resources to simplify operator development and foster community collaboration. By leveraging operators, organizations can automate operations, ensure consistency, and streamline the management of complex workloads in Kubernetes clusters.

Self-healing databases

As the digital age progresses, the role of databases in powering applications becomes ever more significant. Traditional databases, while central to data management, are not without their share of challenges, particularly when it comes to ensuring reliability and data integrity. Enter the era of self-healing databases: a forward-thinking solution designed to address these inherent vulnerabilities. Through automated mechanisms, these databases aim to detect and rectify failures, ensuring seamless operation even in the face of unforeseen issues. In the following section, we'll delve deeper into the intricacies of these self-healing mechanisms, their numerous benefits, as well as the potential risks and limitations that organizations should be aware of.

Traditional database challenges

Databases play a critical role in modern applications, managing the storage and retrieval of data. However, traditional databases often face challenges related to availability, resilience, and **fault tolerance** (**FT**). System failures, hardware issues, software bugs, and human errors can lead to data inconsistencies, downtime, and data loss.

To address these challenges, self-healing mechanisms have emerged as a valuable approach to enhance the reliability and resilience of databases. Self-healing databases are designed to automatically detect, diagnose, and recover from failures or anomalies without human intervention.

Self-healing mechanisms in databases

Self-healing mechanisms in databases encompass a range of techniques that enable automatic fault detection and recovery. These mechanisms can vary based on the database type and architecture but typically include the following:

- **Replication**: Replication involves creating multiple copies (replicas) of data across different nodes or clusters. If a primary node fails, a replica can take over seamlessly, ensuring continuous availability and data durability. Replication mechanisms, such as master-slave or multi-master replication, enable self-healing by providing redundancy and failover capabilities.

- **Automated backup and restore**: Regularly backing up data and automating the restore process is a crucial aspect of self-healing databases. Incremental backups, periodic snapshots, and transaction logs allow for quick restoration of data in case of failures or data corruption. Automated backup and restore mechanisms help ensure data integrity and minimize the impact of failures.

- **Automated failure detection**: Self-healing databases employ mechanisms to detect failures or anomalies in real time. This can be achieved through various techniques, such as heartbeat monitoring, health checks, or anomaly detection algorithms. By continuously monitoring the health and performance of database nodes, self-healing databases can promptly identify issues and initiate recovery procedures.

- **Automatic failover**: Automatic failover is a critical component of self-healing databases, enabling the seamless transition from a failed node to a healthy replica. When a failure is detected, the self-healing system automatically promotes a replica to the primary role and redirects client requests accordingly. Failover mechanisms ensure HA and minimize downtime in the event of node failures.

- **Data consistency and integrity checks**: Self-healing databases incorporate mechanisms to validate and ensure data consistency and integrity. Techniques such as checksums, hashing, and data validation algorithms help detect and correct data corruption or inconsistencies. By regularly performing integrity checks, self-healing databases can identify and recover from data integrity issues.

- **Configuration management**: Self-healing databases include mechanisms to manage configuration settings dynamically. This allows for automatic adjustment of parameters, such as memory allocation, caching policies, and replication settings, based on workload patterns and changing conditions. Dynamic configuration management optimizes database performance, mitigates resource contention, and adapts to evolving requirements.

Benefits of self-healing databases

Self-healing databases offer several benefits for organizations and applications:

- **HA**: By leveraging replication, automated failover, and fault detection mechanisms, self-healing databases provide HA. They minimize downtime, ensure continuous access to data, and improve overall application resilience.

- **FT**: Self-healing databases enhance FT by automatically recovering from failures or anomalies. They reduce the impact of hardware or software failures, mitigating the risk of data loss and minimizing the need for manual intervention.

- **Improved data integrity**: Self-healing mechanisms, such as data consistency checks and automated backups, contribute to improved data integrity. They detect and correct data inconsistencies, protect against corruption, and facilitate data recovery in case of failures.

- **Scalability**: Self-healing databases often include mechanisms for dynamic scaling, enabling them to handle increasing workloads and adapt to changing demands. Automated provisioning and scaling of resources ensure optimal performance and accommodate varying application requirements.

- **Reduced operational overhead**: Self-healing databases automate tasks related to fault detection, recovery, and data integrity. This reduces the operational overhead, freeing up human resources to focus on other critical tasks and reducing the risk of human error.

- **Enhanced reliability**: Self-healing databases enhance the reliability of applications by minimizing the impact of failures. They improve system uptime, reduce service disruptions, and enhance the overall user experience.

Risks and limitations

While self-healing databases offer significant advantages, they are not without risks and limitations:

- **Complexity**: Implementing self-healing mechanisms introduces additional complexity to the database architecture. Designing, configuring, and maintaining self-healing databases require careful consideration and expertise.

- **Performance overhead**: Self-healing mechanisms, such as replication and automated failover, can introduce performance overhead. The additional processing and network traffic required for self-healing operations may impact the overall database performance.

- **False positives and negatives**: Automated fault detection and recovery mechanisms may occasionally produce false positives or false negatives. False positives can trigger unnecessary recovery actions, while false negatives can lead to undetected failures or delayed recovery. Fine-tuning and rigorous testing are essential to minimize these risks.

- **Security considerations**: Self-healing databases must address security considerations to protect against potential exploits or unauthorized access. Automated recovery mechanisms should be carefully designed to prevent malicious activities and protect sensitive data.

- **Dependency on monitoring**: Self-healing databases heavily rely on accurate and comprehensive monitoring to detect anomalies and trigger recovery actions. Inadequate or incomplete monitoring can hinder the effectiveness of self-healing mechanisms and compromise the overall resilience of the database.

- **Data consistency challenges**: Replication and failover mechanisms in self-healing databases can introduce challenges related to maintaining data consistency across multiple replicas. Synchronization delays, conflicts, and network partitions can impact data consistency, requiring careful design and configuration.

It is important to consider these risks and limitations while implementing self-healing databases and to perform thorough testing and monitoring to ensure their effectiveness in real-world scenarios.

Self-healing databases address the challenges of availability, resilience, and FT in traditional databases. By incorporating mechanisms such as replication, automated backup and restore, failure detection, automatic failover, and data integrity checks, self-healing databases enhance reliability, reduce downtime, and improve data integrity. While they offer significant benefits, careful design, monitoring, and consideration of potential risks are essential for the successful implementation and operation of self-healing databases.

Factors influencing self-healing in different databases

Self-healing mechanisms in databases are influenced by various factors, including the database architecture, data model, scalability needs, and the operational environment. Different database types, such as relational, NoSQL, NewSQL, and time-series databases, have distinct characteristics that impact the implementation of self-healing capabilities.

Relational databases

Relational databases are based on the relational data model and use **Structured Query Language (SQL)** for data manipulation. When considering self-healing in relational databases, several factors come into play:

- **Replication strategies**: Relational databases often employ replication techniques to achieve FT and HA. Self-healing mechanisms should consider factors such as synchronous or asynchronous replication, multi-master or master-slave architectures, and conflict resolution strategies. By maintaining replicas of data, self-healing databases can seamlessly switch to a replica in case of primary node failure, ensuring continuous availability.

- **Transaction management**: Relational databases typically adhere to **Atomicity, Consistency, Isolation, Durability (ACID)** properties. Self-healing mechanisms need to ensure that in case of failures, ongoing transactions are handled correctly, preserving data integrity and atomicity. Proper transaction management during the self-healing process ensures that database operations are consistent and durable.

- **Index rebuilding**: Indexes play a vital role in relational databases for efficient data retrieval. Self-healing mechanisms should consider automated index-rebuilding strategies to recover from index corruption or fragmentation and maintain optimal query performance. By automatically rebuilding indexes, self-healing databases can improve query execution efficiency after a failure.

- **Query optimization**: Relational databases rely on query optimization techniques to improve query performance. Self-healing mechanisms need to consider strategies to automatically detect and recover from query performance issues caused by query plan changes, missing or outdated statistics, or suboptimal indexing. By dynamically optimizing queries during the self-healing process, databases can maintain efficient query execution and minimize performance degradation.

NoSQL databases

NoSQL databases provide a flexible data model and are designed to handle large-scale distributed systems. When it comes to self-healing in NoSQL databases, the following factors are critical:

- **Data partitioning and distribution**: NoSQL databases often use sharding and data partitioning to distribute data across multiple nodes. Self-healing mechanisms need to handle automatic rebalancing and redistribution of data when nodes fail or new nodes are added to the cluster. By dynamically redistributing data, self-healing databases ensure that data remains evenly distributed and accessible even in the presence of failures.

- **Eventual consistency**: Many NoSQL databases prioritize availability and partition tolerance over strict consistency. Self-healing mechanisms should consider the eventual consistency model and employ conflict resolution strategies to reconcile divergent copies of data during the self-healing process. By resolving conflicts and maintaining eventual consistency, self-healing databases ensure data integrity and availability.

- **Replication topologies**: NoSQL databases support various replication topologies, such as master-slave, multi-master, or leader-based consistency. Self-healing mechanisms need to align with the chosen replication strategy and handle automated failover, replication synchronization, and conflict resolution. By managing replication effectively, self-healing databases ensure HA and FT.

- **Automatic schema evolution**: NoSQL databases often allow flexible schema changes. Self-healing mechanisms should consider the automatic adaptation of the schema to handle evolving requirements and ensure data consistency during the self-healing process. By automatically updating the schema, self-healing databases can accommodate changes and maintain data integrity.

NewSQL databases

NewSQL databases combine the scalability and FT of NoSQL with the ACID properties of traditional relational databases. When considering self-healing in NewSQL databases, the following factors are crucial:

- **Scalability and sharding**: NewSQL databases utilize sharding and partitioning techniques to scale horizontally. Self-healing mechanisms need to handle the automatic rebalancing and redistribution of data across shards in the event of node failures or new node additions. By automatically managing sharding, self-healing databases can ensure optimal data distribution and availability.

- **Consistency models**: NewSQL databases often offer different consistency models, such as strict serializability, snapshot isolation, or scalable multi-version concurrency control. Self-healing mechanisms should align with the chosen consistency model and handle automatic failover, consistency maintenance, and conflict resolution. By maintaining the chosen consistency level, self-healing databases ensure data integrity and correctness.

- **Distributed query optimization**: NewSQL databases distribute query processing across multiple nodes to achieve high performance. Self-healing mechanisms should consider strategies to automatically optimize query plans, adapt to changing network conditions, and ensure query execution efficiency during the self-healing process. By dynamically optimizing query execution, self-healing databases maintain optimal performance and minimize response time.

- **Automated repartitioning**: NewSQL databases may require automated repartitioning strategies to handle changes in data distribution, node additions, or failures. Self-healing mechanisms should provide mechanisms to adaptively repartition data while maintaining data integrity and minimizing disruption. By automatically repartitioning data, self-healing databases can ensure efficient data distribution and scalability.

Time-series databases

Time-series databases are specifically designed to handle large volumes of time-stamped data. When it comes to self-healing in time-series databases, the following factors are critical:

- **Data ingestion and retention**: Time-series databases typically handle continuous data ingestion and retention of large volumes of time-stamped data. Self-healing mechanisms should handle automated data ingestion failure recovery, data retention policies, and archival strategies. By automatically recovering from data ingestion failures, self-healing databases ensure data completeness and availability.

- **Data compaction and downsampling**: Time-series databases often employ compaction and downsampling techniques to manage long-term data retention efficiently. Self-healing mechanisms should consider automated compaction and downsampling processes to optimize storage and query performance during the self-healing process. By automating compaction and downsampling, self-healing databases can reduce storage requirements and improve query performance.

- **High write throughput**: Time-series databases are often subjected to high write throughput due to continuous data ingestion. Self-healing mechanisms should handle automated scaling of resources, load balancing, and efficient data distribution to ensure optimal write performance during the self-healing process. By dynamically scaling resources, self-healing databases can handle high write loads without sacrificing performance.

- **Time-based partitioning**: Time-series databases typically partition data based on time intervals for efficient querying. Self-healing mechanisms need to consider automated partition management, rebalancing, and redistribution strategies to maintain optimal query performance and data availability during the self-healing process. By automatically managing partitions, self-healing databases ensure efficient data organization and accessibility.

Self-healing mechanisms in databases are influenced by factors such as the database architecture, data model, scalability needs, and operational environment. Relational databases require considerations related to replication, transaction management, index rebuilding, and query optimization. NoSQL databases need to handle data partitioning, eventual consistency, replication topologies, and automatic schema evolution. NewSQL databases require strategies for scalability, consistency models, distributed query optimization, and automated repartitioning. Time-series databases focus on data ingestion, retention, compaction, and time-based partitioning. By considering these factors, self-healing mechanisms can be effectively designed and implemented in different database types to enhance availability, FT, and resilience.

Self-healing in Kubernetes – implementation and best practices

Kubernetes, an open source container orchestration platform, provides powerful self-healing capabilities that help ensure the availability and reliability of applications running in containerized environments. Self-healing in Kubernetes refers to the automatic detection and recovery from failures, ensuring that the desired state of the system is maintained without requiring manual intervention. In this technical summary, we will explore the implementation and best practices for self-healing in Kubernetes.

Key components for self-healing in Kubernetes

To implement self-healing in Kubernetes, several key components and features are utilized:

- **Replication**: Kubernetes employs replication controllers or replica sets to create and manage multiple replicas of a pod, which is the smallest deployable unit in Kubernetes. Replication ensures HA by automatically replacing failed pods with healthy replicas.

- **Health probes**: Kubernetes supports health checks through two types of probes: liveness probes and readiness probes. Liveness probes are used to determine whether a pod is running correctly, while readiness probes check whether a pod is ready to serve traffic. By configuring appropriate health probes, Kubernetes can automatically restart or remove pods that are deemed unhealthy.

- **Pod autoscaling**: Kubernetes offers **Horizontal Pod Autoscaling** (**HPA**) based on resource utilization metrics. HPA automatically adjusts the number of replicas based on CPU or custom metrics, ensuring that the application has sufficient resources to handle the workload. Autoscaling helps in self-healing by dynamically adapting the resource allocation to the demand.

- **Self-healing controllers**: Kubernetes provides self-healing controllers that continuously monitor the state of resources and take corrective actions. For example, the Deployment controller ensures the desired number of replicas is maintained, replacing failed pods as needed.

- **StatefulSets**: For stateful applications that require stable network identities and persistent storage, Kubernetes introduces StatefulSets. StatefulSets ensure ordered deployment and scaling of pods, enabling self-healing for stateful workloads.

Implementing self-healing in Kubernetes – best practices

To effectively implement self-healing in Kubernetes, consider the following best practices:

- **Define proper resource requests and limits**: Specify resource requests and limits for pods to ensure resource allocation and prevent resource contention. This helps avoid performance degradation or pod failures due to insufficient resources.

- **Configure health probes**: Set up liveness and readiness probes appropriately for your application. Liveness probes should accurately reflect the health of the application, and readiness probes should ensure that the pod is ready to serve traffic before it receives requests. Carefully consider the probe endpoints and their response criteria to avoid false positives or negatives.

- **Use replication controllers or replica sets**: Leverage replication controllers or replica sets to ensure HA and FT. By defining the desired number of replicas, Kubernetes automatically maintains the desired state and replaces failed pods.

- **Utilize pod autoscaling**: Enable HPA to dynamically adjust the number of replicas based on resource utilization metrics. This ensures that the application can handle varying workloads and automatically scales up or down to maintain optimal performance.

- **Configure Pod Disruption Budgets (PDBs)**: PDBs allow you to define the minimum number of pods that should be available during disruptive events such as rolling updates or node maintenance. PDBs prevent excessive disruption and ensure that self-healing actions do not compromise the application's availability.

- **Enable logging and monitoring**: Implement robust logging and monitoring practices to gain visibility into the health and performance of your Kubernetes cluster. Effective monitoring enables timely detection of failures or anomalies, allowing for proactive self-healing actions.

- **Implement application-level health checks**: In addition to the built-in health probes, consider implementing application-level health checks within your containers. This allows your application to report its health status, providing more granular control over self-healing actions.

- **Use rolling updates for deployments**: When updating or rolling out new versions of applications, use rolling updates to minimize downtime. Rolling updates gradually replace pods, ensuring a smooth transition without impacting the availability of the application.

- **Implement StatefulSets for stateful applications**: For stateful workloads, use StatefulSets to manage the deployment and scaling of pods. StatefulSets provide stable network identities and persistent storage, allowing for ordered scaling and self-healing of stateful applications.

- **Implement disaster recovery (DR) measures**: Consider implementing DR measures such as backups, snapshots, or replication to remote clusters. These measures enhance self-healing capabilities by providing data redundancy and facilitating quick recovery in case of catastrophic failures.

Challenges and considerations

While implementing self-healing in Kubernetes brings significant benefits, it also poses some challenges and considerations:

- **Complexity**: Kubernetes is a complex platform, and self-healing mechanisms add an extra layer of complexity. It is essential to have a deep understanding of Kubernetes concepts and components to design and implement effective self-healing strategies.

- **Proper monitoring**: Comprehensive monitoring is crucial for self-healing to detect failures or anomalies accurately. Ensure that your monitoring system covers all relevant metrics and events to trigger timely self-healing actions.

- **False positives and negatives**: Self-healing mechanisms should be carefully designed to avoid false positives and negatives. False positives could trigger unnecessary actions, while false negatives could delay or prevent necessary recovery actions. Rigorous testing and tuning are necessary to minimize these risks.

- **Dependency on external systems**: Self-healing mechanisms may rely on external systems for health checks, monitoring, or storage. Ensure that these dependencies are properly managed, resilient, and highly available to prevent cascading failures.

- **Application-specific considerations**: Different applications may have unique requirements or constraints that impact self-healing. Consider the specific needs of your application, such as session affinity, caching, or state management, when designing self-healing strategies.

Conclusion

Self-healing in Kubernetes is a fundamental capability that enhances the availability and reliability of applications running in containerized environments. By leveraging replication, health probes, pod autoscaling, and self-healing controllers, Kubernetes automates detection and recovery from failures. Following best practices such as defining resource requests and limits, configuring health probes, and utilizing StatefulSets and rolling updates ensures effective self-healing in Kubernetes deployments. However, it is important to consider the complexity, monitoring requirements, and application-specific considerations when implementing self-healing strategies in Kubernetes.

Case studies – self-healing databases in Kubernetes

Self-healing databases in Kubernetes bring together the resilience and scalability of Kubernetes with the reliability and data management capabilities of databases. By combining these technologies, organizations can achieve highly available and fault-tolerant database deployments. In this technical summary, we will explore case studies that showcase the implementation of self-healing databases in Kubernetes environments.

Case study 1 – MySQL Operator

The MySQL Operator is an example of a self-healing mechanism for MySQL databases in Kubernetes. It leverages the Kubernetes operator pattern to automate the management of MySQL deployments. The MySQL Operator monitors the health of MySQL pods and automatically performs recovery actions in case of failures.

When a pod fails, the MySQL Operator detects the failure through liveness probes and initiates the recovery process. It automatically creates a new pod to replace the failed one and performs the necessary steps to restore the database state, such as data synchronization, replication, and reconfiguring the cluster. This self-healing mechanism ensures HA and minimizes the impact of pod failures on the application's database layer.

The MySQL Operator also provides features such as automated backups, replication management, and scaling capabilities. It enables database administrators to easily manage and operate MySQL databases in Kubernetes while benefiting from the self-healing capabilities of the Operator.

Case study 2 – MongoDB Operator

The MongoDB Operator is another example of a self-healing mechanism tailored for MongoDB databases in Kubernetes. It simplifies the deployment and management of MongoDB clusters while incorporating self-healing capabilities.

The MongoDB Operator monitors the health of MongoDB nodes and automatically detects and responds to failures. In the event of a node failure, the Operator automatically initiates the recovery process by creating new pods and configuring them to join the MongoDB cluster. It handles tasks such as data synchronization, shard rebalancing, and cluster reconfiguration to ensure the database remains available and resilient.

The MongoDB Operator also provides features such as automated scaling, backup and restore functionalities, and monitoring integration. These additional capabilities complement the self-healing mechanisms, enabling administrators to efficiently manage MongoDB databases in Kubernetes environments.

Case study 3 – Cassandra Operator

The Cassandra Operator is designed to provide self-healing capabilities for Apache Cassandra databases in Kubernetes. It automates the deployment and management of Cassandra clusters while ensuring resilience and FT.

The Cassandra Operator monitors the health of Cassandra pods and automatically handles failures. In the event of a pod failure, the Operator initiates the recovery process by creating replacement pods and performing the necessary operations to restore the cluster's state. It manages tasks such as data repair, node synchronization, and ring rebalancing to maintain the availability and consistency of the Cassandra database.

The Cassandra Operator also provides features such as automated scaling, rolling upgrades, backup and restore functionalities, and integration with monitoring tools. These features enhance the self-healing capabilities of the Operator and empower administrators to effectively manage Cassandra databases in Kubernetes environments.

Benefits of self-healing databases in Kubernetes

The implementation of self-healing databases in Kubernetes brings several benefits to organizations:

- **HA**: Self-healing mechanisms ensure that databases remain available and resilient even in the face of failures or anomalies. By automatically detecting and recovering from failures, self-healing databases minimize downtime and provide uninterrupted access to critical data.

- **Improved FT**: Self-healing databases enhance FT by automatically recovering from failures without human intervention. This reduces the impact of failures on the overall system and mitigates the risk of data loss or service disruptions.

- **Scalability and elasticity**: Kubernetes provides built-in scaling mechanisms, and self-healing databases can leverage these features to scale database deployments based on workload demands. This enables organizations to easily adapt to changing data requirements and handle varying levels of traffic.

- **Simplified management**: Self-healing databases simplify the management of database deployments in Kubernetes environments. By automating tasks such as recovery, replication, scaling, and backup, administrators can focus on higher-level tasks and reduce the operational overhead.

- **Seamless integration**: Self-healing databases integrate seamlessly with the Kubernetes ecosystem, leveraging its features, such as service discovery, load balancing, and resource management. This enables organizations to take full advantage of the capabilities provided by Kubernetes while ensuring database resilience.

Self-healing databases in Kubernetes showcase the successful integration of self-healing mechanisms with database technologies. Case studies such as the MySQL Operator, MongoDB Operator, and Cassandra Operator demonstrate the benefits of self-healing databases, including HA, FT, scalability, simplified management, and seamless integration with the Kubernetes ecosystem.

By leveraging self-healing databases, organizations can achieve resilient and highly available database deployments, ensuring the continuity and reliability of their applications. These case studies serve as examples of how self-healing mechanisms in Kubernetes can be applied to different database technologies, providing insights into best practices and strategies for building self-healing database architectures in Kubernetes environments.

Challenges and future directions

While self-healing mechanisms in databases and Kubernetes have made significant strides in enhancing availability and resilience, there are still challenges to address and opportunities for future improvement. In this technical summary, we will explore the challenges faced by self-healing systems and discuss potential future directions to overcome these challenges and further enhance the self-healing capabilities.

Challenges in self-healing systems

While the idea of systems that can automatically detect and recover from failures is promising, it does not come without its own set of intricacies and challenges. Before diving into the world of self-healing systems, it's essential to have a grasp of the potential obstacles and limitations that might arise. From technical complexities to performance implications, the following points detail the challenges that developers and administrators often encounter when dealing with self-healing systems:

- **Complexity**: Self-healing systems can be complex to design, implement, and manage. The integration of self-healing mechanisms with databases and Kubernetes requires expertise in both areas, as well as a deep understanding of the specific technologies being used. Managing the complexity of self-healing systems and ensuring their correct operation is an ongoing challenge.

- **False positives and negatives**: Automated fault detection and recovery mechanisms may occasionally produce false positives or false negatives. False positives can trigger unnecessary recovery actions, causing disruption and resource wastage. False negatives can lead to undetected failures or delayed recovery, compromising system availability. Reducing false positives and negatives is crucial for the effectiveness of self-healing systems.

- **Performance overhead**: Self-healing mechanisms, such as replication, failover, and monitoring, can introduce performance overhead. The additional processing, network traffic, and resource utilization required for self-healing operations can impact the overall system performance. Balancing the benefits of self-healing with the associated performance overhead is an ongoing challenge.

- **Security considerations**: Self-healing systems need to address security considerations to protect against potential exploits or unauthorized access. Automated recovery mechanisms should be carefully designed to prevent malicious activities and protect sensitive data. Ensuring the security and integrity of self-healing systems is essential for maintaining the trustworthiness of the overall infrastructure.

- **Data consistency challenges**: Replication and failover mechanisms in self-healing systems can introduce challenges related to maintaining data consistency across multiple replicas. Synchronization delays, conflicts, and network partitions can impact data consistency, requiring careful design and configuration. Ensuring data consistency in self-healing systems is critical for maintaining the integrity of the data.

- **Resource management**: Self-healing systems need to effectively manage and allocate resources such as CPU, memory, and storage. Scaling and reallocating resources dynamically to meet the changing demands of the workload can be complex. Optimizing resource management in self-healing systems is crucial for achieving efficient performance and cost-effective operations.

Future directions

As the digital realm continues to evolve, the quest for resilient and efficient systems never ceases. The vision of self-reliance in technology pushes boundaries and reshapes expectations. Looking toward the horizon, the trajectory for self-healing systems is marked by innovations and enhancements that aim to address their current challenges and amplify their advantages. From leveraging state-of-the-art analytical tools to integrating with modern development paradigms, here are some anticipated directions that might shape the next frontier of self-healing systems:

- **Advanced monitoring and analytics**: Future self-healing systems could benefit from advanced monitoring and analytics capabilities. Leveraging ML and AI techniques, self-healing systems could analyze vast amounts of monitoring data in real time, detecting patterns and anomalies more accurately. This could lead to improved fault detection, proactive recovery, and better resource management.

- **Intelligent decision-making**: Future self-healing systems could incorporate intelligent decision-making capabilities. By leveraging advanced algorithms and techniques, self-healing systems could make smarter decisions about fault detection, recovery actions, and resource allocation. This could optimize the efficiency and effectiveness of self-healing mechanisms, reducing false positives and negatives.

- **Self-learning and adaptive systems**: Self-healing systems of the future could incorporate self-learning and adaptive capabilities. By continuously analyzing system behavior, performance, and failures, these systems could adapt and optimize their self-healing mechanisms over time. This could lead to improved FT, performance optimization, and better resource utilization.

- **Integration with DevOps and CI/CD**: Future self-healing systems could integrate seamlessly with DevOps and CI/CD practices. By automating the deployment, testing, and release processes, self-healing systems could ensure that application updates and changes are rolled out smoothly, minimizing disruption and ensuring the continuity of self-healing capabilities.

- **Standardization and interoperability**: Future self-healing systems could benefit from increased standardization and interoperability. Establishing industry standards and best practices for self-healing mechanisms in databases and Kubernetes could promote compatibility, interoperability, and ease of adoption. This could simplify the integration and management of self-healing systems across different environments and technologies.

- **Security and privacy enhancements**: Future self-healing systems need to prioritize security and privacy enhancements. Implementing robust security measures, such as encryption, access controls, and auditing, could protect sensitive data and prevent unauthorized access. Privacy considerations, such as data anonymization and compliance with data protection regulations, should also be taken into account.

Self-healing systems face several challenges, including complexity, false positives and negatives, performance overhead, security considerations, data consistency challenges, and resource management. However, future directions present opportunities for improvement and advancement in self-healing capabilities.

By incorporating advanced monitoring and analytics, intelligent decision-making, self-learning and adaptive mechanisms, integration with DevOps and CI/CD, standardization and interoperability, and enhanced security and privacy measures, self-healing systems can become more robust, efficient, and reliable.

As organizations continue to leverage self-healing systems in databases and Kubernetes, addressing these challenges and pursuing future directions will contribute to the evolution and maturation of self-healing technologies, enabling organizations to achieve highly resilient and self-managing infrastructures.

Summary

Self-healing mechanisms in databases and Kubernetes play a crucial role in ensuring the availability, resilience, and FT of modern applications. By automating fault detection, recovery, and mitigation, self-healing systems reduce downtime, minimize disruptions, and enhance the overall reliability of the infrastructure.

Throughout this comprehensive exploration, we have delved into the core principles of self-healing systems, the implementation of operators in Kubernetes, self-healing databases, factors influencing self-healing in different database types, and case studies showcasing self-healing in Kubernetes. We have also discussed the challenges and future directions of self-healing systems.

Self-healing systems offer numerous benefits, including HA, improved FT, scalability, simplified management, and seamless integration with Kubernetes. These systems automatically detect failures, recover from them, and adapt to changing workload demands, all without requiring manual intervention. By incorporating self-healing mechanisms, organizations can focus on delivering high-quality applications and services while relying on resilient and self-managing infrastructures.

However, the implementation of self-healing systems comes with challenges. Complexity, false positives and negatives, performance overhead, security considerations, data consistency challenges, and resource management are among the key challenges that need to be addressed. Overcoming these challenges requires ongoing research, development, and best practices to ensure the effective and efficient operation of self-healing mechanisms.

Looking toward the future, there are exciting opportunities to enhance self-healing systems even further. Advanced monitoring and analytics, intelligent decision-making, self-learning and adaptive capabilities, integration with DevOps and CI/CD practices, standardization and interoperability, and enhanced security and privacy measures are areas of focus for future advancements. By incorporating these elements, self-healing systems can become more sophisticated, intelligent, and resilient, adapting to dynamic environments and providing optimal performance and reliability.

In conclusion, self-healing mechanisms in databases and Kubernetes have revolutionized the way organizations manage and maintain their infrastructures. By embracing self-healing technologies, organizations can minimize the impact of failures, reduce downtime, and ensure the continuity of their applications and services. While challenges exist, the future of self-healing systems looks promising, with ongoing research and advancements paving the way for even more robust and efficient self-healing capabilities.

As organizations continue to adopt self-healing systems, it is crucial to stay updated on the latest developments, best practices, and industry standards. By doing so, organizations can harness the full potential of self-healing mechanisms and build resilient, scalable, and self-managing infrastructures that enable them to thrive in the ever-evolving digital landscape.

In the next chapter, we will embark on Alex's transformative journey in the realm of AI.

14

Bringing Them Together

In this chapter, we'll embark on Alex's transformative journey in the realm of **artificial intelligence** (**AI**). From the initial steps of implementation, we'll dive deep into the nuances of observability and operations, key components that shaped his AI experience. Along the way, you'll gain insights into both the triumphs and challenges encountered, offering invaluable lessons for anyone venturing into this domain. As we reflect on the past, we'll also look ahead to what the future might hold in this ever-evolving field. Whether you're an AI enthusiast or a seasoned professional, this chapter promises insights that can enrich your understanding. Dive in to discover Alex's story, and perhaps to shape your narrative in the world of AI.

The following topics will be covered in this chapter:

- Alex's AI journey
- Implementation
- Observability and operations
- Lessons learned and future directions

Alex's AI journey

At the renowned **Fictional Company** (**FC**), Alex and his skilled team embark on a mission to integrate an innovative AI solution to revolutionize their operations and customer service. They navigate the intricacies of system architectures, data handling, and security, testing their combined expertise. Their journey reveals the challenges and triumphs of pioneering technological change in a global enterprise.

Introduction and project assignment

Alex had always been fascinated by technology. As a child, he'd dismantled and reassembled old radios, marveled at the seemingly magical abilities of computers, and dreamt of a future where he could play a part in creating such marvels. Now, as the lead **site reliability engineer** (**SRE**) for a globally renowned corporation, FC, he was living that dream. Yet, the exciting landscape of technology continually held new challenges that pushed him to explore and innovate.

FC had recently embarked on a project that would push Alex and his team to the brink of their expertise. The company planned to implement an AI solution that would revolutionize its operations and customer service, aiming to predict and address customer issues proactively, thereby dramatically improving customer satisfaction and loyalty.

However, the path was riddled with challenges, each more complex than the last. Architectural considerations were the first to tackle – the AI solution required a robust, scalable infrastructure that could handle vast amounts of data in real time while ensuring top-tier performance. FC's existing systems were robust but were not designed to handle such demands.

Cost was another significant issue. While FC had set aside a substantial budget for the project, the implementation of AI technologies was known for unexpected costs that could quickly spiral out of control. Ensuring a cost-effective, high-return solution was a major objective.

Operational risks were a constant specter that loomed over the project. Any system downtime could lead to substantial revenue losses and potentially harm FC's reputation. Alex and his team needed to ensure that their AI solution was not just efficient but also resilient and reliable.

Privacy was another significant concern. FC's customers trusted them with vast amounts of **personally identifiable information** (**PII**) data. Protecting this data while utilizing it to power their AI solution was a task that required careful planning, stringent security measures, and full regulatory compliance.

Given these challenges, the project's success depended heavily on the team responsible for it. Alex's team comprised highly skilled professionals, each bringing unique expertise to the table. The team included AI specialists, database engineers, network administrators, and security experts, all led by Alex, whose deep understanding of systems and architectures made him the ideal person to spearhead this endeavor.

Alex was responsible for ensuring the system's reliability, scalability, and security. He was tasked with creating a robust architecture that could handle the demands of the AI solution while ensuring minimal downtime and maximum security. His role also included coordinating with the rest of the team, ensuring seamless collaboration, and making critical decisions that would guide the project's direction.

The AI specialists, led by Dr. Maya, an expert in machine learning and neural networks, were responsible for designing and implementing the AI algorithms. They were to work closely with Alex and his team to ensure that their designs were compatible with the system's architecture and could be seamlessly integrated.

Database engineers were led by Leah, a seasoned expert in both relational and non-relational databases. They were responsible for designing the databases that would power the AI solution, ensuring efficient data storage, quick retrieval, and seamless scaling.

Network administrators, led by Carlos, an expert in network architectures and cloud solutions, were to design the network infrastructure that would support the AI solution. They had to ensure high-speed data transmission, minimal latency, and maximum uptime.

Finally, security experts, led by Nia, a veteran in cybersecurity, were to safeguard the system and the data it processed. They were to design and implement security measures to protect FC's systems and customer data, ensuring full compliance with privacy laws and regulations.

As Alex looked at his team, he felt a sense of anticipation. They were about to embark on a journey that would test their skills, challenge their knowledge, and push them to their limits. Yet, he was confident. They were not just a team; they were a well-oiled machine, ready to face whatever challenges lay ahead. As the lead SRE, Alex was ready to guide them through this journey. The road ahead was long and arduous, but they were ready. This was their moment, their challenge. And they were going to rise to the occasion.

Software and infrastructure architecture decisions

On a crisp Monday morning, the team gathered in their primary conference room. The topic of the day was the software and infrastructure architecture for the AI solution. Alex started the meeting by laying out the agenda: *"Today, we'll discuss and finalize the architecture, the cloud strategy, our AI software frameworks, our operational strategy, and our observability approach."*

Maya was the first to speak, presenting her team's findings on the requirements of the AI application. She painted a clear picture of a system that needed to be fast, flexible, and capable of handling vast amounts of data in real time.

The discussion then moved on to architectural choices: a monolithic versus a microservices architecture. Carlos, the network administrator, highlighted the benefits of a monolithic architecture, pointing out its simplicity, consistency, and the reduced overhead of inter-process communication. Leah, however, raised concerns about scalability, fault isolation, and the long-term sustainability of a monolithic architecture.

Microservices emerged as the preferred choice due to the scalability, resilience, and flexibility they offered in choosing technology stacks for different services. Alex also saw the appeal of smaller, independent teams working on different microservices, reducing dependencies and fostering innovation.

Next up was the choice between cloud-native and on-premises infrastructure. Carlos stressed the advantages of a cloud-native approach, such as the reduced need for infrastructure management, flexibility, and scalability. Nia, however, raised concerns about data security in the cloud, particularly regarding the PII data that FC handled.

An on-premises infrastructure offered more control over data and enhanced security. Still, the team agreed that it could not match the scalability and cost-effectiveness of a cloud-native approach. After an intense debate and a detailed POC on cloud security measures, the team agreed on a hybrid cloud approach. It promised the scalability of the cloud and the security of an on-premises setup.

As the discussion shifted to AI software frameworks and libraries, Maya suggested the use of TensorFlow and PyTorch for their robustness and wide acceptance in the AI community. Alex also suggested the use of **Open Neural Network Exchange (ONNX)** for model interoperability and the AI Fairness 360 toolkit to ensure the AI solution's fairness.

The team then dove into the operational strategy. Alex was a strong proponent of DevOps and SRE principles, emphasizing the importance of an iterative approach, continuous integration, and end-to-end ownership. The team agreed, recognizing the value of these principles in achieving high-quality, reliable software delivery.

Nia then brought up the observability strategy, proposing the implementation of robust monitoring and alerting systems. She insisted on an on-call support strategy, allowing rapid incident response. Alex agreed and added the need for tracing systems for effective debugging. The team acknowledged these suggestions, agreeing on the necessity of comprehensive observability for a project of this scale.

Finally, Alex laid out clear objectives for the team. They needed to ensure scalability, security, cost-efficiency, and regulatory compliance. These objectives would guide the team through the project's life cycle, serving as their North Star.

As the meeting concluded, Alex felt satisfied with their progress. Every team member had contributed, and all voices were heard. They discussed the pros and cons, conducted POCs, and, most importantly, made informed decisions based on solid data and thoughtful consideration. The road ahead was clearer now. Their AI solution was no longer a mere concept; it was taking shape, and the team was ready to turn it into a reality.

Relational versus non-relational databases

The following week, the focus shifted to a critical aspect of the project – the choice of databases. The team gathered, coffee cups in hand, ready to dissect the nitty-gritty of structured and unstructured data requirements for the AI solution.

The session began with the team collaboratively defining the requirements of the system. They discussed what data the AI application would consume and produce, focusing on its structure and the degree of reliability needed. They found that they would need to handle both structured data, such as user profiles and transaction logs, and unstructured data, such as user behavior patterns and complex AI model data.

Once the requirements were defined, Alex steered the conversation toward structured data and the role of SQL databases. He introduced the idea of **Atomicity, Consistency, Isolation, Durability (ACID)** compliance and how SQL databases such as PostgreSQL, MySQL, and Oracle adhered to these principles.

He detailed how ACID compliance ensured data reliability and consistency in every transaction, a critical requirement for structured data such as user profiles and transaction logs. While each had its pros, such as MySQL's high performance and Oracle's advanced features, they also came with cons, such as Oracle's high cost and MySQL's scalability limitations.

Unstructured data introduced its own set of challenges. To address these, Leah suggested using NoSQL databases such as MongoDB, CockroachDB, Couchbase, and Cassandra. She explained their benefits, including schema flexibility, horizontal scalability, and the ability to handle large volumes of data.

However, Leah also highlighted their cons. MongoDB had scalability issues, Couchbase had a high learning curve, Cassandra had complexity and difficulty handling relationships, and CockroachDB had high latency. The team noted these factors, cognizant of the trade-offs each choice presented.

After weighing all the options and running a detailed POC comparing the NoSQL databases, two choices emerged: Couchbase and Cassandra. Couchbase stood out due to its impressive performance, memory-first architecture, and powerful indexing, while Cassandra was chosen for its robustness, linear scalability, and high availability.

Alex then laid out the reasoning behind choosing both SQL and NoSQL databases. For structured data, they needed a SQL database for its ACID compliance and reliable transactions. In contrast, for the vast volumes of unstructured data the AI solution would handle, they needed the schema flexibility and scalability that NoSQL databases offered.

They were also aware of the operational burden and cost that managing these databases would entail. Alex emphasized the importance of automating database operations as much as possible and ensuring a robust backup and disaster recovery strategy.

Lastly, the team examined the data flows and how the microservices would interact with the databases. Nia pointed out potential bottlenecks and proposed solutions to ensure smooth data movement.

The meeting was intense, with each team member contributing their expertise to shape the AI solution's database strategy. It was a session of robust discussions, data-driven decisions, and meticulous planning.

By the time they had finished, Alex could see the project's skeleton forming, the bones of their decisions solid and robust. The AI solution was no longer a concept; it was taking shape, and they were one step closer to making it a reality.

Implementing caching, data lakes, and data warehouses

The project began to take shape, and the discussions in the fourth week reflected a team hitting its stride. They had chosen their databases, and now, it was time to delve into the realms of caching, data lakes, and data warehouses.

The day started with the subject of caching layers. Alex introduced potential options: Redis, Memcached, MongoDB, RabbitMQ, Hazelcast, and Cassandra. The essence of the discussion hinged on the need for rapid data retrieval and the undeniable value it would bring to their AI solution.

Redis was the first caching option discussed, known for its lightning-fast data access and Pub/Sub capabilities, although it required careful data management due to its in-memory nature. Memcached offered simplicity and efficiency but lacked some of the more sophisticated features of Redis.

MongoDB was acknowledged for its caching capabilities but was quickly dismissed as it did not match the specific needs of the AI solution. RabbitMQ was suggested for its effective message queuing service, but the team had doubts about its use as a cache.

Hazelcast emerged as a strong contender with its distributed computing capabilities and in-memory data grid. Cassandra was also a viable option due to its proven scalability, but its complexity became a point of contention.

The team ran small tests and evaluated each option, but eventually, Redis was chosen. It was the balance between speed, rich features, and community support that tipped the scales in its favor.

With caching decided, they moved on to the concepts of data lakes and data warehouses. Their new AI solution would generate vast amounts of data, and managing this data efficiently was a challenge they needed to tackle head-on.

Alex and Leah described the use of data lakes such as AWS S3 for raw data storage. They explained the potential benefits, which included scalability, versatility, and cost-effectiveness, but were also mindful of the potential pitfalls, such as security risks, data governance issues, and the necessity of skilled personnel for managing and extracting value from the data.

Data warehouses, on the other hand, were designed for structured data storage. Snowflake was mentioned as a cloud-based data warehouse that could deliver speed, scalability, and ease of use, but it came with a higher cost.

The discussion turned into a brainstorming session, with each member sharing their insights on how to best leverage these technologies. The team was acutely aware of the cost implications and the operational burden that these technologies could bring. But they also recognized that in a data-driven world, these were tools that could give their AI solution a competitive edge.

In the end, they decided to proceed with AWS S3 for their data lake and Snowflake for their data warehouse. The decision was informed by the nature of their data, cost implications, security concerns, and the performance requirements of the AI solution.

As they wrapped up the day, Alex couldn't help but feel a sense of accomplishment. Their careful consideration of each option, deep discussions, and data-driven decisions were leading them down a path that was as challenging as it was exciting. With each passing week, their AI solution was evolving, and they were growing with it.

Security concerns and solutions

As the project rolled into its fifth week, the team embarked on a journey through the complex maze of security. The global scale of their AI solution and the sensitive nature of their data necessitated an unyielding focus on robust security measures.

Alex started the week by highlighting the importance of security in every layer of their architecture. From the application to the infrastructure layer, each required specific and targeted measures to ensure the safety of their data and services. The term **Defense in Depth** reverberated through the room, emphasizing the need for multiple layers of security.

The team went over several security concepts. Encryption was the first topic on the agenda, and they discussed its role in protecting data both at rest and in transit. They discussed using industry-standard encryption algorithms and considered using hardware security modules for key management.

They explored intrusion detection systems and firewalls, and their role in safeguarding their network and system. Secure coding practices became a hot topic, particularly the need for continuous security testing in their DevOps pipeline.

Then came the talk about key rotation strategy. The team knew this would be an essential part of their overall security, to mitigate risks associated with key exposure or theft. After a lively discussion, they settled on automated key rotation on a regular schedule to provide an optimal balance between security and operational overhead.

The discussion moved on to **Identity and Access Management** (**IAM**) systems. With their solution deployed across multiple regions, the ability to control who has access to what resources was a pivotal issue. They decided to adopt a strict principle of least privilege approach, granting only necessary permissions to each user and service.

Virtual private networks (**VPNs**) also found their way into the conversation, for their ability to provide secure access to the corporate network for remote workers.

Security decisions were among the most difficult the team had to make. For each choice, they had to consider not just the technical merits, but also the cost, operational implications, and potential vulnerabilities. Each decision was weighed against the data they had and the risks they identified.

For example, the team was concerned about the potential for data breaches through injection attacks. Data from the OWASP Top 10 indicated that this was one of the most common security risks. This influenced their decision to include secure coding practices and continuous security testing in their DevOps pipeline.

The choice of these security technologies and practices was fundamentally about ensuring data integrity, confidentiality, and availability. They knew that their AI solution would stand or fall based on the trust their users had in their ability to protect their data.

As the week drew to a close, Alex looked at the decisions they had made. They had confronted some of their most significant challenges yet, making tough decisions underpinned by data and a thorough understanding of their risk landscape. But they had navigated their way through, armed with a clear security strategy and a determination to build a secure, world-class AI solution.

First status update

Alex was asked to submit a stakeholder update at the end of every major milestone. Here is the first project update he sent:

Subject: Project Status Report: AI Implementation - Milestone 1

Dear Stakeholders,

Over the past months, our team has made significant progress in laying the foundational architecture for the proposed AI solution. I am thrilled to share a summary of our work, highlighting key decisions, and outlining our plan for the coming stages:

- *Project kick-off: We've established our team, each member bringing in unique expertise crucial to our project. We've also defined the scope of our problem – to design and implement a robust AI solution that enhances our global operations, keeping the balance between cost efficiency, operational risks, scalability, and privacy concerns.*

- *Software and infrastructure architecture: After careful deliberation, we have decided to adopt a hybrid cloud approach combining the best elements of cloud-native and on-premise infrastructure. This decision was based on multiple factors, including scalability, security, and cost efficiency. We're also planning to adopt DevOps methodologies and SRE principles to streamline our operations and minimize downtime.*

- *Database selection: We've analyzed our data requirements and selected a combination of PostgreSQL, Couchbase, and Cassandra to handle structured and unstructured data. We performed a POC to validate our theories on Couchbase and Cassandra's performance, with positive results confirming their utility for our project.*

- *Caching, data lakes, and data warehouses: We've decided to implement caching layers for rapid data retrieval. Simultaneously, we're preparing to use data lakes for raw data storage and data warehouses for structured data storage to support data-driven decision-making.*

- *Security measures: Security is a high priority, and we've begun implementing robust measures to protect our infrastructure and data. These measures include encryption, intrusion detection systems, secure coding practices, and the use of IAM systems and VPNs.*

Next steps and timeline:

Over the next quarter, we're planning to do the following:

- *Begin the implementation of the chosen technologies (timeline: weeks 1-8)*

- *Set up monitoring and observability for our system using the latest tools and practices (timeline: weeks 3-9)*

- *Develop self-healing systems for high availability and reliability (timeline: weeks 7-12)*

We're also planning to carry out rigorous testing at each stage of implementation to identify and rectify potential issues before they escalate.

As we move into the next phase, we'll continue to keep you informed of our progress and any significant developments. Your support and confidence in us continue to motivate our efforts.

Kind regards,

Alex

Implementation

After laying a strong foundation with cybersecurity, Alex and his team pivoted to exploring DevOps and SRE methodologies to further optimize their AI solution for FC. Delving deep into the intricacies of immutable and idempotent logic, they harnessed the strengths of DevOps practices such as **Infrastructure as Code** (**IaC**) and embraced the significance of immutability in infrastructure. The journey also saw them integrating SRE practices such as error budgets and SLAs. This whirlwind of discussions, tool evaluations, and proof-of-concept experiments was merely a precursor to their next ambitious goal: zero-touch automation.

Utilizing DevOps and SRE methodologies

After ensuring the security layer was diligently prepared, Alex turned his focus onto a different arena – adopting the DevOps methodology and integrating SRE principles into the project's framework.

DevOps, a methodology that emphasizes the integration of development and operations teams, was a crucial aspect to consider. It promised a streamlined communication flow and a more efficient production process by automating the build, test, and deployment workflows with CI/CD pipelines. The team discussed alternatives, such as the traditional waterfall or agile methodologies, but DevOps stood out due to its strong emphasis on collaboration and its ability to accommodate frequent changes and rapid deliveries.

This brought Alex to an essential component of the DevOps ecosystem: IaC. IaC was an integral concept in ensuring idempotent and immutable infrastructure. It allowed the infrastructure setup to be automated, replicable, and maintainable, reducing human error and increasing efficiency. An alternative to IaC would have been a manual infrastructure setup, but the team quickly recognized the downsides – higher risks of inconsistencies, slower time-to-market, and larger overhead costs.

Immutability was a particularly crucial requirement for IaC. Alex explained that an immutable infrastructure was one where no updates, patches, or configuration changes happened in the live environment. Instead, new changes were introduced by replacing the old environment with a new one. This ensured that the environment remained consistent across all stages, reducing the chances of unexpected failures.

Next came the practices of SRE, the discipline that uses software engineering to manage operations tasks and aims to create scalable and highly reliable software systems. Principles such as error budgets, **service-level indicators (SLIs)**, **service-level objectives (SLOs)**, and **service-level agreements (SLAs)** were discussed. These were critical to ensure that the system was both reliable and robust.

For implementing the CI/CD pipelines, several tools such as Jenkins, CircleCI, and Travis CI were considered. Jenkins, with its versatile plugin ecosystem, proved to be a better fit for the project's needs. For IaC, the choice boiled down to Terraform, Chef, Puppet, or Ansible. Terraform, with its provider agnostic nature and declarative language, won the vote. It promised a seamless experience in managing the hybrid cloud approach that the team had decided on.

Through the discussions, debates, and data points, Alex found his team navigating through uncharted territories, making decisions that were best for their context. Every choice was a calculated step toward the overall goal – an efficient, scalable, and reliable AI solution for FC. Their journey was only just beginning, but the excitement in the air was palpable.

The power of immutable and idempotent logic

With the principles of DevOps and SRE methodologies in place, Alex led the team into another essential facet of their project – immutable and idempotent logic. These principles, although sounding complicated, held a simple yet powerful impact on the project's robustness and reproducibility.

The concept of immutability in infrastructure means that once a component is deployed, it is never modified; instead, it is replaced with a new instance when an update is needed. Alex explained how this minimizes the *"works on my machine"* problem and brings consistency across development, staging, and production environments, reducing the risks during deployment.

On the other hand, idempotency ensures that no matter how many times a certain operation is performed, the result remains the same. This meant fewer surprises during deployments and enhanced predictability of the system.

Implementing these principles, though, was a whole other challenge. The team had limited experience with these concepts. They would have to learn as they went, making it a daunting but necessary task. However, the unity and resilience of the team shone bright as they embarked on this journey of learning and implementing together.

Alex proposed using containerization and orchestration tools – Docker and Kubernetes, specifically – to realize these principles. Docker could ensure that the application ran the same, irrespective of the environment, thus providing immutability. Kubernetes, meanwhile, could guarantee that the system's state remained as desired, ensuring idempotency.

The team debated the pros and cons of this immutable strategy. On one hand, it provided consistency and reliability and improved the system's overall security. However, it also meant that every change required a complete rebuild of the environment. This could lead to longer deployment times and could potentially increase costs, but given the scope and size of their project, the benefits significantly outweighed the cons.

The team members rolled up their sleeves, ready to face the new challenges head-on. They conducted multiple POCs to validate their decisions and used the data gathered from these POCs to drive their next steps.

Alex knew the journey toward an immutable infrastructure wasn't going to be easy. The team needed a solid **proof-of-concept** (**POC**) to validate their decision and give them a taste of the challenges ahead.

They chose a small yet essential component of their infrastructure – the user authentication service – for the POC. It was a perfect candidate as it was integral to their AI solution, and any problems with consistency or availability would have significant implications on their service.

The POC started with a shift in mindset – instead of modifying the live instances, every change was going to be a whole new instance. Docker came to the forefront, allowing them to containerize the user authentication service. Alex and the team crafted a Dockerfile that outlined all the dependencies and configurations the service needed, resulting in a Docker image.

For orchestration, Kubernetes was their weapon of choice. It allowed them to define the desired state of their system using declarative syntax. They could now specify the number of Docker containers, or "Pods" in Kubernetes parlance, they wanted to run, and Kubernetes would maintain that state, ensuring idempotency.

With the architecture outlined, the team deployed their containerized user authentication service on Kubernetes. The POC wasn't without hiccups – there were issues with networking configurations, persistent storage, and handling stateful sessions – but every challenge was met with determination and a keen eye for learning.

Once deployed, the team conducted a series of stress tests, emulating scenarios from minor updates to catastrophic system failures. Each time, the service held its ground. Every change was handled by rolling out a new instance without affecting the live service. Kubernetes proved its worth by ensuring the system's state stayed as defined, even in failure scenarios, effectively reducing downtime.

The financial implications of immutable infrastructure were also brought into sharp focus. There was an increase in costs due to the frequent build and deployment processes. But these costs were counterbalanced by the gains. With immutable infrastructure, the team noticed a drastic reduction in the time spent debugging inconsistent environments, leading to higher productivity. The faster recovery times minimized service disruption, which would have a positive impact on user satisfaction and, subsequently, the company's reputation and financial health.

At the end of the POC, Alex and the team could see the benefits of immutable and idempotent logic outweighing the costs. The experiment validated their decision, and although there were challenges to overcome, the POC had given them a playbook to move forward. They now felt prepared to replicate their success throughout the rest of the infrastructure, a crucial step toward a robust AI solution for FC.

The implementation of Docker and Kubernetes was a success, their efforts paying off in a system that now assured consistency and predictability. Through trial and error, learning, and growing together, they were building an infrastructure that promised not just to support but to boost the AI solution's performance they were working so hard to realize.

Embracing zero-touch automation

Following their successful venture into the world of immutable infrastructure, Alex and the team ventured into the realm of automation. Zero-touch automation, to be specific.

In theory, the concept was enticing. By removing manual intervention from as many operations as possible, the team could enjoy greater speed, less risk of human error, and even cost savings. The challenge, however, was in its application.

Infrastructure provisioning was the first area they tackled. They had already laid the groundwork with their use of IaC, so extending that to a complete zero-touch solution was the next logical step. Using tools such as Ansible and Terraform, they were able to automate the creation, management, and teardown of their resources in the cloud. The benefits were immediately evident – consistency in configuration, a reduction in potential human error, and considerable time savings.

Next, they moved to code deployment. The aim here was to create an environment where any code, once committed, would automatically move through the pipeline – testing, building, and deploying. This task was challenging, given the need to coordinate multiple tools and platforms. Still, by using Jenkins to create a CI/CD pipeline, they were able to achieve their goal.

Automation didn't stop at deployment. The team extended it to their testing and monitoring. Using automated testing frameworks, they could ensure their code was tested thoroughly, quickly, and consistently each time changes were made. Monitoring, too, became a hands-off operation. With tools such as Prometheus and Grafana, they set up automated alerts that would inform them of any anomalies or issues, eliminating the need for constant manual monitoring.

However, zero-touch automation wasn't all smooth sailing. The automation scripts themselves needed maintenance and updates, and any errors in the scripts could lead to significant issues, given the scale at which they operated. There was also the factor of losing control – with everything automated, it was more challenging to intervene if something went wrong. Yet, the team mitigated these concerns through thorough testing, monitoring of the automation processes, and a staged approach to rolling out automation.

Zero-touch automation also posed a stark contrast to their earlier manual operations. Where they previously had complete control, they now placed their trust in scripts and machines. But the upsides – speed, consistency, reduction in errors, and last but not least, the freedom for the team to focus on more value-adding tasks – made it a worthwhile transition.

Through each decision and implementation, data drove the team. They evaluated the time saved, the errors reduced, the cost implications, and the impact on their end product. They ran POCs, tested their solutions, and fine-tuned until they were satisfied. And while they knew their journey to zero-touch automation was far from over, they also knew they were on the right path. Alex could see the team working more effectively, and they were eager to see where this path would lead them in their quest for an efficient, robust AI solution for FC.

Update 2

Another month passed, and Alex was back to send a progress report:

Subject: Status Report – Month 2

Dear Team,

I am writing to summarize the progress we've made in the past 2 months of our ambitious journey. We have successfully embraced and implemented zero-touch automation and embarked on the path of immutable and idempotent logic.

Over the past few weeks, our focus has been on automating our infrastructure provisioning, code deployment, testing, and monitoring. Our decision to go this route stemmed from our vision to increase speed, reduce the chance of human error, and optimize costs. Utilizing tools such as Ansible, Terraform, and Jenkins, we've automated the majority of our operations. Now, every piece of code that's committed goes through an automatic pipeline of testing, building, and deploying.

The implications of these transformations are far-reaching. We've observed a drastic reduction in human errors and a noticeable acceleration in our operations. However, this zero-touch automation also brought new challenges, such as maintaining the automation scripts themselves and the necessity of relinquishing control to automation. However, we have managed these challenges through rigorous testing and careful monitoring.

We also tackled the principles of immutable infrastructure and idempotency. The prospect of reduced deployment risks and assured reproducibility were compelling enough to put these principles into practice. Through the implementation of containerization and orchestration tools such as Docker and Kubernetes, we've managed to construct an infrastructure that ensures a higher degree of consistency and reliability.

Again, the impact of this transformation was profound. It has increased the financial efficiency of our operations, notably reducing our recovery times and the need for manual effort.

Moving forward, we will continue to refine and expand upon these automation strategies to further improve our operations. Our next steps will involve expanding our automation to include more aspects of our operations and further enhancing our existing automated processes.

We're also planning to conduct a series of additional POCs to test out new technologies and strategies to see if they could bring further improvements to our operations.

Thank you all for your hard work. The progress we've made has been due to the collective effort of the entire team. I look forward to seeing where the next chapters in our journey will take us.

Kind regards,

Alex

Implementing self-healing systems

The concept of a system that could self-diagnose and self-correct faults was a challenging yet enticing proposition for Alex and his team. They knew that the introduction of self-healing systems would bolster system uptime, user satisfaction, and overall system reliability. The journey to implementing such systems, however, was laden with complexities and challenges.

Kubernetes was the first piece of the puzzle. The orchestration platform was already a vital component of their architecture, and its inbuilt features of auto-scaling and auto-restarting services were naturally inclined toward self-healing. To fully utilize these features, the team designed and configured their services with these principles in mind.

On the database front, the team knew they had a tall order ahead. Their stack included Couchbase, Cassandra, and PostgreSQL, each with its quirks and capabilities.

Couchbase was up first. Couchbase Server had built-in resilience and fault-tolerance features. By using **cross-data center replication** (**XDCR**), they could replicate data across multiple clusters. In the event of a node failure, the replica would seamlessly take over, effectively implementing a self-healing system. They implemented this alongside auto-failover and rebalance features for a robust, self-healing Couchbase system.

For Cassandra, they leveraged its inherent design for distributed systems. The ring design meant that each node was aware of the other nodes in the system, allowing for effective communication and coordination. By using the Gossip protocol and hinted handoff, they ensured that data was not lost in the case of temporary node failures. Upon recovery, the node would collect the data it missed, maintaining the consistency and integrity of the system.

Implementing self-healing capabilities in PostgreSQL, a traditional SQL database, was more challenging. As PostgreSQL was not inherently designed with distributed systems in mind, the team had to be innovative. They implemented a clustering solution using Patroni, which created automated failover. In combination with `pgpool-II`, a middleware that worked between PostgreSQL servers and a database client, they created a load-balancing system with automated connection pooling. This way, even if a database instance failed, the system would redirect traffic to the remaining instances, maintaining the database's availability.

With each decision, the team referenced the data they had collected. Time and cost implications, the potential increase in system availability, and the reduction of manual interventions all played a significant role in shaping their self-healing system.

Though the path to implementing a self-healing system was filled with hurdles, they celebrated their small victories and learned from their setbacks. Every debate and technical deep dive brought them closer to a system that was robust and reliable. Every POC and every metric was a testament to their hard work and dedication. As the final pieces fell into place, Alex looked at the self-healing system they had built. It was far from perfect, but it was a significant step forward. One that they could all be proud of.

Implementing load balancers and scaling

Load balancing had been a pivotal discussion in the team's strategy, and Alex initiated the dialogue with knowledge of Nginx and **Elastic Load Balancer** (**ELB**). Nginx, known for its robustness, could efficiently handle traffic while offering flexibility. ELB, native to AWS, provided seamless integration with other AWS services. However, ELB incurred additional costs that the team needed to justify. The team weighed the features against the potential costs, eventually settling on a combination of both: Nginx for in-cluster balancing and ELB for external traffic routing. The balance of cost and effectiveness tilted the scales in this decision.

Next was the question of scale – vertical or horizontal? Vertical scaling, the act of adding more resources such as CPU or memory to a server, was straightforward but had its limitations. Horizontal scaling, which involved adding more servers to share the load, was more complex to manage but offered better fault tolerance and distribution of load. The team recounted experiences of companies that had failed to scale horizontally, leading to costly downtime during peak usage. Backed by this data, they decided to leverage Kubernetes' horizontal pod auto-scaling, setting rules to scale up based on CPU and memory usage.

Database scaling, however, was a completely different beast. PostgreSQL, being a traditional relational database, preferred vertical scaling. The team knew they could boost its performance by adding more resources, but they were also aware of the constraints. They decided on a read replica approach for scaling reads while leaving writes to the master node. The team also decided to vertically scale the master node if required, accepting the financial implications for the sake of data integrity and performance.

With Couchbase and Cassandra, the route was different. Both NoSQL databases were designed to scale horizontally, fitting well with the distributed nature of their architecture. Couchbase allowed easy addition and removal of nodes in the cluster, rebalancing itself after every change. They set up XDCR for disaster recovery, providing a safety net for their data.

Cassandra's scaling strategy was equally resilient. Its ring design made adding new nodes a breeze. The team planned to monitor the system closely, adding new nodes when necessary to maintain optimal performance.

The benefits of this scaling approach were evident. High availability, fault tolerance, and efficient use of resources were the key advantages. However, there were also downsides. Costs increased with horizontal scaling, and managing a distributed system introduced its own complexities.

As this was a pivotal point in the team's journey, it had to be tested with another POC. This involved examining the scaling capabilities of their chosen databases – PostgreSQL, Couchbase, and Cassandra. The challenge was clear: to simulate high-load scenarios and ensure the database infrastructure could handle it without compromising on performance or losing data.

The first step was setting up the test environments. Alex's team used containerized environments in Kubernetes, each container running an instance of the respective databases. They leveraged the principles of immutable infrastructure and idempotency, ensuring reproducibility and minimizing deployment risks.

For PostgreSQL, they created a master node with multiple read replicas, testing the efficacy of the read replicas under high read traffic. On Couchbase and Cassandra, they implemented a cluster setup, adding nodes to the existing cluster and observing how the databases rebalanced themselves.

They then simulated the high-load scenarios using database load testing tools. The loads were created to mimic real-world traffic spikes, pushing the databases to their limits.

PostgreSQL's read replicas handled the read requests effectively, preventing the master node from becoming a bottleneck. However, when they artificially failed the master node, the team had to manually promote one of the read replicas to become the new master – a critical task that required human intervention and increased the risk of downtime.

On the other hand, Couchbase and Cassandra proved their mettle under high loads. As the load increased, the databases rebalanced, distributing the data evenly among the nodes. When a node was intentionally failed, they observed self-healing properties; the databases quickly readjusted, ensuring no loss of data or service.

However, these processes weren't flawless. Adding nodes to the NoSQL databases increased infrastructure costs, and they also observed a brief period of increased latency during the rebalancing phase. These were important considerations for their operational budget and SLOs.

Despite the challenges, the POC was deemed a success. The team demonstrated the databases' scalability under high-load scenarios, a critical requirement for their global AI solution. The insights from the POC guided them in optimizing their scaling strategies, providing a balance between cost, performance, and data integrity. Furthermore, the reduced manual effort and enhanced recovery speed reaffirmed their faith in immutable infrastructure and idempotency principles.

The POC didn't just answer their questions; it highlighted potential issues that they might face in the future, allowing them to plan ahead. It was a testament to their commitment to data-driven decision-making, reminding them that every hurdle crossed brought them one step closer to their goal.

As the final discussions drew to a close, Alex marveled at their progress. They had navigated through an ocean of complex decisions, making choices that were not just technologically sound, but also backed by hard data. The journey was far from over, but their progress was undeniable. The scale of their ambitions matched the scale of their solution, a testament to their collective resolve and effort.

As he looked forward to the next stages, he knew that whatever challenges lay ahead, they were ready to face them together.

Update 3

Yet another month passed, and Alex sent his usual status update:

Subject: Project Status Report – Month 3

Dear Team,

We've made significant strides in our journey to implement our ambitious AI solution for FC. This report summarizes our achievements from the last two phases of our project – Chapter 9, Implementing Self-Healing Systems, and Chapter 10, Implementing Load Balancers and Scaling.

In the previous month, we fully embraced the concept of self-healing systems. By leveraging Kubernetes' auto-restart and auto-scaling features, we have built a system that can auto-detect and correct faults, thereby reducing downtime. For our database layer, we've implemented this for both our relational (PostgreSQL) and non-relational (Couchbase and Cassandra) databases, which can now detect and correct any deviations, ensuring optimal performance and data accessibility at all times.

Our focus was on load balancing and scaling. We utilized Nginx as our primary load balancer, effectively distributing network traffic and ensuring no single component is overwhelmed. This achievement paved the way for our experiment with both horizontal and vertical scaling. We used Kubernetes to set up auto-scaling rules and events, enabling us to handle traffic spikes more effectively.

Our POC for database scaling proved enlightening. We simulated high-load scenarios and observed how our database layer responded. PostgreSQL demonstrated efficient handling of read requests via read replicas, but we noted a need for manual intervention if the master node failed. Couchbase and Cassandra showed impressive scalability and self-healing properties but at the cost of increased infrastructure costs and a temporary latency spike during the rebalancing phase.

In terms of implications, our POC has provided us with invaluable data on database scalability, infrastructure costs, and performance under high-load scenarios. The insights gathered will guide us in striking a balance between cost, performance, and data integrity.

Looking forward, our next steps will be optimizing the implementation of our chosen technologies based on the insights gained from the POC. We will fine-tune our scaling strategy to minimize latency and infrastructure costs. Moreover, we'll look into automating the master node failover process for PostgreSQL to reduce the risk of downtime.

Finally, I'd like to extend my sincere gratitude to the entire team for their relentless hard work and innovative spirit. Let's keep pushing boundaries and breaking new ground as we continue to shape this AI solution for FC.

Kind regards,

Alex

Observability and operations

In the bustling hub of FC, evolving challenges continuously push the boundaries of innovation and operational excellence. While strategies such as canary deployments and database scaling have propelled the team into new realms of success, the dawn of another day brings the intricate dance of security and compliance into sharp focus. For Alex, the company's visionary, safeguarding data while ensuring steadfast adherence to regulatory standards becomes the next critical chapter in FC's ongoing narrative.

The art of canary deployments

2 months had passed since the last update. In the heart of FC, Alex stood before his team with a new mission at hand. With the core architecture in place and various operational strategies tested, they now faced the challenge of integrating new features into their existing AI strategy. Their approach? Canary deployments.

"Think of it as releasing a canary into a coal mine," Alex explained, noting the puzzled looks on a few faces. *"If the canary thrives, the environment is safe, and the miners can proceed. In our context, if our new feature works smoothly with a small subset of users, we can gradually roll it out to all users. It's about risk mitigation."*

Their first task was setting up canary deployments in Kubernetes. Alex and his team chose Kubernetes for its sophisticated rollout controls, allowing them to control the percentage of users that would receive the new updates. It was a crucial decision driven by the need to ensure system stability and provide the best user experience possible.

After various internal discussions and countless hours of research, the team commenced their journey into the world of canary deployments. The development team was initially hesitant, concerned about the added complexity in the delivery process. But as they ran their first canary deployment, they realized the benefits outweighed the initial discomfort. Issues could be detected early without affecting the entire user base, a significant boost for system reliability. Plus, it created an environment for rapid and risk-controlled innovation.

Interestingly, the data science team found unique value in canary deployments. They relished the ability to test their machine learning models on a smaller, more controlled user group before wide-scale deployment. It was an unforeseen but welcomed outcome that further emphasized the value of the canary deployment strategy.

However, Alex knew it wasn't all sunshine and rainbows. Canary deployments came with potential risks. If not properly managed, a faulty deployment could still impact a substantial number of users. Monitoring and rollback strategies needed to be robust. There was also the risk of inconsistent user experience due to different users accessing different feature sets during the deployment.

Key decision points around canary deployments involved striking a balance. What percentage of users would form the "canary" group? How fast should the rollout be after its initial success? Each decision was backed by data from past deployments and industry best practices. The team used data to understand the impact of their decisions on system stability and user experience, ensuring they were making informed choices.

In the end, Alex and his team decided to adopt canary deployments. It aligned with their strategy of minimizing risks and operational disruption while allowing for controlled innovation. The decision was a calculated one, made from a place of understanding and careful consideration of their specific business needs.

As this chapter closed, the team looked forward to the road ahead, confident in their strategy and ready to embrace the art of canary deployments. Alex knew that the success of this approach would rely not just on the technology, but the people operating it, a testament to the importance of their team's expertise and commitment to the project.

Database scaling

The Sun was just breaking over the horizon, streaming light into the office where Alex sat, coffee in hand, contemplating the new challenge ahead. The success of the AI solution had resulted in a data influx like none they'd seen before. With their expanding user base, it was clear that database scaling was inevitable.

"Scalability is the key to our future success," Alex emphasized at the team meeting later that day, explaining that their databases, the heart of their solution, needed to grow with the demand. But as he well knew, achieving scalability wasn't as simple as flicking a switch.

The team explored several strategies, beginning with partitioning. By dividing their database into smaller, more manageable parts, they expected to improve performance and ease the load. However, this came with the challenge of managing data consistency across partitions, a crucial aspect given the interdependence of data in their AI solution.

Replication followed, a concept that involved maintaining identical copies of their database to distribute the read load. For their SQL database, the team implemented master-slave replication, with the master handling writes and slaves catering to read requests. This approach worked well but introduced a delay in data propagation between the master and slaves, a point that needed careful consideration.

Their NoSQL databases, Couchbase and Cassandra, offered built-in replication support. However, they needed to consider the eventual consistency model, which meant the replicas would not immediately reflect changes, a potential source of outdated data.

Sharding was the third piece of their scaling puzzle. It involved splitting the database into horizontal partitions or "shards," each capable of operating independently. This was a particularly appealing approach for their NoSQL databases due to the inherent support for sharding and the ability to distribute the shards across multiple servers for better performance and fault tolerance.

Despite the potential benefits, Alex was well aware of the complexities of implementing sharding. Deciding on the right shard key to ensure evenly distributed data and minimal cross-shard operations was critical, and missteps could lead to uneven load distribution and increased complexity in queries.

The process of scaling their databases was arduous, but the team found its rhythm. They meticulously recorded their observations, noting performance improvements and bottlenecks. Armed with this data, they navigated the complexities, making data-driven decisions to refine their strategy and achieve the optimal balance of performance, cost, and operational feasibility.

The team made their final decision, choosing a combination of partitioning, replication, and sharding to meet their scaling needs. It was an informed decision, backed by their experiences and the data they had gathered along the way.

As they concluded the scaling operation, they looked back at the journey with a sense of accomplishment. The road ahead was clearer, with their databases now ready to handle the growing data and user base. The AI solution, they realized, was no longer just a project; it was a living, breathing entity, growing and evolving with each passing day, just as they were.

Security and compliance in operations

As the excitement of the launch receded, the team found themselves stepping into a new realm: operational maintenance. They had built a robust, scalable solution, but now, they needed to keep it secure and compliant, a task just as challenging, if not more so, than the initial build.

The importance of operational security quickly became apparent. Alex convened the team, highlighting the need for regular patch management. Every technology they had employed, from PostgreSQL to Kubernetes, received periodic updates, not just for feature improvements but crucially to patch any identified vulnerabilities. Alex understood the risk of ignoring these patches and made it clear: *"patches are non-negotiable."*

A key part of their operational security was access management. The team had grown, and not everyone needed access to all systems. They conducted regular access reviews, revoking privileges where necessary and ensuring a principle of least privilege.

Incident response was another operational reality. One Tuesday evening, their intrusion detection system flagged a suspicious login attempt. The team swung into action, isolating the incident, identifying the cause, and implementing countermeasures. This event, though unsettling, proved the effectiveness of their incident response plan.

Compliance was another matter altogether. Their solution was a global entity, meaning they had to comply with various data privacy laws, including GDPR in Europe and CCPA in California. Every piece of data they collected, stored, and processed needed to adhere to these regulations. *"Compliance isn't just about avoiding fines,"* Alex reminded the team. *"It's about building trust with our users."*

Implementing these measures was not without challenges. Compliance required constant vigilance to evolving global data privacy laws. Operational security added complexity to their day-to-day activities, and incident responses could disrupt their planned tasks.

Addressing this operational burden was crucial. They sought ways to automate repetitive tasks, leveraging their existing DevOps tools and investing in **security orchestration and automated response (SOAR)** solutions. Alex emphasized the concept of "TOIL" – those manual, repetitive tasks that provided no enduring value. *"Let's focus on reducing TOIL so that we can dedicate more time to innovating and improving our solution."*

The team agreed, working together to refine their operations, striking a balance between security, compliance, and manageability. They reviewed data and user feedback, making informed decisions to streamline operations and enhance their solution's reliability and trustworthiness.

Reflecting on their journey, Alex felt a sense of achievement. Despite the challenges, they had successfully navigated the complexities of operational security and compliance. They had learned, adapted, and grown, not just as individuals but as a team, reinforcing the foundation for their solution's continued success. He had another update to send to his team.

Update 4

Yet another month passed, and Alex sent his usual status update:

Subject: Project Status Update – Update 4

Dear Team,

I hope this message finds you well. Here's a brief overview of our recent progress in our AI project.

Over the past few weeks, we adopted canary deployments, improving our roll-out strategy and allowing our teams to make data-driven decisions while enhancing user experience.

We also addressed the necessary next steps in database scaling due to an increasing user base and data volume. We implemented strategies such as partitioning, replication, and sharding, significantly boosting the performance of our databases.

In parallel to that, we emphasized operational security and compliance. Regular patch management, access reviews, and a robust incident response plan have been established, ensuring adherence to global data privacy laws. We are focusing on reducing TOIL to streamline operational processes.

Our journey continues. The challenges we've overcome have made our solution stronger and our team more resilient. Thank you for your unwavering dedication and hard work.

Kind regards,

Alex

Version-controlled environment variables

A few weeks into the deployment phase, Alex found an unexpected email from senior leadership in his inbox. The AI solution they had been working on was gaining attention not only within the organization but also outside. There were requests from sister organizations to deploy a similar solution in their cloud environments. The ask was significant: make the AI solution portable across different cloud accounts, namely AWS and GCP.

Alex knew this would pose a fresh set of challenges. The solution they'd built had been tailored to their specific environment and infrastructure. They had not initially considered the requirement for portability across different cloud providers. It meant that their environment configurations, which were unique to their setup, would have to be generalized and made portable. This is where the concept of version-controlled environment variables became critical.

Environment variables were pivotal in providing configuration data to their application. This data included IP addresses, database credentials, API keys, and more. Alex realized that to ensure portability, these variables would need to be version-controlled and managed securely. It was the only way to guarantee that the AI application behaved consistently across different environments.

The team started exploring tools to help with this task. Git was their first choice as it was already the backbone of their code version control. It provided an easy way to track changes in the environment variables and rollback if necessary. However, storing sensitive data such as credentials and API keys in Git posed a security risk.

This is where Docker came in. Docker allowed them to package their application with all its dependencies into a container, which could be easily ported across environments. But again, storing sensitive data in Docker images was not ideal.

That's when they discovered HashiCorp Vault. It provided the much-needed secure storage for sensitive data. Vault encrypted the sensitive information and allowed access only based on IAM roles and policies. This ensured that only authorized personnel could access the sensitive data.

The team agreed to set up a POC to evaluate this approach. They planned to create a simple application with various environment configurations and tried deploying it on both AWS and GCP using Git, Docker, and Vault.

As dusk settled outside the office, Alex and his team were huddled around a desk, eyes glued to a screen displaying a terminal. They were running the final tests on a POC on HashiCorp Vault. The outcome of this POC would dictate their approach to managing environment variables in a secure, version-controlled manner, a critical requirement for their AI solution's portability across different cloud environments.

HashiCorp Vault was the centerpiece of this POC. It promised secure, dynamic secrets management that met the team's requirement of handling sensitive environment variables, such as database credentials and API keys, in a safe and encrypted manner. Their architectural design involved Vault as a central, secure store for all their application secrets.

The POC was designed to test three key aspects:

- **Securely store secrets**: The team began by storing various types of environment variables, such as API keys, database credentials, and cloud service access keys, in Vault. This step was crucial because mishandling these secrets could lead to severe security breaches. Vault's promise of encrypted storage, combined with role-based access control, offered the security level they needed.

- **Dynamic secrets**: Vault's ability to generate dynamic secrets was tested next. Dynamic secrets are created on demand and are unique to a client. This reduces the risk of a secret being compromised. The team simulated an API access scenario, where Vault generated a unique API key for each session.

- **Version control**: This feature of Vault was particularly appealing to Alex and his team. It allowed them to track the changes in secrets over time and roll back if required. This was put to the test by deliberately changing the credentials for a database, and later restoring it to its previous state.

As the POC went underway, the team faced several hurdles. Configuring Vault to work seamlessly with their existing CI/CD pipeline was a challenge, requiring many iterations and debugging. The learning curve was steep, especially in understanding the nuances of Vault's policies and role definitions.

Yet, when the last test was run past midnight, the relief and satisfaction on the team's faces were palpable. Vault had stood up to the tests. It demonstrated that it could securely manage their secrets, provide dynamic secrets on-demand, and allow version control over these secrets.

The POC had been a success. Alex was proud of his team and their tenacity. They had successfully demonstrated how to manage environment variables securely and in a version-controlled manner, thus unlocking their AI solution's portability. Their efforts and late nights had paid off.

Alex knew there were still challenges ahead as they moved toward a full-scale implementation. But this POC had shown them a way forward. Their AI solution was one step closer to being deployable across various cloud environments.

The implementation of version-controlled environment variables was a turning point in the project. It not only made their AI application portable but also enhanced their deployment process. Now, they had a reliable and secure way of managing environment configurations, a process that could be replicated in any environment.

However, the implementation was not without its challenges. The team had to grapple with complex configurations and a steep learning curve with Vault. Moreover, they had to ensure that the process adhered to all security and compliance standards. But the benefits outweighed the challenges. The team now had a robust, portable, and secure AI solution that could be deployed in any cloud environment.

Reflecting on this journey, Alex was satisfied. It was not just about meeting the new ask, but about the growth that the team had experienced along the way. The team was stronger, their processes more robust, and their AI solution was now truly portable and scalable.

As Alex always liked to say, "*A constraint is not a barrier but an opportunity for innovation*". Indeed, the team had innovated their way through this constraint, opening up new possibilities for their AI solution.

With this, Alex typed up his last update to the team.

Update 5

Project Status Update – Update 5

Dear Team,

I am delighted to share with you the updates and significant progress we've made concerning our requirement to manage environment variables in a secure, version-controlled manner. Our goal has always been to build an AI solution with the flexibility and portability to be deployed seamlessly across different cloud environments. Today, we're one step closer to achieving this objective.

We recently ran a successful POC with HashiCorp Vault, a tool that securely manages and controls access to tokens, passwords, certificates, and encryption keys for protecting our environment variables. Vault's promise of secure, encrypted storage, combined with dynamic secrets and version control, seemed to perfectly align with our objectives. Hence, we decided to test it out thoroughly.

The POC tested Vault's capabilities in securely storing various types of environment variables, such as API keys, database credentials, and cloud service access keys. Vault proved its reliability by dynamically generating unique secrets on-demand, reducing the risk of any secret being compromised.

Moreover, the version control feature was crucial in tracking changes over time, giving us the flexibility to roll back if needed. Although we encountered some hurdles while integrating Vault with our existing CI/CD pipeline, the outcome was highly promising.

Our team's tireless efforts have proven that HashiCorp Vault can manage our environment variables securely and effectively, enhancing our AI solution's portability. With these promising results, we are now preparing for a full-scale implementation.

As we move forward, I want to thank you all for your continued support. Your dedication and hard work are the driving forces behind our success. Let's keep pushing boundaries and achieving new milestones.

Kind regards,

Alex

Lessons learned and future directions

As we reflect on Alex's journey through the complex maze of implementing a scalable, portable, and secure AI solution, it's clear that this expedition has been as much about learning as it was about achieving. This winding journey, fraught with challenges and illuminated by successes, has distilled invaluable insights and lessons that the team will carry forward.

Throughout the journey, there were numerous lessons learned. The most significant of these was the vital importance of designing a flexible architecture that could evolve with the project's needs. From the initial choice of the AI model to the selection of various caching layers, the team recognized the need for adaptability in every component.

The team also learned the value of robust security measures. Ensuring secure access, data integrity, and compliance with global data privacy laws proved challenging but essential. It instilled in them an enduring respect for security-first practices and an understanding of the complex implications of global compliance.

Moreover, the implementation of immutable and idempotent logic demonstrated the power of these principles in ensuring system stability and resilience. The adoption of these principles served as a reminder that following established patterns can often lead to more predictable and reliable outcomes.

However, the journey wasn't just about adhering to established principles. Alex and his team also recognized the need for innovation and out-of-the-box thinking. The implementation of canary deployments, self-healing systems, and zero-touch automation, to name a few, showcased the team's ability to leverage cutting-edge technology and methodologies to solve complex problems.

In terms of future directions, the world of AI technology is rapidly evolving. With advancements in AI technology and changing business requirements, the team's AI solution is primed for continuous evolution. There are opportunities to explore more sophisticated AI models, improve system performance, and refine user experience.

The team's future lies in maintaining its innovative spirit, continuously learning, and staying curious. They understand the importance of being data-driven in their decision-making and the significance of conducting proof of concepts to validate their choices.

As Alex's journey concludes, it's clear that this is just the beginning. The lessons learned have prepared the team for future challenges, and their spirit of curiosity is a testament to their readiness to meet the evolving demands of the AI landscape. The journey ahead is full of potential and, armed with their experiences, Alex and his team are ready to embrace the future.

In the end, Alex's journey serves as a beacon, reminding us that the path to success is paved with data-driven decisions, curiosity, and the courage to embrace new ideas.

Summary

Within the pages of this chapter, you embarked on a transformative journey deep into the realm of AI, witnessing Alex's profound experiences unfold. From the initial steps of AI implementation to the intricate layers of observability and operations, the narrative painted a vivid picture of the triumphs and tribulations faced by the dedicated team at FC. These experiences serve as a testament to the enduring power of acquired wisdom, offering valuable lessons for those venturing into this dynamic field.

While reflecting on the past, the narrative also cast a forward gaze, hinting at prospective directions within the ever-evolving AI landscape. Whether you are an ardent AI enthusiast seeking deeper insights or a seasoned professional aiming to enrich your comprehension, this chapter invited you on an enlightening odyssey.

At its core, this chapter covered the story of Alex, a technology enthusiast, interwoven with pivotal themes. Alex's AI journey was the focal point of this chapter, but it also delved into the early steps and intricate process of implementing AI, shedding light on the strategies employed and the challenges surmounted. Observability and operations were scrutinized, underscoring their pivotal roles in shaping the AI landscape. As a retrospective account, it unearthed invaluable lessons from the past while simultaneously prompting contemplation on the potential trajectories that the future might unfurl within this dynamic field.

In essence, this chapter encapsulated the collective wisdom gleaned from traversing the AI frontier, offering not just a portrayal of Alex's narrative but also an illuminating guide for others, beckoning them to chart their own stories in the ever-evolving space of AI.

In the next chapter, we will learn about specializing in data while utilizing my personal experiences.

Part 5: The Future of Data

In this part, you will take a sneak peek into the author's personal experience and thoughts on what the future might hold in terms of technology and how that might relate to the world of data. With smart IoT devices everywhere, your car, your fridge, and even your pet can generate GBs of data each day – which is then transported, analyzed, and stored in different parts of the world. You will explore the implications of such expanding utilization and demand in relation to new requirements, best practices, and future challenges ahead.

This part comprises the following chapters:

- *Chapter 15, Specializing in Data – The Author's Personal Experience and Evolution into DevOps and Database DevOps*

- *Chapter 16, The Exciting World of Data – What the Future Might Look Like for a DevOps DBA*

15

Specializing in Data

For over 20 years, I've navigated the ever-changing terrain of the tech world. My journey has been both a privilege and a source of immense pride. Not only am I deeply passionate about the roles I've undertaken, but I've also had the fortune to witness and contribute to pivotal shifts in the industry. This chapter seeks to encapsulate my unique experiences, tracing back to my foundational role as a developer at a Hungarian university. My true initiation began at IBM, delving into the intricacies of **high availability** (**HA**) distributed systems. At Lufthansa, I bridged the realms of tech and aviation, spearheading transformative projects. My stint at Symantec focused my skills in security and resilience, emphasizing data persistence. Sky UK deepened my grasp on data persistence technologies, whereas at Oracle, I was at the forefront of developing their maiden public cloud services, concentrating on compute and persistence. My leadership skills shone at Vodafone, overseeing the entire **site reliability engineering** (**SRE**) framework. Now, with **Amazon Web Services** (**AWS**), I'm pushing the envelope in data, analytics, **artificial intelligence** (**AI**), **machine learning** (**ML**), and emerging tech. Reflecting on these two decades, my commitment to innovation and excellence has cemented my position in the global tech panorama.

In this chapter, we will cover the following topics:

- Mastering data – bridging the gap between IT and business

- My first experience, Unix – 2009

- The first signs of DevOps – 2010s

- My first SRE team – 2015

- Steep learning curves – 2017

- Putting it all into practice – 2019

- The landscape of 2023 – data and DevOps united

Mastering data – bridging the gap between IT and business

In today's digital age, data has emerged as a key differentiator for businesses. It is the cornerstone of strategic decision-making and operational efficiency, shaping the way organizations grow and compete. This chapter highlights the imperative role of data in businesses, the relevance of understanding and mastering it for DevOps, SREs, IT professionals, and business executives, and the ways in which a data-driven approach can create tangible business value.

Data, in its essence, is raw information that becomes meaningful and actionable when processed and analyzed. In an organization, data can originate from various sources, such as transactional systems, IoT devices, or customer interactions, and it is typically structured, semi-structured, or unstructured. Understanding the various data types, their sources, and how they flow across an organization's ecosystem is a fundamental step in exploiting the potential of data. By mastering these basics, professionals from both technical and business realms can effectively communicate, making strategic decisions that align with the organization's goals.

In the world of data management, governance is paramount. It encompasses the practices, processes, and frameworks that ensure data quality, security, and accessibility. Adhering to a robust data governance strategy helps businesses uphold data integrity, streamline operations, and comply with regulations such as the **General Data Protection Regulation (GDPR)**. Compliance with such regulations is not merely a legal necessity but also a way to foster trust with customers and partners, emphasizing the company's commitment to data privacy and security.

Data engineering is the bedrock of any data-focused endeavor. It involves designing, building, and managing data infrastructure, which includes databases and large-scale processing systems. For DevOps and SREs, understanding and collaborating with data engineers is critical to ensure the smooth operation of these systems and to maintain the high quality and accessibility of data. Knowledge of tools such as Apache Hadoop, Spark, and data warehousing solutions can aid in this collaboration, contributing to more efficient data handling and system performance.

Data is intrinsically tied to IT operations. It provides insights that help in monitoring and troubleshooting IT infrastructure, thereby improving service delivery. By employing data analytics, IT professionals can identify performance bottlenecks, forecast system failures, and implement preventive measures proactively. This approach not only ensures a robust IT landscape but also contributes to improved business processes and customer satisfaction.

Data-driven decision-making for business executives

For business executives, data analytics can provide a wealth of insights, offering a strategic edge. By applying data science techniques to analyze data, executives can uncover patterns, trends, and correlations that lead to informed business decisions. For instance, customer data analysis can unveil preferences and behaviors, guiding product development, marketing strategy, and customer service enhancements. Several companies have leveraged this data-driven approach to gain a competitive advantage and drive growth. The predictive capabilities of data analytics also allow for risk mitigation and better resource allocation.

AI and ML have dramatically transformed the way organizations manage and analyze data. These technologies enable predictive analytics, automate routine tasks, and enhance decision-making capabilities. For IT professionals, AI-powered tools can offer real-time insights into system health, enabling rapid troubleshooting. Meanwhile, business executives can leverage AI to uncover deeper insights, predict market trends, and personalize customer experiences.

Building a data-driven culture – an enterprise perspective

Creating a data-driven culture is essential for an organization aiming to harness the full potential of its data. This culture encourages data literacy, fosters data-centric decision-making, and promotes a mindset of continuous learning and improvement. Each stakeholder, including DevOps, SREs, IT professionals, and executives, plays a vital role in promoting and cultivating this culture. Their collaborative efforts can lead to better decision-making, innovation, and a more profound understanding of the business landscape.

Mastering data is no longer an optional skill but a critical competency for all stakeholders in an organization. Data not only shapes the business strategies and decisions of executives but also influences the work of IT professionals, DevOps, and SREs. Understanding data, adhering to governance and compliance norms, embracing data engineering, using data for informed decision-making, leveraging AI, and fostering a data-driven culture are the pathways to leveraging data effectively. As organizations increasingly become data-intensive, the mastery of data will be the key that unlocks unprecedented business opportunities and competitive advantage.

My first experience, Unix – 2009

Specializing in data as an AIX system administrator in 2009 was an exciting and demanding role, offering exposure to a wide array of tasks that relied on data management and data manipulation. If you had the pleasure of working in such a team back in the day, you would've spent most of your time maintaining and optimizing the Unix-based AIX system, configuring servers, managing system security, and keeping an eye on the system's performance metrics. Remember – DevOps was nowhere at that time.

Here are some of the core responsibilities that filled most of our working time:

- **System installation and configuration**: As an AIX administrator, one of your main responsibilities was to install and configure the AIX operating system on IBM server hardware. Ensuring the smooth and efficient operation of these systems was critical.

- **Data management**: You were responsible for managing and safeguarding the organization's data. This would involve taking regular backups, performing data restoration as needed, and ensuring high availability of data for the various services running on the servers. You would also handle storage management, including allocating disk space to users and applications and managing disk quotas.

- **Performance monitoring**: Regular monitoring of the system's performance was a critical part of the role. This involved using system commands and tools such as TOP to analyze system metrics (CPU usage, memory consumption, and I/O operations), identifying bottlenecks, and taking corrective actions to optimize system performance.

- **Security management**: One of the key responsibilities was to manage system security. This would involve setting and managing user permissions, configuring firewalls, and staying up to date with the latest security patches from IBM. In addition, you'd handle user account management, including adding, removing, or modifying user accounts, and setting access levels.

- **Script writing and task automation**: Writing shell scripts (probably using Bash or Korn shell, given the time frame) to automate repetitive tasks would be a significant part of your day. You might have used Crontab for scheduling these scripts to run at specific intervals.

- **Cluster management**: If your organization ran critical applications, you'd likely manage HA clusters, using solutions such as IBM's HACMP or Veritas Cluster Server. This would ensure that your applications and services remained available, even if a server failed.

- **Troubleshooting**: No day would pass without some form of troubleshooting. Whether it was addressing user issues, fixing system errors, or resolving network connectivity problems, this would be a regular part of your job.

- **Documentation and reporting**: Last, but definitely not least, maintaining system documentation and generating regular reports about the system's health and performance would be part of your duties.

Obviously, in today's world, most of it is fully automated; a little was back in 2006 when the best automation we had was written in Bash (okay – that's a bit of over-exaggeration, or is it?).

In this role, we interacted closely with other IT professionals, such as network administrators, database administrators, and developers, to ensure that all systems worked together seamlessly. Despite the challenges, I absolutely loved it, sitting at the heart of the IT operations. This was a very similar place to those where DevOps and SRE were eventually born!

The first signs of DevOps – 2010s

The early days of DevOps were fueled by the agile software development movement and its principles of continuous improvement, customer satisfaction, and collaborative working. Agile methodologies provided a framework for software development that encouraged frequent inspection and adaptation, and it paved the way for the integration of operations into the development life cycle.

I first heard about it in 2009 but only experienced it in 2012. The key focus was on bridging the gap between development and operations. This included ideas such as IaC, where infrastructure management was automated and version-controlled, just as with software code. Tools such as Puppet and Chef started to gain popularity, allowing for automated configuration management. CI and CD were also essential elements, enabling more reliable and faster software releases.

Fundamentally, it was about fostering a culture of collaboration, communication, and shared responsibility. It encouraged a work environment where building, testing, and releasing software could happen more rapidly, frequently, and reliably. DevOps represented a significant cultural and practical shift in the software industry.

Support and software engineering in 2012

As a support and software engineer in 2012, during the early days of DevOps adoption within a company ingrained with the traditional waterfall methodology, your day-to-day duties involved a constant interplay between legacy processes and new methodologies. And if that sounds like chaos to you, you are not wrong.

Imagine the following:

You start your day with a review of outstanding support tickets, prioritizing them based on their urgency and impact. As the bridge between customers and the software development process, you interact with customers, ensuring that their concerns are being addressed.

Next, you spend time troubleshooting software issues. This involves replicating problems, diagnosing errors, and patching code. Given that the company follows the waterfall methodology, getting these fixes into a live environment takes time due to the sequential nature of the process.

As part of a company transitioning to DevOps, you participate in several meetings throughout the day. These include stand-ups with your immediate team to discuss daily objectives and blockers, as well as larger meetings with other teams to facilitate better communication and collaboration, a core tenet of DevOps.

After addressing immediate support tasks, you focus on software development. Here, you encounter the clash between the old and new, writing code in short sprints as per Agile practices, but waiting for it to be deployed in the waterfall stages of testing, staging, and production.

Documentation is a crucial part of your role. Keeping track of support issues, coding decisions, and discussions not only provides a reference but also helps in creating a knowledge base for the entire team. This helps push toward the DevOps mentality of shared responsibility and knowledge.

Given that DevOps is still relatively new, you dedicate time each day to self-learning. Whether exploring new tools such as Jenkins for CI, or Docker, which was just beginning to make waves in 2012, you stay on the cutting edge, pushing for more efficient practices in your organization.

At the end of the day, you review your work, update ticket statuses, and prepare for the next day. As someone straddling support and development roles, you continuously balance between customer support and pushing the envelope on the software development process.

Working in this environment is challenging, sometimes frustrating, but also exciting. You are at the forefront of change, helping to transition the company from a rigid waterfall model to a more flexible and collaborative DevOps culture.

My first SRE team – 2015

As an SRE manager in 2015, leading a young team within a traditionally old-school company, your day-to-day work involves a unique blend of traditional processes, team management, and exploration of cutting-edge practices.

You start your day by leading discussions on developing a new type of cloud. Back in the day, this is uncharted territory, and you guide your team as they navigate these challenges. You're experimenting with new technologies, and one of them is Kafka. It's a novel technology for your team, and you're not sure yet how to fully utilize it within your architecture. You spend a significant amount of your time researching its potential use cases, consulting with experts, and planning potential implementation strategies.

A considerable challenge you face is the limitations of your existing infrastructure and virtualization capabilities. You are pushing the boundaries of what your infrastructure can handle, constantly trying to innovate within the confines of your resources. It's a delicate balancing act, ensuring stability while striving for innovation.

Amid the strategic planning and research, operational activities persist. Much of the day-to-day work still involves handling and troubleshooting issues through a lot of Bash scripts. You're working to automate these as much as possible to free up your team's time for more strategic work.

You have started to use Jenkins for CI/CD. As a tool, it's helping you automate parts of your development process, but you're also actively looking for possible alternatives that might offer more efficient or robust solutions. The concept of pipelines is particularly exciting; it promises a more streamlined and automated process.

Collaboration is crucial in your role. Initially, you test a collaboration tool called **Rocket.Chat**. It offers a centralized platform for team discussions, quick updates, and collaborative problem-solving. It's a leap forward in team communication, but then you discover Slack. You're excited about the prospect of switching to a tool that offers integrations with many of the other tools you use daily.

As a manager, a significant part of your role is to manage and mentor your team. You encourage them to learn and adopt new technologies and practices, fostering an atmosphere of constant learning and growth. At the same time, you are aware of the need to manage their enthusiasm, ensuring that the desire to adopt the latest tools does not overshadow the need for stable, reliable systems.

At the end of the day, you review the progress made, reassess your strategy, and plan for the next day. You prepare for future discussions about the adoption of new tools and practices and think about ways to overcome the challenges that you face.

In essence, the role of an SRE manager in this transitioning environment is a challenging one, filled with balancing the demands of operational stability and innovation. You are not only dealing with technological challenges but also guiding a young team eager to adopt new practices within a traditional company. It's a fascinating journey filled with learning, growth, and change.

Steep learning curves – 2017

As an SRE manager in 2017 leading a team specialized in data-persisting technologies, the day-to-day activities consisted of innovation, problem-solving, and in-depth analysis of cutting-edge technologies. The company's forward-looking approach offered a dynamic environment where constant learning and adaptation were the norm.

You start your day brainstorming with your team about new technologies and potential solutions. As this is uncharted territory, for the first time in your career, Google and the existing documentation do not offer ready-made solutions for your problems. The challenge is invigorating; you and your team need to figure out the solutions yourselves, constantly learning, experimenting, and improving.

A significant portion of your day is dedicated to resourcing and running PoCs to determine the best possible solutions. It's a continuous process of proposing hypotheses, running tests, analyzing results, and refining your approach.

Your role includes in-depth analysis of different data-persisting technologies. You conduct comprehensive comparisons of database performance, resilience, cost, and security among technologies such as Couchbase, Cassandra, MongoDB, Elastic, CockroachDB, Kafka, NGINX, and others. You work directly with these companies, leveraging their expertise to get the most out of their technologies.

You're beginning to see the first signs of self-healing technologies, such as Kubernetes Operators. Kubernetes is becoming a force to be reckoned with, bringing significant changes in how you manage and deploy your applications.

You aim to be "multi-cloud," a term you first heard in 2017. You see the potential of using Kubernetes to build clusters across different platforms such as Google Cloud, AWS, and your on-premises infrastructure. This approach promises flexibility, resilience, and cost-effectiveness.

As a manager, you foster a culture of innovation and creativity within your team. You encourage them to experiment, learn from their mistakes, and continuously improve. Collaboration is key, not just within your team but also with the various technology vendors you work with.

You end your day by reviewing the progress made, reassessing your strategies, and planning for the next day. You're constantly looking ahead, anticipating new developments in data-persisting technologies, and preparing your team for the exciting challenges ahead.

In this role, we were not just managing a team; we were leading the charge in an era of fast-paced technological innovation. It was a journey of continuous learning and discovery, full of challenges and triumphs. We were at the forefront of implementing cutting-edge data-persisting technologies, driving change and transformation within the organization. I loved every minute of it!

Putting it all into practice – 2019

As a senior leader, my role is an exciting and challenging blend of technical, cultural, and political leadership, building and leading an SRE organization from scratch in a traditional non-tech native company. The day-to-day experiences I face while pioneering this transformation form a dynamic and fulfilling journey.

The dawn of transformation: Each day, I commence by revisiting the inception of our journey. With only eight of us at the start, we ventured to bring change into a traditionally inclined company, an environment where embracing modern technological practices wasn't the norm. This initial phase was critical in establishing a growth mindset within our team, preparing them for the impending challenges and responsibilities. It was our time to disrupt the status quo and lay the groundwork for a future-ready SRE organization.

Our first major milestone in this journey is the challenging but crucial task of transitioning from manually configured cloud infrastructure to IAC. In practice, this is an arduous task that requires thorough planning and execution. We start by identifying the IAC requirements, working backward from our goals to the current state. This shift requires us to let go of entrenched technologies such as AppD due to their incompatibility with our IAC requirements. It's a tough call, but it's critical for the success of our IAC transformation.

Celebrating early successes: The launch of our IAC-backed production is a resounding success, validating our collective efforts. The volume of support tickets has been reduced dramatically by 93%, our system uptime sees an improvement of 12%, and, most significantly, our infrastructure costs have been reduced by 30%. It's not just the quantitative success that boosts our morale; it's the reassurance that we are on the right path, bringing meaningful and effective change to our organization.

Fresh from our initial successes, we set our sights on the next ambitious milestones. These involve creating on-demand environments and continuously eliminating environment variables. These goals keep us in a state of continual learning and innovation. Each day, we push boundaries, question the established ways, and drive our team toward our shared goals.

Achieving immutable observability: Another significant leap in our journey is the establishment of immutable observability. We construct pipelines and rules to automate the creation of dashboards, alerting rules, and escalation paths, aiming to make our system self-sufficient and intuitive. We collaborate with renowned vendors such as Datadog, PagerDuty, and Elastic, merging their expertise with our vision to create an observability solution that becomes an exemplar for the entire industry.

Automated testing and chaos engineering: The following milestones take us further down the road of automation. We start implementing automated testing as gatekeepers in our CI/CD release pipelines, followed by establishing rigorous controls for environment variables and secret management standards.

Eventually, we introduce CHAOS Engineering into our ecosystem, making it an integral part of our quality control process.

Beyond the technical challenges, my role becomes a journey through the complex cultural and political landscapes of the organization. It's about transforming not just the technical infrastructure, but also the mindset of our stakeholders. I constantly engage in dialogues, negotiations, and discussions with other teams, leaders, and stakeholders. It's a strategic effort to bring everyone on board with the SRE vision and demonstrate its tangible benefits for our organization.

A large part of my role is about managing the growth trajectory. In just 3 years, we grow from a small team of 8 to a massive organization of over 300 dedicated individuals. More impressively, the scope of our responsibility expands from a subset of a single country to a worldwide operational scale. It's a remarkable testament to our hard work, strategic planning, and unwavering commitment to our vision.

As a senior leader, my role grows beyond managing; it's about setting the vision, fostering a culture of innovation, and leading the transformation of our organization into an entity that's prepared for the future. This journey, with all its challenges and successes, is what makes my memories of this particular experience so precious.

The landscape of 2023 – data and DevOps united

The current DevOps and SRE landscape is a fast-evolving terrain, significantly influenced by data engineering, databases, analytical systems, and AI and ML technologies. These components are not just standalone entities but integrated pieces transforming the DevOps and SRE field into an even more complex, yet streamlined and efficient, practice.

Integration of DevOps with data engineering

In today's digital era, data is the lifeblood of businesses, making databases integral to many applications. Accordingly, databases are being integrated into the DevOps life cycle, promoting efficient and seamless workflows.

DevOps, a set of practices that combines software development and IT operations, aims to shorten the system development life cycle and provide continuous delivery with high software quality. When applied to databases, DevOps promotes faster development and deployment of database changes, improves the database's performance and security, and assists in timely bug detection and resolution.

The integration begins with provisioning and managing databases using IaC tools such as Terraform and AWS CloudFormation. These tools enable developers to automate database setup, eliminating the manual effort and potential human error while ensuring consistency across environments.

Furthermore, developers implement CI/CD pipelines for databases, as with applications. Tools such as Liquibase and Flyway are used to manage database schema changes, ensuring that these changes are version-controlled and automatically applied, making deployments repeatable and reversible.

DataOps – revolutionizing data analytics pipelines

DataOps, a new methodology that applies DevOps principles to data analytics pipelines, brings about faster, more reliable, and high-quality data analysis. This practice involves automating and monitoring data pipelines to cut down the time lag from data ingestion to actionable insights, improving the overall business decision-making process.

DataOps requires a tight collaboration among data engineers, data scientists, and business stakeholders. This cross-functional team setup facilitates a holistic view of the business's data needs, promoting a more seamless and efficient workflow. Moreover, it places a high emphasis on automation, CI, testing, and monitoring to improve data quality and speed up the delivery of data workloads.

MLOps – bridging the gap between ML development and operations

ML Operations, or **MLOps**, is a nascent field that seeks to bring harmony between ML system development and operations. It aims to amplify automation and improve the quality of production ML while also concentrating on business and regulatory requirements.

MLOps borrows from the principles of DevOps, intending to reduce the time it takes to deploy ML models into production, improve their performance, and streamline the management of ML systems over time. This process includes practices such as model versioning, model monitoring, automated testing and validation of models, and model retraining and fine-tuning.

AI-powered DevOps/SRE

The integration of AI and ML into DevOps and SRE practices brings about new efficiencies and capabilities. This emerging practice includes AI-powered alerting, anomaly detection, predictive analytics for capacity planning, auto-remediation, and more.

AI/ML can provide significant help in analyzing operational data to predict and prevent incidents, enhance system performance, and automate routine tasks. For example, AI can help categorize and prioritize incidents automatically based on historical data, ensuring a swift and effective response.

Application of SRE principles to data systems

SRE principles are now being applied to data systems, thereby ensuring their reliability, availability, and performance. These principles include defining **service-level objectives (SLOs)** and **service-level indicators (SLIs)** for databases and data pipelines, implementing error budgets for data systems, and treating data incidents and outages with the same rigor as application-level incidents.

Error budgets, a concept introduced by SRE, help balance the need for rapid innovation and the risk of system instability. This principle, when applied to data systems, ensures that they are reliable and meet their users' expectations.

DevSecOps – security in the age of data

With the increasing complexity of data infrastructure and the emergence of stricter data regulations, security is now being integrated into the DevOps life cycle – a practice known as **DevSecOps**.

DevSecOps embeds security practices into the CI/CD pipeline. It includes automating security checks and vulnerability scans, enforcing policy as code, and continually monitoring for potential security risks in data systems. This practice makes security an integral part of software development and operations, enabling early and proactive detection of security issues.

The present DevOps and SRE landscape is characterized by the profound integration of databases, analytics, AI, and ML systems. This integration reshapes established practices and workflows, bringing greater automation, reliability, speed, and security to the development and operation of data-intensive applications and systems. It's a new frontier of DevOps and SRE, where data, AI, and ML are at the heart of operations, creating not only technological challenges but also opportunities for innovation and growth.

Summary

I consider myself lucky, having been able to experience first-hand such an amazing change in the world of Data and DevOps in such a short period of time. The last 14-15 years were nothing but extraordinary, filled with ambiguity, opportunity, and pure passion for innovation.

In 2009, the term "DevOps" was only just emerging, and its principles were far from widespread adoption. Traditional software development was marked by silos, where developers and operations teams worked separately. This disjointed approach often led to significant bottlenecks in the software delivery process, causing delays and conflicts.

Data systems at this time were largely monolithic and on-premises. Relational databases were the norm, and NoSQL databases were just beginning to gain traction. The management of these systems was largely manual, and they were often treated as separate entities from the applications they supported.

CI/CD practices were not as widely accepted or practiced as they are today. Jenkins, one of the pioneers in this area, was just starting to gain popularity. IaC was also a relatively new concept, with tools such as Chef and Puppet starting to emerge.

Monitoring and observability were more reactive than proactive. Tools such as Nagios were used to monitor system health, but the scope of these tools was limited, and they often lacked the ability to provide in-depth insights into system performance.

Security in development and operations was often an afterthought, dealt with at the end of the development cycle, or, worse, after deployment.

Fast forward to 2023, and the DevOps landscape has significantly evolved. DevOps is now the standard approach in software development, promoting a culture of collaboration between developers and operations. CI/CD is a widely practiced strategy, with numerous sophisticated tools available.

Data systems have become more complex and varied. There's a move toward distributed systems, with technologies such as microservices, serverless architectures, and containers becoming more popular. NoSQL databases have matured, and new types of databases such as time-series, graph, and in-memory databases have entered the scene. The rise of cloud computing and managed services has also significantly changed how these data systems are managed.

Monitoring and observability have become more proactive and insightful. The rise of AIOps has enabled teams to automatically monitor, analyze, and manage their systems for enhanced performance and to preemptively address issues before they affect the user experience.

Security has also become a priority, with the rise of DevSecOps, which integrates security practices into the DevOps workflow. Security is now considered at every stage of the development cycle rather than being an afterthought.

In terms of data, there's been a shift from just storing and managing data to using it to drive decision-making and business strategy. This has given rise to practices such as DataOps and MLOps. AI and ML are now commonly used in DevOps for tasks such as anomaly detection, forecasting, and automatic remediation.

Overall, the landscape has evolved from siloed, reactive, and manual processes in 2009 to more integrated, proactive, and automated practices in 2023. The role of data has also evolved from being a byproduct of operations to a central component driving operational and business decisions. While the journey hasn't been without challenges, these advances have led to more efficient, reliable, and secure software delivery and management.

In the final chapter, we will learn about the exciting new world of data.

16

The Exciting New World of Data

In this modern era, data sits at the heart of our digital advancements, offering countless opportunities for growth and innovation. As we approach the conclusion of our journey, this chapter will summarize the key takeaways and anticipate what lies ahead. From the foundational aspects of data management to the broader implications for technology design and ethics, we're about to recap and look forward. Let's dive in and explore what the future holds for the world of data.

This final chapter will cover the following topics (in parts):

- Part 1 – the future of data-persisting technologies
- Part 2 – anticipated changes in AI/ML DevOps
- Part 3 – evolving trends in SRE
- Part 4 – career outlook and emerging skill sets in SRE
- Part 5 – the future of designing, building, and operating cutting-edge systems

Disclaimer: The predictions and suggestions presented in this chapter are entirely speculative and are based on my personal experiences and understanding of current trends in the field of data-persisting technologies. They are not influenced by, nor do they represent the views or positions of, any company or organization that I am currently associated with or have been associated with in the past. These are personal insights and should be viewed as such. The rapid and often unpredictable nature of technological advancements means that the future may unfold differently than what has been outlined here. Therefore, while these predictions have been made to the best of my knowledge and belief, I bear no responsibility for any actions taken based on them. Always conduct thorough research and consider multiple viewpoints when making decisions related to these technologies.

Part 1 – the future of data-persisting technologies

The digital era has pivoted on the axis of data, continuously redefining how we capture, process, and interpret vast information streams. Anchored in this metamorphic landscape are data-persisting technologies, which have been the linchpin in ensuring data's durability, retrievability, and relevance. As we stand on the cusp of new technological frontiers, it's essential to grasp the evolutionary trajectory of these data-persisting methodologies. From relational stalwarts adapting to the demands of the modern data milieu to the agile ethos of NoSQL systems and the blistering pace of in-memory databases, the narrative of data storage and retrieval is poised for transformative shifts. This deep dive unveils the prospective developments and anticipated advancements in the realm of data persisting technologies, outlining a future where data isn't just stored, but seamlessly integrated into our tech-driven narratives.

The evolution of current data-persisting technologies

As we navigate the intricate landscape of data technologies, three major shifts are evident. Relational databases, long revered for their stability, are evolving to handle larger datasets, unstructured data, and real-time processing, intertwined with AI. Concurrently, NoSQL databases are diversifying their features, moving toward stronger consistency guarantees and richer querying capabilities. In tandem, in-memory databases and distributed filesystems are gearing up for enhancements in durability, scalability, and integrated technology applications, signaling a progressive trajectory in our data-centric world.

Predicted advancements in relational databases

Relational databases have been the backbone of data storage for many years. Traditional relational databases such as MySQL, PostgreSQL, and Oracle have been known for their reliability, robustness, and adherence to **Atomicity, Consistency, Isolation, Durability (ACID)** principles. However, in recent years, with the advent of big data and real-time processing needs, there have been growing demands for more scalability and versatility from these systems.

In the foreseeable future, we anticipate advancements that will transform the relational database landscape. Firstly, enhanced scalability will become a standard feature, driven by the ever-increasing volumes of data generated daily. Techniques such as database sharding and the use of distributed database systems will become more common, enabling relational databases to handle larger datasets efficiently.

Secondly, improved support for unstructured data is anticipated. Traditional relational databases primarily cater to structured data. However, as the variety of data types and sources continues to expand, we expect advancements that will enable these databases to store and process unstructured data more effectively. This could involve integrating capabilities of NoSQL databases, leading to hybrid systems that offer the benefits of both structured and unstructured data handling.

Thirdly, we foresee further enhancements in real-time processing capabilities. As real-time analytics becomes more critical in sectors such as e-commerce, finance, and healthcare, relational databases will need to support faster processing and lower latency. This will likely involve advancements in in-memory processing technologies, query optimization, and indexing strategies.

Lastly, expect to see increased integration with AI and ML. This will enable smarter database management, predictive performance optimization, and more advanced data analysis capabilities.

Anticipated developments in NoSQL databases

NoSQL databases, including MongoDB, Cassandra, and DynamoDB, have been popular choices for handling big data due to their scalability, flexibility, and suitability for unstructured data. NoSQL databases are known for their **Basically Available, Soft State, Eventually Consistent (BASE)** properties, which allow for high availability and scalability at the expense of strong consistency.

In the future, we foresee numerous developments in NoSQL technologies. Firstly, there will be a growing trend toward offering stronger consistency guarantees while maintaining high availability and scalability. This could be achieved through advancements in consensus algorithms and distributed system designs.

Secondly, expect to see more comprehensive querying capabilities. One of the criticisms of NoSQL databases is their limited querying capabilities compared to SQL databases. Future developments will likely address this issue, possibly incorporating SQL-like querying features to provide users with more powerful data manipulation tools.

Thirdly, there will likely be greater support for multi-model data storage. This would allow a single NoSQL database to handle different types of data models, such as document, graph, key-value, and columnar. This multi-model support can significantly simplify data architecture and improve data processing efficiency.

Finally, as with relational databases, we anticipate increased integration with AI and ML technologies. These enhancements could lead to better database management, automated tuning, and smarter data analysis capabilities.

Potential evolution in in-memory databases

In-memory databases such as Redis and Memcached offer superior performance for data-intensive applications by storing data in memory rather than on disk. As RAM prices continue to decrease and the need for real-time processing grows, we can expect the adoption of in-memory databases to increase.

Future advancements in this field are likely to involve increased durability and persistence. Traditionally, in-memory databases have been vulnerable to data loss in the event of a power failure or system crash. To mitigate this risk, we can expect advancements in technology that increase the durability of in-memory databases, possibly through improved data replication strategies or integration with persistent storage solutions.

Another area of evolution is scalability. While in-memory databases provide high performance, they're currently limited by the memory capacity of individual machines. Future developments will likely focus on distributed in-memory solutions that can scale horizontally across multiple machines, thus supporting larger datasets.

Finally, we predict an increased focus on security features. As in-memory databases become more prevalent, they will become more attractive targets for cyberattacks. Enhancements in data encryption, access controls, and intrusion detection systems will likely become a priority.

Changes expected in distributed filesystems

Distributed filesystems such as HDFS and Amazon S3 have revolutionized the way we store and access large datasets. They offer high scalability, reliability, and performance by distributing data across multiple nodes.

In the future, we expect to see significant advancements in distributed filesystems. One key area will be performance optimization. This will involve improving data distribution strategies to balance load across nodes effectively and optimizing data retrieval techniques to minimize latency.

Additionally, there will be a focus on improving fault tolerance and recovery mechanisms. As datasets become larger and systems more complex, the likelihood of node failures increases. Advances in technology will aim to minimize the impact of such failures and speed up recovery times.

Finally, expect to see advancements in the integration of distributed filesystems with other data technologies. This could involve better integration with database systems for improved data management, or tighter integration with AI and ML technologies for more efficient data processing and analysis.

This comprehensive view of the anticipated advancements in current data persisting technologies showcases the importance of continuous innovation in this rapidly evolving field. As data generation rates continue to increase and the complexity of data processing tasks grows, we can expect these technologies to continue evolving to meet these new challenges and opportunities.

Emerging data-persisting technologies

Let's review the fascinating world of emerging data-persisting technologies, exploring new advancements designed to enhance the way businesses manage and utilize their growing data repositories. These innovations aim to address the limitations of existing database systems, offering improved scalability, performance, and flexibility to meet the demands of today's digital landscape. From the integration of NewSQL databases, which combine the strengths of both SQL and NoSQL systems, to the specialized capabilities of time series databases for handling temporal data, and the groundbreaking potential of quantum databases, this section provides a comprehensive overview of these cutting-edge technologies. We will examine their technical aspects, understand their potential impacts on data storage and processing, and discuss the challenges and considerations that come with adopting these novel solutions.

Overview of upcoming technologies

As we navigate through the age of digital transformation, new technologies are surfacing to cater to the evolving needs of businesses and their growing volumes of data. One such technology is the rise of the NewSQL databases, which aim to bring the best of both worlds from relational (SQL) and NoSQL databases. They are designed to handle high transaction rates and large numbers of concurrent users, just like traditional SQL databases. However, they also offer the high scalability that NoSQL databases are known for.

Another noteworthy advancement is the rise of time series databases, such as InfluxDB and TimescaleDB. These databases are designed to efficiently store and retrieve time series data, which is data that is indexed by time. As more industries embrace IoT devices and real-time analytics, the use of time series databases will likely become more widespread.

Quantum databases, though still in their infancy, represent another exciting development. Leveraging quantum computing's potential, these databases could offer unprecedented speed and processing power. However, there's still a long way to go before they become mainstream.

A detailed examination of their technical aspects

NewSQL databases, such as CockroachDB and TiDB, take a hybrid approach to data storage. They leverage the transactional consistency of SQL databases and the scalability and flexibility of NoSQL databases. Key technical features include distributed SQL queries, global transactions, and strong consistency, which make them well- suited for high-demand applications that require consistency and scale.

Time series databases store data points indexed in time order, making them highly effective for analyzing trends and patterns over time. Their primary technical aspect involves efficient data compression techniques to store large volumes of time-stamped data and sophisticated indexing strategies to facilitate rapid data retrieval.

Quantum databases, though theoretical at this point, would utilize the principles of quantum mechanics to store and process data. This would involve the use of qubits, superposition, and entanglement, which could potentially lead to exponential increases in processing power and speed.

The potential impacts on data storage and processing

The emerging data persisting technologies could have significant impacts on data storage and processing. NewSQL databases could provide businesses with a scalable yet consistent database solution, which could simplify application development and support more robust applications. Similarly, time series databases could facilitate more efficient storage and analysis of time series data, thereby supporting real-time analytics and IoT applications more effectively.

Quantum databases, while still largely theoretical, could revolutionize data storage and processing. With their potential for vastly increased processing power and speed, they could enable new types of applications and analytics that are currently too computationally intensive.

However, as these technologies continue to evolve, it's crucial to keep in mind that they will also bring new challenges. These could include technical challenges related to their implementation and management, as well as broader issues related to data privacy and security.

By keeping abreast of these emerging technologies and understanding their potential impacts, professionals in the field can better prepare for the future of data-persisting technologies. The importance of continuous learning and adaptation in this rapidly evolving field cannot be overstated.

Future use cases and challenges

This section explores innovative use cases enabled by emerging data persisting technologies, impacting industries from IoT and edge computing to real-time analytics and distributed applications. We will also touch upon the potential of quantum computing applications to solve currently infeasible computational tasks.

However, these advancements bring challenges in technical complexity, security, privacy, and regulatory compliance. To navigate these, we propose a strategy of continuous learning, advanced security practices, and strong governance frameworks. By proactively addressing these issues, we can leverage these novel technologies to unlock data's full potential, fostering innovation and progress across sectors. This section aims to equip professionals and enthusiasts with insights and strategies to navigate and capitalize on these technological developments.

Forecast of novel use cases

As data-persisting technologies evolve and new ones emerge, they will enable a variety of novel use cases that could revolutionize different industries. Here are a few forecasts:

- **IoT and edge computing**: As time series databases become more efficient and widespread, they could greatly enhance IoT and edge computing applications. With their ability to handle vast amounts of time-stamped data, they could enable real-time analytics on IoT devices, leading to more intelligent and responsive IoT systems.

- **Real-time analytics**: With advancements in both relational and NoSQL databases, along with the rise of in-memory databases, real-time analytics will become even more pervasive. Industries including finance, healthcare, and e-commerce that require real-time insights will greatly benefit from these advancements.

- **Distributed applications**: NewSQL databases, with their ability to ensure transactional consistency while being highly scalable, could lead to the development of more robust distributed applications. These applications could maintain high performance and reliability even when dealing with vast amounts of data and users.

- **Quantum computing applications**: Although still theoretical, quantum databases could open up entirely new areas of applications. Tasks that are currently computationally prohibitive, such as complex simulations or optimization problems, could become feasible, leading to breakthroughs in areas such as drug discovery, climate modeling, and cryptography.

Discussing the predicted challenges

Despite the exciting potential of these advancements, they will inevitably come with new challenges:

- **Technical challenges**: The implementation and management of these advanced and varied data-persisting technologies will require specialized skills and knowledge. Issues such as ensuring data consistency in highly distributed environments, managing real-time data processing, and navigating the complexities of quantum databases will pose technical challenges to professionals in the field.

- **Security and privacy**: As data-persisting technologies become more sophisticated and widespread, they will become increasingly attractive targets for cyberattacks. Ensuring data security and privacy will be a significant challenge, requiring advanced security measures and continuous vigilance.

- **Regulatory compliance**: With the increasing complexity and global nature of data-persisting technologies, ensuring regulatory compliance will become more challenging. Different jurisdictions have different data protection and privacy laws, and navigating this landscape will be a complex task.

Proposed solutions to tackle these challenges

Addressing these challenges will require a combination of technical prowess, forward-thinking strategies, and strong governance:

- **Upskilling and education**: To deal with technical challenges, continuous learning and upskilling will be essential. This could involve formal education, online courses, and on-the-job training. A solid understanding of the fundamental principles, combined with practical skills in the latest technologies, will be critical.

- **Advanced security measures**: To address security challenges, advanced security measures will need to be implemented. This could involve encryption, secure coding practices, intrusion detection systems, and regular security audits.

- **Robust governance frameworks**: To ensure regulatory compliance, robust governance frameworks will be needed. These frameworks should provide clear guidelines on data management practices and should be regularly updated to keep pace with evolving regulations.

While the path forward may be challenging, it's also exciting. With the right skills, strategies, and mindset, the future of data-persisting technologies holds great potential for those ready to embrace it.

Part 2 – anticipated changes in AI/ML DevOps

As the digital realm accelerates, blending algorithms with operational praxis is paramount. Enter MLOps – an amalgamation of ML, DevOps, and data engineering practices – which, while nascent, promises to redefine the success trajectory of ML projects. Embarking on this exploration, we'll delve into the genesis and essence of MLOps, survey its current state of play, and forecast its transformative evolutions. Through this lens, we'll unveil the burgeoning opportunities, imminent challenges, and the very blueprint of the future of ML operations. Let's dive in and understand how MLOps is setting the stage for smarter, more efficient, and integrated AI-driven endeavors.

Advancements in MLOps

MLOps, the integration of ML, DevOps, and data engineering, is emerging as a vital discipline in addressing unique challenges in ML projects. Currently, in its early stages, tools such as Kubeflow and MLflow are pioneering the field, hinting at a future dominated by automated model training, continuous monitoring, and improved traceability. These evolutions promise swifter model development, heightened accountability, and seamless collaboration across teams, driving successful ML projects with significant business value.

The need for MLOps

MLOps, or DevOps for ML, is the practice of combining ML, DevOps, and data engineering to efficiently manage the ML life cycle. It has become increasingly important due to the unique challenges posed by ML projects, such as the need for continual data validation, model training, testing, and deployment, as well as monitoring and management.

The current state of MLOps

Today, MLOps is in its nascent stages, with many organizations only beginning to establish practices around it. MLOps tools, such as Kubeflow, MLflow, and Seldon, have started to gain traction, offering capabilities such as automated model training and deployment, model versioning, and performance tracking.

The predicted evolution of MLOps

Looking ahead, MLOps is poised to become a mainstream practice in ML projects. Here are some key advancements we foresee:

- **Automated model training and tuning**: The process of training and tuning models could become largely automated, using techniques such as AutoML and hyperparameter optimization. This would not only speed up the model development process but also lead to better-performing models.

- **Continuous model monitoring and updating**: We expect more robust solutions for continuous model monitoring and updating. As models in production can degrade over time due to changes in data patterns, continuous monitoring is crucial to maintain their performance. When performance degrades, models should be retrained, and the updated models should be deployed, ideally with minimal manual intervention.

- **Improved traceability and reproducibility**: As the need for explainability and accountability in AI increases, we predict advancements in model versioning and experiment tracking. These will offer better traceability of models and their associated data, code, and hyperparameters, ensuring that results can be reproduced and audited.

- **Better integration with DevOps and data engineering**: MLOps will likely be more tightly integrated with DevOps and data engineering practices. This would involve closer collaboration between ML engineers, data engineers, and DevOps teams, leading to more efficient and reliable ML life cycle management.

The implication of these advancements

These advancements in MLOps will enable more efficient and reliable ML project management. They'll result in faster model development, better model performance, increased accountability, and closer collaboration between different teams. This will ultimately lead to more successful ML projects, with higher-quality models, shorter time to market, and more tangible business value.

Future use cases and challenges

MLOps is revolutionizing ML, enabling automated decision-making, proactive business intelligence, and personalized customer experiences. However, it introduces challenges in technical complexity, data privacy, and model transparency. To address these, organizations must invest in skills development, establish robust data governance, and prioritize model explainability. Despite the challenges, MLOps presents a significant opportunity to enhance ML projects and drive business value.

Predicted novel use cases

MLOps is poised to transform the way organizations handle ML projects. As it evolves, it could enable a range of novel use cases:

- **Automated decision-making**: With advancements in model training and monitoring, organizations could delegate more decision-making tasks to AI. This could involve decisions related to customer service, logistics, resource allocation, and more. With continuous monitoring and updating, these AI systems could maintain high performance even as data patterns change.

- **Proactive business intelligence**: As MLOps practices mature, organizations could move from reactive to proactive business intelligence. They could continually analyze business data and update their ML models to predict future trends and make proactive decisions.

- **Personalized experiences**: With more efficient model development and updating, businesses could offer more personalized experiences to their customers. This could involve personalized recommendations, targeted marketing, personalized pricing, and more.

Expected challenges

While MLOps holds much promise, it will also bring new challenges:

- **Technical complexity**: Managing the ML life cycle is a complex task that involves diverse tasks such as data validation, feature extraction, model training, deployment, and monitoring. Navigating this complexity will require specialized skills and knowledge.

- **Data privacy and security**: As organizations delegate more decision-making to AI, they'll need to process more sensitive data, raising data privacy and security concerns. They'll need to ensure that their MLOps practices comply with data protection regulations and that their data is secure.

- **Explainability and trust**: As AI systems make more decisions, the need for explainability and trust will grow. Organizations will need to ensure that their models are transparent and accountable and that their decisions can be explained and audited.

Potential solutions for these challenges

Tackling these challenges will require strategic planning, technical prowess, and robust governance:

- **Skills development**: To deal with the technical complexity, organizations will need to invest in skills development. This could involve training their existing staff, hiring new talent, and fostering a culture of continuous learning.

- **Robust data governance**: To ensure data privacy and security, organizations will need robust data governance frameworks. These frameworks should provide clear guidelines on data handling practices and should be regularly updated to reflect changes in regulations and technologies.

- **Model explainability**: To foster trust in AI, organizations will need to ensure that their models are explainable. This could involve using techniques such as SHAP, LIME, or counterfactual explanations, and incorporating explainability considerations into their MLOps practices.

While the road ahead may be challenging, the potential benefits of MLOps are immense. With the right approach, organizations can leverage MLOps to transform their ML projects and realize significant business value.

Career impacts and future skill requirements

MLOps' rise is set to reshape careers in AI and ML, with increased demand for MLOps professionals and a shift in data scientist roles toward interpretation and strategy. This change will necessitate more cross-disciplinary collaboration and new skills, including proficiency in MLOps tools such as Kubeflow and MLflow, improved communication abilities, and a deeper understanding of data privacy and ethics. To navigate these shifts, continuous learning and a comprehensive grasp of the ML life cycle are essential. By embracing these changes, professionals can thrive in the evolving AI and ML landscape.

Anticipated career impacts

As MLOps becomes more mainstream, it's likely to have significant impacts on careers in AI and ML. Here are some key predictions:

- **Increased demand for MLOps professionals**: As organizations look to adopt MLOps, there's likely to be a surge in demand for professionals with skills in this area. This could include roles such as MLOps engineers, data engineers with MLOps expertise, and even MLOps-focused data scientists.

- **A shift in data scientist roles**: As more tasks related to model training and deployment become automated, the role of data scientists could shift. Instead of spending most of their time on model development, they may focus more on interpreting model outputs, communicating results to stakeholders, and guiding strategic decisions.

- **Cross-disciplinary collaboration**: The integration of MLOps with DevOps and data engineering practices is likely to result in more cross-disciplinary collaboration. Professionals will need to work effectively in teams and understand aspects of the ML life cycle that might fall outside of their traditional areas of expertise.

Future skill requirements

In light of these anticipated career impacts, here are some key skills that professionals in the field will likely need:

- **Specialized tooling**: Understanding various MLOps tools (such as Kubeflow, MLflow, and Seldon) and practices will be crucial. This includes knowledge of automated model training, model versioning, continuous monitoring, and more.

- **Collaboration and communication**: As MLOps fosters more cross-disciplinary collaboration, soft skills such as effective communication and teamwork will become more important. Professionals will need to effectively communicate complex ML concepts to stakeholders and work effectively within diverse teams.

- **Data privacy and ethics**: As ML systems become more pervasive, understanding data privacy regulations and ethical considerations will become increasingly important. Professionals will need to navigate the complexities of data protection laws and understand the ethical implications of their work.

Recommendations for preparing for these changes

To prepare for these changes, professionals should consider the following:

- The field of MLOps is rapidly evolving, and continuous learning is key. Professionals should stay up- to- date with the latest tools and practices and be open to learning new skills.

- Understanding the broader context of ML projects, including aspects of data engineering and DevOps, will be beneficial. Professionals should aim to build a holistic understanding of the ML life cycle, beyond just model development.

- Understanding data protection regulations and the ethical implications of ML is crucial. Professionals should familiarize themselves with key laws and ethical considerations, and factor them into their work.

- The rise of MLOps presents both opportunities and challenges for professionals in the field. By proactively developing the necessary skills and adapting to these changes, professionals can position themselves for success in the future landscape of AI and ML.

Part 3 – evolving trends in SRE

As we further entrench ourselves in a digital-first world, the stability and performance of our systems have become paramount to organizational success. Standing at the crossroads of this digital frontier is **site reliability engineering** (**SRE**), intertwining its software engineering prowess with operational challenges. With its foundations being fortified by current technological tenets such as DevOps, microservices, and Kubernetes, SRE is now on the precipice of transformation. This section traverses the ongoing evolutions and imminent revolutions within the SRE landscape, setting the stage for a future punctuated by AI-centric operations, proactive system testing, and a richer understanding of our digital infrastructures. Let's embark on this insightful journey into the shifting sands of SRE.

Changes in the SRE landscape

SRE has emerged as a crucial approach in ensuring system scalability and reliability, especially in our digitized era. Presently, SRE's growth is bolstered by DevOps, microservices, and tools such as Kubernetes, with observability and chaos engineering central to enhancing system dependability. As we look forward, AI-driven operations, a shift-left in reliability, expanded chaos engineering, and comprehensive observability promise to reshape the landscape, potentially elevating system resilience, reducing manual interventions, and offering deeper insights into system functionalities.

The emergence and importance of SRE

As discussed countless times throughout this book, SRE is a discipline that applies aspects of software engineering to IT operations problems to create scalable and reliable systems. Its importance has grown as organizations have recognized the need to effectively manage the reliability and uptime of their systems in an increasingly digital world.

Current trends in SRE

In recent years, SRE practices have been on the rise, aided by DevOps practices and the widespread adoption of microservices architecture. Tools such as Kubernetes and Terraform are now commonly used for automating infrastructure provisioning and management. Moreover, practices such as observability and chaos engineering are helping organizations improve the reliability of their systems.

Anticipated developments in SRE

Looking ahead, several trends are set to shape the future of SRE:

- **AI-driven operations**: With the growing complexity of systems, manual monitoring and troubleshooting are becoming increasingly difficult. We expect a rise in AI-driven operations, where AI and ML are used to monitor systems, detect anomalies, and even automate responses.

- **Shift-left in reliability**: As organizations aim to catch and fix issues earlier in the development cycle, we expect a "shift-left" in reliability. This means integrating reliability considerations earlier in the development cycle, right from the design phase.

- **Increased use of chaos engineering**: To proactively improve system reliability, the use of chaos engineering is expected to increase. Chaos engineering involves deliberately introducing failures into a system to identify weaknesses and improve its resilience.

- **Holistic observability**: With the increasing adoption of microservices and distributed systems, the need for holistic observability of systems is expected to grow. Observability goes beyond traditional monitoring to provide a deeper understanding of system behavior and the interdependencies between components.

Implications of these developments

These trends have significant implications for organizations. AI-driven operations could greatly reduce the manual effort needed to maintain system reliability and speed up response times. A "shift-left" in reliability could result in fewer issues making it to production, leading to improved user satisfaction. Increased use of chaos engineering could make systems more resilient and reduce downtime. Lastly, holistic observability could provide organizations with better insights into their systems, helping them optimize performance and troubleshoot issues more effectively.

The role of SRE in future IT operations

The integration of SRE into IT operations marks a transformative shift toward more resilient and efficient systems. Leveraging software engineering principles, SRE is poised to play a pivotal role in managing complex infrastructures and ensuring system reliability. By embracing automation, AI, and proactive risk management, SRE is evolving to meet the demands of modern IT operations. The future of SRE promises enhanced system performance, reduced downtime, and a relentless focus on user satisfaction.

SRE at the heart of IT operations

With the anticipated developments in the SRE landscape, we can expect SRE to play an even more central role in IT operations. SRE principles, such as maintaining **service-level objectives** (**SLOs**), implementing error budgets, and managing incidents will be integral to managing the complex IT infrastructures of the future.

Automation and AI in SRE

The use of automation and AI will likely be a key part of future SRE work. AI-driven operations can help automate routine tasks, provide proactive alerts, and even automate remediation actions. This can free up SREs to focus on strategic tasks, such as improving system design, implementing reliability strategies, and consulting with development teams.

Anticipating and mitigating risks

With the shift-left approach and chaos engineering, SREs will increasingly focus on anticipating and mitigating risks. Instead of reacting to incidents after they occur, SREs will work on proactively identifying potential weaknesses and taking steps to improve system resilience. This can lead to more reliable systems and less downtime.

Managing complex system interactions

Holistic observability will become a critical part of managing complex system interactions in microservices and distributed architectures. By providing a detailed view of the system's behavior, observability can help SREs understand these interactions, troubleshoot issues more effectively, and optimize system performance.

Ensuring user satisfaction

Ultimately, all of these developments aim to ensure user satisfaction. By maintaining reliable systems, managing incidents effectively, and providing a seamless user experience, SREs can help ensure that the organization's digital services meet user expectations.

In conclusion, SRE will continue to evolve as a critical discipline in IT operations, using a mix of sophisticated tools and methodologies to manage complex, distributed systems, with a primary focus on ensuring user satisfaction.

Part 4 – career outlook and emerging skill sets in SRE

In today's digitally-driven landscape, ensuring the smooth functioning and reliability of systems is no longer a luxury – it's a necessity. Nestled at the heart of this technological renaissance is SRE, a discipline that marries software engineering with IT operations, ensuring systems are both scalable and dependable. As this field burgeons, so does the horizon of opportunities for the aspirants. Whether you're a novice contemplating a leap into the SRE domain or a seasoned professional looking to sharpen your toolkit, this section offers a comprehensive map to navigate the terrains of SRE careers. From understanding the vast scope of opportunities to grasping the multifaceted skills that'll set you apart, let's decode the dynamics of carving a niche in the realm of SRE.

SRE careers – opportunities, skills, and preparation

In today's complex digital ecosystem, SRE stands out as a cornerstone of reliability and performance. Let's dive into the expanding horizons of SRE careers, the essential skills for success, and how to prepare for this dynamic domain.

Career opportunities in SRE

As SRE becomes central to IT operations, the demand for professionals in this field will rise. Organizations will need skilled SREs to manage their increasingly complex and distributed IT infrastructures. This will create a wealth of opportunities for professionals interested in this field, from entry-level roles to senior positions.

Skill set requirements

The future of SRE will require a unique blend of skills:

- SREs need a deep understanding of the systems they manage, including knowledge of networking, systems, cloud technologies, and automation tools. Proficiency in one or more programming languages is also crucial as SRE involves writing code to automate tasks and improve systems.

- With the rise of AI-driven operations, understanding AI and ML concepts will be beneficial. This includes knowledge of how to apply these technologies to improve system monitoring and automate responses.

- As SREs shift their focus toward anticipating and mitigating risks, skills in systems design and risk management will become increasingly important. This involves understanding how different system components interact, how to design reliable systems, and how to identify and mitigate potential risks.

- SRE involves close collaboration with other teams, including development and operations. Effective communication skills are vital as SREs need to coordinate with these teams, share insights, and advocate for reliability practices.

Preparing for a career in SRE

For those interested in a career in SRE, here are some recommendations:

- Hands-on experience is crucial for developing SRE skills. This could involve working on projects that involve managing systems, automating tasks, or implementing reliability practices.

- The SRE field is rapidly evolving, so it's important to stay up- to- date with the latest trends. This could involve following relevant blogs, attending industry conferences, or participating in online communities.

- Don't neglect soft skills. Effective communication, problem-solving, and teamwork skills are just as important as technical skills in SRE.

- The future of SRE looks promising, with a wealth of career opportunities and a growing importance in IT operations. By developing the right skills and staying abreast of the latest trends, professionals can position themselves for a successful career in this evolving field.

Innovations in data persistence technologies

Data persistence technologies have evolved from traditional relational databases to a wide range of databases, including NoSQL, NewSQL, cloud-native, time series, and graph databases, each catering to specific needs. These advancements address growing data volumes, varied structures, and the demand for real-time processing, but challenges remain, such as data consistency and privacy. Looking forward, the horizon is marked by innovations such as automated data management, multi-model databases, and, potentially, quantum databases, all promising enhanced capabilities but also posing new challenges, necessitating adaptive strategies and skill development.

The current state of data persistence technologies

In the ever-evolving landscape of data management, understanding how data is stored, retrieved, and utilized is paramount. From the classic frameworks of traditional relational databases to the cutting-edge innovations in time series and graph databases, this section delves into the progression, strengths, and challenges inherent to the diverse data persistence models available today. As we venture deeper, we'll uncover how these models have transformed in response to the multifaceted demands of modern applications.

Traditional data persistence models

Data persistence is a critical aspect of software applications that ensures data remains intact and available over time and across systems. Traditionally, data persistence has been handled through relational databases such as MySQL or PostgreSQL. These databases use a **structured query language** (**SQL**) to manage data, ensuring ACID properties.

Shift to NoSQL databases

As data volumes grew and data variety increased, NoSQL databases emerged as an alternative, providing flexibility, scalability, and performance that traditional relational databases could not provide. NoSQL databases such as MongoDB, Cassandra, or Redis are designed to handle structured, semi-structured, and unstructured data, providing support for a variety of data models including key-value, document, columnar, and graph formats.

Emergence of NewSQL databases

To combine the benefits of SQL and NoSQL databases, NewSQL databases such as CockroachDB and Google Spanner have been developed. These databases aim to provide the scalability of NoSQL databases while maintaining the ACID properties and SQL interface of traditional relational databases.

The advent of cloud-native databases

With the rise of cloud computing and microservices architecture, cloud-native databases such as Amazon Aurora and Google Cloud Spanner have emerged. These databases are designed to exploit the cloud's flexibility, scalability, and resilience, providing features such as automatic scaling, replication across regions, and automatic backup.

The rise of time series databases

With the growth of IoT and real-time analytics, time series databases such as InfluxDB and TimescaleDB have gained popularity. These databases are designed to efficiently handle time-stamped data, providing fast data ingestion, compression, and query capabilities.

The popularity of graph databases

With the increasing need to handle complex, interconnected data, graph databases such as Neo4j and Amazon Neptune have become more popular. These databases use graph structures to store, map, and query relationships, providing high performance for data-intensive applications.

Current challenges

Despite these advancements, challenges persist in the world of data persistence. These include handling massive data volumes, ensuring data consistency, managing data privacy and security, and meeting the demands of real-time processing. Solutions to these challenges are actively being sought, paving the way for further advancements in data persistence technologies.

Future outlook – next-generation data persistence technologies

The rapidly evolving landscape of data persistence technologies is on the cusp of a major transformation, influenced by emerging trends and innovations. As we navigate toward this future, automated data management is expected to become more prevalent, utilizing AI and ML for various tasks. Additionally, the rise of multi-model databases and the potential integration of blockchain and quantum computing are set to offer new levels of efficiency, security, and speed. Professionals and organizations alike must adapt to these changes, developing essential skills and adopting strategic approaches to fully leverage the capabilities of next-generation data persistence technologies.

Anticipated trends and innovations

Several trends and innovations are set to shape the future of data persistence technologies:

- **Automated data management**: As data volumes continue to grow, the use of AI and ML to automate data management tasks such as data classification, anomaly detection, and optimization of data storage and retrieval is likely to increase.

- **Multi-model databases**: The future may see a rise in multi-model databases that can handle different types of data structures (for example, key-value, document, graph, and time series) within a single, integrated backend. This would offer more flexibility and efficiency in handling diverse data types.

- **Immutable and decentralized databases**: Blockchain technology may shape the future of databases by introducing immutability and decentralization. This could offer enhanced security and transparency, particularly in sectors such as finance, supply chain, and healthcare.

- **Quantum databases**: With advancements in quantum computing, we may eventually see the development of quantum databases. While still theoretical, they could offer unprecedented speed and efficiency in data processing.

Potential implications

These innovations could significantly impact how organizations store, manage, and use their data:

- Automated data management could greatly reduce manual effort and improve data quality

- Multi-model databases could simplify data architecture and improve performance

- Immutable and decentralized databases could enhance data security and transparency

- Quantum databases, while still a long way off, could revolutionize data processing

Dealing with future challenges

While these innovations are exciting, they will also bring new challenges:

- As AI and ML are used for data management, there will be an increased need for data privacy and ethical considerations

- Implementing multi-model databases will require sophisticated data modeling and management practices

- Blockchain-based databases will need to overcome scalability issues and legal uncertainties

- Quantum databases will require new skills and computing infrastructures

In short, the future of data persistence technologies looks promising but will require organizations to adapt to new technologies and manage emerging challenges.

Preparing for the future – skills and strategies in data persistence technologies

The future of data persistence technologies is poised for transformative change, driven by several key trends and innovations. Automated data management is expected to gain traction, utilizing AI and ML for tasks such as anomaly detection and data optimization, while multi-model databases will offer flexible and efficient data handling. The advent of immutable, decentralized, and potentially quantum databases promises enhanced security, transparency, and processing speed, albeit with new challenges in data privacy, management complexity, and the need for advanced skills and infrastructure.

Essential skills for the future

As data persistence technologies evolve, a specific set of skills will become increasingly valuable:

- Proficiency in different types of databases, including relational, NoSQL, NewSQL, and future databases such as multi-model, will be crucial. This involves understanding how these databases work, their strengths and weaknesses, and their suitable use cases.

- As automated data management becomes more prevalent, having experience with AI and ML will be beneficial. This includes understanding how these technologies can be used to enhance data management tasks.

- If blockchain-based databases become more widespread, familiarity with blockchain technology, including how it works and its implications for data storage, will be essential.

- While still in its infancy, learning the basics of quantum computing and keeping an eye on its developments could be advantageous in the long run.

Adopting the right strategies

To effectively leverage future data persistence technologies, organizations should adopt certain strategies:

- **Staying updated**: Given the fast pace of change, organizations need to stay updated on the latest trends and innovations in data persistence technologies. This can involve attending industry events, following thought leaders, and participating in relevant communities.

- **Investing in skill development**: Organizations should invest in developing the skills of their workforce through training programs, workshops, and other learning opportunities. This could involve training in new types of databases, AI/ML, blockchain, and even quantum computing.

- **Experimenting with new technologies**: Organizations should be open to experimenting with new technologies. This can involve running pilot projects or setting up sandbox environments to explore the capabilities of new data persistence technologies.

- **Planning for transition**: If adopting a new technology, organizations should carefully plan the transition. This can involve considering the compatibility with existing systems, planning for data migration, and ensuring sufficient support for the new technology.

By focusing on these areas, organizations can prepare for the future of data persistence technologies and be better equipped to leverage their potential benefits.

Part 5 – the future of designing, building, and operating cutting-edge systems

As we stand on the brink of a new technological era, system design and development are undergoing a radical transformation. The burgeoning technologies presented in this section are not just reshaping the foundational pillars of IT infrastructure, but are also redefining the boundaries of what's possible. While they usher in unprecedented opportunities, these advancements also bring forth intricate challenges, necessitating a holistic approach to system design that prioritizes agility, security, ethics, and inclusivity. Let's dive in and understand the tapestry of these innovations and their implications for our digital future.

Emerging technologies in system design and development

Emerging technologies in system design and development, such as cloud-native architectures, edge computing, AI-driven development, quantum computing, and blockchain, are transforming how organizations operate and deliver value. While these technologies promise enhanced capabilities, they also introduce unique challenges, from cybersecurity and ethical considerations to infrastructure investments and talent acquisition. To harness their potential, organizations will need to embrace agility, prioritize security, invest in new skill sets, and ensure ethical and inclusive deployment.

Cloud-native architecture and serverless computing

As we move toward a cloud-dominated future, organizations are increasingly adopting cloud-native architectures, which are designed to fully exploit the capabilities and flexibility of the cloud. This includes the use of microservices, containers, and serverless computing. Serverless computing, in particular, offers an opportunity to offload infrastructure management tasks to cloud providers, allowing developers to focus on writing code that delivers business value.

Edge computing

With the growth of IoT and real-time applications, edge computing is becoming more important. By processing data closer to its source, edge computing can reduce latency, conserve bandwidth, and improve privacy. This requires a different approach to system design and operation, one that can manage distributed data processing and handle potential connectivity issues.

AI-driven development (AIDev)

AI is now starting to be used to automate various aspects of system development. This includes AI-assisted coding, automated testing, intelligent debugging, and more. AIDev could make system development faster, more efficient, and less error-prone.

Quantum computing

While still in its early stages, quantum computing has the potential to revolutionize system design and operation. Quantum computers could potentially solve certain types of problems much faster than classical computers, opening up new possibilities in fields such as cryptography, optimization, and machine learning.

Blockchain technology

Blockchain technology can provide a decentralized and transparent approach to data management. It can be used to design systems where transparency, traceability, and lack of a central authority are key requirements. However, it also presents unique challenges in terms of scalability and privacy.

Security by design

With increasing concerns about cybersecurity, there is a growing emphasis on incorporating security principles from the earliest stages of system design. This includes practices such as threat modeling, secure coding, least privilege design, and regular security testing. Cybersecurity is no longer an afterthought, but an integral part of system design and operation.

Potential implications and challenges in designing, building, and operating cutting-edge systems

As we stand on the brink of a technological revolution, the way we design, build, and operate cutting-edge systems is undergoing a profound transformation. From the integration of agile and flexible development practices to the imperative of real-time processing capabilities and the potential advent of quantum computing, the landscape is shifting rapidly. Alongside these exciting advancements, the industry faces a plethora of challenges, including ensuring robust security measures, addressing ethical and regulatory concerns, and equipping the workforce with necessary new skills. This section aims to delve into these varied aspects, highlighting the potential implications and challenges that lie ahead in the journey of designing, building, and operating the innovative systems of tomorrow.

Transformation of development practices

As technological landscapes evolve, the methodologies and practices in system development are undergoing significant shifts:

- **Agility and flexibility**: Cloud-native, serverless, and AI-driven development will enable more agile and flexible development processes. However, they may also require new tools, practices, and mindsets.
- **Real-time processing**: The shift toward edge computing will necessitate real-time processing capabilities. This will challenge developers to design systems that can handle the demands of real-time analytics and decision-making.
- **Quantum-readiness**: While still nascent, preparing for a quantum computing future might require fundamental changes in algorithms and computational strategies.

Security considerations

In an age where data breaches and cyberattacks are increasingly common, integrating robust security measures into emerging technologies becomes paramount.

- **Cybersecurity concerns**: With the complexity of new technologies, security risks may increase. A security-by-design approach is necessary but may require significant changes in development practices.

- **Blockchain's double-edged sword**: While blockchain can enhance transparency and integrity, it might also introduce challenges in privacy and scalability.

Ethical and regulatory challenges

As we integrate advanced technologies into our systems, the moral compass and legal boundaries must evolve in tandem to ensure responsible development and deployment:

- **AI ethics**: AI-driven development must consider ethical implications, such as bias and decision transparency. Regulatory compliance might also influence how AI is utilized in system development.

- **Data privacy and governance**: The distributed nature of edge computing and the immutable nature of blockchain may raise new privacy and governance concerns that must be addressed.

Skill development and talent acquisition

In an ever-evolving technological landscape, the human capital element remains pivotal, underscoring the necessity to nurture and onboard talent with aptitudes aligning with the future:

- **The need for new skill sets**: The adoption of emerging technologies requires new skill sets, creating challenges in training and hiring

- **Cross-disciplinary knowledge**: Understanding multiple domains, such as AI, cybersecurity, quantum mechanics, and legal considerations, may become crucial

Infrastructure and investment requirements

Transitioning to new technologies may require significant investment in infrastructure, tools, training, and support.

Integrating cutting-edge technologies with existing systems may be complex and risky, requiring careful planning and execution.

Environmental and social considerations

As technological advancements reshape the digital realm, it's paramount that their broader impacts on our planet and diverse societies are also taken into account:

- **Sustainability**: Building and operating energy-efficient systems, particularly with the expansion of edge computing, becomes an important consideration

- **Inclusivity**: Ensuring that the benefits of cutting-edge technologies are accessible and equitable across different segments of society is a key challenge

In summary, the future of designing, building, and operating systems with emerging technologies presents exciting opportunities but also complex challenges. Strategic planning, thoughtful implementation, ethical consideration, and continuous learning will be key to successfully navigating this evolving landscape.

Strategies for success – preparing for the future of designing, building, and operating cutting-edge systems

In the fast-evolving landscape of technology, organizations must adopt comprehensive strategies to successfully design, build, and operate cutting-edge systems. This entails a strong emphasis on continuous learning, security, responsible innovation, collaboration, and adherence to regulatory standards. By doing so, businesses can navigate the complexities of the future, ensuring both success and resilience in the face of transformative change.

Investing in continuous learning and skill development

In the rapidly evolving landscape of technology, the significance of staying updated cannot be overstated:

- **Training programs**: Implement continuous training programs for teams to keep up with the latest technologies and methodologies
- **Cross-disciplinary education**: Encourage learning across different domains, such as AI, quantum mechanics, cybersecurity, and ethics, to prepare for a multifaceted future

Adopting a security-by-design approach

In an era where cyber threats are ever-present and evolving, a proactive stance on security is paramount:

- **Early integration of security measures**: Include security considerations from the inception of a project, rather than as an add-on
- **Regular security assessments**: Conduct regular security tests and assessments to ensure ongoing robustness and compliance

Exploring emerging technologies responsibly

As the frontier of technological innovation expands, it's essential to approach new tools and methodologies with both enthusiasm and caution:

- **Pilot projects and prototyping**: Test new technologies through pilot projects and prototyping to understand their real-world implications and potential benefits
- **Ethical considerations**: Evaluate the ethical implications of technologies such as AI and blockchain, ensuring that they align with organizational values and societal norms

Fostering collaboration and innovation

In an era where the intersection of diverse disciplines can spark groundbreaking solutions, nurturing a culture of teamwork and creativity is paramount:

- **Interdisciplinary collaboration**: Foster collaboration between different departments and experts to facilitate cross-disciplinary innovation

- **Open innovation**: Encourage innovation through hackathons, innovation labs, and partnerships with academia and startups

Strategic planning and risk management

In a rapidly evolving technological landscape, forward-thinking and proactive measures are essential to navigate uncertainties and capitalize on new opportunities:

- **Long-term planning**: Develop strategic plans that consider both the opportunities and risks associated with emerging technologies

- **Risk mitigation strategies**: Implement comprehensive risk management strategies to identify, assess, and mitigate potential challenges and pitfalls

Emphasizing sustainability and social responsibility

As the global focus shifts toward sustainable solutions and equitable technology deployment, organizations must align their initiatives with these principles:

- **Sustainable practices**: Consider the environmental impact of technologies and adopt practices that promote sustainability

- **Community engagement**: Engage with communities to ensure that technologies are inclusive and beneficial to all stakeholders

Adhering to regulatory compliance and standards

In a landscape increasingly shaped by legal and industry benchmarks, ensuring alignment with prevailing regulations and norms becomes paramount:

- **Regulatory awareness**: Stay updated on regulatory requirements related to privacy, security, and ethical considerations

- **Standardization**: Work with industry bodies to contribute to and comply with emerging standards in cutting-edge technologies

In my opinion, the future of designing, building, and operating cutting-edge systems is filled with exciting prospects. Organizations that wish to thrive in this environment should prioritize continuous learning, responsible innovation, collaboration, strategic planning, and a strong commitment to security, ethics, sustainability, and social responsibility. By focusing on these aspects, they can position themselves to leverage emerging technologies effectively while navigating potential challenges and risks.

Summary

Hey, are you tired of all the buzzwords I've just used in this chapter? Shall we recap what we were saying in this chapter, and more or less in this book? Let's take a quick tour!

Part 1 dived into the world of data – you know, all the things that keep our information secure and accessible? Right now, we're talking about things such as NoSQL and in-memory databases. But looking forward, imagine automated data management and even quantum databases! It sounds complex, but with the right skills and an eagerness to learn, we can keep up with these changes.

Part 2 dived into AI/ML DevOps. This is where AI meets development and operations. Pretty cool, huh? Imagine automated pipelines and continuous integration, all working seamlessly. The future here is even more automation and collaboration, but also being mindful of ethics and explainability. It's all about aligning tech with our core values.

In *Part 3*, we learned all about SRE. Ever wondered how tech companies balance being innovative with keeping things reliable? That's what SRE does! It's a mix of goals, error budgets, and smart automation. What's next? Think AI-powered monitoring and more intelligent alerting. It's about being agile, but stable too.

Part 4 was for those tech-savvy folks who design, build, and operate these amazing systems. We're already seeing things such as edge computing and blockchain, but the future? Wow, it's filled with possibilities such as AI-driven development and quantum computing! Of course, there are challenges, such as the need for new skills and dealing with security, but with the right approach, we're all set to thrive.

Finally, *Part 5* zoomed out to look at the big picture. From cloud-native architecture to security by design, there's so much happening. But what's even more exciting is the road ahead. There's potential for huge transformation, but also a need to think about ethics, sustainability, and inclusivity. If we're smart, we can design a future that's not just innovative but responsible too.

So, there you have it! This was a wild ride, filled with exciting opportunities and complex challenges. Whether it's data, AI, reliability, or the very way we design and build technology, the future is calling. Are you ready to answer?

Index

C

Other Books You May Enjoy

If you enjoyed this book, you may be interested in these other books by Packt:

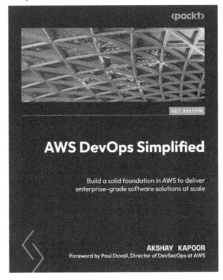

AWS DevOps Simplified

Akshay Kapoor

ISBN: 9781837634460

- Develop a strong and practical understanding of AWS DevOps services
- Manage infrastructure on AWS using tools such as Packer and CDK
- Implement observability to bring key system behaviors to the surface
- Adopt the DevSecOps approach by integrating AWS and open source solutions
- Gain proficiency in using AWS container services for scalable software management
- Map your solution designs with AWS's Well-Architected Framework
- Discover how to manage multi-account, multi-Region AWS environments
- Learn how to organize your teams to boost collaboration

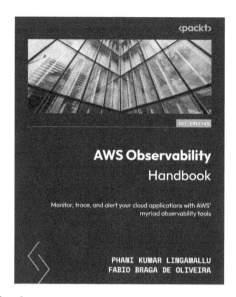

AWS Observability Handbook

Phani Kumar Lingamallu, Fabio Braga de Oliveira

ISBN: 9781804616710

- Capture metrics from an EC2 instance and visualize them on a dashboard
- Conduct distributed tracing using AWS X-Ray
- Derive operational metrics and set up alerting using CloudWatch
- Achieve observability of containerized applications in ECS and EKS
- Explore the practical implementation of observability for AWS Lambda
- Observe your applications using Amazon managed Prometheus, Grafana, and OpenSearch services
- Gain insights into operational data using ML services on AWS
- Understand the role of observability in the cloud adoption framework

Packt is searching for authors like you

If you're interested in becoming an author for Packt, please visit `authors.packtpub.com` and apply today. We have worked with thousands of developers and tech professionals, just like you, to help them share their insight with the global tech community. You can make a general application, apply for a specific hot topic that we are recruiting an author for, or submit your own idea.

Share Your Thoughts

Now you've finished *DevOps for Databases*, we'd love to hear your thoughts! Scan the QR code below to go straight to the Amazon review page for this book and share your feedback or leave a review on the site that you purchased it from.

`https://packt.link/r/183763730X`

Your review is important to us and the tech community and will help us make sure we're delivering excellent quality content.

Download a free PDF copy of this book

Thanks for purchasing this book!

Do you like to read on the go but are unable to carry your print books everywhere? Is your eBook purchase not compatible with the device of your choice?

Don't worry, now with every Packt book you get a DRM-free PDF version of that book at no cost.

Read anywhere, any place, on any device. Search, copy, and paste code from your favorite technical books directly into your application.

The perks don't stop there, you can get exclusive access to discounts, newsletters, and great free content in your inbox daily

Follow these simple steps to get the benefits:

1. Scan the QR code or visit the link below

https://packt.link/free-ebook/978-1-83763-730-0

2. Submit your proof of purchase
3. That's it! We'll send your free PDF and other benefits to your email directly

www.ingramcontent.com/pod-product-compliance
Lightning Source LLC
Chambersburg PA
CBHW060647060326
40690CB00020B/4541